Human Resource Management for Tourism, Hospitality and Leisure

Human Resource Management for Tourism, Hospitality and Leisure

An international perspective

Tom Baum

THOMSON

Australia • Canada • Mexico • Singapore • Spain • United Kingdom • United States

THOMSON

Human Resource Management for Tourism, Hospitality and Leisure: An International Perspective
Tom Baum

Publishing Director
John Yates

Publisher
Jennifer Pegg

Editorial Assistant
Natalie Aguilera

Production Editor
Stuart Giblin

Manufacturing Manager
Helen Mason

Marketing Manager
Leo Stanley

Typesetter
Photoprint, Torquay, Devon

Production Controller
Maeve Healy

Printer
Zrinski d.d., Croatia

While the publisher has taken all reasonable care in the preparation of this book the publisher makes no representation, express or implied, with regard to the accuracy of the information contained in this book and cannot accept any legal responsibility or liability for any errors or omissions from the book or the consequences thereof.

Products and services that are referred to in this book may be either trademarks and/or registered trademarks of their respective owners. The publisher and author/s make no claim to these trademarks.

British Library Cataloguing-in-Publication Data
A catalogue record for this book is available from the British Library

Contents

Preface

The international tourism, hospitality and leisure sector continues to be one of the fastest-growing sectors within the global economy, despite riding the effects of major setbacks during the early years of the twenty-first century, notably the events of 9/11 in the United States and their aftermath, SARS and avian flu, conflict and war in many locations, and famine and natural disasters in Asia and Africa. A reasonable estimate of global employment in tourism, hospitality and leisure is that it included a workforce of over 200 million people in 2000 and that this figure will grow to in excess of 250 million by 2010. Growth is most rapid in those parts of the world where tourism is a relative newcomer, notably East and South-East Asia. The industry is highly labour intensive, notwithstanding the impact of technology on all aspects of product and service development, distribution and delivery. People, therefore, are central to the commercial and cultural future of tourism, hospitality and leisure in both the developed and developing world.

Tourism, hospitality and leisure are closely related concepts and, in many respects, are mutually dependent upon each other. While a general understanding of how the three concepts relate to one another is quite easy to achieve, closer analysis identifies areas of overlap and also exclusivity which makes attempts to measure key attributes of this amalgam of a sector problematic at times. This book is not overly concerned with definitions that will separate the three concepts, although this theme is addressed in Chapter 1. Of far greater importance are the strands that bind them together and the ways in which such common ground manifests itself in the common work that employees across all three areas have to undertake and the similar role that is exercised in working with customers. Therefore, in this book, 'tourism, hospitality and leisure' is frequently used as a collective term, designed to address the wide range of activities that fall under this generalized umbrella. At times, specific reference is made to features of or data relating to a specific part of the three and this is then made explicit. At other times, there is a conscious fudging of the distinction between them.

This book is not a standard human resource management text for the tourism, hospitality and leisure sector. The student and practitioner markets for such texts are very well served in most countries. Rather, this book seeks to explore some of the many themes and contradictions that become apparent through a study of human resource themes within tourism, hospitality and leisure in different countries, cultures and contexts. The book is designed to provoke thought and debate and to encourage its readership to challenge the conclusions that are reached in this volume. It is also intended to stimulate further reading and research, within the tourism, hospitality and leisure environment but also beyond it, and to bring the outcomes of this research back to discussion and debate on themes in this book. Therefore, use of an eclectic range of academic and general sources is a deliberate feature of this book, intended to show the reader that the management of people in tourism, hospitality and leisure cannot be seen in isolation from developments across a wide range of allied areas in society.

This book aspires to be truly international in its discussion and its use of sources and examples. This has proved to be a very challenging aspiration in that there is a clear imbalance in the material available about tourism, hospitality and leisure and the sector's people between developed and developing countries. It is clear that many of the assumptions that prevail about work and employment in tourism, hospitality and leisure are constructed from a developed-country perspective and there is a clear need for a research-driven reappraisal of such assumptions in the context of the developing world.

This book draws, conceptually and in some of the material that is used, on my 1995 book, *Managing Human Resources in the European Tourism and Hospitality Industry. A Strategic Approach*, also published by Thomson. Since 1995, the world of tourism, hospitality and leisure has altered dramatically, as a result of global political, economic and social change but also because of significant developments within the sector itself in its products (the expansion of low-cost airlines in Europe and Asia, for example), marketing (the growth of the internet as a major distribution tool) and markets (the expansion of China in both in-bound and outbound terms). Tourism, hospitality and leisure is increasingly global in its outlook and behaviour and, therefore, a book that is place-bound within one continent faces major limitations. The speed and flexibility of modern-day travel means that, as consumers, we increasingly behave globally and, therefore, discussion of a key business theme, such as people management, needs to adopt a similar perspective, Likewise, thinking about people and work has moved significantly and we have seen the introduction and use of concepts that are of considerable significance to tourism, hospitality and leisure – such as work–life balance, lifestyle employment and aesthetic labour – become commonplace.

This book owes much to discussion and friendship with valued professional friends who are too numerous to mention here by name. They include colleagues in the University of Strathclyde with whom I have shared discussion about the nature of work, employment and people management in tourism, hospitality and leisure, both in Glasgow and when working on our overseas assignments in diverse locations. Enjoyable work with my own doctoral students, who come as they have from over a dozen countries, has taught me much about work and employment in our industry but also about the nature of culture and communications and I am indebted to them for this. Fellow researchers across the globe have shared ideas and collaborated with projects over the years in the best spirit of the Academy. Tourism, hospitality and leisure industry professionals whom I have met and worked with over the years have influenced my thinking and opened my eyes to particular facets of how things work (or do not work) in our industry and I am grateful for their unfailing courtesy and time. I am particularly grateful for the assistance and friendship of staff in Fáilte Ireland in Dublin, many of them former colleagues of mine from the 1980s, who continue to demonstrate some of the best examples of good practice to be found in our field. To all the above, my heartfelt thanks and acknowledgement for the contribution you have made to the ideas in this book.

For Alexander and Brelda

Companion Website

Visit the *Human Resource Management for Tourism, Hospitaility and Leisure: An International Perspective* website at www.thomsonlearning.co.uk/baum to find further teaching and learning resources for lecturers, including:

For Students

Weblinks
Key weblinks to organizations and other sources are provided so that students can enhance their learning through research and further exploration of key issues addressed in the text.

For Lecturers

Instructors' Manual
This addresses the main pedagogical and academic focus of the book, chapter by chapter, and provides guidance to Instructors on options available in using the material in class.

PPTs

A suite of PowerPoint slides are provided for each chapter. These give instructors the backbone of each chapter in content terms and will allow for adaptation/modification to meet local requirements.

Case Studies

Case studies in the book complement the main content and instructors' notes are intended to provide ideas and guidance with respect to their use in the classroom.

People in international tourism, hospitality and leisure: an introduction

Chapter objectives

This chapter sets the scene for the book. While the focus of this book is on the role of the people who deliver services within tourism, hospitality and leisure, it is important that we understand how the role of people is affected by the wider context in which they and the businesses within which they are located operate. Therefore, the aims of this chapter are:

- to set tourism, hospitality and leisure in their historical, geographic, political, economic, cultural and technological contexts;

- to demonstrate how tourism, hospitality and leisure are clearly embedded within the contextual systems within which they are located and to illustrate what this embeddedness means for people and work in tourism, hospitality and leisure;

- to explore what is meant by the key activity areas covered in this book, tourism, hospitality and leisure, highlighting their interdependencies but also the senses in which they differ;

- to identify who tourism, hospitality and leisure's people are and the role they play in the sector.

These are important first steps because without them it is impossible fully to understand the role that people play in the delivery of tourism, hospitality and leisure services.

The context of tourism, hospitality and leisure

The organization and structure of each of tourism, hospitality and leisure is demonstrably different in different parts of the world according to national and regional characteristics; consider the differences to be found in Ireland, India, Italy, Iran and Iceland, for example. These countries offer very different tourism products, have contrasting hotel operations, operate widely divergent social and economic systems, and provide access to leisure opportunities to their citizens based on differing opportunity afforded according to a wide range of factors including history, geography, gender, caste or economic status. Here we will explore some of the main drivers that shape how tourism, hospitality and leisure operate in diverse locales and will take initial steps to raise questions about these drivers in terms of what they mean for the work people do in the sector and the management of the human resource function.

First we will examine the factors that drive divergence in tourism, hospitality and leisure.

Historical factors

Historical factors have impacted upon the development and characteristics of tourism, hospitality and leisure in all locations. Tourism in the United Kingdom, for example, can trace its origins back over 200 years so that the development of destinations such as Bath, Brighton and the Scottish Highlands has been one of evolution in response to and as part of wider social and demographic change over an extended period of time. Likewise, the emergence of a hospitality sector in parts of Europe can be traced back hundreds of years – in the case of the Posthotel Adler in Hinterzarten in the German Black Forest, the hotel has been in the one family since 1462. Tourism, hospitality and leisure in many parts of northern and western Europe have evolved slowly over an extended period and their products and facilities reflect this slow process over time. By contrast, many tourism destinations in Asia, the Caribbean or Africa have developed very recently and very rapidly over a short span of time. Products and facilities, as a result, tend to be much more modern but also rather more homogeneous in character. They are also far more remote, economically and, frequently, physically, from the communities within which they are located.

The gradualist argument, in terms of tourism and leisure developments in Europe, must be set alongside key 'big bang' events which have prompted the growth of tourism, hospitality and leisure. Access to leisure time, for example, was directly related to the emergence of statutory paid holiday entitlements in industrialized countries in the late nineteenth and early twentieth centuries. Today, we are witnessing similar developments in the more recently developed world, as countries such as Malaysia and Singapore introduce their citizens to greater opportunities for leisure and travel. The former, for example, has reduced Saturday working for public servants in order to encourage greater participation in domestic leisure and travel.

Similarly impactful was the advent of technological development in transport. This has also created dramatic change to the nature of mass tourism travel at various points in the past 150 years, acting as a liberating force for many people otherwise restricted in their travel options. The advent of the railways in the nineteenth century in Europe and North America contributed significantly to the creation of tourism's footprint and helped to establish many resorts that remain important on the tourism map today. Likewise the motor car and its infrastructural requirements and facilities for travellers impacted significantly on travel patterns in the United States from the 1930s onwards and in Europe after the Second World War. Road transport, particularly the development of motorways, impacted on the nature of mobility in terms of both leisure (more localized) activity and tourism, expanding travel horizons and time frames. The legacy of road transport developments at a local level in many countries can be seen in the development of out-of-town retail and leisure facilities such as sports stadia and cinema complexes. Air travel has also shaped the historic landscape of tourism, hospitality and leisure, notably with the advent of both wide-bodied long-haul aircraft and low-cost jet travel in the early 1960s. North Europeans, especially the British and Germans, were able to abandon domestic holiday resorts for the warmth of Spain and other Mediterranean destinations at highly competitive prices. Long-haul mass air transport spelt the death knell of trans-atlantic and intercontinental travel by liner and created major changes in the operation of sea travel, ultimately offering an opportunity for the new growth area of cruising.

Historical factors also influence the range of tourism attractions that exist at a national or destination level. Monuments, buildings and sites of major events such as battlefields are major attractions to both domestic and international visitors and their presence impacts greatly upon tourist movements. The presence of visible evidence of ancient civilizations in China, Egypt, Greece, Italy, Iran and Mexico has done much to shape the structure and organization of tourism in those countries. Likewise, battlefield sites such as Culloden in Scotland, Gettysburg in the United States and the Somme in northern France are much visited destinations in their own right and have led to the creation of significant tourism infrastructures in support of visitation.

Similarly, leisure pursuits, whether active or passive, also reflect wider dynamics of a society as it has developed over time. Mass participation spectator sports such as football or American football are phenomena which emerged out of the industrialization of major European and North American countries and would have been inconceivable within the rural, agrarian societies that preceded the growth of large, industrial cities. Colonial history, likewise, can be said to be directly responsible for the popularity of cricket as a participant and spectator leisure activity in countries such as Australia, Barbados, India and Pakistan.

Implications for people and work in tourism, hospitality and leisure

The impact of history on the role of people and the nature of work in tourism, hospitality and leisure has been and continues to be very strong. The leisure pastimes of a community are shaped by history, as we have already seen, and this, in turn, determines the skills that workers in areas of sports, culture and heritage must possess in order to instruct and support such activities. Some of these skills are generic while aspects of them may be very specialist to the community in which they are located. A coach of Gaelic football or hurling in Ireland requires a range of skills that are common with a large number of other athletic, team games (football, rugby, Australian rules football, field hockey, for example) but also requires specialisms that are unique to the sports and are only in demand in Ireland and within a very limited number of migrant Irish communities overseas. The same is true in the cultural industry where notions of authenticity tend to restrict access to and interest in skills associated with Balinese dancing, Chinese opera or Scottish piping to communities with strong hereditary ties to the respective cultures. Some manifestations of local culture have been globalized and the skills associated with them are no longer the preserve of their communities of origin. Dances of Latin American origin, for example, are popular worldwide and the skills of teaching associated with the activity are likewise dispersed.

A similar picture emerges when we look at the skills required to support the tourism and hospitality sector. The reasons people visit a country or a location can be strongly influenced by historical factors – for example, the genealogical interest of black, Irish and Scottish Americans returning 'home' to West Africa and north-west Europe respectively. Historical interest in major battlefield sites such as those in northern France and the Pacific may be driven by family connections but can also relate to a wider interest in world history. The skills of those charged with interpreting environments such as these for visitors with differing interests are both locally based and generic. The structure of the industry is also a reflection of history and accounts for the large number of very small accommodation providers (hotels, bed-and-breakfast businesses) to be found in the countries of the British Isles. This structural factor reflects historical origins and influences, in turn, the nature of work and careers available within hospitality.

Historical links also shape the education that is provided to prepare people for work and careers in tourism, hospitality and leisure. Many countries that have historical colonial links to Europe have developed educational systems that clearly have their origins in that of the former colonial power. Tourism, hospitality and leisure education in Malaysia and Singapore, for example, are modelled closely on the British system although the ties do loosen with the passage of time. Hong Kong, with its return to Chinese sovereignty in 1997, has seen major changes which have pulled its educational system away from its British roots although evidence of former links is still strong. Taiwan, never a US colony, nevertheless has an educational system that closely reflects the strong economic and cultural ties between the two countries since 1949. These links and others with France (for example in North and West Africa) and Russia (in former Soviet republics) also manifest themselves through overseas study in the partner country. This further reinforces and perpetuates the historical ties and their manifestation within roles played by people who work in the tourism, hospitality and leisure sector.

Geographical factors

Geographical characteristics, notably climate, topography and population distribution, have a great influence on the nature of tourism, hospitality and leisure that exists within a locality. Activities that tourists wish to undertake are linked to the natural environment, whether mountains, rivers or the sea, and the use that is made of these resources varies according to climate and seasons. Likewise, climate greatly influences the propensity of a local population to travel overseas. The demand for travel to sunshine destinations such as Dubai and Thailand during the northern winter months is particularly high in Nordic countries where the dark and cold create demand for 'escape to the sun' opportunities. Similarly, the misery of wet summers in the United Kingdom creates increased demand for holiday packages to Mediterranean destinations.

The design and organization of hospitality operations is influenced by what visitors do (water-based activities, skiing) and by the demands of climate (should rooms be heated or air-conditioned?). As examples, hotels located in tropical climates can provide dining and leisure facilities which are substantially out of doors, while hotels in ski resorts must cater for the wear and tear of outdoor ski footwear on floor coverings.

Leisure activities, whether indoor or outdoor, are influenced in terms of demand within the local community by climate, by the impact of seasonality and by population distribution. Some aspects of leisure provision are only economically viable when organized to be within ready access of large population concentrations. This concern was a major determinant in locating Disneyland, Paris, within easy reach of large urban concentrations in France, Germany, England and Benelux.

Geographically, the physical distribution of tourism, leisure and hospitality is subject to different pressures than is the case with other sectors of the economy. Where people wish to visit is influenced by climate, technology, facilities and fashion, among other things. Thus, enhanced transport links enabled people to abandon Northern European resorts for those of the sunnier Mediterranean while Florida's appeal is partly due to the development of a concentration of attractions facilities in the one location. Tourism, leisure and hospitality are also less subject to the pressures of globalization on where they locate. While certain support functions in the sector can relocate off-shore (call centres moving from Europe to India, for example), most aspects of tourism, leisure and hospitality are place-bound. The sector is one of the few within the broader services economy in the United Kingdom not to be disproportionately concentrated in the south-east of England, although London is by far the major destination attraction in the country.

Implications for people and work in tourism, hospitality and leisure

Geographical impact on the nature of tourism, hospitality and leisure translates clearly into the range of skills required by employees in the sector. Obviously, tropical island destinations such as the Maldives require an employee skills set that is based around water activities and the country's cultural assets while the focus of skills in landlocked Andorra is much more on the requirements of mountain and winter sports.

Geographical peripherality or remoteness also has major consequences for people, work and training in tourism, hospitality and leisure. The industry is widely dispersed in many countries: the outback of Australia, small islands off northern Norway, safari parks in Kenya and Tanzania and eco-lodges in Borneo. Recruiting skills appropriate for the tasks required to deliver service to contemporary international travellers in such locations is a real challenge in parts of the world. This is because such skills may not be available locally or, as in the case of some of Egypt's Red Sea resorts, urban dwellers may be reluctant to relocate to more remote parts of the country. This is a challenge further highlighted by general tendencies in many countries towards migration away from rural areas (where much tourism, hospitality and leisure employment is located) to the large urban centres where perceived opportunity is greater.

A lack of major urban centres also means that local education and training for the sector is frequently unavailable, thus both initial and in-service training must be accessed at some distance from home. Potential tourism, hospitality and leisure workers in the Faroe Islands or in Åland (Baum 1996b), for example, need to travel to Denmark and Sweden respectively to undertake any form of skills or managerial training for the sector. Peripherality, in this sector, is not just about geographical remoteness. Many workers in tourism, hospitality and leisure find access to learning difficult because of the working hours demanded by the sector, essentially offering services to guests at times when much educational provision is offered. Fáilte Ireland (2005b, p.22) recognizes this challenge in the Irish context.

> Small tourism businesses in peripheral locations are rarely able to avail of the scale benefits which larger organisations can provide to both their craft and management employees ... Tourism SMEs in Ireland can struggle to provide an environment within which sustained and developmental learning takes place. This in turn mitigates against the capacity of the sector to innovate and create new product, marketing and financial opportunities.

Distance or electronic learning via the internet or other technologies can provide part of the answer to the challenges of remoteness and the range of opportunities now available, both through companies and educational providers, does ameliorate some of the disadvantage. Scandic, the North European hotel chain owned by Hilton International, has properties located in fairly remote parts of the Nordic countries and operates a comprehensive 'Sigge Skole' for employees, covering all levels of training from induction to management development.

Political factors

The national political environment has considerable influence of the character of tourism, hospitality and leisure within a country. Political considerations may determine whether citizens of particular countries are permitted to travel overseas for touristic purposes. The Chinese authorities, for example, have recently relaxed the rules under which their citizens are allowed to travel abroad and have stipulated the countries where visitors may go, either as part of organized tours or as individual travellers. This relaxation has opened up much of the world to visitors from the most populous country on the planet and has the potential to fundamentally alter in-bound tourism in many parts of the world. In the past, many political regimes placed travel restrictions on their citizens, notably the former Soviet Union and other eastern bloc countries. These countries also limited the locations and interactions that in-bound visitors could include in their itineraries. Foreign visitors to the Soviet Union were prohibited from access to the now independent Republic of Kyrgyzstan, for example, on grounds of national security. Cuba today retains vestiges of such tensions in that tourism workers have recently been prohibited from fraternizing with foreign visitors.

On the supply side, many tourism businesses have been and continue to operate within public ownership and are, thus, subject to political influence.

Airlines are the most prominent sub-sector within tourism that remains significantly located within full or partial state ownership while operational control in the sector remains subject to close regulation in many countries in areas such as route allocation, safety and security. Railways, airports, cultural venues such as museums and major attractions such as national parks also remain under public control in many countries. Finally, the key function of destination marketing is widely accepted as a responsibility of public sector agencies at both a local and national level.

Hospitality as a sector too can be subject to political influence. In many countries, hospitality businesses have also been or, indeed, remain within public ownership and, therefore, are subject to political influence in terms of their business focus, investment decisions and, indeed, future strategy. Most hotels in former socialist Eastern Europe were state-owned and employees within them were government employees. This also remains the case in China and, in the Republic of Ireland, the Great Southern hotel chain remains part of a state company that has been subject to significant levels of political interference in recent years.

Leisure and access to leisure time can also be highly politicized in some countries. The health of the population across a wide range of areas (general fitness, obesity, smoking, alcohol consumption, exposure to the sun) are widely accepted as legitimate concerns for government and, in countries such as Scotland, are subject to political controversy and debate. How we spend our free time in leisure and what we consume during such times, therefore, becomes politicized and subject to government initiatives and policy. Such policies have underpinned public provision of leisure facilities (swimming pools, sports centres) in industrialized countries, particularly urban areas, since the nineteenth century. In many countries, such facilities continue to operate with high levels of public subsidy in order to ensure that access is possible for the whole community, irrespective of income. Similar thinking influenced the development of the concept of social tourism, creating opportunity for those with least access to leisure and travel for economic reasons to participate in heavily subsidized holiday opportunities. Social tourism was a feature in former socialist and fascist states in Europe but also remains a feature in countries such as France through trade unions and social welfare organizations for the elderly or disadvantaged. Ironically, perhaps, a significant proportion of the summer camp movement in the United States was and continues to be focused on meeting the needs of otherwise socially excluded children from the major urban centres. In Singapore, the role of the government-sponsored Social Development Unit (SDU) is to facilitate social and even romantic contact between young professionals in order to compensate for the pressures of modern working life. Within SDU activities, a wide range of leisure activities are featured and social tourism, in the form of subsidized trips away for selected members, is also an important aspect of SDU activity.

Implications for people and work in tourism, hospitality and leisure

Tourism, hospitality and leisure are a sector that is widely recognized by governments for its employment creation potential. This is true both in developed countries such as Australia, Ireland and the United Kingdom as well as in poorer countries committed to the development of tourism. Employment creation has long been recognized as a major driver in government commitment to the development of tourism, hospitality and leisure (Baum, 1994) but the challenge in countries where skills shortages are increasingly problematic alongside relatively full general employment is to ensure that jobs created in the sector have a high knowledge and skills component. Fáilte Ireland (2005b), on behalf of the Irish Government, focuses on this issue at a strategic level. The Information Society Commission at the Department of the Taoiseach noted that:

> the most important property is now intellectual property, not physical property. And it is the hearts and minds of people, rather than traditional labour, that are essential for growth and prosperity. The emergence of the knowledge society means an ever-increasing demand for a well-educated and skilled workforce across the whole economy (cited in Fáilte Ireland 2005b, p.36)

The challenge which the tourism, hospitality and leisure sector faces is ensuring that there is recognition of the knowledge dimensions of its diverse skills set at a political level in order that the sector is valued in terms of investment in education necessary for it to maintain its contribution to the economy in developed countries. In developing countries, the role accorded to tourism, hospitality and leisure is somewhat different in that the political challenge is to create employment for a potentially disenfranchised population, particularly the young. This is one of the main political motives behind the development of tourism in Iran, for example.

Political management of the tourism, hospitality and leisure work environment can take other forms. With regard to China, for example, Zhang, Pine and Lam (2005) discuss the impact of political controls on ownership, management and compensation in Chinese hotels. They map the development of employee compensation structures from the time of pre-economic reform in the 1970s when pay scales were autocratically determined by government, through a process of gradual ceding of power so that a relatively free-market economy now operates with respect to pay. The role of government in the management of human resource matters, however, has not disappeared. As recently as 1998, the Chinese Government determined that individuals in government, military or police positions could not own or manage private enterprises in order to eliminate conflicts of interest.

Within the European Union, the political debate over working hours has significant implications for businesses in tourism, hospitality and leisure, particularly in regions where seasonality and other forms of stochastic demand are a dominant feature of the operating culture. The sector in a number of European countries has been one of the main opponents of restrictions on the number of hours that employees can work within any one week.

Economic factors

The economic characteristics of countries and regions also influence how tourism, hospitality and leisure are configured. Much contemporary consumption of tourism, hospitality and leisure products and services is based on commercial transactions which, inevitably, exclude a proportion of any community on the basis of the costs involved. In developed countries of the West, exclusion from participation in certain sports or pastimes as well as the inability to avail of some forms of vacation options or luxury hotels is generally but not exclusively related to the ability to pay. Some activities do exclude on the basis of social status, ethnicity or gender, an issue with respect to some major golf clubs, for example. The existence of relatively low-cost facilities such as public sports complexes and golf courses as well as free museum access in Scotland, for example, does go some way to ameliorate exclusion on purely economic grounds. At the same time, statutory provision for paid holidays ensures that the time is provided for participation in tourism, even if the costs may still exclude many people. Such holiday entitlements, beyond core religious days, are far less common in developing countries, with the result that the time to partake in formalized leisure is largely denied people in poorer environments.

The nature of economies in many Western countries has changed dramatically in the past two to three decades and this has also impacted significantly on the role that tourism, hospitality and leisure plays. In particular, the decline of traditional, often heavy manufacturing sectors has physically changed the landscape of cities and old industrial areas and has also created major economic change. Cities such as Baltimore, Glasgow and Liverpool have had to reinvent themselves as centres for tourism and leisure as old industries, such as ship-building, have all but disappeared from the map. In their place, cultural and leisure attractions (museums, sporting venues, retail centres) have developed on a large scale. Some derelict industrial zones have been converted directly for leisure use. For example, a former open-cast coal-mining location has been reborn as a water-sports leisure complex in Rother Valley in Yorkshire, England. A further impact of post-industrial society in developed countries has been the decline in the importance of traditional industrial holidays or 'fortnights' as they are known as in Scotland, reducing the time-dependence of much vacation taking.

In poorer countries, economic exclusion from participation in tourism, hospitality and leisure is even more strongly evident. Within rural communities, where subsistence agriculture predominates, for example, participation in tourism and leisure may not be an option for both direct economic and practical reasons because tending livestock or cultivating land does not readily allow time away from work. Urban populations in the sprawling cities of Asia, Latin America and Africa are substantially excluded from participation in tourism and formal leisure on economic grounds but also because many live in unregulated economies where time off to take part is non-existent or severely limited. Participation in tourism, both domestic and international, is generally the prerogative of small, economic elites. Organized leisure is also out of the reach of a substantial proportion of the population, both urban and rural, although this is not to say that leisure activities, particularly among children, do not take place. Images of street football in Brazil and cricket on any available patch of wasteland in South Asia belie the notion that leisure must operate within a sophisticated, organized and commercial context.

Implications for people and work in tourism, hospitality and leisure

Economic links to tourism employment are closely allied to political considerations in that the creation of gainful employment in tourism, hospitality and leisure within a country brings considerable economic benefits to the country and community alongside political gains. The structure of the economy at a local and national level influences the role that tourism, hospitality and leisure work play in terms of recognition and priority of investment by governments and the private sector. In developed economies, compensation levels for tourism, hospitality and leisure are generally at the lower end of the competitive scale and this acts against the sector in terms of attracting the best employees and students into college and university programmes. In transition economies such as Kyrgyzstan (see the case study later in this chapter), multinational tourism, hospitality and leisure companies are able to compete very favourably with established sectors of the economy such as the public sector and old-style manufacturing, with the result that they are able to attract the most able workers from other organizations and from universities. In the remaining planned economies today, for example China, Zhang *et al.* (2005) report that salary and wage systems in the hotel sector remain largely rigid and are based on seniority rather than performance or responsibility. Therefore economic policy with regard to compensation, they argue, continues to discourage potential candidates from joining the hotel industry and contributes to high labour turnover levels, particularly among the young. In particular, Zhang *et al.* report that a major consequence of government economic control over remuneration is that the tourism, hospitality and leisure sector is not wage-competitive alongside sectors such as finance, information technology and commerce. As an example, they report that, in 2002, the national average income in China was RMB 39 678 whereas the annual income for Beijing's hotel workers was RMB 9580.

In the context of market-driven economies, employment and work security is closely tied to the prosperity or otherwise of a country at any particular time. A consequence of the 1997 economic crisis in Asia was widespread layoffs of or reduced salaries for employees across national economies; in particular within tourism, hospitality and leisure as people ceased to travel within the region. The recovery of regional economies led to the return of employment opportunities and enhanced remuneration but insecurity of this type (as well as that caused by other crises) does leave a scar on perceptions of the industry as a sector of stable employment.

Cultural factors

Cultural factors also create diversity in the nature of tourism, hospitality and leisure at a national and regional level and even within communities. National and regional culture are, in themselves, major attractions for visitors interested in a wide range of cultural manifestations including music, visual arts, dance and theatre in both traditional and contemporary forms. The attraction of formal presentation of culture to tourists visiting diverse destinations such as Bali, Liverpool, Milan and Prague illustrates this point. Culture is also informal and living and tourists participate in this dimension when visiting live, impromptu music events in Irish pubs or joining in sporting events at Highland Gatherings in Scotland.

Cultural factors also influence participation in tourism, hospitality and leisure. Women, for example, may not be permitted to be part of some aspects of culture, whether as actors or spectators, in some traditional cultures. In some countries, such exclusion was present historically in that, at the time of Shakespeare, all female roles in his plays were taken by young men. It is also manifest in countries where religion and culture prohibit mixed participation in leisure. In Iran, for example, men and women cannot share swimming as a leisure activity in either pools or the sea. In 2005 protests and violent police reaction in Pakistan were the result of a ban on men and women running in road races together (Goodenough 2005). Exclusion may also be based on social and peer pressure rather than custom or legal restraint. Boys who engage in dance as a leisure activity, for example, are much less common than is the case with girls of the same age in many Western countries, largely for reasons of this kind.

Implications for people and work in tourism, hospitality and leisure

The impact of cultural factors on people and work in tourism, hospitality and leisure is a significant determinant of variation between countries and regions. The employment structure of the sector in terms of gender and ethnic groups can be greatly influenced by cultural traditions and religious law. Some Arab cultures, for example, forbid or severely circumscribe the role that women can play in employment while, historically, strict Hindus in India were unable to work in food-related positions in the hospitality sector.

Demand for the public consumption of culture as part of both tourism and leisure also impacts upon opportunities for work and the nature of employment that is created. Major European cities such as Vienna, Prague and Barcelona attract large numbers of visitors specifically because of their cultural assets and this, in turn creates a wide range of work opportunities that are culturally based in museums, galleries and performance auditoria. The same can be seen in cities such as Agra in India (location of the Taj Mahal) and Cairo in Egypt. The role of culture in creating employment opportunities in tourism, hospitality and leisure is not exclusively built upon the traditional and 'high brow'. There is increasing recognition of the value of popular culture within a destination's culture port-folio and, as a consequence, cities such as Liverpool (The Beatles), Nashville (Country and Western), Hollywood, California and a wide range of film loca-tions have been able to create a range of employment opportunities allied to interest in their particular dimension of popular culture. Centres of pilgrimage such as Mecca, Lourdes and Jerusalem are also examples of how culture through religion can create large numbers of work opportunities across special-ist cultural positions to more routine service positions.

Specialist culturally related skills in the performing and visual arts, literature, restoration and preservation and aspects of heritage such as food and sport also create a requirement for dedicated training and skills development, in terms of both perpetuating heritage and culture within communities and promoting such activities for visitor consumption. Educational programmes to ensure the continuance of culture are important elements in the preservation of such skills throughout many different contexts worldwide.

Structural factors

What might be called structural factors also influence the nature of tourism, hospitality and leisure at a national or regional level. One of the most significant of these structural considerations relates to the impact of seasonality on demand for tourism, hospitality and leisure (Baum and Lundtorp 2000). Many activities that are attractive to tourists but also play a significant role in leisure consumption at a local level are highly seasonal in terms of when it is feasible and enjoyable to engage in them. Skiing, for example, plays a role in both tourism and leisure but is an activity confined to winter months in most localities. Likewise, outdoor activities dependent on warm weather (water sports, for example) are limited to summer months in all but tropical and sub-tropical locations. In many cases 'the season' can be exceedingly short in what might be called 'extreme' tourism destinations (Baldaccino 2006), lasting little more than six weeks to two months, during which time suppliers of tourism services seek to generate sufficient income to cover the full year. The impact of seasonal variation can be very significant in some countries. According to the ILO (2001):

> In Austria, there is a 26 per cent variation in employment in the sector; in Spain the figure is 47 per cent; in Italy it is more than 50%, while in Denmark the number of employees in the sector doubles during the summer months. (p.10)

Structural considerations, however, extend beyond seasonality. Location and distance from key centres of population, while essentially geographical in nature, can lead to the impact of peripherality on tourism, hospitality and leisure provision. Peripheral locations suffer from poor communications and access, for example, and may face competitive disadvantage in relation to destinations offering similar facilities and opportunities but located closer to major urban areas or transport nodes. Island locations, for example, have been the subject of extensive study because of the particular influence that insularity has on the nature and performance of the tourism sector (for example, Conlin and Baum 1995; Lockhart and Drakakis-Smith 1997; Apostolopoulos and Gayle 2002).

A further consideration that can be included as a structural consideration is that of business ownership within the sector. The balance between small, independent operators and large, chain-owned multiples within each of tourism, hospitality and leisure shapes the way that the sectors operate and how they organize their business. In many parts of the developed world, there is a tendency towards increasing multiple ownership and operation, either through a direct model or through various forms of management or franchising. Brand identity within tourism, hospitality and leisure is growing rapidly so that names such as TUI, Thomas Cook, Hilton, Shangri-la, Living Well and David Lloyd are becoming increasingly well recognized. However, independent, private ownership is still very important in most countries and all three sectors remain dominated by small, indeed micro, operations. This is particularly evident in peripheral locations where the impact of multinational brands is generally marginal; examples are Iceland and the Åland Islands in the Baltic (Baum 1996b), where there is evidence of business integration across sectors, involving locally controlled businesses to the exclusion of outsiders (shipping, accommodation, finance, supplies).

In rather newer destinations, particularly in the developing world, the tourism, hospitality and leisure enterprises exhibit extreme contrast between large multinational operations and the micro operations of local entrepreneurs in the souvenir, food or activities markets. Some countries in the developing world, having driven the early stages of growth in tourism, hospitality and leisure on the back of multinational investment (also known as foreign direct investment or FDI), now recognize the importance of micro businesses to the future sustainability of their industry. Wong (2004), in the case of Malaysia, outlines the importance of FDI to the early growth of the sector but recent government initiatives have stressed the need to raise operational standards in the micro-business sector, particularly in food service and accommodation.

Some structural dimensions in tourism, hospitality and leisure are relatively fixed and slow to change. Traditionally, seasonality was seen to be an element within the sector in which marginal change was achievable but where fundamental change was unlikely. In some cases, such as that of the winter ski season in the northern hemisphere, this remains substantially true; shifting dependence on specific seasons has been successfully addressed in destinations such as Hawaii. Ownership structure in tourism, hospitality and leisure is dynamic in many countries and is subject to considerable and ongoing change over time. Lloyd (2003), for example, reports on the structure of the fitness industry in the UK and notes that just over half of fitness clubs are independent, single-site operations. However, she further notes that 'these independents are gradually declining in significance as they are taken over or put out of business by the rapidly growing fitness chains' (p.9).

Implications for people and work in tourism, hospitality and leisure

Structural impacts on work and employment in tourism, hospitality and leisure are very significant. Variation in demand, whether seasonal or located within shorter and less predictable time frames, impacts directly upon the stability and continuity of employment. It can also affect the quality of life of tourism, hospitality and leisure workers in the sense that, for example, split shifts, often resulting from volatile demand in the restaurant sector, can be identified as a contributing cause of alcoholism and anti-social behaviour among workers in this sector in some countries. Seasonality, especially of an extreme nature in peripheral locations, undermines sustainability of employment and careers in the tourism, hospitality and leisure sector and this, in turn, has serious implications for the delivery of sustained quality. Use of specialist skills, for example those of a ski instructor, may require the worker to migrate between the northern and southern hemispheres if she or he wishes to focus full-time on the use of these skills, something that, in practice, is difficult to manage. As a result, as Adler and Adler (2004) point out, many workers with such skills drift into other forms of tourism, hospitality and leisure work out of season in order to make ends meet.

Business size and structure influence the nature of work and the employment opportunities that are offered in the tourism, hospitality and leisure sector. In Europe, there are 2.7 million small and medium-sized (SMEs) operating in the hotel, catering and tourism sector (ILO 2001), of which 94 per cent are micro enterprises employing fewer than ten people. In Portugal, for example, the average number of people employed in a hotel or catering business in 1996 was 3.3 while the figure across the then 15 members of the European Union was 4.6 (ILO 2001). The major role that SMEs, indeed micro businesses, play in most countries and across a majority of sub-sectors has major implications in this regard. Small businesses require considerable workplace flexibility from employees who are likely to be required to undertake work across a range of functional areas. Such businesses are also frequently family ventures and this can act as a barrier to career development if you are not from within the owning family. At the same time, major growth, worldwide, in tourism, hospitality and leisure is vested substantially in larger, increasingly multinational organizations. These companies do offer opportunity and career mobility but this takes place within the constraints of a corporate culture.

Technological factors

The effects of technological change on tourism, hospitality and leisure also play an important part in shaping the sector as it is found in various parts of the world today. When we talk about technology, generally the reference is to, on the one hand, change in the equipment and facilities that underpin the way that the sector operates (aircraft, theme-park rides, hotel security locks, refrigeration) and, on the other, to information and communications technology (ICT) (computers, the internet, telecommunications, entertainment).

What we might call the 'operating' or 'process' technology of tourism, hospitality and leisure is subject to constant change but such development is frequently uneven in its impact. Advances in transportation, for example, have the capacity to benefit destinations that receive direct advantage from such change but, at the same time, other locations may be bypassed and lose out as a consequence. The advent of longer-haul aircraft, for example, has reduced the number of stopovers airlines are required to make on major trunk routes. As a result, stopover locations such as Bahrain, Gander, Honolulu and Shannon have lost out badly over the past 25 years as long-distance aircraft overfly them on transcontinental routes. Likewise, road bypasses and express train services disenfranchise smaller locations en route between major cities. High-cost technology has also impacted upon food production, preparation and delivery with consequences that mean small businesses or those in poorer countries are unable to compete with global production and distribution. High-cost leisure technology in, for example, the fitness industry has changed the manner in which the developed world enjoy themselves and has created options that are inaccessible to those in poorer countries. Food processing and preservation technologies have impacted on the availability of menus across a wide range of outlets that previously would not have attempted the level of diversity that they do include, creating both greater choice for consumers and greater competition between operators.

Developments in ICT have already revolutionized the lives of most people living in the developed world and have the potential to impact upon much of the developing world in years to come. Mobile telephones, the internet and the globalization of entertainment options are examples of technologies that have impacted upon both access to and cost of many services in tourism, hospitality and leisure. Access to such technologies is not equal and disparities exist on the basis of socio-economic, geographical, educational, attitudinal, generational or physical disability factors. This notion of a digital divide (Cullen 2001) relates to the gap between the availability of ICTs and the levels of access and utilization of them in developed nations, as well as the situation in less developed countries (Blanning, Bui and Tan 1997; Clark and Lai 1998; Espiritu 2003; James 2005). Thus, technologies do not in themselves solve social and economic discrepancies within societies, but they can often exacerbate them. Quay (2001) notes that the digital divide is not just an issue of access but that it relates to those who are able to use the internet to improve the quality of their lives and those who are not.

Technological developments in ICT also mean that the consumer has gained far greater control over the process of distribution, particularly in tourism and hospitality. As a result, the role of intermediaries, particularly travel agents, has changed and, to some extent, been bypassed because tourists can obtain information as well as making bookings directly with suppliers (car hire, theatre, airlines, hotels). However, Baum (2004) argues that the requirements of ICT access in availing of low-cost and flexible travel in itself creates social exclusion so that the technology revolution in travel is every bit as exclusive as it can be in other sectors of economic activity.

Implications for people and work in tourism, hospitality and leisure

As we have already suggested, technological development acts in a number of ways with respect to work and employment in tourism, hospitality and leisure. On the one hand, process technology can act to simplify and de-skill many areas of work in areas such as restaurant kitchens and aircraft flight decks. The impact of technology, accompanied by a simplification of service processes through standardization, has contributed greatly to processes that fall under the umbrella of what Ritzer (2004) called 'McDonaldization'. In this sense, technology acts to dehumanize the workplace and to sacrifice all vestiges of creativity and flair in the interests of standardization and cost reduction. At the same time, technology can act to make services more reliable and to allow service staff to focus on delivering a better and more individualized service to guests in tourism, hospitality and leisure.

ICT, as we have seen, has acted to reduce the importance of some work roles in tourism, hospitality and leisure, notably in traditional travel agencies because consumers can take control of aspects of their own information-seeking and reservations. At the same time, ICT has created new opportunity through internet travel companies such as Expedia and Lastminute.com. Of particular significance is the growth of remotely located call centres for reservations and marketing purposes in tourism, hospitality and leisure. A concentration of these now exist in India, drawing on locally available ICT and language skills at much lower costs than is the case in Europe and North America.

The impact of technology on work in tourism, hospitality and leisure in developing countries has been much more limited. With low labour costs and a high demand for employment opportunity, there is less incentive to invest in technology substitution. Furthermore, local populations are not digitally active to the extent that their counterparts in developed countries are and this means that more traditional access and distribution methods still predominate.

Globalization

The impact of globalization on tourism, hospitality and leisure products, services and market behaviour draws upon a number of the drivers of diversity that we have already considered. In some respects, the logic of globalization is that it should work to reduce diversity but, at the same time, there is evidence that the relationship between a local environment and global forces is not necessarily common across time and place. As an example, the presence of McDonald's in different countries has excited divergent reactions from apparent delight when first introduced (Russia, China) to hostility on cultural and religious grounds (France, India).

Globalization, in itself, is a process that is highly contentious and has become the focus of concentrated protest in many countries of both the developed and developing world. The longer-term impact of this trade process on developing countries in particular is certainly not clear and there are cogent arguments within the debate that see many aspects of globalization as tilted unfairly in favour of those countries and multinational companies that can readily avail of its benefits. Lall (2003) address the impact of globalization on employment in developing countries and argues that, certainly in the short term, the process will have many damaging effects on established economic sectors in poorer countries, notably agriculture and manufacturing. Tourism, hospitality and leisure activity may also suffer, especially in terms of the employment benefits of infrastructure development, if such activity is substantially imported into developing countries.

Wong (2004) talks about the role that foreign multinationals play in creating labour market competition within destinations and, as a consequence, imposing spillover effects, in the form of enhanced skills and greater investment in training, upon local tourism, hospitality and leisure operators. In this context, globalization acts to enhance the overall skills levels and the investment in human capital within the sector.

Globalization as a process also has implications for tourism, hospitality and leisure in an indirect manner. Changes in the structure, technology and trade in global agriculture has resulted in farmers facing over-production and declining returns on traditional crops and husbandry while their rural communities suffer from depopulation. Diversification through tourism has been a widespread response, initially in the developed world, that is now being considered in developing countries as well, such as Karnataka in India (ILO 2001).

Implications for people and work in tourism, hospitality and leisure

The impact of globalization on work and employment in tourism, hospitality and leisure is certainly mixed and is felt in somewhat different forms in developed and developing countries. Tourism, hospitality and leisure is not a sector that can be centralized, it is an industry where factories of the field operate in a dispersed manner. Thus, the process of globalization in tourism, hospitality and leisure, at one level, cannot take the form of concentrated production found in the automobile sector or in textiles. There will always be demand for skills, albeit relatively routine ones, in every community and country. However, globalization is having the effect of concentrating control of large sectors of the tourism, hospitality and leisure industry (airlines, hotels, theme parks) in the hands of a small number of companies. As a result, opportunities for innovation and strategic involvement may be centralized even when actual service delivery is not.

Globalization has also created significant opportunity for some people within the tourism, hospitality and leisure to experience work and careers across different countries and cultures. Baum (2000) considers some of the varied ways in which globalization has affected education for tourism, both in terms of opportunity and threat, and the contradictory tensions which see it as both parochial within countries and borderless in terms of online and corporate learning. The impact of globalization in agriculture and the opportunity that this has created for new tourism, hospitality and leisure businesses has also generated new employment opportunities in communities that previously may have been off the tourism trail.

Impact of market perception

Our final driver is what might be styled the impact of market perception. In other words, a combination of the factors addressed above can shape the manner in which key stakeholders in tourism, hospitality and leisure perceive a location and this, in turn, influences the way in which the sector is shaped in that location. Political events such as terrorism or conflict create an image for a location, country or, indeed, whole region, and this impacts upon the choices (or otherwise) of visitors when choosing to visit that destination. A country like Iran, very peaceful on the ground to those visitors who do choose to visit, faces major perceptual obstacles as a destination. This, in turn, impacts on the range of products and services it is able to offer, shaping the sector in a significant manner. Northern Ireland has, over 25 years, been likewise influenced. Such influences, however, can be of much shorter duration, as in when potential visitors react to major crises and disasters such as the Heysel Stadium football tragedy in 1985, foot and mouth outbreak in Britain in 2001, SARS in Asia in 2003 and the tsunami of 26 December 2004. Each of these events combined physical, human and perceptual impacts and influenced the manner in which tourism, hospitality and leisure services were perceived and organized.

Implications for people and work in tourism, hospitality and leisure

Crises drive change in the organization of tourism, hospitality and leisure and such change, in turn, has major implications for those working in the sector. In the immediate aftermath of crisis, many people working in the sector can lose their jobs as was the case in the UK with foot and mouth, in Hong Kong with SARS and in the Indian Ocean countries affected by the 2004 tsunami. Recovery can be slow but, even where it is more rapid, many sector employees will have moved on to other employment and their skills may be lost to tourism, hospitality and leisure. There can also be a major impact on perceptions of the sector for future employment among school and college students and their families – people reacting by rejecting the sector as unstable and not offering long-term prospects (Subramonian *et al.* 2005). There is certainly anecdotal evidence to support such perceptions in the manner in which applications to study in the sector from potential students in East Asia reduced significantly at the time of SARS. Where conflict is sustained over an extended period, the impact may be somewhat different in that tourism, hospitality and leisure are not seen as careers of choice and people choose not to work in the sector.

The above list of the drivers of divergence in the shape of tourism, hospitality and leisure at a national or regional level is by no means exhaustive. Neither is our consideration of some of the implications of these drivers for people and work in tourism, hospitality and leisure. It is possible to look at how the three areas operate so differently in different countries and regions and identify links and influences across a wide range of other factors. In the context of this book, how tourism, hospitality and leisure are configured and operate are considerations of major importance to our understanding of the role of people in the delivery of services and how this role is also subject to major variation across different countries and regions. These issues are touched on in our discussion of the implications that are outlined above and will receive further elaboration as discussion as this book unfolds.

Case Study *Tourism, hospitality and leisure in Kyrgyzstan*

Kyrgyzstan is one of the more impoverished of the former Soviet republics in Central Asia, with a 2002 per capita gross national income (GNI) of US$290, which is significantly below the regional average and that for Asia as a whole. Against most of the World Bank's indices of economic progress, the country's position is in the bottom 50 per cent and, in many cases, the lower 30 per cent of countries and Kyrgyzstan has seen only limited progress in any of the key areas over the past five years. It is a country that remains subject to political instability, as witnessed in changes to the political landscape in March 2005, and some areas to the south are subject to civil unrest for religious reasons.

Kyrgyzstan has a population of five million people and is a landlocked country, bordering on Uzbekistan, Kazakhstan, China and Tajikistan. The country is multi-ethnic and linguistic, with Kyrgyz the official language and Russian the language of communication between communities. The majority religion is Islam although there is a substantial Russian Orthodox minority. Religious observance as a legacy of the Soviet era is relatively low. Literacy levels remain high also as a result of the Soviet era. Kyrgyzstan is a small, poor and mountainous country with a predominantly agricultural economy. Cotton, tobacco, wool and meat are the main agricultural products, although only tobacco and cotton are exported in any quantity. Industrial exports include gold, mercury, uranium, and natural gas and electricity. Kyrgyzstan has been fairly progressive in carrying out market reforms, such as an improved regulatory system and land reform and, as such, was the first Commonwealth of Independent States (CIS) country to be accepted into the World Trade Organization. With fits and starts, inflation has been lowered to an estimated 7 per cent in 2001, 2.1 per cent in 2002, and 4.0 per cent in 2003. Much of the government's ownership of enterprises has been sold. Drops in production had been severe after the break-up of the Soviet Union in December 1991, but by mid-1995 production began to recover and exports began to increase. Growth was held down to 2.1 per cent in 1998 largely because of the spill-over from Russia's economic difficulties, but moved ahead to 3.6 per cent in 1999, 5 per cent in 2000 and 5 per cent again in 2001. On the positive side, the government and the international financial institutions have been engaged in a comprehensive medium-term poverty reduction and economic growth strategy. Further restructuring of domestic industry and success in attracting foreign investment are keys to future growth.

Former republics of the Soviet Union such as Kyrgyzstan face major challenges as they move from planned economic structures to the competitive environment of the free-market world. Losing the economic and political protection of a parent super-power means that countries in the region must seek new economic opportunities in the services sector. International tourism is seen as a major strategic opportunity by most of these countries but engaging competitively in this sector requires significant investment in facilities, infrastructure and, above all, in skills development. A key objective in supporting the development of tourism in transition economies such as Kyrgyzstan is the creation of new employment opportunities in countries traditionally highly dependent on heavy industries and agriculture.

The most recent figures published by the World Tourism Organization for Kyrgyzstan report 140 000 international visitors in 2002, representing a seven-fold increase over 1995. Given that, prior to 1990, the country was closed to international visitors, a very low starting base is not surprising and there has been significant growth since then, assisted by improved air links to Europe and within the region. In 1995, international receipts were US$5 million and the equivalent figure for 2001 was US$24 million. The support provided by Kyrgyzstan to the international coalition during the invasion of Afghanistan in 2002, particularly through use of its airbases, has generated sustained military and diplomatic business for the capital city.

International investment in the tourism, hospitality and leisure sector in Kyrgyzstan is limited to three hotels in the capital, Bishkek, one of which is part of a major international chain and the other two of which are owned and operated by foreign entrepreneurs. Some tourism and hospitality businesses remain in state hands but the majority today are locally owned, small businesses. Organized leisure, where it exists, is pre-independence and operates within public ownership.

Kyrgyzstan's main attraction to the international visitor is its relatively unspoiled natural environment, comprising mountains and lakes. Its location, in close proximity to the fabled Silk Road, also generates interest in the country and its culture. Facilities in support of these attractions were developed during the Soviet era and, although there has been some foreign investment in the accommodation stock over the past 15 years, the majority of providers in all sectors offer fairly basic services and facilities by modern international standards. Leisure facilities available to both the local community and visitors are old and in need of investment and, as a consequence, pose safety issues. There are few modern facilities for those wishing to explore rural and wilderness areas of the country.

Case prepared by the author from personal research and published sources.

Case discussion questions

1. In what ways have historical, geographical, political, economic, cultural and structural factors influenced the contemporary shape of tourism, hospitality and leisure in Kyrgyzstan?

2. Identify and research other countries and regions that may have been subject to similar influences to Kyrgyzstan in the development of their tourism, hospitality and leisure sectors.

Defining tourism, hospitality and leisure

'Tourism', 'hospitality' and 'leisure' are interrelated concepts, the precise meaning of which varies according to country and context and has also changed over time. Indeed, we could also add recreation and travel as commonly used alternatives to complete what could be seen as definitional confusion! So, some care is necessary when looking for definitions including the need to check the source for its country of origin and date so as to be sure of the intended sense. Definitions of these concepts are not always entirely in agreement – the terms are such that their interpretation and usage varies considerably according to the context in which they are employed and the particular interests of the author. It is worthwhile looking at some of these definitions.

Tourism and the tourist

The sum of the phenomena and relationships arising from the interaction among tourists, business suppliers, host governments, host communities, origin governments, universities, community colleges and non-governmental organisations, in the process of attracting, transporting, hosting and managing these tourists and other visitors. (Weaver and Oppermann 2000, p.458)

Tourism is the study of man away from his usual habitat, of the industry which responds to his needs and of the impacts that both he and the industry have on the host's socio-cultural, economic and physical environments. (Jafari 1990, p.36)

Tourism is the sum of the phenomena and relationships arising from the interaction of tourists, business suppliers, host governments and host communities in the process of attracting and hosting these tourists and other visitors. (McIntosh and Goeldner 1996, p.4)

Four criteria can be considered. First, there is itinerary: domestic or international or both. Second, minimum or maximum duration of trips can be indicated ... A third criterion (not essential) is minimum distance travelled. A fourth is distinctive behaviour which can be indicated by saying that tourism revolves around leisure. (Leiper 2000, p.590)

Defining 'tourism' is not really helpful unless we also understand who the tourist is, so it is worthwhile to add a further definition of 'the tourist'. Therefore, the tourist can be seen as:

Any person who travels to a country other than that in which s/he has his/her usual residence, but outside his/her usual environment for a period of at least one night but not more than one year and whose main purpose of visit is other than the exercise of an activity remunerated from within the country visited. This term includes people travelling for leisure, recreation and holidays, visiting friends and relatives, business and professional health treatment, religious pilgrimages and other purposes. (WTO 1995, p.24)

'Travel' sits alongside 'tourism' as a key component.

Travel involves movement from place to place. This is a fundamental aspect of tourism, and in its absence there would be no tourism. (Wall 2000, p.600)

Hospitality and the hospitality industry

Friendly behaviour towards visitors. (*Longman Dictionary of Contemporary English 2001, p.691*)

Friendly and generous reception and entertainment of guests or strangers. (*Oxford Quick Reference Dictionary and Thesaurus 1998, p.424*)

The method of production by which the needs of the proposed guest are satisfied to the utmost and that means a supply of goods and services in a quantity and quality that is acceptable to him so that he feels the product is worth the price. (Tideman 1983, p.1)

A harmonious mixture of tangible and intangible components – food, beverages, beds, ambience and environment, and behaviour of staff. (Cassee 1983, p.xiv)

Commercial organisations that specialise in providing accommodation and/or food and/or drink through a voluntary human exchange, which is contemporaneous in nature, and undertaken to enhance the mutual well being of the parties involved. (Brotherton and Wood 2000, p.14)

Leisure

The time available to an individual when work, sleep and other basic needs have been met. (Cooper *et al.* 2005, p.11)

Two views of leisure, the Greek with an emphasis on the mind and quality of life and an undercurrent of elitism and the Roman with an emphasis on rest and entertainment and an undercurrent of social control, characterise the two dominant views of leisure throughout much of history. (Smith and Mannell 2000, p.354)

Relatively freely undertaken non-work activity. (Roberts 1978, p.3)

Within leisure and tourism as well, recreation can be seen as the

Pursuit engaged upon during leisure time. (Cooper *et al.* 2005, p.11)

Recreation's links to leisure are also emphasized.

Recreation is a pleasurable, socially sanctioned activity that restores the individual, concomitant with the experience of leisure. (Simmons 2000, p.488)

The definitions that we have looked at are just a sample of a very wide range that can be found in the literature. What may be evident from this exercise are the links that exist between the concepts but also that the links are not always complete and involve some degree of compromise. For example, most business travel is not undertaken for leisure purposes (but may contain a leisure component) and therefore does not sit comfortably within a definition of tourism that focuses on leisure time. However, we can draw a connecting line between them which is not totally inclusive of all the elements included but provides a useful framework to assist in our understanding. This linking line can look something like this:

Leisure involves discretionary time free from work

⇓

Recreation is structured use of leisure time centred on one or more activities

⇓

Travel involves movement from one place to another place for purposes which may include tourism

⇓

Tourism is what we do (business, leisure and recreation) once we have travelled to our destination

⇓

Tourists are individuals who engage in tourism

⇓

Hospitality provides core services (accommodation, food and drink) to the visitor when at a destination but also when at home during periods of leisure

It should be clear from the exercise that these concepts are closely interconnected but each one has specific aspects that distinguish it from the others. They are also closely related to other concepts, notably time, place and work and the development of definitions of tourism, hospitality and leisure all build upon these implied links. To travel and to be tourists and, thus, be part of tourism, to benefit from hospitality and to enjoy leisure, to participate in leisure activities, we require time and, in most cultures, this time is thought of as periods when we are not committed to work. If we are working, we are not at leisure. However, we can be tourists while, at the same time, engaging in work. To do so, we must accept definitions that include business travel as part of tourism. Just as leisure can include recreational activities that are not part of tourism (playing football, meeting friends in the shopping mall, reading at home) so tourism includes activities that are not necessarily leisure- or recreation-related (business meetings, conferences, trade shows). Travel and tourism also imply devoting time (generally when we are not working) to activities away from our normal home. In other words, there is a geographical or place component to travel and tourism which is not necessarily present in hospitality or leisure. This removal from normality is a theme that we will address at various points later in this book in terms of what this means for those who work in the sector and provide services for visitors.

People in tourism, hospitality and leisure – who are they?

People in the tourism, hospitality and leisure sector, the workforce who own and operate the enterprises in the industry's private sector and provide support roles within the public sector, are a group characterized by diversity in terms of all their dimensions. This diversity presents one of the main difficulties in understanding the challenges faced within the sector and to seeking a route towards sustainable human resource practices in the sector. Diversity in part reflects structural considerations addressed above but, in this context, is driven by a range of further considerations, including:

- people working in widely differing sub-sectors which include attractions, culture/heritage, events, transportation, accommodation, catering, facilitation, retail, sports and fitness all of which employ diverse people in terms of their technical and interpersonal skills and management functions;
- people working in what might be styled 'adjacent' sub-sectors – businesses such as non-tourist retail, security, border services and agriculture which include direct involvement with tourism, hospitality and leisure even though their business and operational *raison d'etre* may not lie within the sector and as workers they may not think of themselves as located within tourism, hospitality and leisure;
- people located in businesses which provide for either in-bound or out-bound tourism activity or, in some cases, both, from whom differing operational, cultural and linguistic skills and sensitivities are demanded;
- people working in the public sector, private organisations, voluntary organisations and through forms of community participation, each with differing motivational business/employment objectives and cultures;
- people benefiting from tourism, hospitality and leisure's capacity for social inclusion and ability to accommodate employees from diverse social, cultural, ethnic and capability backgrounds;
- people working in operations of differing business size, structure, ownership and ownership motivations;
- people who provide highly personalized and individual services for their clients, often outwith the structure of a formal organization, whether as personal fitness trainers or sex workers;
- people faced with the impact of stochastic demand patterns, particularly in terms of flexible, part-time, seasonal, casual and 'lifestyle' work; and
- people faced with the diversity of organizational structures, skills levels and operational responsibilities that emanate from the above.

Given the above variety, it is clear that tourism, hospitality and leisure's people are anything but a homogeneous group. Essentially, the common factor in defining the tourism, hospitality and leisure workforce is not governed by what they do nor for whom they work but rather by the relationship which their role plays in terms of meeting the needs of visitors and leisure consumers in a country, region or community. People are part of tourism, hospitality and leisure so long as the role they fulfil (even if only for part of their working and community lives) meets this criterion. Therefore, tourism, hospitality and leisure's people include those working in mainstream tourism, hospitality and leisure businesses (hotels, airlines, leisure centres, museums), those working in administration to support the sector (government, semi-state bodies, local authorities), those contributing at a community or voluntary organizational level (sports clubs, heritage organizations, local cultural events) and those with an occasional, transitory association with visitors (bank employees, police, immigration officials, petrol retailers). From a human resources perspective in the context of tourism, hospitality and leisure, this diversity creates real challenges in that stakeholders in the sector do not think or act collectively, do not respond to common 'stimuli' in terms of problem recognition and ownership and, in any case, have diverse traditions in meeting their people management and development requirements.

Managing people, managing human resources

This book is not about functional human resource management in the sense that the field is addressed in a wide range of textbooks in this field. Human resource management is frequently seen in terms of a three-part cycle, which contains all of the functional responsibilities that managers with responsibility for this role are required to address. This human resource cycle can be summarized as:

1. Attract an effective workforce
   - labour markets
   - human resource planning
   - recruitment and selection
   - flexible approaches to employment
   - retention.

2. Develop an effective workforce
   - performance and appraisal
   - education, training and development
   - career development and succession planning.

3. Maintain an effective workforce
   - rewards – formal and informal
   - welfare
   - teamwork and empowerment
   - employee involvement and employee relations
   - grievance and discipline
   - equality and diversity.

This book addresses most of these functional concerns but does so in a manner that contextualizes them under a number of key themes, some of which have direct convergence with elements of the cycle and some of which do not. In identifying the main components of the cycle, the purpose of this book is to consider them within their wider setting, relating them to themes across the spectrum of connections to history, geography, politics, economics, culture and technology, among other themes. In this way, the management of people is considered in an integrated and integrative manner.

Case Study *Southwest Airlines*

Southwest was founded by Rollin King and Herb Kelleher over 30 years ago when they got together and decided to start a different kind of airline. They began with one simple notion: if you get your passengers to their destinations when they want to get there, on time, at the lowest possible fares, and make sure they have a good time doing it, people will fly with your airline.

What began as a small Texas airline has grown to become one of the largest airlines in America. Today, Southwest Airlines flies more than 65 million passengers a year to 59 great cities (60 airports) all across the country, and they do it more than 2800 times a day.

In May 1988, Southwest were the first airline to win the coveted Triple Crown for a month – Best On-time Record, Best Baggage Handling and Fewest Customer Complaints. Since then they have won it more than 30 times, as well as receiving five annual Triple Crowns for 1992, 1993, 1994, 1995 and 1996, and no other airline has contributed more to the advancement of the commercial airline industry than Southwest Airlines. Southwest were the first airline with a frequent flyer programme to give credit for the number of trips taken and not the number of miles flown. They also pioneered senior discounts, Fun Fares, Fun Packs, a same-day air freight delivery service, ticketless travel, and many other unique programmes.

Aspects of the Southwest operational model have had a great influence on low-cost airlines in Europe, notably Ryanair and easyJet.

Southwest illustrates that human resource management is not something which can be compartmentalised into its core activities. This case demonstrates the value of an approach to human resources matters which lies at the heart of the company's mission statement and underpins all its statements about itself. It is all about joined-up thinking and connected practice in all areas of business.

Southwest's approach to people management starts with the company's mission statement and its elaboration:

The mission of Southwest Airlines is dedication to the highest quality of customer service delivered with a sense of warmth, friendliness, individual pride and company spirit.

> At Southwest Airlines, our Mission Statement has always governed the way we conduct our business. It highlights our desire to serve our Customers and gives us direction when we have to make service-related decisions. It is another way of saying, 'we always try to do the right thing!' Our Mission Statement has also led the way to the airline industry's best cumulative consumer satisfaction record, according to statistics accumulated and published by the U.S. Department of Transportation. That is why we are sharing it with you.
>
> In keeping with the spirit and intent of our Mission Statement, and as evidence of our wish to continually meet the expectations of our valued Customers, Southwest wants you to have a basic understanding of how we operate. We want you to have confidence in our airline and Employees, and we want you to be aware that there are, or may be, circumstances that can have an impact on your travel plans, purchase decisions, or your overall expectations.

▶

Foremost, we want you to know that it is never our wish to inconvenience our valued Customers. We tell our Employees we are in the Customer Service business – we just happen to provide airline transportation. It is a privilege to serve your air travel needs.

The Employees of Southwest Airlines understand our mission, and we are happy to share it, and the following information, with you, our valued Customer. Our Customer Service Commitment was designed and written in such a way as to clarify many of the most commonly questioned terms and conditions of our Contract of Carriage and provide you with insight into some of our policies and procedures. For that reason, it only made sense to make it a part of our Contract of Carriage. And, Southwest is proud to incorporate its voluntary Customer Service Commitment in its official Contract of Carriage reinforcing our pledge to provide safe, affordable, reliable, timely, courteous, and efficient air transportation and baggage handling service on every flight we operate, as well as produce a fair return on our Shareholders' investments. We offer you this information in recognition of the great importance that we place on your business and your confidence.

The role, responsibilities but also the benefits of working for Southwest underpin the relationships they seek to establish with other key stakeholders, particularly shareholders and customers.

Southwest's approach to its people is demonstrated across a wide range of indicators. Their personnel credo includes the following catchy lines which illustrate what they are all about:

- Southwest Airlines is a service organization.
- Employees are No. 1.
- Think small to grow big.
- Manage in good times for bad times.

- Irreverence is OK.
- It is OK to be yourself.
- Have fun at work.
- Take competition seriously, not yourself.
- Hire for attitude and train for skills.
- Do whatever it takes.
- Always practise the golden rule, both internally and externally.

In addition, however, they put the overall people philosophy into practice through a range of staff benefits, including the following:

Passes/travel privileges One of the special benefits of working at Southwest is flying free. Effective the first day of employment, employees, spouses, eligible dependent children and parents of employees have unlimited space-available travel privileges on Southwest. Discounted travel arrangements with other carriers are also available through the Southwest Airlines Pass Bureau, subject to eligibility requirements and other restrictions.

ProfitSharing and 401(k) Participation in the ProfitSharing Plan is offered to all eligible employees. The plan is funded by company contributions to profit-sharing accounts. Company contributions are made when the company meets profitability goals set each year. The 401(k) Plan is designed to help employees to prepare for the future. Eligible employees may contribute up to 50 per cent of their pay to the plan on a pre-tax basis. A company match is offered based on employee groups. Rollovers are accepted from the employee's former employer's qualified plan.

Stock Purchase Plan This plan was specially designed to allow employees to share in the success of the company. Through the plan, employees may invest in Southwest Airlines Co. stock through payroll deductions. Employees pay only 90 per cent of market value for the stock. The company pays broker commissions on stock purchases.

Medical insurance Employees may choose from several different medical plan options depending on their lifestyle, needs and priorities through a cafeteria style flexible benefits programme. PPO Network and HMO plans are included. Most medical plan options are available to employees at no cost with family coverage available at minimal cost.

Dental insurance Dental coverage is offered through several dental plan options. Basic dental coverage is available to employees at no cost. Optional additions and family coverage are available at minimal cost. All dental coverage options include preventive, basic, major and orthodontic coverage.

Vision Vision coverage is offered to provide affordable vision care for employees and their families. Coverage under the vision plan includes complete eye exams and lenses and frames or contact lenses. Under some plans, vision coverage is available only to certain work groups.

Life insurance Basic life insurance is provided to all employees at no cost. Coverage is based on annual salary. Optional employee and dependant life insurance are also available.

Sick leave, vacation and holidays Depending on employment classifications, employees are able to accrue time off for personal illness and vacation. Employees celebrate several paid holidays throughout the calendar based on their employment classifications.

Other benefits Long-Term Disability Insurance • Dependant Care Spending Account • Healthcare Spending Account • Adoption Assistance Reimbursement Benefit • Child and Elder Care Resource and Referral Program • Mental Health Chemical Dependency/ Employee Assistance Program

Southwest is undoubtedly the most successful airline operation in North America and one that has withstood the problems faced within aviation in America since 9/11 in far better shape than any of its competitors. Part of this success is operational but a significant contributor has also been the airline's people. Treating people right makes good business sense is a view that the airline endorses in practice and its record speaks for itself. As a result, it is one of the most in-demand employers in the USA.

Prepared by the author for Fáilte Ireland from published sources and reproduced here with permission.

Case discussion questions

1. What does the Southwest case illustrate in relation to people management in tourism, hospitality and leisure?

2. Is the company likely to be a good one to work for?

3. Can Southwest's employment principles be transferred to other countries?

Review and discussion questions

1. How do the contextual themes addressed in this chapter impact on work and employment in tourism, hospitality and leisure in all of the location types indicated below and in settings with which you are familiar:
   - town or city
   - country
   - region?

2. Review the range of definitions of tourism, hospitality and leisure from a conceptual (what do they mean?) and technical (what are the main features?) point of view. Draw a chart that shows where the concepts overlap and where they stand independently. On completion, consider problems you may have encountered with this exercise and list reasons why these may have been encountered.

3. Think about the country or region where you are currently studying or where you come from. How might an understanding of tourism, hospitality and leisure be different to that pictured in the definitions given in this chapter and why might these differences exist?

4. Consider the importance of the tourism, hospitality and leisure industry to the economy of a community, region or country with which you are familiar. In what ways is this importance evident and what strategies are pursued by the public and private sector in support of the industry, particularly in terms of work and employment?

5. To what extent do the wide range of sub-sectors and jobs within tourism, hospitality and tourism reflect a coherent and cohesive industry?

2

The development of tourism, hospitality and leisure and the nature of employment

> ## Chapter objectives
>
> The aims of this chapter are:
>
> - to place tourism, hospitality and leisure in their historical and social context;
>
> - to address the work and employment implications for tourism, hospitality and leisure of key historical and social dimensions.

In Chapter 1, we considered some of the broad contextual characteristics of tourism, hospitality and leisure and developed these themes by exploring the human resource implications of these characteristics. We also addressed definitional aspects of the concepts, noting the interrelationships between them. Finally, we highlighted the diversity of people who work in tourism and the varied roles that they play. This chapter develops some of these themes in more detail.

The notion of leisure time

Smith and Mannell's (2000) description of leisure points to the fact that concepts such as leisure, recreation, travel and tourism evolve and change over time but also mean different things in different cultures and societies. The definitions quoted in Chapter 1 come, primarily, from authors who look at the subject from a developed-world perspective. In other words, they are all based in Australia, North America or Europe and this, inevitably, colours the way in which they see things.

Leisure time, as our starting point, is essential for participation in recreation, travel and tourism. In societies that are substantially agrarian and where farming is focused on subsistence rather than commercial, for-profit production, working on the land is a year-round, week-round commitment with time off generally confined to religious observance and religious or family holidays. European society, prior to the Industrial Revolution of the eighteenth and nineteenth centuries, was largely agrarian with the vast majority of people living off

the land as subsistence smallholders, tenants or serfs. There was little entitlement to free time or, indeed, the economic resources to indulge in it. In many developing countries today, rural communities face the same dilemma – commitments to the land are such that there is no opportunity to participate, significantly, in non-land and non-work activity. Leisure or non-working time, for those outside of the ruling, professional or mercantile elite, was and in many parts of the world remains confined to specific religious or cultural holidays the weekly holy day in Christianity, Islam and Judaism or annual festivals such as Eid, Passover, Chinese New Year or Easter.

The exceptions, in both pre-industrial Europe and the contemporary developing world, were and are a small economic and professional elite, people in leadership positions in the societies in question – the ruling political classes, merchants, doctors and lawyers. Their economic resources, education and lifestyle allowed and permitted leisure time and the freedom to engage in recreation, travel and tourism. Europe in eighteenth century saw the Grand Tour, educational tourism by the sons of the British elite to the main historic and cultural centres of France and Italy for extended periods of up to a year. Outbound tourism today, from some of the poorest countries in the world, in a sense, represents a similar phenomenon.

The concept of leisure, as defined by Cooper *et al.* (2005), is substantially a product of industrialization and urbanization. Industrialization created a middle class and, subsequently, an urban working class with the economic freedom to use their leisure time in the pursuit of recreational activities, travel and tourism. It also created working patterns that were not slavishly tied to the agricultural calendar. It is possible to close a factory for a week or two weeks in a way that livestock cannot be neglected for a similar period. Many European countries introduced statutory entitlement to holidays with pay in the mid- to late nineteenth century and industrial holidays such as the Glasgow Fortnight in July became commonplace. At the same time, there was also extended free time available for many workers at weekends from one day to one and a half days to two days. These moves created a new leisured society with the economic resources to purchase leisure time activities, whether at home (cinema, football matches, organized sport) or further afield (day trips, more extended vacations). Indeed, the organization of regular mass participation and spectator sports, such as football in Western Europe, dates from the time when large numbers of people in urban areas had, for the first time, the time and resources to join local clubs and to attend the matches of their local teams.

Leisure time, therefore, is the product of economic change and more recent experience in other parts of the world suggests that leisure time is something that has also increased in more recently industrialized countries such as Mexico and Brazil in parallel to the industrial and economic growth of those countries. In other words, the greater the prosperity of a country, the more likely it is that employers, employee organizations and governments will collaborate to provide workers with shorter working hours and a greater leisure/vacation-time entitlement. In Malaysia and Singapore the reduction in Saturday working for public employees in recent years is a good example of this process.

The growth in leisure time in nineteenth-century Europe coincided with technological change that provided opportunity for the newly 'leisure enfranchised' (those with free time to engage in leisure) to make use of this time. They did this by travelling in large numbers to newly emerging tourist resorts by the sea or in the mountains. The development of the railway system in Europe in the mid-nineteenth century provided the technology to carry large numbers of people, with speed and at low cost, from the industrial urban centres such as Manchester in England to resorts such as Blackpool on the coast. Initially such travel was in the form of day trips but, subsequently, it also took place for longer periods of time. Access to leisure time, therefore, enabled people to travel (using technology such as the railways) and travel opportunity provided the spur for the development of mass tourism. Technological change also provided further opportunity to extend travel and tourism possibilities during the twentieth century. The advent of low-cost independent motoring, initially in the United States in the 1920s and 1930s, gave those with leisure time the freedom to travel both locally and further afield. At the same time, bus and coach transport complemented and, in some places, superseded rail travel as a low-cost, flexible mode of travel for a growing mass tourist market in North America and Europe. In the latter half of the twentieth century, availability of low-cost, jet air travel created the modern package tourism market as it exists in Europe, North America, Australia and Japan today. Air travel provided advantages of access and speed with which other modes of transport could not compete in catering for the limited leisure time of industrial and office workers. The most recent stage in the travel revolution has seen the launch of low-cost air travel in the United States, Europe, Australia and, latterly, in Asia. Low-cost airlines employ entirely new business models and compete very successfully against traditional legacy carriers such as Lufthansa, Malaysian Airlines and Qantas (Pender and Baum 2000; Kua and Baum 2004). Low-cost airlines, on the face of it, enhance access for disadvantaged travellers and enable them to participate in international travel in a manner previously impossible. However, there is evidence that the operating model adopted by low-cost airlines is, in fact, socially exclusive in that those on the economic and educational margins of society are unable to access low-cost flights (Baum 2004, 2007 forthcoming).

Access to leisure time is not only a concern for those in employment. Increased participation in full- and part-time education (school, college) means that access to leisure time is also dictated by the school calendar. School holidays are period in many countries where demand for travel and tourism reaches a peak and these breaks act as a focus for the utilization of leisure time by those in employment.

Many developed countries are experiencing major changes to their demographic structure and this also has an important impact upon understanding and utilization of leisure. The structure of the workforce has changed and continues to do so, with participation by women in work outside of the home growing in all developed and many developing countries. This has consequences for leisure time and recreational participation by women and their children. Unpaid work, whether in the home or in a voluntary capacity in the community, is frequently undervalued in many societies and does not receive the same leisure-time entitlement that external paid work does.

In most European, North American and some Asian societies, improved health care and other factors mean that people are living far longer than was the case in the past. Retirement ages from work have come down with the combined result that older citizens in these countries have both the time and financial resources to participate actively and more often in leisure-time activities, including recreation, travel and tourism. Recreational sports such as sailing, golf and hiking have seen great increases in the number of senior participants and this has included activity at home and while away from home as tourists.

At the same time as an ageing seniors population, these societies also have a declining number of younger people. This change also impacts on leisure and travel/tourism participation in that the traditional pre-eminence given to school holidays in travel and tourism choice may be reduced. In the context of this book, a declining youth population in developed countries has significant repercussions for recruitment from tourism, hospitality and leisure's main source of labour, a theme that will be further developed in Chapter 7.

The development of tourism, hospitality and leisure – from elite to mass participation

In order to understand the human resource environment within the contemporary international tourism, hospitality and leisure industry, it is necessary first of all to review the origins of tourism and hospitality and the sector's growth to its present status as a mass participation industry. This analysis must then be complemented by parallel consideration of the changing human resource environment which has evolved in support of the growing tourism, hospitality and leisure industry. We will now consider the development of the sector from being the minority privilege of the elite in the eighteenth century to becoming an industry of international mass participation. The driving forces behind this change, as we shall see, combine social, cultural, economic and technological factors. These same impulses have driven change with respect to employment in tourism, hospitality and leisure.

It would be naive to attempt to view the development of tourism, hospitality and leisure, internationally, as homogeneous. As we have seen in Chapter 1, the tourism, hospitality and leisure industry is highly diverse in its product as well as its structure and organization. For a variety of cultural, social, economic, political and technological reasons, tourism, hospitality and leisure has evolved in patchwork form, some locations reaching maturity some considerable time before others were recognized as destinations of any significance. It would be beyond our scope here to attempt anything that goes beyond a selective and thematic appraisal of the development of tourism, hospitality and leisure and how this has impacted on employment within the sector. In doing this, the focus will, inevitably, be on those countries most clearly associated with the move towards mass tourism, primarily Britain but also other countries in the northwest of Europe and North America.

Europe, or to be more precise, Western Europe is the cradle of modern tourism and leisure as we know it or, as Pompl and Lavery (1993) put it, 'it was in Europe, particularly in Great Britain, that the tourist industry was invented, refined and developed' (p.xi).

The tourism, hospitality and leisure industry can be traced back to the growth of urbanization and conquest in Ancient Egypt, Greece and Rome. In her consideration of the origin of hotels in Britain, Borer (1972) notes that: 'The first inns in this country, where travellers could eat, drink and sleep after a day's journey, were built before the English ever arrived here, for they were introduced by the Romans' (p.9). These establishments, as elsewhere in the Roman Empire, were designed to support the efforts of war and colonial administration and were thus focused at specific rather than general travel markets, to place the activity in a contemporary context.

However, the true antecedents of modern mass tourism can be identified in the 'Grand Tour' which flourished during the period from the sixteenth to the nineteenth centuries. Originally a selective, primarily aristocratic prerogative, the classical tour, mainly originating in Britain, included France, Italy, Switzerland, Germany and the Low Countries and is well described as 'a tour of certain cities in Western Europe undertaken primarily, but not exclusively, for education and pleasure' (Towner 1985, p.301).

The original conception of the Grand Tour and related journeying to fashionable resorts and spas of the eighteenth century was very much as an extension to the normal pattern of aristocratic living and this is reflected in the employment structure that existed in support of travel at this time. Essentially, the rich and well-bred travelled with all or part of their normal retinue of servants. In the case of domestic travel to Bath, Deauville or Weymouth this could well consist of much of the household. Accompaniment on the Grand Tour was, generally, on a rather more modest scale but would probably include a tutor plus one or more personal servants. Accommodation was found in the great houses of families from the same class and background and only on rare occasions would commercial establishments be frequented during travel. Thus, the employment impact of travel at this time was limited and the development of identifiable tourism-related jobs cannot be really attributed to this period.

While the Grand Tour had its heyday in the eighteenth century, one significant feature of its evolution is the length of time committed to the experience, which fell from an average of 40 months in the mid-sixteenth century to just four months in the 1830s at the dawn of railway travel (Towner, 1985, p.316). This propensity to shorten the experience over time is a characteristic of the development of tourism generally and continues to be an important feature in market trends today. It reflects changes in lifestyle; social, economic and working conditions, the impact of improved transport and other technologies; but, probably most significantly, the popularization of the experience from selective to relatively mass participation. Buzzard (1993) rightly argues that industrialization in Europe provided the main focus for this change, in that modern tourism arose 'as a broadly accessible form of leisure travel no longer based in the overt class and gender prerogatives of the Grand Tour' (p.18).

This link between industrialization and the development of mass tourism accounts, in part, for the importance of Britain in the development of tourism as an industry. According to Feiffer (1985), even in the era preceding the impact of the railways, by 1820 about 150 000 British travellers a year were visiting Europe, representing a considerable growth from the time that has been described as the cultural 'golden age' of the Grand Tour (Poon 1993, p.30). Similarly, in the United States, travel was elitist. Zimmerman (undated) notes that the upper class and members of the aristocracy went on holiday for months at a time. The working class, for the most part, did not travel. When on the road, travellers would stay in one place for weeks at a time either in a hotel or enjoying the hospitality of a friend or person to which they had a letter of introduction. They did not travel light. Besides lugging trunks filled with gowns and other finery, the aristocratic traveller would often bring along various 'extras': a nurse for the children, a secretary, a cousin or distant relative to act as a pseudo-servant.

Initially, the pattern of this change was one which represents replication in that the growing affluence of the new, urbanized middle classes developed tourism in a way that included much that had featured in the elitist travel experiences which preceded their own ventures. Thus domestic travel, for example, gravitated towards the seaside locations made famous by royal and aristocratic patronage, such as Brighton and Weymouth in England and Deauville in France. At the same time, some specific resorts such as Blackpool developed to meet the needs of the newly 'enfranchised' tourist classes. Similarly, the new post-Industrial Revolution model of European travel from Britain followed the same main arteries as the Grand Tour, but on a scale which would have been impossible without the technology of the railways and the organizational and entrepreneurial skills of travel industry innovators such as Thomas Cook. Young (1973), in discussing Cook, points to the latter's unique contribution when he says that 'his originality lay in his methods, his almost infinite capacity for taking trouble, his acute sense of the needs of his clients, his power of invention and his bold imagination' (p.21).

Cook pointed the way towards the industrialization of tourism, its presentation as a consumer commodity available to all who could afford the time and cost. The packaging of the tourist's experience, which was a key feature of this process, implicitly gave recognition to the complexity of assembling the diverse components of tourism which was beyond the expertise of most potential travellers, especially among the newly affluent middle and skilled working classes. These groups of new travellers were primarily from the growing urban centres, benefiting from changes to the technology of travel but also from factors such as access to financial resources available to only a small group prior to the Industrial Revolution, the advent of paid holidays and the impact of increasingly universal education in many European countries.

The advent of leisure participation in a formalized sense is something which was influenced by similar drivers to those which created activity with respect to tourism and hospitality. The origins of much commercialized and formalized leisure, as it is presented today within our globalized economy, is primarily European in origin, drawing on traditions that have their roots in a combination of, among many influences, Ancient Greece (the Olympic games, for example), Roman civilization in drama and spectacle, Medieval European carnivals, sport and festivities and the collective activities of urban communities in the industrial age including major sporting events and, subsequently, cinema. Veal and Lynch (2001) identify the Industrial Revolution as a key point in the history of leisure, when a sense of time changed radically from that experienced in a previously agrarian society. This was the time when people moved from task-orientation, within which intensive periods of work (to gather in the harvest, for example) alternated with periods of idleness, particularly in the winter months, to a society where behaviour was governed by a much greater time orientation. The demands of industrial, capitalist production processes imposed an overpowering structure on working and, therefore, leisure lives. The organization of leisure and, indeed travel and tourism, stems from the structure imposed on people's lives by factory and office life. Developed countries do not have a universally common history in terms of the evolution of leisure as each country's experience was influenced by a different range of factors. In the Australian context, Veal and Lynch (2001) identify two major influences on contemporary culture and leisure. These come, on the one hand, from traditional Aboriginal traditions and, on the other, from European, particularly British, origins. These very different influences can be seen to manifest themselves in Australians' pride in and love of the outdoors and the wilderness, reflecting Aboriginal influences, and also their fanatical devotion to organized sports of all kinds, pointing to European cultural and leisure antecedents.

The true commercialization of leisure time owes much to the American influence of the early twentieth century and the impact of technology – film, radio and television. Commercialization of leisure activity came hand in hand with the democratization of access to pastimes, whether sporting, cultural or, in some way, 'uplifting'. Most leisure activities in Western society are accessible on a mass scale and their organization is highly commercialized in order to facilitate universal access. This is true of sports, entertainment and 'hobby' activities such as do-it-yourself (DIY). All these are increasingly provided by large, frequently global, organizations.

Leisure in the developing world operates along very different lines and is far from democratic in terms of participation. Even where time is not a barrier, for example among children in South Africa, facilities and equipment to allow participation in sport may not be readily available. Akyeampong and Ambler (2002) provide a wider insight into the much more recent development of leisure and the use of non-working time in Africa. Their starting point is to consider leisure in terms of three phases: colonialism, post-colonialism and the development of modern models of consumer capitalism. They note that, 100 years ago, leisure time and the consumption of leisure were totally unknown concepts in most of Africa, reflecting both economic but, probably more importantly, lifestyle factors. With the advent of colonialism and the formal organization of time, the trend towards leisure development starts to mirror aspects of similar developments in developed countries, particularly in terms of early domination by a moneyed, educated and cultured elite. Akyeampong and Ambler's analysis focuses on the development of participation sports, notably football and boxing, and note the impact of world stage success on local village participation in countries such as Senegal and Cameroon.

Participation in leisure activity has not only been denied to people on grounds of economic or social class division. Political and religious reasons have also created barriers to participation. Veal (2002) points out that in the Puritan England of the seventeenth century a ban was in place prohibiting sports and entertainments on Sundays. In contemporary times, similar limitations can be found on freedom of participation in leisure pastimes in some communities in Israel on the Sabbath and on Sundays in the Western Isles of Scotland. Restrictions have also been placed on participation of certain groups in leisure activities. Nazi Germany banned Jewish people from using swimming and sports facilities in the 1930s; leisure participation was segregated in the southern states of the United States until the 1960s; and Iran today denies women access to stadia during football matches.

Williams (2002) argues that, notwithstanding the major changes through which tourism, hospitality and leisure have developed into the modern phenomenon we know today, there are themes and issues that have remained substantially the same over the past 200 years. These themes and issues relate to neo-colonial relationships between visitors and hosts as well as to the largely extractive relationship between tourists and the natural environment.

> Early nineteenth century tourism focused on exploration, hunting and trading in colonial territories. This was a fact of colonial conquest and hence was linked to the issues of the alienation of land and natural resources with underlying ethnic, racial, class, and gender dynamics. This form of tourism and its gains were controlled by the colonial powers, tour operators, and owners of steamships and domestic railroads within the countries. Tourism was primarily extractive and depleted natural resources such as skins, ivory and fauna in order to sustain the wealthy. The development of mass tourism in the 1950s and 60's led to the inclusion of the middle class into 'fun and sun' adventures in the developing world. But even the new forms of tourism of the 1980's and 1990's carry echoes of the past as tourism increasingly returns to the themes of exploiting the 'exotic' and the natural. This is seen for example in the development of modern day 'adventure tourism': hiking, backpacking, trekking and 'eco-tourism.' These forms of tourisms are no more in the sole control of developing countries nor do they deplete and extract fewer natural resources than previous tourism cycles. (pp.3–4)

Changes in the pattern and structure of the tourism, hospitality and leisure industry (and in particular its commercial packaging) had inevitable consequences for the nature of work in the industry. In many ways, this represents a clear parallel to the much more widely recognized changes which occurred within other industry sectors, notably manufacturing, mining and, latterly, agriculture. Supporting the travel of the aristocratic rich, whether while in transit or at a temporary destination, was in reality an extension of the home routine for the travellers and their retinue, little different from the movement between, for example, London, Bath and the country house which reflected the social seasons in Georgian England. Thus, those employed were the normal serving staff of the travellers or of their hosts and the nature of work as well as the relationship between the travellers and those that served them derived from existing 'upstairs–downstairs' conventions in the great aristocratic homes of most European countries.

The advent of travel by the middle classes or the bourgeoisie initiated significant change in this respect because, first, these new travellers were not able to avail themselves of the hospitality of their social peers in the resorts and cities that they visited and thus were required to make use of commercial accommodation as well as public transportation, initially the stage coach and subsequently the railway and steam packet. Second, they did not have the retinue of serving staff to allow the transfer of whole households to new locations. Local assistance during travel and while at the destination was required to support the tourist experience. Finally, the new travellers did not have the leisure time traditionally available to the aristocratic rich. For commercially driven business families, leisure provided a limited and controlled change from the normal working routine for maybe one or two weeks; thus the impracticality of moving the full household was further underscored.

The circumstances of employment in support of the fledgling commercial tourism, hospitality and leisure industry may have changed as a result of widening participation but consumer expectations were much slower to develop. Thus the master/mistress and servant culture remained central to the provision of travel, hotel and associated services to the tourism industry of the nineteenth century and indeed beyond, reflecting not only its origins in the master–servant working connection but also the clearly defined relationships between social groupings at that time. Tourism was by no means a democratic activity but was largely confined to a relatively small (if growing) minority of the population in most European countries, and the nature of work in commercial enterprises in support of the industry reflected this elitism. The subsequent development of employment in tourism has continued to 'track' the main features of the industry's development and can be linked to the model of imitation which has characterized its change from elite to highly populist activity.

The process of replication from the exclusive in holidaymaking to mass participation in like activities and similar locations is one that has been repeated throughout the development of tourism as a popular and increasingly universal activity. A loose analogy to Archimedes and the notion of displacement can be used as an analogy of how participation in tourism, hospitality and leisure evolved.

The initial stage is one where the first contact between the fashion trend-setters, the rich or the adventurous (whom we may call Group A visitors), with a specific tourism destination or wider locale is made. This early phase relationship survives for a limited period of time, whereupon increasing numbers (Group B visitors), perhaps more hedonistic in focus and more restricted in their access to time and monetary resources, follow. Larger-scale and cheaper travel and accommodation provision is developed and the price of the destination decreases or, put another way, its affordability becomes more widespread. The total value of the new tourist influx may not be significantly greater than that of the original visitors and, certainly, the environmental and social impact will be much greater. The popularization of the destination leads to its abandonment by the pioneering visitors who established its status for tourism and they move elsewhere, frequently further afield or to other relatively undeveloped locations.

This process is repeated at both ends of the spectrum. Continued development of the original destination and the downward pressure on cost attracts visitors in larger numbers and from groups previously unable to avail themselves of the resort for cost and access reasons (Group C). This influx, in turn, will result in the migration of members of Group B to new destinations, possibly those to which Group A moved earlier. This group, in turn then, moves on to destinations new and the process continues in effect in a continuous spiral, ever wider as the ripples in a pool after a stone has been thrown into it. The drive for change comes from a combination of economic, fashion, lifestyle and technological factors which work together to provide tourism and leisure opportunities to an increasingly large proportion of the population. This process is essentially that which Steinecke (1993) calls one of 'imitation-segregation'. Steinecke illustrates this process in tabular form and his ideas are presented and extended in Table 2.1.

This model looks at the displacement concept with respect to a finite and defined population, within primarily the Western European context. Thus it is possible to map the development of tourism in, say, Britain or Germany by applying the successive stages. There are arguments which suggest that this notion of replication or displacement is over-simplistic in that it does not cater for models of tourism, hospitality and leisure development which omit one or more of its stages. Blackpool, for example, developed as a resort to cater for the leisure needs of the industrial working classes in the north-west of England and did not go through a prior period of catering for aristocratic or middle-class markets. Steinecke, of course, focuses on the development of tourism in a European context. A similar process of replication, popularization and democratization of participation could be drawn up with respect to use of wider leisure time in Europe and, indeed, in terms of growing participation in tourism,

Table 2.1 Periods in the development of tourism in Europe

Period	Class Landed classes/ celebrities	Bourgeoisie	Mass market	Causes of change
17th/18th century	Grand Tour			
18th century	Spa	Grand Tour/ educational journey		Growing industrial middle class
18th century/early 19th century	Seaside resort	Spa		
Mid 19th century	Mediterranean in winter/Rhine tour	Seaside resort (domestic)	Excursion by train	Advent of railway travel/paid holidays
Late 19th century	Alpinism/Mediterranean in summer	Rhine tour/ Mediterranean in winter	Seaside resort (domestic)	
Early 20th century	World tour	Alpinism/ Mediterranean in summer	Seaside resort/ spa/(domestic); holiday camps	Early impact of the motor car on leisure travel
Mid 20th century	Multiple vacations; cruise travel	Travel further to destinations	Mediterranean in summer	Jet air travel; reduction in travel documents
Late 20th century	Multiple vacations; activity holidays	Multiple vacations; short and longer cruise travel	Travel further; all-inclusives	Jumbo jet
Early 21st century	Elite destinations; space travel	Multiple vacations; cultural breaks	Long-haul travel; cruise travel	Low-cost airlines; security concerns; health concerns

Increasingly blurred distinctions between three market segments within developed countries. Mass travel from some developing countries

Adapted and developed from Pompl, W. and Lavery, P. (1993), *Tourism in Europe: Structures and Developments*, Wallingford: CABI.

hospitality and leisure in some newly industrialized or developing country environments.

Steinecke's model is one that draws on the notion of economic change and development within market-driven or relatively open economies and does not cater for the development of tourism within developing countries or parts of Eastern Europe and the former Soviet Union. In these countries, the development of low-cost social tourism, organized through agencies such as trade unions and community organizations, enabled participation on a mass scale without the barriers imposed by access to major economic resources. Clear similarities with socio-political tourism organized for, in particular, young people in Nazi Germany during the 1930s can be seen. Primarily domestic in focus, this form of tourism was, according to Hall:

> viewed as essential to the well-being of citizens and to their economically productive capacities. The availability of leisure and tourism was an important component of the cycle of production and reproduction. Being strictly subordinated to political and ideological considerations, however, domestic tourism had a largely organized, group character. (Hall 1991, p.84)

Hall continues by quoting Halász who outlined Hungarian provision for this form of tourism in the late 1950s as including:

> a widespread network of holiday resorts. On the recommendation of the trade unions, the workers can enjoy holidays at reduced prices, or, as a special reward, even free. There are special holiday resorts for mothers with small children. Through the nurseries, schools and youth organizations many thousands of children and young people spend their vacation in the summer holiday camps either entirely free or for a very small sum. (Halász in Hall 1991, p.85)

Social tourism was, of course, not an exclusively Eastern European phenomenon and continues to operate in countries such as Belgium, France and Singapore as well as, to some extent, under the auspices of charitable organizations in Britain and the United States, where parts of the summer camp movement provide a good example of social tourism in operation. Richards (1992) traces the origins of social tourism in Western Europe back to the 1930s and the passing of laws on paid holidays. He proposes three models of social tourism as identifiable in the 1980s. One is that already discussed in the context of Eastern Europe, where all forms of tourism were social in their focus. The Northern European model emphasizes individual consumption, with social tourism by the state limited to the most underprivileged groups. The third model, akin to the first, is that which prevailed in Southern Europe, which was more collective in focus and emphasized state provision of low-cost accommodation for low-income groups, with distribution controlled by social services and trade unions (Richards 1992 p.R1).

The Steinecke model implies that there is no replication or infilling at the levels which the mass tourist market from developed countries have just vacated. In a sense, this is true as the evidence of declined seaside resorts such as Seaton Carew in north-east England and Bangor and Bray in Ireland testify. However, at an international level, the model may well take on a transnational dimension, with resorts or destinations which have been vacated by the 'lower class' categories of Germany or the Netherlands meeting the needs and aspirations of travellers from Eastern Europe instead. Hotels in Hong Kong have adapted to a similar change in accommodating groups of first time international travellers from mainland China.

The Steinecke model also has relevance when we consider the growing importance of domestic and outbound tourism within emergent developing countries of, for example, Asia. India, with its increasingly important middle classes, and more industrialized countries such as South Korea, Malaysia, Taiwan and Thailand all provide cases of the Steinecke model at work, albeit with somewhat different locational examples but with the key difference of time scale. These countries are moving through a very rapid displacement process so that widespread tourism participation has been achieved within 20 to 30 years, compared to the two centuries of development in Europe.

Extending Steinecke's model effectively maps the development of tourism from an elitist occupation of a small minority of the population to one where there is mass participation within most developed societies. As with all models, it must be treated with some caution in that there are dangers of simplification and a tendency to ignore the complex interrelationship of many factors in creating change within tourism. However, it is indisputable that the development of tourism to its mass participation status within most developed economies represents one of the most wide-reaching social phenomena of the second half of the twentieth century. Looking to the future, the adapted model suggests that the clear distinctions which have existed in terms of 'class' participation in tourism, hospitality and leisure over the past two centuries may well blur as technology makes travel cheaper and more accessible, in terms of time, to larger sections of the population. The speed with which new phenomena such as space tourism become affordable to a relatively wide market will indicate the extent to which traditional divisions persist. Differentiation, in terms of tourist participation, may well become increasingly determined by interest as opposed to fashion.

Steinecke's model focuses, of course, entirely on the behaviour and perspective of the growing number of tourists and appears to assume a passive response from host communities. Models of sustainability as well as widening demands for community involvement within tourism planning and development (Murphy 1985), question the simple assumptions of tourism as solely led by consumer demand in its growth, especially when a contemporary and speculative future gloss is imposed. A lack of passivity by the local community is by no means new. For example, local friction between tourists, especially as the number and profile of visitors changed, and residents has been a common if under-reported theme in the development of tourism. Berry (1992), considering the 1890s, notes disquiet at the 'takeover' of San Remo by the British during the winter, especially the development of facilities which included 'a Presbyterian Church and two Church of England Churches, an English Druggist, an English Nurses Institute and four English doctors' (p.211) in competition with local providers. Other communities decide that tourists are detrimental to the environment within which they live. The residents of Niagara-by-the-Lake in Canada, for example, instituted measures to discourage excessive visitation because of congestion and privacy concerns. Thus the development of tourism, hospitality and leisure is not entirely externally driven by factors within originating countries and locations. The local environment and the responsiveness of the host community to the tourist invasion can, in its own right, influence the nature and volume of visitor arrivals.

The model, as extended after Steinecke, represents the movement of tourism, hospitality and leisure from a minority, elite activity to one where, in developed countries at least, tourist activity in its broadest definition is accessible to the vast majority of the population. Tourism can be viewed as a normal consumer activity, competing with other commodities for a share of the discretionary income of most households, but nonetheless part of everyday consumption. Burton (1994) quotes figures regarding the proportion of the population of Western European countries who travel abroad and, without defining the time frame within which the figures operate, points to international travel rates of 69 per cent for Germany, 67 per cent for Belgium, 65 per cent for the Netherlands, 50 per cent for Sweden, 35 per cent for the UK, 8 per cent for Spain and 7 per cent for Greece. With the advent of widespread access to low-cost air travel since Burton wrote, these figures will, almost certainly, have increased significantly. Clear inferences about links to, on the one hand, geographical factors and, on the other, the economic strength of the country can be made. Alternative sources look at overall vacation participation rates, including domestic tourism, in different countries and this leads to figures of around 80 per cent in Scandinavian countries and a range of between 50 per cent and 75 per cent in other north-western European countries but lower figures for Southern and Eastern Europe.

This change from elite to mass consumption, which can be traced over a 200-year period – with considerable acceleration since 1945 – may be attributed to a diversity of social, economic, political and technological/communications factors. It is easy to pinpoint key factors such as legislation to ensure paid vacations for employees; the railways, the motor car and the advent of fast and cheap air travel; and the relaxation of travel restrictions by most countries. However, the reality represents a complex amalgam of determinants, reflecting change in the wider social and economic environment of most countries. It is impossible, therefore, to attribute one of the most significant changes of the twentieth century to any single factor or, indeed, to any specifically definable group of factors. Despite the antecedents to mass tourism which have been pinpointed in this chapter, the scale and scope of participation in travel today is an entirely new phenomenon, which has no real parallel before the mid-nineteenth century or even later.

International tourism, hospitality and leisure – the development of work and employment

The scale of employment in support of contemporary tourism, hospitality and leisure reflects the range of changes that have taken place in most developed countries so that the industry can now claim to be the world's largest sector employer. The development from work which was essentially an extension of the normal serving function in the home to that which has organizational characteristics akin to other industry sectors, especially within services, has been dramatic and has been driven both by the scale of change and by its social and economic features. Therefore, the historical origins of the hotel and catering workforce in developed countries lie in the work of domestic servants who worked the homes of the ruling classes in the latter half of the nineteenth century and the first half of the twentieth.

Thus, the prevailing relationships between those in service and those being served in the emerging tourism, hospitality and leisure industries of Europe in the nineteenth century were closely modelled on the prevailing domestic service models that existed in most countries. As Scanlon (1998) points out, it is precisely aversion to this concept of being 'in service' in a semi-feudal society that prompted many Europeans to seek new lives across the Atlantic in North America. As a result, models of hospitality and service that emerged in the United States sought to avoid this 'in service' basis to hospitality relationships and replace it with a more democratic approach. However, Scanlon further argues that much of the antipathy of Americans to service work stems from a failure to understand the history and traditions of European service.

In other cultures, the modern tourism, hospitality and leisure employee has also grown out of centuries-old tradition. Dale (undated) talks about her experiences as a bar hostess in Japan.

> The hostess, I learned, was the modern equivalent of the geisha, a centuries-old and highly venerated profession that attracts Japanese girls like a vocation. Geishas are the embodiment of that enduring Japanese icon: feminine perfection. They exist to serve men and preserve the traditional arts such as singing, dancing and playing classical instruments like the samisen.
>
> Her modern counterpart, the bar hostess, has exchanged silk kimonos for cocktail dresses, and the samisen for a karaoke box. She is considerably less expensive than her predecessor yet she shares the same values: to be the feminine ideal, to entertain, to listen, to be serious, to dazzle with her wit and charm. It is not considered a demeaning job. Certainly no sexual favours are expected – just mild flirtation, perhaps a glimmering eroticism. Many Japanese girls claim to be proud to serve men in this way and to be recognized for their 'skills'. The pursuit of this feminine ideal is revered in Japan like an art form. (p.1)

Returning to the Western context, Saunders (1981) argues that the growth of the hotel industry in the early twentieth century came at the same time as domestic service faced its first phase of serious decline and that many serving employees made the transition to hotel work as a result of a combination of 'push' (increasing domestic technology necessitating fewer serving staff) and 'pull' factors (more attractive and secure conditions). Thus, the change was a reflection, in part, of the effects of industrialization and urban living on the home. It is argued here that the origins of this change actually lie earlier, in the mid-nineteenth century, and reflect the effects of increasing industrially generated affluence and the consequent growing level of participation in tourism by the urban middle and subsequently working classes. However, there is little argument about the process involved which saw an initial transfer of employment from one sector to another.

Because of its early industrialization, the process discussed here took place rather sooner and in more pronounced fashion in Britain than in other

European countries, but similarities can be seen in the process of industrialization within the hotel and catering sector in France and Germany. However, in countries or regions which faced expansion of tourism and hospitality without a significant industrial or urban history, the move into employment in related sectors was, inevitably, somewhat different. The growth in tourism- and hospitality-related jobs in the countries of the Mediterranean or the rural areas of western Ireland and Scandinavia has much in common with similar more recent transitions in the developing tourism economies of, for example, the Caribbean, Malaysia and Thailand, where the shift is directly from agricultural subsistence or employment to tourism, hospitality and leisure sector work. A seasonal combination of work across sectors was and remains a significant feature in these countries.

Little is documented about the origins of employment in the myriad of other sectors which comprise tourism, hospitality and leisure beyond the dominant hotel and catering sub-sector. However, it is reasonable to speculate about a number of areas which have their antecedents in the social fabric and culture of many countries. Good examples lie in the fields of entertainment and traditional crafts where occupations which are now focused, in a predominant way, towards meeting tourist needs and extracting the tourist dollar have their origins in traditions carried out in communities and the home for centuries. It is argued that many of these activities could and would not survive without the support and impetus of tourist interest; it is also arguable that the authenticity of much traditional culture and art has been compromised by its 'packaging' for tourist consumption. Long and Wall (1996) argue that this effect is in evidence in Bali. The 'industrialization' of traditional craft production processes and marketing, frequently advocated within tourism planning in the developing world, inevitably has a major impact on the nature of work in the sector and moves production and ownership from the level of the cottage to that of the factory. A similar process can be identified with respect to traditional dance and music in many countries. It is arguable that some of the highly stylized forms of employment offered in theme parks and similar environments have a direct linkage to traditional entertainment forms and thus can be seen as a modern manifestation of the commercialization of tradition. In the context of Disneyland, Paris, which represents American and therefore 'alien' culture, this is clearly a highly contentious issue and one which purist supporters of French culture may seek to refute.

Other areas of tourism employment also owe their origin to activities which had been part of the local landscape long before the emergence of tourism. Examples include the work of the ski instructor in the Alps and that of offering fishing and pleasure trips along Europe's entire Atlantic seaboard. Here again, a merging of employment with other sectors is evident, providing more than one source of work and income to the local population on a seasonal basis. The relatively recent prominence given to agritourism also depends on this model, where people's traditional occupation and income, which are derived from the land, are supplemented by work which uses those same agricultural resources to meet tourism and hospitality needs, but often involving their working to complementary peak seasons. Agritourism, while by no means a new concept, is to be found in a wide range of countries in Europe as well as in Australia, New Zealand, South Africa and the United States and is increasingly being advocated as part of tourism development measures countries such as Malaysia. Diversification of this kind from agriculture has been strongly supported by both national governments and transnational agencies such as the European Union in an attempt to reduce reliance on subsidies within the agricultural sector and to maintain rural employment.

Tourism, hospitality and leisure's development has also provided opportunities to extend existing economic activity, and therefore employment, from services designed primarily for the local community to meeting the needs of visitors. A wide range of business areas can fall into this category, including banks, clubs, garages, pubs, restaurants, shops and taxi cabs, all of which may have commenced trading with a primarily local market focus and have changed and frequently grown through the patronage of tourists. Many retain dual markets but the growth of the tourism and hospitality industry has not only distinctly affected the character of the establishments but also the level, sustainability and nature of employment available in them. While the businesses in question may well survive in the absence of tourist clientele, it is unlikely that they could employ the same level of staff as they are able to do within a mixed market. Of course, the success of existing businesses in attracting tourist trade frequently results in the establishment of dedicated establishments, catering almost exclusively for visitors and thus creating new employment opportunities within the existing skills base.

This phenomenon of the merging of local consumption with tourist consumption, of businesses serving what are, on the face of it, two very distinct markets, is characteristic of locations which are seasonal in their operations and have evolved into tourist centres rather than those which have been purpose built. Thus a study of businesses and employment in towns such as Clifden in Connemara, Ireland, Callander in Scotland and Georgetown in Penang in Malaysia illustrates how employment in tourism, including self-employment, has developed on the lines of the above model through a combination of local business market diversification and expansion as well as new, dedicated investment. By contrast, 'created' tourist resorts such as Brighton and Bournemouth in England, Magaluf in Majorca, Golden Sands in Bulgaria and Langkawi in Malaysia have developed with businesses and employment primarily focused on meeting tourist needs.

Tourism, hospitality and leisure work in developed countries has not evolved exclusively in such clear form out of traditional, existing employment activities. In common with most industries, new categories and types of employment have been created to cater for technological-, market- and service-led change during the transition to mass tourism. Airline crew represent an interesting but hybrid example of this process. Airline pilots and related support staff have, evidently, a recent history and it can be argued that their antecedents lie in hobby and military flying. This is reflected in the number of military pilots in particular drawn into civil aviation during the post-war period, but the military still remains a source of recruitment for many airlines today. By and large, however, the work is recent in its creation. In contrast, cabin staff in aircraft as well as those involved in ground handling, while relatively new positions in themselves, undertake work which has much in common with other areas of tourism employment, notably in hotels. Indeed, recruitment by airlines of staff with hotel backgrounds is quite common. Tourism, hospitality and leisure today also generates highly technical employment which has little by way of origin in other employment areas, although contemporary parallels exist in other sectors. This is true of areas such as financial management and information handling in tourism, hospitality and leisure businesses as well as the technical and technological aspects involved in theme park and fitness centre management.

Changing patterns of work in tourism, hospitality and leisure

A historical perspective on the growth of tourism, hospitality and leisure points to the development of changes in work patterns in response to the structure of the industry which evolved, focusing on the emergence of influences which altered the focus of work in the sector but also created significant differences in the manner in which work relations evolved in developed and developing countries. These influences were partly economic but were also a result of the impact of cultural-, consumer- and technologically driven evolution. The growth of different employment structures can be linked directly to the changing demands of the industry as it evolved to mass participation status in the developed world in response to changes in consumer expectations and demand. Adler and Adler's (2004) discussion of employment in the hotel sector in Hawaii points to a structure and basis for the allocation of roles in the workplace which reflects task factors (what work needs to be done and when), consumer preferences (who visitors wish to see doing the work), social and ethnic status (which employee groups do what work) and employee choice and lifestyle (how workers want to organize their time and manage their resources). This suggests that the nature of work in tourism, hospitality and leisure is determined by an amalgam of factors which are far more complex than may have been the case in the emerging years of commercial tourism, hospitality and leisure in the nineteenth and early twentieth centuries.

Seasonality has already been mentioned in the context of work which is combined with other activities, such as agriculture, fishing or, in Ireland, local authority capital projects (Baum and Lundtorp 2000). Seasonality is not exclusive to tourism, hospitality and leisure and was not new to much land-based activity. The insecure and transitory nature of the seasonal work of sheep shearers and harvest-time employees, for example, pre-dates the industrialization of agriculture but was given particular impetus by new divisions of labour on the land from the nineteenth century onwards.

However, mass tourism in those areas where it is overwhelmingly concentrated into a relatively short period of the year created demand for labour on a scale and in skills areas previously unknown. It also created demand for work that, inherently, was unstable and did not offer sustained opportunity for advancement and growth. Seasonal tourism, which can be of little more than three months' duration in some peripheral regions of Europe, North America and elsewhere, developed so that labour was drawn from a number of sources. Local employees were attracted through accommodation with their existing main source of work (as has already been indicated), and this pattern is common in many Greek islands as well as on the western fringes of Northern Europe. Alternatively, tourism drew on the local, non-working population, such as women in the home, the long-term unemployed, as well as school and college students during their vacations. Tourism-related employment has offered the first experience of paid work to a large section of the population in areas that have a high dependency on visitors. Finally, the development of tourism created new patterns of employment migration, with people moving temporarily to work opportunities in holiday resorts in the south of France and the English coastal resorts as well as Spain and Greece. This is a phenomenon which remains in evidence in traditional work areas such as hotel and restaurant services but is also exemplified, at a somewhat more contemporary level, by the movement of tour company representatives, entertainers and timeshare salespeople from Northern Europe to the Mediterranean during the summer months. Thus a process of seasonal movement in response to tourism work opportunities has developed a strongly international flavour, facilitated by cheap and available transportation as well as the easing of travel and working restrictions.

Migration to support seasonal demand for employees in tourism, hospitality and leisure has also developed permanence as demand for labour in some sub-sectors of the industry exceeded local supply beyond the core season. In Chapter 6 we discuss this phenomenon in terms of its impact upon ethnic diversity in the workplace. The large-scale migration of workers for the tourism, hospitality and leisure sector from Eastern Europe and elsewhere to countries such as Ireland and Scotland has significantly changed how work is organized but has also impacted on the nature of the service proposition offered to guests in these destinations. There can be little doubt that there has been an effect on the culture of service and that this impact has been frequently to enhance the professionalism and commitment of the service on offer while also internationalizing it to the point where debate is emerging about the authenticity of its cultural delivery. Bird (1989) also touches on this theme when she talks about the very rapid growth of tourism in Langkawi, Malaysia, from the mid-1980s onwards and the practice of 'importing' workers on a large scale from the mainland of peninsular Malaysia, people with a different cultural background, not islanders and, therefore, less able to deliver authentic Langkawi hospitality.

Baum (1993b) discusses the traditional patterns of work-related migration within European tourism which has a long-standing history from the 'periphery' regions of Europe to the 'centre', the main urban centres. It was, historically, particularly prevalent among Irish, Italian and Spanish employees during the off-season and Baum notes that this can result in permanent loss of skills to the 'periphery' as workers settle to full-time and non-seasonal employment in the larger European cities. These movements are considered in greater depth in Chapter 6. In a general sense, the impact of seasonality, with the inevitable workforce instability that it creates, can be very significant in terms of operational standards within the industry, the pressure to provide adequate and rapid training, staff motivation and loyalty, and also in the insecurity that is induced among employees.

The relationship between seasonality and work in tourism, hospitality and leisure is increasingly addressed in the literature. Likewise, another dimension of the new working environment within tourism, hospitality and leisure, flexible working arrangements, is also subject to increasing research and consideration (this is discussed in greater detail in Chapter 5). Wood (1997), while neglecting the impact of seasonality on employment within hotels and catering, gives in-depth recognition to part-time and flexible work and reports a number of studies which address the effects of this growing work form on both hospitality businesses and on their employees, especially women. The nature of demand in the tourism industry is such that part-time options have long been recognized as an important strategy to meet labour requirements at peak times. Thus in the industry there is a well-established tradition of utilizing a regular pool of casual or part-time staff within banqueting, stewarding and housekeeping departments, and this practice may have derived from traditions inherited from entertaining in the great houses of the eighteenth and nineteenth centuries. Casual work in tourism, hospitality and leisure has also become increasingly subject to formal organizational arrangements through the presence of dedicated employment agencies (Lai and Baum 2005) which establish long-term supply relationships with employers in the sector. Other tourism and hospitality industry sectors have daily demand patterns which require flexible work. Bed-and-breakfast establishments and youth hostels, for example, may only offer work for limited periods of the morning while infrequent flight and shipping schedules to islands in Scotland and Greece do not require full-time staffing in support at the local stations. In the leisure context, the demand for specialist skills in water sports, equestrian skills or traditional music may be highly variable and result in the establishment of transitory or casualized working relationships between customers, organizations and service providers.

Flexible work has evolved as a natural response to the requirements of the business cycle within tourism. In many tourism, hospitality and leisure organizations, flexible work models operate alongside a core of full-time, long-service employees with relative harmony, although facing the personal pressures of insecurity and poor remuneration which can be a characteristic of this form of work. However, until relatively recently, the basic employment model in tourism, hospitality and leisure in developed countries remained that derived from the industrial and agricultural sectors: full-time employment with the expectation of continuing work with a single employer. Until the post-war period, however, this was without employment protection and security. The implicit expectation was that, should business levels require, full-time working opportunities would emerge instead of the part-time work on offer. This remains substantially the case in many developing countries where the very low cost of labour allows employers to sustain employment notwithstanding fluctuation in demand. As a result, the presence of workers operating to flexible employment models is much less common than in developed countries.

However, economic restructuring in many developed countries has seen the growing importance of service sector employment, with a far greater structural reliance on a part-time, flexible and predominantly female workforce. This restructuring reflects in part a major underlying change within the economies of many countries, but it is a change that has been actively facilitated by a complex amalgam of environmental changes relating to market competition, globalization and free trade as well as organizational matters such as employment security and employee entitlements. These issues and their social impact are considered in rather greater depth in Chapter 5. The change has, at its heart, a recognition by governments and employers that flexible work practices allow companies to fine-tune their labour needs both to changes in the business cycle (on a daily, weekly or longer time-span basis) and in response to more fundamental restructuring, such as alterations in market profile, shifts in guests' expectations and the introduction of technological alternatives to labour. They also reflect changing expectations of those in the labour force with respect to their personal balance between working and non-working time, both in the short term and in a longer, career-orientated sense. There is a general sense, globally, that international and national agreements have in recent years have been designed to facilitate flexibility in the workforce by reducing employment protection from some workers and eliminating wage controls but it is unclear how the debate in this area will conclude in the longer term.

The outcome, however, is clearly in evidence with an increasingly high proportion of new employment opportunities in Britain, for example, being offered on a flexible basis within the service sector. Within this, tourism, hospitality and leisure and, especially, hotel and catering have been responsible for a significant element in employment growth. The growth of employment in the sector has been twice that in the service sector in general, and the increase, for women, has been almost exclusively part-time. Part-time jobs also account for over two-thirds of new positions held by men in the service workforce. This growth in part-time employment has taken place at the expense of full-time employment, especially among women. Westwood (2002) cogently questions the quality of new work in the service sector on the basis of these trends in Britain and elsewhere.

The nature of much tourism, hospitality and leisure work is that it is readily accessible to those with relatively little specific training (Baum 2002a). At the same time, conditions and rewards are such that employees frequently are drawn to alternative, allied sectors such as contract or institutional catering where these attributes have traditionally been more attractive. Thus, labour turnover in some sectors of the tourism industry is high, although this situation is by no means new and was noted by George Orwell (1933) on the basis of his experiences in pre-war Paris. As a result, levels of worker mobility are high, both at the unskilled and the managerial level. Wood (1997) discusses a number of studies into aspects of labour turnover, primarily at the unskilled level. At the professional level in the hotel industry, Baum (1988) found that managers in Irish hotels moved to new posts, on average, within 15 months of taking up appointments. In part, high labour turnover is a factor of seasonality but also derives from what Riley (1996) describes as the characteristically weak internal labour market of much of the tourism industry. Riley compares the features of strong internal labour markets which are characteristic of professions such as medicine with the contrasting features of tourism, hospitality and leisure and, in particular, hotel and catering. Further discussion of Riley's work will be found in Chapter 3.

However, as is the case with various models of flexible work, there is some evidence that the introduction and maintenance of an ethos of temporary employment can be attractive to some service industry sectors. The fast-food industry has, arguably, pioneered this approach, building its staffing on the short-term expectations of primarily students and young people who do not wish to enter into long-term or career-focused commitments. The approach allows for the introduction of highly repetitive and de-skilled work routines which high energy and, generally, well-educated employees can follow without the danger of longer-term motivation problems. Other benefits to the company are flexibility and low wage costs (Ritzer 2004). The temporary, revolving work-force, however, represents a model which can be attractive to tourism, hospitality and leisure businesses with a large number of low-skilled positions, and which can systematize and standardize a substantial number of working routines as well as having a relatively transitory customer base. From an employee point of view, impermanence and the uncertainty of flexible working can create problems but can also be seen as an advantage. Lai (2005) found that international agency workers, employed for work in major London hotels, valued the flexibility of their working arrangements which permitted them to take period out of work (to return home) without any form of penalty to their status.

Tourism, hospitality and leisure in developed countries, therefore, has become a mass participation sector with increasing trends towards the creation of a workforce which mirrors its consumer market in its breadth. The growth of seasonal, part-time and temporary working opportunities in most sectors of the industry means that, for many young people and women returning to work, positions in tourism-related companies represent an early exposure or reintroduction to the world of employment. At the same time, these same employees are, frequently, relatively seasoned tourists in their own right and have participated in both domestic and international travel to a considerable extent. Thus, for the first time, we have tourism, hospitality and leisure employees who are versed and experienced in the needs that their customers have, and the gap between the two groups no longer has the importance that it did in the past.

The changes in patterns of work within tourism, hospitality and leisure would not have been possible had the overall guest–worker relationship remained the same as it was during the early days of the sector's development. Tourism, hospitality and leisure within most countries in the developed world has developed to a point where, with respect to a substantial proportion of both visitors and those working in the industry to meet their needs, there is no longer a significant difference in their attitudinal, social and economic backgrounds. This is most apparent when we consider the relationship between visitors and those working to meet their needs in resorts such as Blackpool and Benidorm, but is an increasing feature of tourism within developed economies worldwide. Yet the master–servant relationship which lay at the root of the early history of tourism, hospitality and leisure employment has much less potency within modern tourism, although vestiges of it still do exist and to a certain degree are perpetuated by the trappings of businesses within the sector, for example on cruise liners and in hotels and restaurants.

One of the driving forces behind this change process has, of course, been economic in that overall prosperity in developed countries combined with a general reduction in the real-term cost of participating in tourism, hospitality and leisure means that consumer participation is much more affordable. But the democratization of participation and work in tourism, hospitality and leisure is not exclusively an economic phenomenon. The nature of work has changed from its predominantly technical basis to include a range of, arguably, sophisticated generic skills, covering areas such as communications, languages and information technology as well as emotional and aesthetic labour inputs; themes that we will return to in Chapter 5. As a result, sectors of tourism, hospitality and leisure attract employees, maybe only in the short-term, who are able to deliver on the emotional and aesthetic labour requirements of work and this brings them into much closer proximity with their customers. For some employers, their need is to recruit what Nickson, Warhurst and Witz (2003) call 'style' workers, people who physically and emotionally match their work surroundings and are able to identify with the products and services they are selling and fully empathize with the expectations and buying objectives of their customers. Guerrier *et al.* (1998) refer to this process in the Singaporean context where retail and hospitality workers are highly brand-conscious in their choice of workplace, so that:

> The modern young Singaporean is disinclined to work in service unless the image of the product accords with her own sense of fashion. Working in Gucci means that the product becomes part of her own accessory range. (Guerrier *et al.* 1998, p.34).

Therefore, it is evident that democratization of participation in both consumption and work has become widespread in developed countries, creating what might be called narrow or non-existent social distance between the workers and customers in tourism, hospitality and leisure. As a result, there is a total interchangeability of roles between customers and employees who, literally, can move from one side of the counter to the other without any sense of being out of position. The Ritz Carlton's motto that 'We are Ladies and Gentlemen serving Ladies and Gentlemen' is a well-stated case in point. In another sense, airline magnate Niki Lauda set a standard of 'democratic' symbolism in the 1990s when his then-airline, Lauda Air, redesigned their cabin staff uniforms to match the normal attire of their business customers – including jeans – to 'create an environment that is casual but polite, and leads to a more personal contact with customers' (Churchill 1994). With his new airline, Niki Lauda has also taken radical steps in the design of his cabin crew uniform, allowing employees to wear their own casual clothes under a dramatic, reflective silver ensemble described by fellow cabin crew at airlinecrew.net as 'the most embarrassing uniform ever', 'wrapped in aluminium foil' and 'the poor girl that modelled Niki's uniform looks like she's off to go bowling' (airlinecrew.net accessed at http://www.airlinecrew.net/ubbthreads/showflat.php?Cat=&Number=130011 &Main=129712 on 23 May 2005).

In many respects, these examples bring us to a position in developed economies that is in complete contrast to the one where we started, when traveller and server were totally detached in social, economic and cultural terms. In the past, both parties fully accepted this social distance, tacitly buying into the Malthusian notion that divisions in society were part of the natural order of things and that each person had their own place and role. The democratization of tourism, hospitality and leisure has created an environment where – in theory at least – server and guest are equal. Critical to this process has been the exposure of tourism, hospitality and leisure workers to travel and international guest status in their own right, something unthinkable at its current level and scale even 40 years ago.

Let us move this discussion away from a developed-world context and take a look at the situation in poorer, developing countries which are also more recent participants in the development of international tourism, hospitality and leisure. Here, the social distance between customers and guests is very considerable, as it was in the early days of commercial tourism, hospitality and leisure in what are now the countries of the developed world. There are evident economic barriers to participation in tourism, hospitality and leisure by those who work in the sector in the poorer countries of Africa, Asia and the Caribbean. However, as we have already indicated, social distance is not an exclusively economic phenomenon and, in many parts of the developing world, takes on a cultural and political dimension as well. The manner in which international tourism, hospitality and leisure are presented and the sector's operating culture is predominantly Western-centric and is far more remote from the everyday lives of people living in India, Tanzania or Cuba than it is from residents of Australia, Canada or the Netherlands. It is this combination of divergence (economic, cultural, political) which creates the high level of social distance between tourism, hospitality and leisure's customers and the sector's workforce in developing countries.

Case Study *The Club Sandwich Rule*

The club sandwich is an almost universal menu item in international standard hotels from Buenos Aires to Birmingham and Washington to Windhoek. Officially, the club sandwich can be described as 'a sandwich with cooked chicken breast and bacon, along with juicy ripe tomatoes and crisp lettuce layered between two or three slices of toasted bread with mayonnaise' (Stradley 2004) but its preparation varies across countries and time, responding to cultural consideration (the absence of bacon in Muslim countries) and time ('healthier' versions available in the early twenty-first century than was the case in the past). Indeed, the Australian Institute of Sport include a particularly healthy version of the club sandwich among their 'Survival of the Fittest' menus (AIS undated).

Stradley traces the club sandwich back to the late nineteenth century in the Saratoga clubhouse in upstate New York although this is widely disputed. What is not in doubt is that the concept did originate in the United States and it gained popularity with the rich and famous over the first half of the twentieth century. It was a particular favourite of King Edward VIII of England and his American wife, Wallis Simpson. Today, as Stradley notes, the club sandwich is most often associated with hotels around the world.

The notion of a Club Sandwich Rule as a metaphor of social distance within tourism, hospitality and leisure work came about during a discussion in the coffee shop of a major hotel in Kingston, Jamaica in the early 1990s. The author of this case (to his shame) ordered a club sandwich instead of an authentic Jamaican dish. When the waitress returned, she struck up conversation along the following lines:

'You see this club sandwich. It will cost you US$ 7.95 [or something like that]. Do you know how long I have to work to earn enough to buy one of these?'

The author of this case confessed that he did not know.

'About 16 hours. I get about 50 cents an hour here so I am never going to be able to afford one of these and still have enough left over to feed my kids at home.'

Clearly, the Jamaican waitress in this hotel could not aspire to relax after her shift and purchase a club sandwich (or, indeed, any other item from the menu) in the hotel where she worked. Economic factors precluded any form of convergence between consumption

▶

and employment in this tourism, hospitality and leisure context. Very clear social distance between guests and those serving them was evident. This experience led the author of this case to look at the relationship between price of a club sandwich and the average earnings of those serving the dish in major hotels across a number of countries and continents.

At the same time, the purchase of a similar club sandwich in a hotel in Stockholm would have cost the waiter(ress) 1 hour 30 minutes of work to purchase, very similar to San Francisco. In London (before the introduction of a minimum wage), the figure at the time was 2 hours 30 minutes. In Singapore, the time required to purchase the club sandwich was six hours and in Mumbai, India, it was close to 11 hours. In Hanoi, Vietnam, an extreme of over 45 hours' work was necessary to purchase the same product.

On the basis of this unscientific club sandwich survey, it is reasonable to suggest that, while never a cheap purchase alongside local food or alternative street cafes, it is eminently reasonable for hotel employees in Australia, Europe and North America to afford the luxury of a club sandwich in their own hotel should they choose to visit the establishment as a guest. Elsewhere, this dual role of worker and consumer is virtually impossible to imagine, for both economic and cultural reasons.

The Club Sandwich Rule, therefore, is an illustrative measure of social distance between consumption and employment in tourism, hospitality and leisure. Where dual participation (as a worker and consumer) is feasible, social distance is low. Where dual participation is inconceivable, social distance is very high.

Original case written by the author.

Case discussion questions

1. Price a club sandwich in an international hotel with which you are familiar, compare this to the average hourly wage of a waiter in that business and calculate an approximate measure of social distance for the location.

2. Why is the club sandwich a good item to select as an indicator of social distance?

3. What problems might be encountered in applying the club sandwich rule?

Review and discussion questions

1. Consider aspects of the history of the tourism, hospitality and leisure industry in a town or region with which you are familiar. What are likely to have been the main reasons for its development? What were the main features? Does any evidence remain of the original form of the industry in your locality?

2. With reference to a town or region with which you are familiar, can you find any evidence in the local history of tourism and hospitality to support or reject Steinecke's replication or displacement model?

3. Consider the vacation and travel opportunities that you and your family (immediate, grandparents) have enjoyed over the past 40 to 50 years. Does any identifiable pattern emerge in the type of holidays that were taken, the locations that were visited and their distance from home? Can you account for changes to your family vacation patterns over that time frame?

4. Utilizing your own work experience or other contacts, interview a senior and mature tourism and hospitality employee or someone, now retired, who

used to work in the industry. Try to establish the main changes that have occurred in that person's experience in the nature of work that was undertaken and that which is prevalent in that occupation today. Consider the reasons for such changes and their implications.

5. What are the implications of decreasing 'social distance' between guests and employees for the management of a tourism, hospitality and leisure business?

6. Does serving guests in the tourism and hospitality industry need to be servile?

3

Tourism, hospitality and leisure labour markets

What are tourism, hospitality and leisure labour markets?

We have already demonstrated that the tourism, hospitality and leisure industries are characterized by diversity both on the basis of intra-national (within countries) and international (between countries) criteria. Diversity is compounded by imprecision in defining the actual boundaries of the tourism, hospitality and leisure sector and variation between countries in how they actually attempt this exercise. The porous parameters of the industry which, at its margins, merges into a variety of other economic sectors, is a characteristic to which we are driven to return repeatedly. It is a source of frustration to those who prefer to work within the precise and comforting boundaries provided by absolute definitions, whether derived from official or other sources. It can also be a source of challenge when it is recognized that the heterogeneous range of activities which constitute tourism, hospitality and leisure are bound together by their contribution to a common goal, that of meeting the comfort, logistical and leisure needs of the traveller away from home.

As we have seen in Chapters 1 and 2, the characteristics of the international tourism, hospitality and leisure industry have a major impact on the nature of work in the sector. Thus the range of sub-sectors, the size of businesses, their ownership, the markets they serve and the impact of seasonality illustrate the factors which contribute to determining, for example, the range of tasks which are undertaken, the numbers employed and the skills required. However, while these associations are undoubtedly very important, they cannot be seen as the exclusive determinants of the tourism and hospitality labour market.

In its broadest sense, the labour market comprises the total working environment at local, regional, national or transnational level. Thus we can talk about the labour market of a small town, such as the location of the 1994 Winter Olympics, Lillehammer in Norway; of a metropolitan city, for example the 2004 Summer Olympics venue, Athens in Greece; of a distinct region of a country, such as Calabria in Italy; of an entire nation state; or, finally, of the whole Association of South-East Asian Nations (ASEAN) region or, indeed, the total continent of Europe. A labour market consists of all industry sectors, their personnel requirements and skills needs, as well as those currently outside the actual workforce, whether unemployed, temporarily unable to work because of illness or injury, or undergoing specific vocational training or more general preparation for the workforce within the schools system. Economists and others who view labour markets from a macro or theoretical perspective tend to describe the environment as one akin to a well-oiled machine, driven by supply and demand within a free market. However, as Riley (1996) rightly points out:

> Labour markets run on information, but they are invariably less than perfect mechanisms. What both buyers and sellers are left with is their perceptions and assumptions of supply and demand. We may think that there is no current demand for our skills, yet it may be that there is. (p.7)

Perfect labour markets, however, do not exist in the real free-market world and, despite major investment in labour planning, the total management of the labour market was not a conspicuous success in the planned economies of Eastern Europe either. This is because labour markets at macro or micro level represent a complexity of interactions which do not lend themselves to management and balancing in the manner demanded by the theoretical model.

> At any one time, people will be seeking employment or trying to change their jobs. Simultaneously, employers will be seeking new employees. Wage rates will be set, recruitment policies implemented, people will need training, and people will have to move. This is the daily life of labour markets. Thousands of independent decisions made by employers and employees make up the trends in mobility, the surpluses of or shortages of supply, the excesses or lack of demand. In other words, whatever the state of supply and demand in a labour market, it is brought about by the independent and unconnected decisions of thousands of people. (Riley 1996, p.7)

In addition to this, the character of this wider labour market is determined by a wide range of macro environmental factors, some of which pertain specifically to the geographical unit in question (town, county, region, country, etc.) while others are shared with other units. Some of these factors include:

- the culture and history of the locality or unit;
- the economic system within which it exists (free market, planned economy, etc.);

- the development status of the economy (developed, transition, developing);
- the range of existing wealth-creating industry sectors (agriculture, heavy industry, light industry, services including tourism, etc.);
- changes to the industrial structure of the unit (the decline of coal mining and steel production and the rise of light assembly work in South Wales is one example while another is that of Liverpool where the decline in traditional port employment has been paralleled by growth in the leisure and tourism sector (McDonald 1994));
- the profile of businesses in terms of size and ownership – multinational companies tend to have a very different relationship to a local and even national labour market than that characteristic of a small, family-owned business;
- local, national and, indeed, global economic performance, factors which will influence demand for good and services produced, the price that will be paid for them and the level and character of employment that will be generated as a result;
- the demographic structure of the unit and trends within it (the falling birth-rate and increasing longevity of older people in most developed countries, for example);
- the range of skills available within the existing workforce and among school leavers and college graduates and how these relate to industry demand;
- competition between companies and industry sectors for available skills within the workforce and among school leavers and college graduates;
- the structure, organization and focus of educational and vocational training provision within the unit;
- the extent of inward and outward labour mobility to and from the unit in question and the barriers and incentives that exist to such mobility (for example, rights of free labour movement within the European Union or at a national level);
- policies enacted at a local, regional, national and transnational level by governments, councils, legislative and representative assemblies with respect to matters which may include:
  - fiscal/economic policy
  - education and training
  - employment creation and related incentives
  - employment protection measures
  - workplace conditions and practice
  - health and safety at work provisions
  - support for export
  - attraction of inward investment
  - migrant labour, both legal and illegal
  - employment of expatriate labour.

A labour market, therefore, is a dynamic concept responding to a diversity of factors some of which can be controlled at a local, regional or national level but also including others which are entirely beyond such management and which cannot be treated as static and unchanging. This reality has major consequences for the manner in which, at a micro level, managers plan and initiate all aspects of their human resource policies within a company. At the macro level, likewise, planning with respect to areas such as vocational education provision and the introduction of special measures to alleviate youth unemployment, for example, must be responsive and flexible in recognition of constant change within the labour market. Recognizing the dynamic nature of the labour market environment and the consequences that this has for planning human resource needs at a macro level is a central theme within Chapter 9 of this book.

What is the value of understanding labour markets?

What is the practical value and purpose of an understanding of the labour market to those involved, as employers and employees, within it? From the employer's perspective, the labour market external to the company provides the source for the recruitment of new staff as well as the pool which personnel made redundant or released for other reasons join. The wider labour market also provides the major benchmark against which it is possible to gauge a range of major human resource policies and practices, some of which are discretionary and some of which are externally imposed. Thus a company's policies with respect to the full range of human resource functions are influenced by the characteristics of the labour market in which it operates. Depending on the nature of the company's business, its skills requirements and a range of other factors such as labour mobility, the labour-market reference point for any particular business may be local, national or even international. For example, the recruitment of semi-skilled kitchen or cleaning personnel will necessitate action within different labour-market parameters than will be the case with respect to staff with specialist technical skills. Labour-market considerations determined by the range of influences which we have addressed above will impact upon a company's policies and practices with respect to a large number of areas. These may include:

- recruitment of personnel in the open market, from schools/colleges and through to head-hunting from other employers;
- staff training and development;
- promotion and enhancement policies;
- severance/redundancy policies;
- employment of part-time, casual and seasonal staff;
- contracting or franchising out of functions to supplier companies (catering, cleaning, office services, etc.);
- rates of remuneration, including overtime, bonus payments, profit sharing, etc.;
- conditions of service such as hours of work, flexible time-keeping, paid holiday entitlements, maternity and similar benefits;
- trade union representation;

- social and other benefits; and
- health and safety provision.

Riley (1996) does not fully accept the above argument that a company's internal environment is essentially a response to external factors of the kind listed above. He argues that, within companies, independent rules may be established to determine how some or all of the above operate in practice. Riley distinguishes the external labour market at whatever geographical level we wish to consider it. This is basically governed by the range of macroeconomic, social and political actors that we have considered earlier, and the internal labour market within the company (or arguably the industry sector) itself. He argues that:

> The concept of the internal labour market is based on the idea that sets of rules and conventions form within organizations which act as allocative mechanisms governing the movement of people and the pricing of jobs. Such rules are about promotion criteria, training opportunities, pay differentials and the evaluation of jobs, but most importantly, they are about which jobs are open to the external labour market. It is the concept of openness which represents the interface between what goes on inside the organization and the external labour market. (Riley 1996, p.12)

We will address the consequences of this distinction between internal and external labour markets in greater depth later in this chapter.

Likewise, from an employee perspective, an understanding of the main features of the labour market provides the basis for decisions with respect, for example, to educational and training choices, both at the initial stage and as retraining, selection of employment and employer, negotiating strength with potential and current employers, career promotion and enhancement, mobility between employers as well as geographical mobility within a region, country or internationally, participation in special schemes during periods of unemployment, and participation in trade union and related activities, as well as a range of attendant considerations.

As regards both the company and the individual, the relationship with the labour market in which they exist, whatever parameters are used to define its geographical boundaries, is highly individual. It is possible to review the characteristics and structure of the labour market in question against the range of determining factors that we have already considered and many of these will impose similar constraints on all employers as well as all employees. However, it is also important to recognize differing circumstances, constraints and needs within both groups (companies and workers) and these will impact upon the way in which members of both groups relate to the labour market.

Global labour markets

In keeping with trends in all aspects of business, labour markets, even at a relatively local level, are increasingly dependent on the international and even global context in which they exist. Historically, labour markets could exist in relative isolation from events and developments in the next town, in the neighbouring country or on the other side of the world. To some extent, this remains the case within agrarian communities in many developing communities, although the impact of globalization of agricultural produce procurement by major supermarkets, for example, has started to effect even remote and traditional communities in East Africa, Central America and South-East Asia (Blythman 2004). Industrialization started the process which has destroyed the virtual self-sufficiency of communities in developed countries and created the complex range of dependencies which characterize modern business. Migration of labour to the new industrial locations occurred on a scale which previous mobility had not permitted. At the same time, opportunities in new labour markets, especially in North America, attracted migrants to leave their primarily rural homes in Europe and travel overseas on a scale previously unknown. Economic migration, as opposed to the political mobility of those avoiding persecution in their own land, has taken place on a previously unknown scale and scope during the past 150 years. It is something which has occurred both domestically (Scots moving to London, for example) and, probably more significantly, internationally. Examples include European and especially Irish migration to the United States and Australia since the 1840s; immigration from former colonial possessions into the Netherlands, France and Britain from the 1950s onwards; movement out of locations such as Vietnam and Hong Kong to Australia, Canada, Europe and the USA since the 1970s; and, over the past decade, widespread migration from virtually every relatively poor country in the world, whether in Eastern Europe, Asia, Africa or South America, to perceived better lives in the economies of the developed world.

Migration into and out of labour markets is a reflection of a combination of push and pull factors. Movement may be driven by appalling conditions at home, whether economic, political or geographical, so that people are literally pushed out of their home countries in order to escape from abject poverty, political persecution and warfare, or natural disasters. Much of the movement of people to Europe, North America and Australia is portrayed as caused by the push of conditions at home. However, labour markets in developed countries are facing major shortages of skills in a wide range of working areas from health and transport to tourism, hospitality and leisure. As a result, their labour markets, facilitated by governments, exert a pull effect on those able and willing to move into work in developed countries. Such migration is complemented by a global trend to relocate expensive work processes, where possible, into cheaper labour markets. This is a process very easy to identify in the manufactured goods sector but is also increasingly in evidence within services, including tourism, hospitality and leisure, where IT functions, reservations call centres and financial processing are examples of activities that have relocated from Europe and North America to India and elsewhere in the developing world. The nature of service delivery and work in tourism, hospitality and leisure, however, reduces the likelihood that more widespread out-migration of activities will take place. Some of the consequences to the tourism, hospitality and leisure industry of migration within the sector are considered in more detail in Chapter 6.

Globalization of markets and business structures as well as the political will to remove the barriers to trade and labour mobility has had the effect, on the one hand, of creating truly international labour markets. This is especially the case in certain vocational sub-sectors, while at the same time blurring the geographical boundaries of others which have traditionally been fairly local in their focus. As a result, some specialist skills are the cause of truly international recruitment searches at an individual or collective level. Shortages of specific computing skills, for example, have led major US companies to actively recruit in South Asia. Alternatively, within the increasingly global economy, companies are willing to relocate their operations to countries and localities where availability of skills is greater and the cost of such skills is lower than is the case in the labour market within which they have previously been operating. The relocation of clothing manufacturing plants from the United States to neighbouring Latin American countries is an example of this process as are movements in South and East Asia to relocate highly labour-intensive industries out of expensive locations such as Hong Kong, Singapore and Taiwan into China. This process of globalization of the world's labour force is a relatively controversial subject and its impact depends on whether it is seen from the perspective of the beneficiary or the loser.

The European Union model of free movement of labour can be seen as an important step within the process of globalization and is one that may be followed by other regional trade blocs such as the North American Free Trade Agreement (NAFTA) and ASEAN. Overall, it is likely that, in terms of skills which are in short supply throughout the world, the net beneficiaries of mobility will be the most advanced industrial countries while, for the poorer countries, globalization of labour means the relocation of low-wage, high-polluting industries from the developed to the less-developed world. A similar analysis can be applied in considering the potential impact of the General Agreement on Tariffs and Trade (GATT) free-trade arrangements.

As we have already noted, labour globalization and relocation is not a widely exercised option within the tourism, hospitality and leisure industry because the tourist attraction, which visitors come to see, generally cannot be moved to alter native locations, although this process may occur in specific technical support areas such as aircraft maintenance. In other respects the recruitment of cheaper labour from elsewhere to meet low-skills requirements in the tourism, hospitality and leisure industry is commonplace. As we will consider in more detail in Chapter 6, migration within Europe is from peripheral countries such as Ireland, Italy, Portugal and Spain in order to work in the hotels of London and other North European cities. This is a long-standing tradition and the consequences of this process are discussed by Baum (1993b), who refers to:

> the pull of the 'core' regions, offering the attractions of different lifestyles, higher rewards, year-round employment and associated benefits. This issue is one that is, perhaps, critical within the whole economic development of the 'New Europe' and has implications for regions not currently within the European Community. The main flow of tourists (international and domestic) within Europe, is essentially from 'core' to 'periphery', although some 'honey pot' locations are identifiable in the 'core' areas (London, Paris). By contrast, the traditional flow of labour is from the 'periphery' to the 'core' (for example Irish emigration to London and the movement of Italian and Spanish labour to France and Germany, a process directly in reverse of the main tourist flows). Greater facility for labour mobility is likely to increase this flow of workers. Migration within Europe and to

Europe has greatly increased in recent years, for a diversity of reasons (economic, political and cultural) and this process has already increased through a 'rippling' process, incorporating areas further and further from the economic core of Europe, such as Turkey, North Africa and the countries of Central and Eastern Europe. As a consequence, the 'peripheral' countries face the prospect of losing their trained and skilled tourism labour to those countries in the 'core'. This, in turn, is likely to adversely affect standards of product and service in the regions losing their skilled labour. There is every reason to believe that this process will continue, providing cheaper labour for the tourism industries of the 'core' countries and drawing skills away from the periphery. (pp.81–2)

Transnational economic integration also provides the basis for major changes to assumptions about traditional labour markets. In particular, the free movement of labour within the European Union (EU), alongside the free movement of investment capital, means that on the one hand companies can locate activities in countries or localities where the skills and labour cost environment are most favourable to their needs. On the other hand, labour has the theoretical opportunity to seek out employment openings wherever they exist within the EU and Baum (1993) above details how this process operates in the tourism, hospitality and leisure industry. Former UK Government Minister Norman Tebbitt's much-quoted advice to job seekers from areas of high unemployment to 'get on their bikes' and avail themselves of job opportunities elsewhere in Britain now has an increasingly global dimension.

Tourism, hospitality and leisure labour markets

Within the context of wider labour-market considerations, it is possible to give particular attention to the characteristics of labour markets within specific sub-sectors of the economy. Such sub-labour markets, while in no way operating in isolation from the wider economic, social and political contexts which drive the broader external labour-market environment, have features and behavioural patterns which set them apart to greater or lesser degrees from those wider contexts. Thus, it is possible to identify a tourism and hospitality labour market at all the geographical levels that we have already considered – local, regional, national and transnational.

In Chapter 1, we identified some of the major features of the international tourism, hospitality and leisure industry. One of these was that commonality is not always easy to identify at a transnational level and that the industry is characterized by inevitable diversity for geographical, historical, cultural, political and social as well as business and market reasons. However, there are a number of broad features which can be identified as representative of tourism, hospitality and leisure and these, when set alongside the range of generic determinants discussed earlier, provide the main influences on the labour market within the sector. These features include:

- an industry dominated by small businesses with a high level of family or self-employment in a number of its sub-sectors (hotels, restaurants, retail activities, fitness) alongside large, multinational enterprises (e.g. in entertainment, accommodation and transport), some of which are state owned;

- an industry which experiences high levels of fluctuation in demand for its services in terms of annual seasonality as well as variation within the time frame of the typical week and day. This has major consequences for the supply of labour, especially in the context of the small business operation;

- an industry constrained by its service-sector characteristics (which we shall consider in greater detail in Chapter 4) including the inseparability of production and consumption; the intangibility of the product; its perishability, meaning that it cannot be stored or warehoused; and the local nature of its demand, which means that it cannot be offered centrally to the market;

- an industry where traditions in terms of the style and ceremony of service remain very important in some countries, but where varying influences of standardization and automation as well as the impact of emotional and aesthetic considerations in service delivery create tensions that have important consequences for the nature of work and its flexibility;

- a labour-intensive industry in most of its sectors and this characteristic, despite the impact of technology, is unlikely to alter substantially in the foreseeable future;

- an industry which, as a consequence of its labour intensity, is dominated in many sub-sectors by relatively unskilled and semi-skilled jobs. There have been various attempts to describe the skills structure of tourism, hospitality and leisure. Riley (1996), with reference to the hotel and catering sub-sector in the UK, proposes a breakdown whereby 64 per cent of staff are semi-skilled and unskilled operatives, 22 per cent are skilled crafts persons, 8 per cent hold supervisory positions and 6 per cent are managers. Azzaro (2005) considers the structure of the whole tourism sector in Malaysia and proposes a breakdown of the workforce on the basis of unskilled (19 per cent); skilled/semi-skilled (42 per cent); middle management (24 per cent), executive management (9 per cent) and senior management (6 per cent). Azarro's skills model points to a sector in a developing economy that is far more intensively 'managed' than is the case in the developed economy of the United Kingdom;

- an industry which, because of this mixed skills profile, is readily accessible to workers with a minimum of formal training and where training focuses on widely transferable skills, especially in the customer contact zone. This 'openness' can work to the advantage of the industry, especially in locations where a high seasonality factor is in operation, in that it is relatively easy to draft additional labour into the industry as demand increases and to shed employees at times of reduced demand. However, the negative corollary means that trained tourism and hospitality employees are readily 'poached' by other industry sectors because of their generic and readily transferrable skills;

- an industry within which some sectors are dominated by traditions of low pay and perceived poor conditions, as we shall see in Chapter 5.

Riley (1996) also analyses the tourism, hospitality and leisure labour-market environment in terms of the concept of internal labour markets. Riley differentiates between the structural features of strong and weak internal labour markets and this differentiation goes some way in explaining the characteristics of employment within many sub-sectors of the tourism, hospitality and leisure industry in developed countries. Exhibit 3.1 identifies the features of the two internal labour-market types. It is Riley's contention that the labour market within the tourism, hospitality and leisure industry in developed countries meets most of the criteria for 'weak' status. This analysis is based, primarily, upon observation of the industry in the United Kingdom and the fit is quite good in this respect. Certainly, when comparisons are made against these criteria between access to management within some sub-sectors of the industry such as hotels and professional careers in medicine, the contrast between strong and weak internal labour markets can be seen in relatively clear relief. However, as is the case with any framework, what we see is a simplified representation of the real situation and Riley's argument does not portray an absolute description of the situation within tourism, hospitality and leisure on an international basis.

It is clear, therefore, that Riley's model does not necessarily transfer comfortably across into all areas of tourism, hospitality and leisure. The diversity of the industry, encompassing as it does sub-sectors as wide-ranging as sports coaching, museums and other attractions, heritage sites and transportation as well as hotels and restaurants, includes many working environments or internal labour markets which exhibit predominantly strong characteristics. Such employment opportunities include museum curators, airline pilots and tourism consultants, where the open employment environment characteristic of lower skills areas is not typical. However, even these relatively protected areas are weakening to some extent. During Ronald Reagan's presidency, the US Government's willingness to replace the highly specialized skills of established air traffic controllers through recruitment and training of alternatives when threatened by the consequences of strike action represents a good example of a weakening labour market. Likewise, the Irish airline Ryanair employed less expensive Eastern European pilots during the mid-1980s when the cost of labour prohibited the use of local alternatives.

Riley's model poses further challenges when it is applied to many developing country contexts where there is evidence of rather stronger labour market characteristics. Indeed, it is arguable that any formalized employment environment in a situation where a high proportion of the population live outside organized and sustainable employment, is relatively speaking a strong labour market. This is particularly true where multinational companies bring their global workplace practices into a developing country where equivalent local employment is poorly remunerated and of low status. Hilton International, as the only multinational tourism, hospitality and leisure employer in Kyrgyzstan, has a work ethos that is far 'stronger' in character than its local competitors', partly because of the calibre of workers it is able to attract but also because of the culture it has brought with it into the country. There is evidence that the process of development in countries such as Malaysia and Singapore has seen significant weakening of their tourism, hospitality and leisure labour markets as general affluence increases.

The tourism, hospitality and leisure sector internationally is an amalgam of sub-sectors which represent both weak and strong labour markets. Overall labour-market management by governments in most developed countries is undergoing a general process of weakening, so as to facilitate greater flexibility within the workforce at lower cost to both the state (through training and

---

Exhibit 3.1 Features of strong and weak labour markets

Strong   Weak

Specified hiring standards   Unspecified hiring standards
(representing the extent to which specific jobs demand a particular qualifications and experience profile for entry to the organization)

Single port of entry   Multiple ports of entry
(representing the extent to which recruitment for particular posts are restricted to one source in terms of qualifications and experience or whether applicants with a diversity of backgrounds are eligible to apply for the post)

High skill specificity   Low skill specificity
(representing the extent to which the job demands specific technical, knowledge-based or other skills)

Continuous on-the-job training   No on-the-job training
(representing the extent to which specific and ongoing training is necessary in order to progress within the job or, alternatively, where initial training provides the totality of expected training for the job)

Fixed criteria for promotion   No fixed criteria for promotion
and transfer   and transfer
(representing the extent to which further training and experience are identified as requirements for promotion and/or transfer)

Strong workplace customs   Weak workplace customs
(reflecting the strength of organized and professional labour control over pay and conditions, especially in terms of protecting the status and reward differentials between higher skills posts and those at a lower level)

Additional dimensions to those proposed by Riley are:

Fixed roles/responsibilities   Flexible roles/responsibilities
(reflecting the extent to which rigid job demarcations exist in the workplace or to which flexibility in work roles/multi-skilling applies)

Primary use of full-time, core staff   Use of part-time, casual or outsourced
                                              staff
(reflecting the relationship between the internal company labour market and the wider external labour market)

Source: Reprinted from Riley (1966) *Human Resource Management in the Hospitalty and Tourism Industry*, with permission from Elsevier. Italics indicate this author's additions

benefits) and the employer through wage costs and additional benefits. A range of legislation in, for example, the United Kingdom since the early 1980s has been designed to meet these ends, eroding the position of trade unions within the workplace, deregulating a wide variety of workplace practices, supporting the de-skilling of tasks within both the public and private sectors and removing minimum wages protection in a number of industries. However, national minimum wages (NMW) operate within most countries of the European Union and undoubtedly act to strengthen the labour market to a limited extent. As we shall see in Chapter 5, the European Union's Social Chapter is also, on the face of it, a move in the direction of strengthening the labour market. However, much of the impetus for change is driven by the private sector and it is unlikely that the Social Chapter can wholly counteract the effects of such developments. Examples above from the US and Ireland illustrate the process of labour-market weakening at work in the tourism, hospitality and leisure sector.

Flexibility in the tourism, hospitality and leisure workplace

The issue of flexibility in the workforce is one that is central to the weak–strong labour market debate and has been added to Riley's model within Exhibit 3.1. Flexibility has a number of important dimensions when we consider the tourism, hospitality and leisure labour market. There are a number of different forms of flexibility, of which the most significant here are numerical and functional flexibility. Employers seek flexibility in terms of the numbers that are employed within a business in order to cope with cyclical variation in demand, whether based on annual seasonality, peaks and troughs within the week or day or in order to cater for the high demand created by special events; whether a wedding in a hotel or transport to the Olympics or other 'one-off' sporting events. Flexibility in the workplace allows employers to manage their labour costs in line with income and, in extreme situations like that which occurred in Hong Kong during the SARS crisis, downsize their workforce dramatically in the face of minimal or no demand.

Numerical flexibility can be defined as the ability of organizations to increase or decrease employment quickly in line with fluctuations in business demand, and to improve the competitiveness of firms through adopting this flexible policy (Atkinson 1984; Lai 2005; Lai and Baum 2005). Ruiz-Mercarder, Ruiz-Santos and McDonald (2001) identify four types of numerical flexibility.

- Contractual working time flexibility – This relates to the use of temporary/short-term and part-time contracts, both of which are commonplace within hospitality's variable demand environment.
- Distancing flexibility – When the firm utilizes outside employees who have commercial contracts to undertake an activity, such as through subcontracting and home working on the basis of self-employment.
- Exit flexibility – This involves the simplification of administrative procedures and reducing the dismissal costs involved in shedding labour when demand decreases.

- Internal flexibility or time flexibility – This relates to the duration and planning of working time, for example, extra hours, annual contracts on hours worked, and the use of shift working.

Numerical flexibility models normally employ 'human hours' as instruments while utilizing labour-force flexibility strategies. Companies predict their requirements for human resource (based on hours needed or skill required), and adjust their human resource supplies. To achieve greater success in balancing demand and supply, companies have to obtain the ability to utilize employment and deployment.

The traditional response to the need for numerical flexibility has been reliance on part-time, casual, short-contract and seasonal staff. All sub-sectors of the tourism, hospitality and leisure industry have employed this approach to flexibility which is manifest in the work undertaken by, for example, representatives employed by tour operators and located in resorts for the duration of the season, seasonal hotel and airline staff, breakfast kitchen and service staff in small hotels, banqueting staff in hotels and convention centres, and self-employed tour guides. Such staffing arrangements are attractive to employers in that labour is only costing them when it is required. However, control over matters such as operational and service standards may be jeopardized by the lack of permanence within the workforce. Problems can also arise at times of peak labour demand because other employers may offer better or more extended employment to those in the pool from which a company normally draws in order to exercise its need for flexibility. The personnel involved are permanent and fully trained members of staff and cannot opt to work elsewhere as is the case with other arrangements.

There are alternative responses to numerical flexibility that can accommodate both the flexibility needs of employers and their employees. Traditional flexibility models have been driven by the demand cycle and by the requirements of employers. Flexibility in how long and when people work is also a matter of considerable concern to employees. ILO (2001) cite examples of responses to reductions in the working week in France to 35 hours which are built around permitting employees to determine their most suitable times for work within an 11-hour, seven-day week in an electronic travel agency, permitting flexibility to accommodate both the work output required and the lifestyle requirements of employees.

The second aspect of flexibility relates to the tasks that are undertaken by employees within the workplace and is known as functional flexibility in that flexibility is achieved through widening the responsibilities, often across departments, of employees. Functional flexibility is the ability of managers to extend the range of tasks a worker can perform. This normally applies in core, permanent staff inside organizations in the form of a multi-skilling scheme. The organization expects employees to take on different functions and work between various departments. For example, a hotel receptionist checks in/out guests in the morning and cleans guest rooms as a chambermaid after the morning rush. If employees were multi-skilled, this gives companies greater flexibility to act quickly and smoothly while reacting to the problem of staff shortage. Functional flexibility implies that the same labour force changes its activities within the organization, in both the short and medium term (Atkinson 1985). Within tourism, hospitality and leisure, there is considerable debate regarding aspects of functional flexibility because multi-skilling in the sector rarely involves diversity in the skills utilized (for example, customer care) but rather variation in the context within which they are applied. Employees are thus multi-tasked rather than multi-skilled. In other words, employees are required to employ the same skills but in differing contexts rather than developing a new range of skills which could be of greater value to them, both personally and vocationally.

In the past, workplace demarcation was relatively fixed in many sectors of the tourism, hospitality and leisure industry. The classical *parti* system in hotel kitchens, for example, identified the specific tasks which lay within the responsibility of each member of the kitchen brigade and little interchange of functions took place. The notion that kitchen staff could work outside of that specific domain, for example through participation in service functions, may have been beyond comprehension to many who worked within that system. Vestiges of the classical *parti* system still exist in some countries, although working practices combined with the advent of more advanced food-processing and production technology and the de-skilling of some tasks through the use of alternative, convenience products has eroded its significance. Similarly clear role definitions have been features of work within airlines, railway systems and other sectors of the tourism, hospitality and leisure industry.

Inflexible working practices have made it difficult for businesses to respond to variable demand and, especially within small businesses, to compete effectively while at the same time maintaining cost competitiveness in the marketplace. The manufacturing sector has pioneered a response to the need for flexibility in this sense by developing a core of permanent full-time employees who are trained in a variety of skills in order that they may move from function to function as required. The weakening of the internal labour market within tourism and hospitality can be seen in the extent to which similar approaches have been adopted within the sector. Small hotels have long practised flexibility through the employment of personnel who can work in a number of departments and who, typically, may face a working day which involves service at breakfast, housekeeping functions during the morning and bar or restaurant service at lunchtime to complete the day. Baum and Odgers (2001) discuss the case of the London Hilton where multi-task training across all customer contact areas is in place for all new service staff and is a requirement for permanent status and promotion within the organization. Similar flexibility requirements are evident in new working practices, especially of smaller airlines where cabin staff may well be involved in a variety of other functions, including check-in, baggage handling and related tasks. This has the effect of reducing the requirement for ground station staff at small airports where the airline offers limited services. Examples include the Loganair Scottish island services as well as those operated by low-cost airlines in Asia, Australia, Europe and North America. The low-cost airlines are particularly interesting in this context because they require cabin crew to execute a range of tasks traditionally reserved for specialists including boarding flights and tidying the cabin at the end of journeys (Pender and Baum 2000).

Functional flexibility can include elements of job redesign and enrichment, used both as a means of enabling the employer to achieve greater flexibility within the existing workforce and as a perceived means of motivating and rewarding staff. Whether this can work depends on the nature of redesign and enrichment that is offered to staff and is also dependent upon a desire by such staff to take aboard additional responsibilities in their work. Ng, Boo and Ingram (2005) cast doubt on the value of job redesign in the hospitality sector in Singapore. They report a survey of staff in hotels that have implemented job redesign and noted broadly unfavourable responses from respondents, with little evidence that such change will influence their propensity to remain with that organization in the future. Of particular note here is the fact that much of the job redesign reported constituted change of technical nature in the workplace with little reference to soft skills pertaining to interpersonal, emotional, aesthetic or empowerment domains.

Guerrier and Lockwood (1989) were, perhaps, the first to consider flexibility issues in the context of the tourism, hospitality and leisure sector. Their discussion looked at the organization in terms of the relationship of various groups of employees to the 'core' of the company. Guerrier and Lockwood applied Atkinson's (1985) flexible firm model to the hotel industry in the United Kingdom. They divide the core staff of a multi-unit hotel company into three components. First, there are 'company core staff' consisting of the cadre of senior and middle management within the hotel such as the general manager, deputy or resident manager, assistant managers and graduate trainees but usually excluding department heads. They are so defined because they operate within the company's career structure and potentially have access to career opportunities elsewhere within the group. Normal progression includes periods with responsibility for a number of functional areas in the hotel. Traditionally, but less so today, this route has required a period in food and beverage management as a prerequisite for general management. Thus, this group of staff are expected to exhibit maximum functional flexibility and are a highly skilled, versatile and committed group which the company cannot afford to lose in any great number. Career-tracking schemes which companies such as Hilton International have instituted focus on this group of core staff and contribute to the planning of both their geographical and functional progression within the organization.

According to Guerrier and Lockwood, the second group of core staff are unit based, with access to career opportunities within a single unit but less so within the whole corporate structure. The unit core consists of heads of department, supervisors and some operative staff. This group lack functional flexibility and work in their specialist areas of food preparation, housekeeping, food and beverage service, etc. Flexibility comes in terms of their ability to 'trade down' to operative tasks as and when required. This group constitute the most stable within a hotel by contrast with more transitory senior managers and peripheral staff. Mobility within the company is limited and enhancement tends to be achieved by movement to alternative but local opportunities.

The third core group is that of skilled operatives, notably in the kitchen, front office, housekeeping, and food and beverage service. These personnel are performing key functions in the hotel in a relatively functionally inflexible way, but are in high demand within the labour market and have the opportunity for considerable mobility if they wish. Thus building a stable core within a hotel at this level can be difficult. Mobility can be accommodated within a larger company while loyalty can be sought through incentive and promotion schemes at unit or company level. The Swiss hotel industry makes interesting use of this core group in that the positions in many hotels remain stable with defined operative functions attached to each. However, links to hotel schools provide a guaranteed source of stagiers, mainly from abroad, who rotate through the positions on a six-monthly cycle, providing core stability but with different personnel filling the actual posts.

Outside these core groups of staff, Guerrier and Lockwood address those staff who exist at the periphery of the organization. The first group of peripheral workers consist of full-time employees with limited security and career opportunities. They have many characteristics in common with the operative core and undertake similar functions in the hotel. The main difference relates to labour turnover as this group is frequently drawn from groups in the labour market with little long-term interest or commitment to the company or, indeed, to the industry. The group may consist of skilled 'cosmopolitans' seeking to exercise their skills as a means of supporting lifestyle choices – the Australian and New Zealand influence on tourism businesses in terms of provision of transient employees, in Dublin, London and elsewhere, exemplifies this as do students, transient foreign workers and others with no interest in the security available to core staff. This group may have greater interpersonal, aesthetic and emotional skills than those normally available within the local labour force but, because this group is essentially transient, problems may arise with regard to attaining and maintaining a consistency of service to the expected levels.

The second peripheral group consists mainly of part-time and casual staff living locally to the hotel. The part-timers may have a long-term commitment to the hotel but such loyalty is less frequent among casuals, who will, typically, be on the 'pool' of a number of hotels at the same time. The final component that Guerrier and Lockwood identify on the periphery is that of distancing or outsourcing strategies. Such approaches may involve contracting out various functions within hotels, frequently laundry requirements, maintenance and cleaning contracts, as well as the provision of pastries to the kitchen. The range may extend considerably beyond these areas and include the employment of agency or subcontracted staff for lobby shops, the leisure centre and car-park operations. Similar strategies not identified by the authors are also used in housekeeping and security. Guerrier and Lockwood do not identify core hotel activities as likely to be 'distanced' in this way. However, Baum and Hallam (1996) point to a growing practice among hotels of restaurant franchising, either to an individual or group operation. This practice is well established in North America, where some major hotel/restaurant chain alliances can be found. The advantages to the hotel of using external sources of labour are flexibility in response to cyclical demand and a reduction in the permanent payroll. It is also a means by which the sector in highly unionized locations, such as major cities, can reduce the influence of trade unions because outsourced companies are much less likely to be subject to trade union agreements (ILO 2001).

Guerrier and Lockwood's model provides a useful vehicle for the analysis of the labour environment in the tourism, hospitality and leisure sector and has applicability beyond the specific of hotels in the United Kingdom. Indeed, it is arguable that the model probably has greater relevance today in more traditionally structured work economies of developing or transition economies. In the United Kingdom and the United States, workplace flexibility is probably at its most advanced in the tourism, hospitality and leisure sector and core employees of the type described by Guerrier and Lockwood are much less common than in the past. In some European countries and elsewhere, more traditional industrial structures remain and the core and periphery model has, perhaps, greater application.

In essence, the process of increasing all forms of flexibility within the tourism, hospitality and leisure workforce is one that can only reinforce and increase the weak nature of its labour market. Flexible working practices go entirely contrary to the major features of a strong labour market. The same can be said for the process of de-skilling which is a feature of work in most industrial sectors and has certainly had some impact in tourism and hospitality.

Flexible working in tourism, hospitality and leisure are generally seen as a management tool that enables the organization to achieve more effective use of its human resources. There are, however, strong arguments that flexibility also contributes to improving the working lives of employees, by meeting their objectives for balance between work and their personal lives outside the workplace. DTI (2001) note that:

> It's not just a question of family-friendly policies. It's also about respecting and accommodating individual needs. For some that may mean caring for an elderly relative or altering working practices so that their disability may be taken into account. Often relatively minor changes can make the difference between recruiting or retaining valued employees and missing out entirely – both for employer and the potential employee.
>
> For others flexibility may mean the chance to pursue a course of learning or an interest such as golf or art – or to seize an opportunity to give something back to the local community. (p.7)

This report goes on to identify the main reasons why employees seek flexibility in their working lives. These reasons are varied and underpin the wide range of reasons why people work they way they do in organizations.

- *Childcare* – Looking after the children – or sharing care with a partner, perhaps.
- *Eldercare and other caring responsibilities* – There are almost six million carers in the UK who look after frail, sick or disabled relatives or friends.
- *Further education or training* – Earning while learning, at any age.
- *Health (including mental) or disability* – Flexible working arrangements or working from home may enable people to find or continue in paid employment.
- *Transport/distance from work* – Where people live can affect their availability for work. Making their base their home alters the focus and may turn an impossibility into an option.
- *Arts and sports* – For a lot of people it's crucial that they can support themselves financially while they're a struggling actor or dancer, a painter or sculptor, writer or musician, for example.
- *Other interests* – There are many reasons people give for wanting flexible work – such as voluntary work, starting up a business, painting, playing in a

band, taking part in amateur dramatics, home improvements, going to the gym, training for a marathon, gardening, keeping horses or other animals, travelling – the list is endless.

- *Quality of life* – Some people are willing and able to trade money for more time to improve their work–life balance.
- *Approaching retirement* – If retirement's looming, it's often better to ease into it gradually, reducing the number of hours worked before stopping completely. And if it's a partner who's retiring, an employee may want more flexible working arrangements so they can spend more time with them. (p.27)

Given employee concerns, there are a wide range of models that can be adopted in order to accommodate their requirements. DTI (2001) identify a number of these:

a) *Flexi-time*, giving employees choice about their actual working hours, usually outside certain agreed core times.

b) *Staggered hours*, which give employees different start, finish and break times.

c) *Compressed working hours*, which allow people to work their total number of agreed hours over a shorter number of working days.

d) *Annualized hours systems*, which organize working time on the basis of the number of hours to be worked over a year rather than a week.

e) *Part-time work*, which has no legal definition in many countries. UK Government statistics define it as less than 30 hours a week. Usually it simply means working less than the normal full-time hours – it can range from working only a couple of hours a week to just less than full-time working.

f) *Job sharing*, involving two people carrying out the duties of a post that would normally be done by one person. Each person is employed part-time but together they cover a full-time post and divide the pay, holidays and other benefits.

g) *Term-time working*, meaning employees can remain on a permanent contract, either on a full or part-time basis, but have unpaid leave of absence during the school holidays.

h) *Temping or casual work*, involving working for an employer for short periods, often to fill in for an absent employee or during a period of recruitment.

i) *Shift working*, which allows staff to extend the use of facilities as groups of workers or individuals work their hours on the same job one after another, often through a 24-hour period.

j) *Shift swapping*, which means employees can negotiate working times to suit their needs and re-arrange shifts amongst themselves or within teams – provided the needs of the business or service are met.

k) *Self-rostering*, giving team members more control over their work times. Parameters can be set first about the numbers of staff and the skill mix required during each working day and then staff work together to ensure that all tasks and responsibilities are covered.

Clearly, these flexible working models are not always suitable for all contexts within tourism, hospitality and leisure organizations. However, they do provide an indication of the range of options that are available within the labour market to make flexible working operate effectively from an employee as well as an employer perspective.

Case Study *Using flexible labour – agency staff in hotels*

Airport Express Hotel is located at an airport within the Greater London area. It is listed as a four-star full-service property and is part of an international hotel chain group. The main target markets for this hotel are business travellers, holiday makers and airline crew. Hotel occupancy is influenced to a great extent by airport operations. There is not a very significant peak and drop over the year. However, at Christmas, occupancy rates can drop to below 30 per cent because of the closure of airport. Overall, the average annual occupancy rate is 85 per cent. The hotel has 791 bedrooms, in terms of standard, family, executive rooms and suites. In 2004, the average room rate was £71 per room night.

Airport Express Hotel relies on employment agencies to supply hotel staff in a range of areas and for positions such as housekeeping attendants, kitchen stewarding staff and banqueting waiter/ess, and to fulfil the hotel's need for flexibility. For example, the hotel housekeeping department uses one employment agency, Room Clean Agency, as their labour supplier to provide staff, in terms of room attendants, house porters and linen-room attendants. The hotel employs 29 permanent full-time housekeeping staff. On top of these core members of staff, on average, 50 agency staff are required for housekeeping work on a daily basis.

Room Clean Agency charges the hotel either by the number of hours worked, or by the number of rooms cleaned in the case of housekeeping room attendants. The average hourly rate paid to the agency was around £6.26 an hour in April 2004. This fee is equiv-alent to the sum of agency staff's direct wages and the fee chargeable to cover agency costs. In Airport Express Hotel, the Room Clean Agency provides not only the housekeeping labour force (e.g. housekeeping staff), but also various services, such as an in-house agency coordinator, staffing support, staff payroll, induction training, on-the-job training assistance and staff transportation. Because of the hotel's location and the competition with the nearby airport for the local labour market, the hotel faces difficulties in recruiting permanent full-time employees. The partner agency is aware of this difficulty and realizes that this is where their niche market lies. Therefore, the agency provides minibus services and thus 'imports' their staff from central London to Airport Express Hotel every morning and transports them back to the city centre at the end of daily shift.

This agency charge is negotiable and the more staff a hotel requests the cheaper price it pays. However, because of high competition in the industry, the charge rates are generally similar amongst agencies and the profit margin are less than 17 per cent. There are no binding contracts signed between Airport Express Hotel and the Room Clean Agency. This enhances the hotel's buying power over their partner agency and also gives them more flexibility to choose with whom the hotel wants to work. However, the partnership between the hotel and the agency goes back over 20 years and, therefore, the working relationship between the hotel and the agency is close in terms of regular communications and various forms of mutual support. An unofficial partnership between the hotel housekeeping department and their partner employment agency is evident.

Hotels use agencies in order to gain labour flexibility, cost effectiveness, ease of termination, a good quality workforce and protection against total outsourcing. In addition, some relatively involuntary motivations for using agency services can be found, such as the pressures of a 'no-recruitment' company policy and recruitment difficulties for this type of worker in the location in question. It is noted that, in Airport Express Hotel, achieving labour flexibility and reacting to recruitment difficulties were two main motivations for the hotel to use such a significant proportion of agency staff in their housekeeping department.

Agency staff also perceive the benefits of this form of working arrangement. Many are immigrant workers from Eastern Europe and the Far East, notably Vietnam. Their objective is to earn sufficient money to be able to send their surplus home on a regular basis. Agency work permits them to work extended hours in the hotel when such work is available. They also have the flexibility of choosing when and for how long they want to work. They are, for example, able to take extended leave and vacations to visit their home country without difficulties in the secure knowledge that other agency work will be available to them on their return.

The executive housekeeper in the Airport Express Hotel noted that she would consider herself as the 'employers' of a hotel's agency staff, due to the long-term working relationship between the hotel and the Room Clean

Agency. In fact, according to new agency legislation in the UK, the employer of agency staff is the employment agency which places them to work in client's workplace. Agency staff are entitled to similar benefits as a company's permanent member of staff, such as holiday pay and sick pay.

In managing agency staff, fair treatment between agency labour and the hotel's permanent members of staff is common practice. In other words, both sets of workers (hotel and agency) receive similar training and supervision, and take the same staff meals in the same staff canteen. This fair treatment reduces staff morale problems and also helps to retain staff, both agency and permanent staff.

In general, Airport Express Hotel is satisfied with the services and products provided by their partner agency, Room Clean Agency. The hotel will continue to use agency staff as part of their labour flexibility strategies. In reality, the hotel enjoys the benefits of having agency staff working on a long-term basis without the costs of a long-term commitment to individual staff.

This case was prepared by Peichun Lai of the University of Strathclyde for this book, using original research material. Included with permission.

Case discussion questions

1. What are the benefits to a hotel of using agency staff?

2. Why might hotel staff prefer to work through an agency?

3. What are the potential problems with using agency staff in a hotel?

De-skilling and the tourism, hospitality and leisure workplace

As Wood (1997) notes, the issue of de-skilling and degradation of work is one of the most important themes in recent industrial sociological debate and represents a complex amalgam of theoretical discussion and empirical analysis of the nature of work within a diversity of industry sectors. Wood cites Braverman

(1974) as the originator of much of the discussion about de-skilling from a Marxist perspective. Braverman approaches the issue on the basis that, within a capitalist economy, the objective of the owners and managers of capital is to maximize control over the labour force as a means of ensuring increased profits. The argument which Braverman pursues is that scientific management – or Taylorism – has been key to this process of increased control because it divorces the conception from the execution of work, defining a clear distinction between the roles of management and labour, thus degrading and de-skilling the role and contribution of the latter. Braverman's argument has much in common with that of Ritzer, although the latter does not place his analysis within the theoretical construction of Marxism. According to Ritzer, control of and in the workplace is one of the central aspects of the process which leads to de-skilling in a variety of service areas. At the centre of this process is the substitution of human by non-human technology.

> Historically, organizations gained control over people gradually through increasingly effective technologies. Eventually, they began reducing people's behaviour to a series of machinelike actions. And once people were behaving like machines, they could be replaced with actual machines. The replacement of humans by machines is the ultimate stage in control over people; people can no longer cause uncertainty and unpredictability because they are no longer involved, at least directly, in the process. (Ritzer 2004, p.106)

Ritzer applies this analysis to a number of case sources in the service sector, notably but not exclusively within fast food.

> Much of the food prepared at McDonald's arrives at the restaurant preformed, precut, presliced, and 'preprepared'. All they need to do is, where necessary, cook, or often merely heat, the food and pass it on to the customer … The more that is done by nonhuman technologies before the food arrives at the restaurant, the less the workers need to do and the less room they have to exercise their own judgements and skill. (Ritzer 2004, pp.107–108)

Wood (1997) discusses theoretical constraints within the de-skilling debate but also presents considerable evidence which is fully consistent with Ritzer and supports the contention that, despite the low skills starting point, further reduction in the skills requirements in some sub-sectors of the tourism, hospitality and leisure industry is a widespread and ongoing process. Other examples can be found in the airline business where the everyday application of skills has been considerably reduced in the piloting of commercial aircraft. Automatic systems can effectively take over virtually all pilot functions. However, the presence of the skills in the flight deck crew remains essential in order to cater for the eventuality of an emergency or system failure. Robotic control of other means of transport such as trains and monorails (for example, the airport transfer train at Kuala Lumpur International Airport) is also becoming commonplace and has thus substituted as well as reduced the skills requirements in certain areas. In many respects, substitution, de-skilling and flexibility go hand in hand because the simplification of one task or a range of tasks may well place it within the skills reach of employees who also have other responsibilities and who previously would not have been able to undertake the tasks in question – pilots assuming engineering and navigational roles in aircraft is an example of the combination of de-skilling and flexibility.

There is an inherent contradiction in this discussion of de-skilling within the tourism, hospitality and leisure labour force. This will become manifestly evident in Chapter 4 where a central theme is the use of empowerment strategies to upgrade the responsibilities and demands of jobs at the front line within the tourism and hospitality industry and thus to improve a company's competitive position in terms of service delivery. Empowerment is certainly incompatible with the control dimensions of McDonaldization, and what we are seeing is an increasing divide within the tourism and hospitality industry and the creation of distinct service cultures and strategies to cater for very different markets and market philosophies. Contradictory directions appear to have evolved with respect to control on the one hand and empowerment on the other. In the 'old' type of organization activities are segmented into discrete compartments and isolated from their context on the basis of a non-systems approach. This is in contrast to McDonaldization where the process of segmentation of work acts to inhibit creativity and innovation in the workplace, something which empowerment is claimed to encourage.

Returning to the macro environment

In concluding this chapter about tourism, hospitality and leisure labour markets, it is useful to return to the macro environment within which they operate. Riley, as we have seen, links many of the key issues which face sectors of the industry – some of which we will return to in later chapters – to the weak nature of the internal labour market that operates within these sectors. The attributes of the weak labour market provide both benefits and difficulties, whether you view the industry from an employer or employee perspective. It is worth going back to a relatively early analysis of tourism, hospitality and leisure labour markets. Pizam (1982) addresses labour market attributes in the context of unskilled and semi-skilled labour in the tourism, hospitality and leisure industry from two wider environmental perspectives, which he designates societal characteristics and industry characteristics. Figure 3.1 summarizes these influences in relation to some of the main issues facing the industry at the level to which Pizam is referring.

The characteristics of society which Pizam identifies as important determinants provide an important classification of the influences on labour markets in general, not necessarily specific to tourism and hospitality. They certainly reflect the optimism of the early 1980s in some respects but have only qualified validity over a decade later. What consideration of Pizam's analysis does emphasize is the changing nature of factors which influence the labour market within tourism and hospitality. Thus any consideration of this environment cannot afford to be static but must respond to a dynamic and ever-changing combination of both macro and micro environmental factors.

Certainly the growing importance of services within all developed economies remains an important attribute and the restructuring of global economies has seen increasing dependence both on high technology such as information and financial services and on labour intensive areas of the sector, notably tourism, hospitality and leisure. Traditional industries in the manufacturing, agricultural and extractive sectors have declined in most developed countries and further concentration of these into relatively small geographical areas – or, indeed, to other parts of the world – will further reduce their significance.

Pizam identifies greater leisure time as his second social impact. In many respects, his analysis is accurate although projections that this process would continue and result in a general reduction in working time have not really been fulfilled. In the United Kingdom, for example, the last few years have actually seen an increase in average time worked by those in employment, particularly in situations where an organizational culture exists that makes lifestyle prioritization in preference to work difficult. What remains true is that, whatever the availability of theoretical leisure time, people are increasingly investing a higher proportion of such time on activities within tourism and hospitality.

| Figure 3.1 | Tourism's work environment and its determinants |

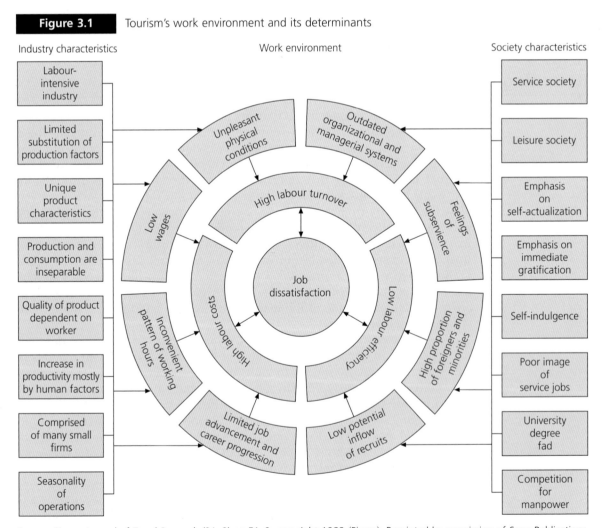

Source: Pizam, Journal of Travel Research (21, 2) pp.51–9, copyright 1982 (Pizam). Reprinted by permission of Sage Publications.

Demographic factors in developed countries, notably an increasingly healthy and active older population, may further reinforce this trend. However, in some countries such as the United Kingdom, pressure on the labour market and a crisis over pensions for those planning to retire means that early retirement may be on hold, people may be required to work longer rather than shorter years and these factors may well have an impact on access to and use of leisure time.

Pizam identifies greater emphasis on self-actualization as an important social trend and implies the need of the tourism and hospitality industries to cater for such employee needs. A sustainable approach to human resource management implies support for an employment model which offers greater scope and responsibility to employees. In the next chapter, we address the concept of empowerment among front-line staff, and this also is consistent with offering a motivational environment which is in tune with the pinnacle of Maslow's hierarchy (as elaborated in Chapter 10). However, there are counter-trends in tourism, hospitality and leisure and within the service sector in general, notably the impact of labour-saving technology, standardized service delivery and de-skilling (a theme that we have already touched upon in this chapter), encapsulated in the work environment portrayed so effectively by Ritzer in his book, *The McDonaldization of Society* (2004). In his thesis, Ritzer analyses the impact of the processes of efficiency, calculability, predictability and control on the working environment within a wide range of service employments and his conclusions do not paint an optimistic scenario for the achievement of self-actualization within much tourism and hospitality work.

Pizam defines the demand for immediate gratification as an emphasis on immediate material benefit which impacts to the detriment of a working environment such as that in the tourism and hospitality industry. In particular, the dead-end nature of many semi-skilled and unskilled positions in the industry, together with a lack of evident pathways for progression in terms of monetary reward and responsibility, combine to alienate many young people from working in the sector. Again, recognition of the notion of sustainability in the human resource domain may lead employers to create working environments where progression paths are more clearly defined and the prospect of enhanced rewards enunciated. However, an understanding of Riley's concept of the weak internal labour market suggests that the very characteristics which create a low-paid, low-skills environment also provide considerable opportunity for rapid, meritocratic promotion within the industry.

Self-indulgence as a social phenomenon has many links to the demand for immediate gratification. Pizam uses the social trend by way of contrast with the conditions faced by the lowest-skilled and poorest-paid members of the tourism, hospitality and leisure workforce. In many respects, this is not a new social attribute. In Chapter 2, we addressed the notion of social distance between tourists and those who serve them and, on the whole, it is a distance that has decreased within developed economies as tourism has moved to become more democratic and mass participatory in character. Many tourism, hospitality and leisure employees, even among the lower-skilled and poorer-paid, have the expectation of a degree of role reversal as they are also able to indulge in various forms of vacation and leisure activities. Such expectations do not exist among employees in the developing world, where the gap between international visitors and those that provide for them has, if anything, greatly increased following the economic instability in Eastern Europe born of political changes in the early 1990s.

The image problem of some service jobs, especially those in the low-skills category, is a problem that hospitality and tourism share with like sectors. Pizam approaches this issue at a macro level from the point of view of equating servitude and service, thus linking work in the service sector to a perceived status of inferiority, especially in parts of the developing world with a colonial legacy. The new and fast-evolving tourism, hospitality and leisure environment in parts of Eastern Europe also faces this problem. Again, in the context of the preceding discussion about self-indulgence, moves towards the democratization of many societies and of the customer–worker relationship can contribute to reducing this image problem.

Pizam also notes that growing participation rates in higher education, or what he describes as the 'university degree fad', creates an educated workforce who are reluctant to seek employment in the unskilled and semi-skilled employment areas of tourism and hospitality. Pizam could have argued further that, taking their lead from practice in North America where upwards of 60 per cent of all graduates have worked for McDonald's at some point in their high-school or college careers, in many European countries these graduates are basing their reluctance to commit to a career in tourism, hospitality and leisure on exposure to the industry through part-time and seasonal work. Such work may be in the fast-food sector, but also in bars, restaurants, hotels, as timeshare salespersons or tour operator representatives in Mediterranean or Alpine resort locations. Furthermore, exposure to work at the semi-skilled or unskilled level influences attitudes to careers in management or specialist areas within the industry.

Pizam's final environmental influence returns us to our earlier discussion of macro labour-market determinants because he notes that, in many countries, the tourism and hospitality industry is facing an increasingly competitive market environment for quality labour. As he rightly notes, 'those industries and firms that have the ability to reward employees with high wages and pleasant working environments constantly win this competition and attract the best employees' (Pizam 1982, p.7). As we have argued at some length earlier, the tourism, hospitality and leisure industry has such diverse sub-sectors that parts of it will be net beneficiaries of such competition but, by and large, the mass of semi-skilled and unskilled positions on offer are not attractive by Pizam's criteria.

The industry-specific side of Pizam's model deals with a range of issues which form themes in subsequent chapters of this book. Labour intensity; limitations on substitution; the nature of the tourism, hospitality and leisure product; the inseparability of production and consumption; and, implicitly, the issue of professionalism are all addressed in Chapter 4 and its focus on the service quality–human resource management link. The issue of working conditions is at the centre of Chapter 5 while training concerns are central to Chapter 8.

Case Study *The Headland House Hotel, Cornwall, England*

The Headland House Hotel is an independently owned 20-bedroom hotel located close to a small coastal village on the Lizard Peninsula in Cornwall. The hotel has a first-class restaurant that has 60 covers and is open all year round. The restaurant specializes in locally caught seafood with other food supplies being sourced from local growers and suppliers, and it enjoys a good reputation with both tourists and local residents. The restaurant is jointly managed by the chef and a restaurant manager. Other than a key assistant manager in each area the restaurant is staffed by three specialist full-timers in the kitchen and restaurant alike, with the addition of ten regular part-timers who are multi-skilled in that they are able to work in either of the two areas.

Due to its location the restaurant has seasonal variances in demand; this is not only due to the traditional tourist season but also with all year round business on a day-to-day basis from the local business community and residents. The restaurant closes on Mondays and Tuesdays during the low season from mid-October to mid-April but still suffers from fluctuating demand on other weekdays during this period. The impact of this fluctuation in business means that labour costs which are predominantly fixed are regarded as too high at 32 per cent of sales.

To cope with this variable demand it was agreed with part-time workers to introduce a scheme for standby working arrangements with them. This scheme worked on the basis of three levels:

1. guaranteed working hours to represent the core of their contracted hours at agreed set times at a standard hourly rate.

The remaining hours, including overtime, were split between:

2. being on-call for one day each week at a rate of 25 per cent of their normal pay but receiving their normal hourly rate if called into work; and

3. being available to work at certain times but, being subject to 24 hours' advance notice as to their requirements for this, it was agreed to pay a 25 per cent bonus rate per hour.

The overall impact of this arrangement once teething problems had been sorted out was a significant reduction in labour costs of more that 15 per cent; they now represented 29 per cent of sales over a similar period. This showing more than a 4 per cent increase in profitability.

The scheme also proved popular with staff at the restaurant in that those living locally were loyal employees, there was less sickness and staff turnover for part-time employees showed a significant reduction.

Case prepared by the Peter Odgers of Brighton University for Fáilte Ireland. Reproduced with permission.

Case discussion questions

1. Why is functional flexibility more commonly associated with small businesses than larger operations?

2. In what ways do numerical flexibility strategies support lifestyle needs of staff?

3. How does the business benefit from introducing flexible work patterns?

Review and discussion questions

1. In relation to a destination with which you are familiar, identify some of the major factors which influence the structure and characteristics of the local labour market.

2. To what extent are Riley's strong and weak internal labour-market features applicable to different sub-sectors of the tourism and hospitality industry?

3. Does the extent to which the tourism and hospitality industry exhibits weak internal labour-market characteristics vary between different countries of Europe?

4. How useful and realistic is it to consider a global labour market for the tourism, hospitality and leisure industry?

5. Apply Guerrier and Lockwood's core and periphery model to a sub-sector of tourism and hospitality industry other than hotels. How useful is it in understanding the structure of human resources in that sector?

6. Identify examples of technology substitution, de-skilling and flexibility in the tourism and hospitality workplace. What do they contribute to an understanding of Riley's labour-market model?

7. Pizam identified the societal and industry characteristics which impacted upon the tourism and hospitality labour environment as long ago as 1982. How relevant are they to today's tourism, hospitality and leisure industry in both developed and developing countries?

Tourism, hospitality and leisure:
a service focus and the role of people

Chapter objectives

In this chapter, we shall consider the importance of delivering good service to customers and the nature of service quality as a business strategy within the international tourism, hospitality and leisure industry and demonstrate the central role that human resource management plays in attaining this quality. Recognition of this link has been implicit in much of the discussion to this point.

The specific aims of this chapter are

- to demonstrate the role of people in the delivery of quality service in tourism, hospitality and leisure;

- to explore the nature of service delivery in tourism, hospitality and leisure;

- to explore the pressures faced by front-line staff in the delivery of service;

- to consider the contribution of empowerment and organizational citizenship to the delivery of good service by front-line staff.

Service quality and the tourism, hospitality and leisure environment

As a starting point, it is useful to raise the question as to why the delivery of good service by contact personnel is important. In contemporary society in most cultures, the importance of good service is taken, in part, as read and the opposite, the delivery of poor service by front-line staff, is widely condemned. These assumptions are based on notions of consumerism within which the customer has choice and discretion in the purchases that they make. Clearly, this is by no means always the case, particularly in situations where demand greatly exceeds supply as was frequently the case in pre-1989 Eastern Europe. To some extent, some of today's low-cost airlines perpetuate this form of relationship when they argue that customers come to them for price only and other considerations are only of marginal importance in the delivery of the service. Some such carriers have totally rejected the service 'values' of traditional carriers, stated bluntly by Ryanair CEO, Michael O'Leary:

> We don't go in for all the old bullshit that British Airways and other airlines have gone on with for years ... What we're trying to do is to wean people off this notion that air travel is some first class, intercontinental, Titanic-like experience – it isn't, this is a bus service. (Calder 2002, p.218).

At the same time, low-cost airlines have brought air travel to markets and destinations which previously did not enjoy access to this form of transport.

This said, however, Bateson and Hoffman (1999), among others, identify a number of reasons why organizations in tourism, hospitality and leisure can benefit from the delivery of good service. The first of these is based on social and cultural considerations in that good service portrays a good image of a people, a country and/or an organization. This is particularly true when this represents the natural courtesy of a people and is used effectively in the marketing of destinations such as Thailand. A further reason can be described as economic in that good service by staff of an organization or at a destination level can enhance the guest's or user's sense of well-being and may induce higher spend. Restaurant staff who are particularly attentive and warm in their service are more likely to facilitate the purchase of an additional bottle of expensive wine than is likely to be the case when the service is cool, detached and perfunctory. In addition, good service may well increase chances of repeat business and, through word of mouth, may support the generation of new business. There are also managerial benefits when companies focus on the delivery of good service. Satisfied customers are generally easier to manage than those who are unhappy with their experience and, as a result, businesses and their staff face fewer difficulties at an operational level. This is true of the front-line staff members who have to handle guests in real time on aircraft and in fitness clubs as well in terms of back-of-house personnel who are likely to handle fewer complaints and other follow-up problems. Finally, contemporary consumers expect good service as the norm when participating in tourism, hospitality and leisure and have been 'educated' to expect this from their experiences at home and while travelling internationally.

The notion of quality, particularly in relation to service, has traditionally been associated with luxury and personalization. Thus, consumers were entitled to good service as part of a high-cost, high-value transaction but purchases from a street vendor, bottom-end bed-and-breakfast or hawker stall were perceived to carry no guarantees in terms of courtesy, interest in the customer or recognition of customer needs. This argument is not so widely accepted today and many companies, offering a low-cost proposition to the market, pride themselves on the quality and sensitivity of their front-line service. Service quality, therefore, is not a concept that is incompatible with low cost and value, notwithstanding claims by some low-cost airlines that price is the only real driver of choice. It also means that all consumers, irrespective of social, economic, religious or cultural status, are entitled to expect good service.

This is an important change which has clear links to our earlier analysis of the historical context of work within the tourism and hospitality industry. The era of mass participation in travel and tourism, the consumption of hospitality products and the democratization at the centre of change within the guest–server relationship have created a level of expectation concerning the overall experience provided by the industry that transcends the luxury–budget divide. Service quality, it is now recognized, is not some absolute standard, immutable and fixed for all time and part of the defining differentiation between what customers can expect from, on the one hand, the Savoy Hotel in London or the Shangri-la in Penang, Malaysia, or, on the other, the Prom View Guesthouse in Blackpool or hawker stalls along the seafront, also in Penang. Rather, it is a concept which rides on the back of expectations that the customer brings to the particular business, whether it is five star or unclassified. Thus, the customer has clear expectations of service and its quality hallmarks, whether he or she is travelling first class or economy, eating in the Cafe Royal or a fish and chip shop, attending a gala performance at Covent Garden or the pier head bingo evening. While this notion of relative quality in service has been increasingly recognized by successful companies in tourism and hospitality, it is by no means universally applied. There are award-winning airlines from both Europe and the Far East where the standard of service for economy passengers is not noted for its quality. The accolades, however, come from their first- and business-class products. Other airlines, by contrast, have laid great stress on meeting the needs of all their customers and creating appropriate levels of service quality wherever on the aircraft their passengers are located.

Service quality is frequently presented as primarily a marketing-orientated concept, designed to assist companies to win and keep customers. This approach leads to consideration of the concept of relationship marketing. Relationship marketing is, broadly, the ability of companies to build up genuine loyalty in their customer base which protects the level of repeat business that is so important to all tourism, hospitality and leisure operations. The quality of service, and especially the personalized, flexible and individualized response which frequently makes all the difference to the customer and determines whether he or she will return, are essential marketing tools within this model. Harker (1999) considers 26 definitions of relationship marketing and arrives at a composite description of the process on the basis that:

> An organisation engaged in proactively creating, developing and maintaining committed, interactive and profitable exchanges with selected customers [partners] overtime is engaged in relationship marketing. (p.16)

In 1981 Levitt described the essential nature of the relationship to be found in the service encounter in somewhat more prosaic terms.

> The relationship between a seller and a buyer seldom ends when the sale is made. The sale merely consummates the courtship. Then the marriage begins. How good the marriage is depends on how well the marriage is managed by the seller. That determines whether there will be continued or expanded business or troubles and divorce, and whether costs or profits increase.
> ... It is not just that once you get a customer you want to keep him. It is more a matter of what the buyer wants. He wants a vendor who will keep his

promises, who'll keep supplying and stand behind what he promised. The age of the blind date or the one-night stand is gone. Marriage is both more convenient and more necessary. In these conditions success in marketing, like success in marriage, is transformed into the inescapability of a relationship. (Levitt, in Lewis and Chambers 1989, pp.65–6)

Relationship marketing, while addressing a wide range of stakeholder relationships, focuses in particular on the customer and, therefore, has major implications for the role of front-line staff in service organizations. Therefore, it has implications for the manner in which a tourism, hospitality and leisure company relates to its overall business environment because maintaining stability and good relations with all critical groups in that environment (for a hotel, these groups may include suppliers of food and other products, travel agents who influence customer choice, the existing and potential labour market as well as those who influence it such as employment agencies, and the staff of the hotel as an internal market) becomes a matter for active concern for all staff and not just passive acquiescence. Of course, if all parties are themselves tuned into relationship marketing, the matrix of relationships becomes highly mutually supportive and enhances the business performance of all concerned. In terms of front-line staff, however, effective implementation of relationship marketing practices provides an additional challenge and source of pressure in their working lives.

Characteristics of service

The delivery of service within tourism, hospitality and leisure is frequently located firmly within marketing. Service enters the discussion through a consideration of the characteristics of tourism which set the industry and its products apart from other industries and products. Cooper *et al.* (2005) identify three characteristics which separate tourism as a service from manufactured goods and present these distinctions in what is called a 'goods and services continuum', as shown in Figure 4.1.

This continuum applied within the tourism context in turn owes much to the work of Albrecht and Zemke (1985), although focusing on just three of the concepts which the American authors employ. Mahesh (1988, p.10) takes Albrecht and Zemke's classification of the differences and develops them further. He highlights the difference between services and products as follows. The first seven points are derived from Albrecht and Zemke, the final two being his own additions.

Figure 4.1	SERVICE	PRODUCT
Services and goods continuum	Intangibility	More tangible
	Perishability	Often storable
	Inseparability	Standardizable

Source: Cooper *et al.* (2005) *Toursim: Principles and Practice*, 3rd ed., p.574 with permission from FT Prentice Hall

- Sale, production and consumption of a service take place almost simultaneously, while there is usually a long lead time between production and sale of a product – in other words the concept of inseparability as used in the continuum. Also known as 'heterogeneity', 'inseparability' means that it is difficult to distinguish between the production of the tourism service and its consumption, especially when the customer is personally part of that production process. This has important implications for the management of quality in the tourism and hospitality industries, in that the level of checks and inspection characteristic of the manufacturing sector cannot be applied.

- A service cannot be centrally provided, inspected, stockpiled or warehoused – it is usually delivered where the customer is by people who are beyond the immediate influence of the management. This feature includes the notion of perishability, by which a hotel room, vacant exercise machines, an empty car on a theme park ride or an aircraft seat unsold at time of departure represents a loss which cannot be recouped. Yield management systems are used by airlines, hotels and other service providers to ensure optimum use of facilities and these are usually focused on pricing and marketing strategies. However, there is also a strong human resource dimension to the process; for example, in some hotels front-office staff may take responsibility for agreeing tariffs with late check-in guests and so must have the skills and authority to do so.

- A service cannot be demonstrated, nor can a sample be sent for customer approval in advance of purchase. This notion of intangibility also has strong marketing implications and attempts are made to overcome the problems that it causes at a marketing level through interactive use of websites and other technology as well as some element of sampling – for example, offering potential customers a free weekend in a timeshare complex. However, such substitution does not overcome the inherent problems caused by the individual nature of the tourism, hospitality and leisure experience and its dependence on the human element for its delivery.

- Following on from the above, a customer receiving the tourism, hospitality and leisure service generally owns nothing tangible once the service has been delivered – its value is frequently internal to the customer.

- The tourism, hospitality and leisure experience is frequently one that cannot be shared, passed around or given away to someone else once it has been delivered. The experience is, in some respects, unique, even among members of a group who are ostensibly sharing the same itinerary or facilities. This is a result of their differing expectations, previous experiences, motivations in taking part in the experience and a variety of other concerns which may be affecting them at that time. This phenomenological argument need not be taken to extremes and from a marketing point of view it would be difficult to do so, but from the human resource management perspective, recognizing and responding to this individuality among customers is a very important skill. 'Have a nice day' may be an apt and sincerely meant farewell, appropriate to a group embarking on a day's sightseeing, but would cause offence to customers setting off for a funeral!

- Delivery of a tourism, hospitality and leisure service usually requires some degree of human contact – the receiver and the deliverer frequently come together in a relatively personal way. Although technological substitution for some aspects of service delivery has become important in some sectors of the industry (for example, automatic check-in and check-out at airports and in hotels), there is a probably a limit as to how far this process can go and consumer demand may be for increased personal service rather than its reduction.

- Quality control over a tourism, hospitality and leisure service requires the monitoring of processes and the attitudes of all staff. This, inevitably, presents certain problems in the industry, largely because of the heterogeneous nature of the delivery of these services.
- Unlike a bad product, bad service cannot be replaced – at best, it is possible to be sensitive to customer dissatisfaction and recover the situation with such good service that the customer may both forgive and forget the bad service received earlier.
- It is both difficult and undesirable to attempt to standardize service – the more spontaneous and custom-built a service, the greater its value in the customer's eyes. This is probably the most contentious dimension within the classification in that there are many examples from the tourism and hospitality industry where companies have attempted to standardize service delivery, for example in fast food, budget hotels and theme parks. This is an issue discussed at some length by Ritzer (2004) and will be developed in more detail later in this chapter.

Human resource implications of a service quality focus

Mahesh (1988) derives five major implications from these differences which impact upon the management of businesses in the tourism and hospitality industries, all of which are directly related to human resource concerns. In this chapter, we will use Mahesh's five implications in order to provide a structure to the discussion of the role of human resources in achieving quality service within the tourism and hospitality industries. The five are summarized by Mahesh as follows:

First, the customer's perception of service quality is more directly linked to the morale, motivation, knowledge, skills, and authority of front-line staff that are in direct contact with customers, than in the case of a product selling organization. Secondly, rather than being responsible for their staff, management should become responsive to staff. This is easier said than done for most line managers tend to view their jobs as control centred rather than freedom centred. The supervisors and managers of front-line staff should have the managerial skills to motivate their staff to be effective. Thirdly, traditional tools of quantification of output and work measurement have to be replaced by the subjective tool of customer satisfaction. Fourthly, as a service cannot be stockpiled and customers are in direct touch with staff, the power of the union to pressurize management increases manifold. Fifthly, bureaucratic organization structures and mega-organizations that suffer from what Tofler calls 'gigantiasis' a disease whose major symptoms are the hardening of decisional arteries and their ultimate breakdown, are ill-suited to excellence in service. The structure has to be adaptive, decentralized, and downsized to respond speedily to changing customer needs. (Mahesh 1988, pp.10–11)

Let us examine Mahesh's analysis in a little more detail, taking the five implications that he identifies point by point.

Front-line staff

Mahesh first of all focuses on the critical role of front-line staff in the service encounter and their 'packaging' in terms of such diverse attributes as morale, motivation, knowledge, skills and authority. This analysis is fairly widely accepted within many service organizations but, perhaps, owes its most effective conceptualization to Jan Carlzon, past president of Scandinavian Airline Systems (SAS). Carlzon introduced the concept of the 'moment of truth' into the service vocabulary (Carlzon 1987). Carlzon described a 'moment of truth' as every point of contact between the customer and front-line staff of the company, thus applying it to every contact, however seemingly trivial, that a customer has with a staff member of the company in question. All major tourism, hospitality and leisure organizations, as a result, have thousands of 'moments of truth' each day, encounters between the organization through its front-line personnel and the customer base. 'Moments of truth', although they may individually be small in scale (hotel check-in, drinks service in an aircraft, the purchase of duty-frees in an airport, assistance with a theme-park ride), are make-or-break occasions, when the company has the opportunity to disappoint the customer by failing to meet his or her expectations, to get it right by matching those expectations, or to excel by exceeding those expectations. From an organizational and management perspective, while it is heartening to exceed expectations, the key objective must be to consistently meet customer expectations and to minimize occasions when customers are disappointed.

Carlzon conceived of 'moments of truth' at a time when personal contact predominated in service encounters and he was very much thinking in terms of uniformed members of the SAS staff physically encountering customers throughout their service experience or, at least, engaging with them over the telephone. In today's tourism, hospitality and leisure sector, a significant element of a customer's contact with service-providing organizations is electronic, most notably through PCs, mobile phones and other devices in order to make direct bookings on-line, e-mail enquiries and pass on or receive information through automated telephone systems. 'Moments of truth' as a concept does have relevance to such electronic engagements. As consumers, we are now highly speed-demanding in that, unless a telephone reply system or a website can give an immediate response to an enquiry, we will move on to seek a similar product or service from an alternative supplier. Thus, if I have choice in the airline with which I can fly from, for example, Mumbai to Chennai and all service providers offer online booking, if Airline A does not provide me with the details I require (price, schedule, availability) within a matter of seconds, I am likely to move onto Airline B to seek that information and, if satisfied with the proposition, to purchase. Likewise, if a consumer in the United States is looking for bed-and-breakfast accommodation in Connamara in the west of Ireland and e-mails an enquiry regarding availability, it is unlikely that he or she will wait more than a day or so for a response before trying alternative bed-and-breakfasts. He or she may start off by sending a number of similar enquiries and may ultimately select from those that provide a response within what he or she sees as an acceptable time frame. In both these examples, 'moment of truth' does not relate to the face-to-face encounter that Carlzon was thinking of but, rather, to the quality, speed and interactivity of electronic communications media, notably e-mail and the organization's website.

The tourism, hospitality and leisure industry also presents particular challenges in managing 'moments of truth' because of the fragmentation of the experience for many customers. Within a hotel, for example, guests come into contact with a wide range of staff attached to different organizational units within the establishment (front office, housekeeping, restaurant, business centre, etc.) even during a relatively brief stay. Plotting the 'moments of truth' for a typical guest stay in a hotel can be highly illuminating in this respect.

Even more complex is the range of 'moments of truth' encountered by the customer of a typical package holiday company. From the purchaser's perspective, he or she is buying from one company and yet the reality is that a wide range of intermediaries are likely to contribute to the total experience. These may include businesses over which the tour operator has some level of control and can monitor service standards but will also include exposure to organizations or individuals where no such control exists, although the 'moments of truth' will be judged by the customer with the umbrella company in mind. These intermediaries may include:

- the retail travel agent – both 'high street' and virtual such as Expedia or Lastminute.com;
- insurance companies;
- ground transport to the airport;
- airport handling agents;
- airport services (shops, food and beverage outlets);
- the airline;
- immigration and customs services;
- local ground transportation;
- the hotel or apartment;
- tour services at the destination;
- companies and individuals selling a diversity of goods and services (retail, food and beverage, entertainment, financial establishments, timeshare vendors); and
- service providers on return (e.g. photo processing).

Many of these companies and organizations are, of course, beyond the control of the tour operator and most customers would not directly attribute problems with them to the company through which they booked. However, good or bad experiences or 'moments of truth' with the local police, beach vendors and taxi companies will colour the visitor's perceptions of the total experience in a way that does not really apply with respect to the purchase of other goods and services. Some organizations, not directly in the tourism, hospitality and leisure business, recognise their role with respect to visitors' 'moments of truth'. Immigration officials at Singapore's border points, notably Changi Airport, greet visitors with a smile, a display or orchids on the desk and the offer of a sweet while documentation is checked. Tour operators, of course, may be legally responsible under consumer protection legislation in many countries for the satisfactory delivery of many of the components within the package tour experience, but such liability cannot include the full range of bodies listed above. One response from the tourism and hospitality industry is to reduce the risk of inconsistent or unmanaged 'moments of truth' within the holiday experience by maintaining as close regulation and control over as many of the intermediaries as is possible. This may be achieved by vertical integration of as many of the providers within the tourism system as possible.

Such integration may result in tour operators acquiring their own retail travel agents and airline as well as hotels and ground tour operators at the destination. There are other benefits besides greater control and consistency in the delivery of service but the potential to manage and control as many 'moments of truth' within the guest experience as possible is one of the main attractions of vertical integration. This process may involve outright ownership of the various components or, alternatively, the establishment of a network of partners, all of which operate to agreed standards and systems and may even adopt the sponsoring company's branding. A good example of a company that has achieved effective integration of all the main elements of the holiday experience is the German multinational, TUI.

At an operational level, organizations in tourism, hospitality and leisure have sought to offer a very wide range of services to guests 'under the one roof', partly in order to isolate the guest from many uncontrolled variables, or 'moments of truth', at the holiday destination. The British holiday camp of the 1950s perhaps pioneered this approach, which was developed further by organizations such as Club Méditerranée and is now offered by different types of operators, be they Centerparcs, all-inclusive resorts or cruise liners. The guest will typically only come into contact with employees selected and trained by the sponsoring company in relation to all the activities that the guest may wish to undertake, and so the guest will be insulated from the uncertainty of contact with the diverse range of local providers which typically contributes to the make-up of the vacation experience.

This level of control and standardization of service is not feasible with respect to many tourism, hospitality and leisure destinations, nor, indeed, would it be seen as desirable by many visitors themselves. The local encounter is a central attraction within the vacation experience, whether it is in an Irish bar in Connemara, a nightclub in Paris or as part of a farm holiday in Hungary. In a very real sense, then, the range of 'moments of truth' which the visitor will encounter can involve the total population of the destination locality and not just those specifically employed to meet guest needs. The welcome and assistance that the visitor receives from the community as a whole becomes an important factor in ensuring an extended or return visit to the locality or in helping to decide that 'once is enough'. In many communities, there is certain ambivalence to visitors, who may create congestion on roads and in facilities, behave in ways that are not compatible with local practice or exhibit levels of conspicuous affluence unattainable within the host location. A major challenge for the tourism industry in both the public and private sector is to support the education of the local community about the sector and its consumers, so as to ensure a welcome or at least to avoid outright hostility. At the same time, tour operators have the responsibility to ensure that their visitors are sensitive to local customs and culture and behave accordingly. Tourism awareness programmes at community and national levels have become quite widespread in locations as far apart as Hong Kong, Hawaii and South Africa as well as in some European destinations. Likewise, responsible tour operators do provide information and briefings for visitors on the locations they are visiting as well as behaviour that is and is not acceptable. These strategies will all contribute to ensuring that the uncontrolled variables within the 'moments of truth' cycle are positive in their outcomes and do not negatively affect the overall perception that the visitor derives from his or her visit.

Creating a true service culture at company or national level implies that the term 'front-line' must be used in its widest possible sense. For a community or nation to continue to attract visitors, especially those returning after the initial visit, ensuring positive 'moments of truth' at each commercial service and less formal encounter becomes imperative. The whole population are part of the relationship-marketing effort. In societies where traditions in work as well as in a wider social context have made people suspicious of the stranger and indifferent or hostile in their attitude to service, creating this environment is a major challenge. The transition economies of Eastern Europe historically faced this challenge as probably their main human resource issue. As Airey (1994) pointed out, 'In Central and Eastern Europe it is only recently that the satisfaction of the customer has become a key issue' (p.8). In practical terms, companies developing tourism, hospitality and leisure enterprises in Eastern Europe responded to the problem of a lack of a service culture by circumventing the issue. When the Sofitel in Bucharest, Romania, first opened in the 1990s, it employed no front-line staff with hotel experience, preferring to rely on enthusiastic but untrained young people to meet their needs. Likewise in Russia, within the same hotel group, it was seen that a hotel preferred to train via its own means, by hiring unprepared candidates who, at least, have no bad habits.

Vikhanski and Puffer (1993) report the same approach with respect to McDonald's in Moscow, where front-line staff was selected on the basis of having no prior work experience:

> The idea was that it would be easier to instil McDonald's work habits and standards in people who knew no other way to work than to disabuse people of unacceptable work habits they had acquired in previous jobs. (p.104)

Other reported strategies include resort hotels in the Crimea recruiting front-line staff from former care employees, nurses, social workers and the like because these are deemed to be the only group to whom the notion of customer care has any realistic meaning.

The delivery of quality service in tourism, hospitality and leisure not only places significant responsibilities on the staff at the front line who deliver such service but also places considerable onus and responsibility on staff members who, as we shall see in the next chapter, are frequently the lowest-paid and least-valued members of the organization's workforce. Bateson and Hoffman (1999) discuss the work of these key members of staff in terms of their boundary-spanning roles, responsibilities that provide the critical link between the organization and the environment in which it operates including, crucially, its customers. In a marketing context, they note that 'strategically, contact personnel can be the source of product differentiation' (p.59). The primary purpose of boundary-spanning personnel is for information transfer and representation on behalf of the organization. In this sense, contact or boundary-spanning staff collect information from the environment, particularly customers, and feed it back to the organization. This is a very significant role provided that the organization, in turn, is willing and able to listen to the information it receives through such channels. At the same time, boundary-spanning personnel communicate with the environment on behalf of the organization, often conveying bad news on behalf of their employers. For example, first information about a flight delay is often communicated to a passenger by front-line staff at check-in. Boundary-spanning roles in tourism, hospitality and leisure take on particular significance because of the operating features of the sector, particularly because of the high number of customer contact zones that exist within the sector and the consequently intense level of contact with consumers that takes place. In addition, the dispersed nature of the business sector means that there are high levels of unsupervised work undertaken by boundary-spanning personnel, involving decision-making and action with respect to information flows in both direction between the organization and its environment.

Therefore, the role that personnel play in representing the organization in this way does not come without its costs and Bateson and Hoffman elaborate further with respect to the role stress that is inherent in undertaking work at the organization's boundaries. They note, in particular, that boundary-spanning roles are often characterized by low status combined with high stress and the potential for conflict. Rafaeli (1989; in Bateson and Hoffman 1999, p.64) discusses four main sources of stress, based on his work in the retail sector. These are:

- The inability of boundary-spanning personnel to create a social network with fellow employees due to customer demands that the staff be attentive solely to the needs of the customer. Unlike those work environments where customer contact does not feature, in these environments there is little opportunity for workers to engage, socially or otherwise, with colleagues during working hours when on duty at check-in in an airport, as a museum guide or at hotel reception. Demanding customers, themselves often stressed because they are out of their normal life context, require levels of attention which make communication with colleagues, beyond the banal and brief, impossible.

- In many service encounters, the encounter between service provider and customer is brief and therefore does not permit a normal social interaction. Many service encounters are time-circumscribed by the organization for which the front-line operative works. For example, customer service staff in reservations or call centres may be required to handle a specified number of queries or reservations within a set period of time and thus cannot engage with clients beyond a nationally set time period. Alternatively, the time allocated to service encounters may by constrained by customer expectations or impatience: most of us want to move through many service engagements at airport check-in, in a shop or in a self-service cafe as rapidly as possible, particularly at critical times such as lunch breaks or when travelling during rush hour. Obviously, there are interactions which are less time constrained, when the purchase in a travel agency is for a significant sum of money or where we are uncertain of the options available to us, but pressure still exists for boundary-spanning staff in that they may need to be conscience of the needs of other customers waiting for service. Thus, the service context does not permit any depth of social or personal engagement between front-line personnel and their customers and the former are expected to progress through the preliminary social rituals of engagement many times within the one shift without actually developing the relationship further. This work-based version of 'speed dating' can be very stressful for those working at the front line.

- The challenge of role conflict and role ambiguity relates to situations where boundary-spanning staff members are required to represent their company in situations where their true sympathy may lie with the customer. An episode of the British television documentary *Airline* (ITV 2005) showed the case of a passenger wishing to travel in order to attend her father's funeral who arrived at the airport after the designated closing time for check-in. The airline employee at check-in empathized with the plight of the passenger (as, in all probability, did most viewers) but, despite this, could and did not alter company policy with respect to latest check-in times. Particularly in developed countries, we have already noted that there is significant role crossover between those who serve in tourism, hospitality and leisure and those who are served so that the social distance between them, in terms of their experiences of tourism, hospitality and leisure, is narrow. Thus, role ambiguity can also be born from the fact that 'we've all been on the other side of the fence' at various times and can certainly see the other person's viewpoint. Such situations place servers in positions of considerable stress.

- Front-line stress is also the result of the fight that can occur in service encounters for control of the situation. Boundary-spanning staff may find themselves in a competitive situation with clients or travellers, with both seeking control of the service situation. Control of information can provide a good example of stress induced by such competition. A travel agent who is checking travel options for guests using a company intranet may angle the computer monitor so as to have exclusive sight of the information presented. That way, she can control the service situation and provide only that information that she wishes. When the guest seeks to re-angle the monitor or moves round the desk to get a personal view of the options available, many travel agents react very negatively to such loss of control. McGrath (2005) reports a trend within the travel sector that will further exacerbate this tension. She notes that, increasingly, holiday-makers believe that they know more about their planned destination than their travel agent. Thus, a traditionally advantageous position held by travel agents as controller of information is in danger of being undermined, creating self-doubt and role stress. Likewise, tour or museum guides can react very negatively to clients who demonstrate a level of knowledge about a specialist subject that may exceed that of the guide, because this represents a reduction in the guide's control of the encounter.

Role stress in boundary-spanning roles in tourism, hospitality and leisure is particularly prevalent because of the high level of customer contact that is evident within the sector. Indeed, it is part of customer's expectations when purchasing in the sector that such contact does take place, often extending to staff members whose normal function is not at the front line. Thus cruise ship passengers feel entitled to the privilege of dining with the ship's captain and frequent guests in luxury hotels are invited to a general manager's cocktail party as a special benefit. Travellers, in particular, represent customers out of their normal routine and, as a result, may also experience high levels of stress when they encounter air travel or arrive in unfamiliar hotel environments. A further cause of role stress in tourism, hospitality and leisure is caused by the high level of delegation and quasi-empowerment that is common throughout the sector. Giving people responsibility without necessarily recognizing this through status or reward can also place significant and, perhaps, unwanted stress on boundary-spanning staff members (Lashley 1997). Empowerment or delegation initiatives within service companies rarely provide opt-in or opt-out clauses for personnel. They are generally imposed without exception across companies and departments.

Alongside Rafaeli's work to identify stress in boundary spanning roles, Bateson and Hoffman (1999) extend this discussion to address the potential for conflict faced by staff in such positions in tourism, hospitality and leisure organizations. In doing so, they draw on the work of Shamir (1980), who identified a number of sources of conflict in boundary-spanning roles, some of which are closely allied to the causes of stress in these roles. These sources include:

- Inequality dilemmas, the result of the efforts of front-line staff to put the customer first leading them to feel belittled or demeaned.
- Balancing feelings against behaviour whereby contact personnel are often required to hide their true feelings and present a 'front' or 'face' to the customer. This can result in role conflict as the server does not identify with the role they are expected to act out. Such tension can be overt in organizations such as Disney where cast members are expected to act prescribed roles at all times and never to slip out of role, even when faced by severe provocation or challenge by their guests.
- Territorial conflict whereby contact personnel often establish their own personal space, defending this space against clients and other servers, often leading to actions which conflict with the server's role.
- Organization versus client tensions within which contact personnel can receive conflicting instructions from the client and the organization resulting in a three-cornered fight. If such conflict is mishandled, any resulting compromise may leave the server dissatisfied.
- Interclient conflicts occur when two or more customers have different and opposing demands, for example where one requires extended assistance in

interpreting a city's geography while the next person in the queue seeks a quick answer to a question. As a result, an argument may arise between the two guests to which the front-line staff member is a spectator. This type of conflict can result in the server having to step out of role and act as an arbitrator or referee.

Generally, such role stress and conflict situations for boundary-spanning personnel produces dissatisfaction, frustration, and increased turnover intentions for the personnel concerned. In effect, it creates a workplace environment which staff members seek to avoid. As a result, personnel may begin to avoiding the customer in order to avoid stress that contact brings or they may move into a 'people-processing mode' so as not to get too close to customers and be faced with stress-producing decisions. Clearly, any of these reactions will be detrimental for a service-focused organization in tourism, hospitality and leisure and there is a need for careful management of such situations in order to avoid the worst effects of role stress and conflict.

Responsive management

We have considered the importance of every 'moment of truth' to the total guest experience and as a central feature within the achievement of quality service. The management of the 'moments of truth' cycle is a critical process and, according to Albrecht and Zemke (1985), requires a fundamental mind shift from traditional control-based supervision and management: 'When the moments of truth go unmanaged, the quality of service regresses to mediocrity' (p.31). Interestingly, in following up their service concepts after the onset of the information age, Albrecht and Zemke (2001) point to a major deterioration in customer service as a direct result of the electronic revolution. E-business, according to Albrecht and Zemke, has made many companies into virtual vending machines, with mindless use of digital technology depopulating the customer interface and thus detracting from a focus on service driven by quality, personalized service and 'moments of truth'. This concern, while valid in some areas of tourism, hospitality and leisure, is unlikely to impact in others such as luxury hotels, airline service in the air and personal fitness.

The traditional approach to managing relationships within a company can be seen to operate on a hierarchical basis, as in Figure 4.2. What is important in this model is that the decision-making process flows from the base of the pyramid to its apex, the senior management level. The customer contact zone is figuratively and, frequently, literally adrift at the bottom. A caricature of this model at work, which has more than a touch of reality in it, is the situation where staff in a busy hotel restaurant swarm to serve the general manager when he arrives for lunch and, in doing so, neglect the needs of paying guests. Staff at each level in this model are primarily concerned to satisfy their immediate superiors within the hierarchy, even if this means neglecting the real customers of the business. Figure 4.3, by contrast, shows what is known as the inverted service triangle, a philosophical inversion of traditional management hierarchies (Mahesh 1994).

This simple reversal of the triangle (in Figure 4.3) has major ramifications for the operation of service within tourism, hospitality and leisure businesses. The energy flow remains upwards but is the complete reverse of that which operates within the traditional model. In this approach, the customer contact zone becomes the most important component within the management of the organization. Everything else is subservient to that aspect of the service process. Back in the 1980s, Jan Carlzon of SAS saw the relationship between front-line staff, those responsible for handling the many thousands of 'moments of truth' on a daily basis, and the technical, supervisory and management functions as one of service, with the back-of-house team existing primarily to facilitate the critical work of those at the front line. Carlzon (1987, p.4) put it like this: 'If you're not serving the guest, your job is to serve those who are.' Disney's application of this principle is to consider all employees as cast members, with those at the front-line sharp edge as 'on stage' and those working behind the scenes as 'off stage'.

Figure 4.2

Traditional management hierarchy

Figure 4.3

The inverted service triangle

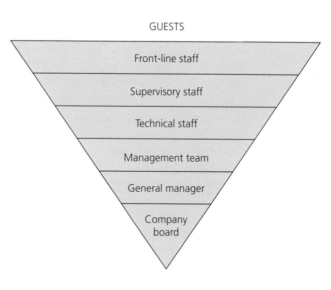

The inverted triangle demands an approach to management that is not control based but is designed to facilitate the work of operational staff. Management are there to assist their front-line colleagues in providing a better service to guests. By providing this superior service, of course, a tourism or hospitality company is enhancing its competitive position and increasing the likelihood that repeat business will be generated.

Organisations in tourism, hospitality and leisure that are particularly successful in terms of their service delivery are those that:

- are highly focused and consistent in everything they do and say in relation to employees;
- have managers who communicate with employees;
- facilitate rather than regulate their employees' response to customers;
- solicit employee feedback about how they can do things better;
- stress the importance of teamwork at each level of the organization; and
- plan carefully the organization's recruitment and training needs.

The link between service quality and the management environment within tourism, hospitality and leisure companies can also be seen in terms of four key principles in the development of customer care within organizations.

1. Customer care is a top-down concept, even if its delivery depends heavily upon front-line staff. This means that commitment to the principle of customer care must emanate from senior management levels within an organization. Successful management is not only about right management style but also an attitude, ethos or culture of the organization which overrides the management techniques used, so that that in the absence of other instructions these values will dictate how an employee will behave.

2. Customer care is totally inclusive within organizations. It is not just about front-line staff. Any contrary view only serves to reinforce the electricians' or administrators' opinion that the standard of service they give in support of front-line staff is not important. How can back-office staff do the right job unless they fully appreciate the customers' needs and the importance of their role? High standards of customer care cannot be achieved by ignoring seasonal, part-time or voluntary staff who represent the face of the business to many customers.

3. Companies need to recognize that if you take care for your staff they are, in turn, more likely to care for your customers. Too often organizations look first to the customer, whereas the emphasis should be placed on the staff. Improving the working experience for staff encourages a better service and a better experience for customers. More customers are obtained thereby improving the climate in which management and staff work. Investment and greater professionalism follow success and a cycle of achievement is reinforced.

4. Finally, it is important to see the management of service as a continuous process, meaning that customer care in tourism, hospitality and leisure is not a short-term project but a long-term commitment.

This analysis places considerable emphasis on the internal marketing process. 'Internal marketing' means applying the principles and practices of marketing to people who serve the external customers so that the best people can be employed and retained and they will do the best possible work. A compelling conclusion from this analysis is that service quality is much more likely to be delivered within a supervisory and management culture that focuses on the effective management of its people than in one that neglects such matters.

The concept of internal marketing and the application of a supportive management culture which enables the delivery of quality service lead to the notion of empowerment of front-line staff, which is a concept that has gained considerable currency within service-focused companies. 'Empowerment' is frequently taken to mean a process that enables and encourages front-line staff to make decisions that will help to solve customers' problems or meet their needs without reference to an interminable management hierarchy. The ability to deal professionally and competently with immediate queries, problems and complaints is an attribute that is rated very highly among customers of tourism, hospitality and leisure organizations and makes a major contribution to effective relationship marketing.

Harley (1999) notes that:

> Advocates of empowerment tend to promote it with considerable fervour, claiming that it has the potential to generate the kind of 'win-win' outcome beloved of unitarists. That is, while improving organizational performance and contributing to the 'bottom line', it simultaneously (and necessarily) leads to improvements in the experience of work for employees. (p.42)

He further describes the practice as follows: 'Empowerment involves delegation of responsibility from management to employees, non-hierarchical forms of work organisation and sharing of information between, and within, different levels of organisation' (p.43).

Lashley (1997), while a cautious advocate of empowered workplace responsibilities, also notes that adding responsibility to a person's job can 'increase the burden of work, produce more stress and represent an intensification of work' (p.11).

One common manifestation of empowerment is the no-quibble goods return policy that is adopted by many retailers. Customers purchase with greater confidence but front-line staff are also in a position where they can contribute to overcoming customer problems and complaints by immediate refund or replacement. This is not total empowerment but rather recognition, by management, that the customer care zone requires clear operating guidelines to which staff can work.

Similar absolute policies are more difficult to apply when the purchase is less tangible than that from a shop, for example a restaurant meal, theme-park ride or transportation arrangement. It is not possible to replace an unsatisfactory hotel experience, although the establishment can attempt to recover its position through a full or partial refund or the offer of a future complimentary stay. Thus, front-line staff need to be able to assess and evaluate each particular situation with confidence and authority and have to be empowered to provide a solution in so far as one is available. Guidelines are clearly important so as to enable front-line staff to respond in a consistent manner, and in some cases relatively standard provision may be acceptable – for example, a complimentary meal for delayed airline passengers and compensation, within specified scales, for those off-loaded due to over-booking. However, generally speaking, effective empowerment is 'ring-fenced' in so far as financial decisions are concerned so that staff have the authority to act up to a specified level without reference to supervisory or management authority. The American Ritz Carlton company permit all employees to change anything, on behalf of guests, up to a specified value. Rather greater freedom may be available if no direct financial consequences are involved. Novotel, part of the French Accor group, use the word 'subsidiarity' to describe their approach to empowerment. 'Subsidiarity' can be seen as another way of saying that employees should be encouraged to take responsibility for decisions. Whatever decisions employees make, at least they have made them. If they cannot make a decision on a problem then they pass it to the next person above them and they try to make it. Subsidiarity can lead to employees making the wrong decision, but the Novotel argument is that it is important that staff have made the decision for themselves and have the opportunity to learn from mistakes. Such a system requires the total absence of a punitive environment when mistakes are made or employees will avoid making decisions of any consequence.

Empowerment, also implies trust and confidence by management in the front-line workforce. For example, many traditional service organizations, where empowerment is not a concept that is fully adopted, restrict access to annual capital budgets and operating plans to management ranks only and on a 'need to know' basis. By contrast, the Disney Corporation claims to provide operational personnel with full access to these tools, entrusting them to translate the strategic plan from the boardroom to the point of action within the theme parks.

Empowerment of front-line staff is not solely a matter customer handling. If we accept definitions of relationship marketing to include, in addition to customer markets, those relating to suppliers, employees, referrals, 'influencers' and the internal environment, it is logical to think of empowerment extending to the management of and interaction with these groups as well. Thus front-line staff require training and support in order to take responsibility and make decisions with respect to a wide range of external groups, all of whom, ultimately, contribute to the success or otherwise of the business.

Real empowerment of staff, however, is not something that takes place as a result of a head office circular and attached guidelines. Empowerment is a direct factor of, on the one hand, effective human resource development policies which give staff the skills and confidence to act autonomously and, on the other, a supervisory and management culture that is based on trust and partnership and not control and censure. Thus front-line staff will only be able to act outside prescribed boundaries if they are equipped with the information and skills to do so but also, more importantly, if they know that their managers will support whatever action they decide upon and will not penalize or undermine such decisions.

Empowerment is, therefore, the result of a combination of corporate and senior management commitment with appropriate training and support at all levels. Sparrowe (1994), in an empirical study of the factors which contribute to the fostering of empowerment, identified two such factors:

First, the relationship employees have with their immediate superiors appears to be a significant element in the development of empowerment. To the extent that supervisors are unable to develop positive exchange relationships with employees because of job demands, frequent shift rotation, or burnout, those employees are less likely to enjoy meaning, choice, impact, and competence in their work activities. Policies and procedures that enable supervisors and employees to establish effective relationships over time would function to support empowerment efforts. Second, the importance of culture in efforts to foster empowerment. Constructive norms and shared behavioural expectations appear to facilitate employees' experience of meaningfulness, impact, choice, and competence at work. (Sparrowe 1994, p.69)

The effects of a genuine empowerment of front-line staff can also have a significant effect upon reducing the social distance between customers and those providing the tourism and hospitality services. When management demonstrates, in a public way, that all their staff has autonomy and the full trust of the company, they are stating their own evaluation of these staff, both as employees and as people. Guests, in the presence of this attitude, are much more likely to respond to those serving them on the basis of equality. Mahesh (1994) argues cogently for a trust in the better side of human nature, and this attitude is at the root of effective empowerment. The issue of social distance or the service/servitude conundrum is one that we have already reflected in our discussions in Chapter 2 . Real empowerment of the kind espoused by the Ritz Carlton organization in the United States, where guests and staff are seen as social equals temporarily undertaking different roles, can make a real contribution to overcoming problems in this area, providing that macro social and economic conditions permit.

The case for empowerment is by no means conclusive. In Chapter 4, we considered the work of Ritzer (2004) and the concept of McDonaldization. Bryman (2004) extends similar thinking to a range of other service organizations, including Disney. Such processes seek to reduce the human input to service delivery to an absolute and well-controlled minimum and deny the employees a perspective on the total production or service delivery system. Control of the workforce is a central tenet within successful fast-food businesses and others in the tourism, hospitality and leisure sector. Control is incompatible with empowerment in its true sense because empowerment means relinquishing control while at the same time ensuring that front-line staff have the skills and confidence to represent the company to customers and help to meet their needs in the best possible way.

Case Study *Flight Centre, Australia*

Flight Centre Limited opened its first store in Sydney in 1981. In two decades, it has grown to become one of the world's largest independent travel retailers with more than 1200 stores in the UK, Australia, New Zealand, South Africa, the USA, Canada and Hong Kong, employing more than 5500 people. Since floating in 1995, the company's share has risen sharply. In 2003, the company achieved global revenue and pre-tax profit of

▶

£245 million and £34 million, a growth of 30 per cent and 13 per cent respectively over the previous year.

How could a small travel agency selling cheap flights and holiday packages to cost-conscious travellers, with low profit margins and low technological inputs grow so fast? The recent awards they received might give some clue. As a new entrant of the competition, Flight Centre has in two consecutive years (2003 and 2004), been voted the third and fourth best company to work for on the *Sunday Times'* list of 100 best employers in the UK. It received similar awards in Australia, Canada, South Africa and New Zealand. What makes this achievement valuable is that compared with other high-profile winners, such as Microsoft, Flight Centre has succeeded in an industry that has low regard, has low pay and suffers persistent crises of skill deficiencies.

Empowerment and staff engagement are widely used clichés. In a low-pay sector with a tradition for high staff turnover, making meaningful empowerment work across a range of cultural and economic environments presents a real challenge. The key to Flight Centre's success is the empowerment of its people. Empowerment is a sense of control of an individual over the work environment. Flight Centre achieved this with a combination of unique approaches. First, its organizational structure is instrumental to the empowerment of people. The company is organized in four layers – 'families' (teams with three to seven people), 'villages' (four to five geographical teams), 'tribes' (areas or regions) and global SWOT (Strengths Weaknesses Opportunities Threats) and company board. This lean structure helps to control bureaucracy, create an egalitarian environment and involve staff into decision-making.

Second, staff are given 'financial and emotional ownership'. On top of the standard pay arrangements, Flight Centre has an uncapped sales-driven commission system. Staff in Flight Centre earn higher salaries than the industrial average, with no ceiling. The company also provides a further range of benefits: discounted travel, the Inceto Award (internal incentive – given to high achievers) and share options or a business ownership scheme (BOS). Seventy per cent of staff own company shares. It is not surprising, then, that many staff in Flight Centre feel that they run their own business.

Beyond these incentives, a bright career is the biggest reward for staff. The company cultivates a productive environment and possible opportunities for staff to develop. Training starts on day 1 and lasts through their career within the company. Recently, Flight Centre opened a business school to allow staff to gain degrees at a low cost. Comprehensive training helps keep their best talents and improve staff competence. Ninety per cent of team leaders have been promoted internally. In 2004, the company won a special award from the *Sunday Times* competition in recognition of the excellence of its in-house 'Learning Centre'.

That Flight Centre's approach to human resource management works is, according to the company, demonstrated by its performance against a range of indicators, notably business performance, staff participation in the company, internal staff promotions and public recognition through awards. In summary, there is no secret to Flight Centre's success: in their own words 'our company is our people'. With this belief, they practise all the approaches to foster environments that enhance the empowerment of people, involve them as an organic part of the business and thereby enhance their commitment and ultimately organizational effectiveness. Flight Centre's model is flexible and allows staff to buy into all, some or none of its features, depending on circumstances and lifestyle. There also are no upper limits in terms of what staff can earn from the scheme.

Case prepared from published sources for Fáilte Ireland by Andrew Martin of The Robert Gordon University, Aberdeen. Reproduced with permission.

Case discussion questions

1. What are the main features of Flight Centre's approach to empowerment?

2. What is unusual about these features?

3. How might this model of empowerment work in organizations with which you are familiar?

Organizational citizenship – taking empowerment further

'Empowerment', a concept that originally comes from the notion that the individual can take charge of decisions within his or her own life, has, arguably, been hijacked by those more interested in its application as an organizational tool. As a result, we are 'empowered' to behave within boundaries prescribed by our employers and empowered behaviour therefore loses any sense of individual control and of spontaneity. The circumscription imposed by many organizations exists precisely because companies may be afraid that their staff will become too empowered and start to make real decisions that, in turn, may act against the collective perception of what customers should be able to expect in the service encounter. As a result empowered actions by employees in many tourism, hospitality and leisure organizations constitutes what Organ (1988; 1990) describes as 'in-role behaviour', prescribed and circumscribed by the organization and available for use if required. In-role behaviour, defined by Barksdale and Werner (2001) as being part of one's job, incorporates most applications of empowerment. It is likely to be rewarded extrinsically but also be subject to sanctions, both formal and informal. The other side of the coin to in-role behaviour is described by Organ as 'extra-role behaviour', which is not part of the normal, daily job and, as a consequence, is rarely extrinsically rewarded and its non-performance is rarely penalized. Both in-role and extra-role behaviours may be intrinsically rewarding to the individual but, where the latter conflicts with the former, employees may face sanctions as a result. The notion of extra-role behaviour, provided that it is deemed positive by the organization (and this is an important caveat), has been described by Organ (1988) as organizational citizenship behaviour.

Organ (1988) defines organizational citizenship behaviours as

> The discretionary behaviours that are not directly or explicitly recognized by the formal reward system and that, in the aggregate, promote the effective functioning of the organization. (p.4)

'Discretionary', in this context, refers to behaviour that is not an enforceable requirement of the job, in terms of one's job description or contract. It refers to behaviour that is a matter of choice in such a way that failure to behave this way will not lead to punishment. Important within Organ's definition is the notion that the behaviour in question does promote the effectiveness of the organization, in other words is consistent with the company's business and operational objectives. In the context of service delivery in tourism, hospitality and leisure, going beyond normal expectation to assist a guest or customer with a particular problem may fall within this definition provided that, in stepping outside the normal boundaries of the job, other guests or customers do not suffer as a result. Thus, focusing additional attention and time on the needs of one participant in a fitness class because she is entered for the city's 15km road race may exhibit positive discretionary behaviour provided that, as a result, other class members are not neglected or alienated.

Organizational citizenship behaviour has a number of key dimensions (Organ 1988). These are altruism, courtesy, sportsmanship, civic virtue and conscientiousness. 'Altruism' constitutes discretionary behaviour that has the effect of helping a specific person, generally a customer or colleague, with an organizationally relevant task. This dimension is widely recognized as an important dimension of organizational citizenship (George and Jones 1997). Examples of altruism include assisting colleagues facing a work backlog during busy periods and assisting a colleague who may have difficulty learning new IT skills. 'Courtesy' is related to altruism but there are some differences. Courtesy is generally taken to relate to behaviour that helps a colleague avoid work-related problems or reduces the impact of a problem that has been anticipated. Reminding colleagues in advance about an anticipated rush is an example of courteous behaviour. 'Sportsmanship' refers to a willingness on the part of employees to tolerate less than ideal circumstances or inconveniences without complaint. This attribute demonstrates a willingness to make personal sacrifices on behalf of colleagues and the organization. 'Civic virtue' relates to behaviour whereby employees participate in the wider life of the organization in a manner that goes beyond the requirements of their post. Such participation may be in the form of engagement in the political life or governance of the organization (membership of staff associations, social clubs) or a willingness to volunteer to represent the organization externally in a variety of roles. Finally, 'conscientiousness' relates to behaviour that goes considerably beyond the minimum that might be expected in terms of attendance, observing company rules, taking breaks and the like. Punctuality, good attendance and adherence to rules are examples of such behaviour. Good organizational citizenship does not necessarily involve all these dimensions at the same time and may, indeed, go beyond these attributes. Furthermore, it is likely that these dimensions will overlap with each other at times and, therefore, cannot always be readily isolated for recognition.

Turnipseed (2003) argues that organizational citizenship behaviour can increase labour productivity at a minimal direct cost to the organization. Given the labour-intensive nature of most tourism, hospitality and leisure operations, this has the potential to be of significant value to businesses in the sector. Therefore, this reinforces the notion that it is in the interest of organizations to create a climate within which organizational citizenship actions are more likely to take place, by recognizing such behaviour through formal and informal rewards and benefits.

There is evidence that the presence of a culture that fosters and encourages good organizational citizenship is conducive to the delivery of excellent customer service (Cheung 2006). Particularly for those working on the front line, doing extra in service organizations in tourism, hospitality and leisure in support of your colleagues and your company is very likely to have a direct impact upon the customers you are serving. If your good citizenship actions help to speed up the check-in process at an airport or help a colleague to overcome a computer glitch in the ticket office of a sports arena, customers are likely to benefit directly and, as a result, their perception of the service they receive is more likely to be positive. Hemdi and Nasurdin (2005) take this link a step further when they posit that organizational citizenship behaviour contributes to enhanced service quality, particularly when this is supported by a company environment where perceived procedural justice is present. In other words, their work in Malaysia suggests that where people feel that they are being treated in a fair way by management, they will be more likely to engage in organizational citizenship behaviour and such actions will, in turn, enhance the customer's experience of service. However, there is a need to maintain balance between good citizenship in the interests of the company and behaviour which, as a consequence, may actually be detrimental to the wishes of the guest. The case study below illustrates how one citizenship dimension, that of conscientiousness, can be taken too far and result in dissatisfied customers.

Case Study *Early morning toast at the airport*

A busy airport restaurant offered customers the opportunity to make their own toast, using a toaster with a continuously rotating conveyor belt upon which bread is placed by the customer. Unfortunately, when the bread rotated through one circuit of the system, it produced warm but untoasted bread while repeating the process resulted in an overdone, burnt outcome. Either way the product was inedible, with the result that a large pile of burnt toast soon accumulated to the side of the machine. One employee took it upon herself to address this matter by scolding customers who added to the pile of burnt toast, complaining loudly that this represented waste and was very costly to the company. Pointing out the problems with the toaster had no impact upon her attitude and customers left without their toast but hungry, frustrated and angry.

Case discussion questions

1. How is organizational citizenship behaviour illustrated in this case?

2. How might the employee have addressed the problem, as she saw it, without alienating customers?

Organisational citizenship behaviour, when it does contribute to guest satisfaction and business effectiveness in a wider sense, can be seen as valuable to operations in the tourism, hospitality and leisure sector provided that it does not place the needs of the company before those of the customer in the unreasonable manner illustrated in the toaster case study. A culture where staff recognize the needs and best interests of the organization in a practical and responsive manner is of particular value in environments where, as we have seen, demand is unpredictable and the management of staff resources imprecise. It can be in the culture of an organization for staff members to help each other out and work beyond their shift in an airport hotel because a group of delayed passengers have to be catered for late in the evening. This is clearly of huge value to an organization and may be achieved either by compulsion (in which case it does not constitute organizational citizenship behaviour) or through an awareness of immediate need by staff, in which case it can be said to be an example of organizational citizenship behaviour. There is, however, a fine line to be drawn between fostering and benefiting from a culture of organizational citizenship and forcing staff to work outside their contractual obligations through threat and intimidation. Such threat may be overt but also can be tacit in the sense that team members find it difficult to disengage from and leave an uncompleted task because their boss and colleagues are continuing to work. The sacrifice they may make in such circumstances to family and external interests is probably not recognized by organizations. The 'macho' culture to be found in some organizations, whereby staff do not leave work until their superior does so in order to undertake additional, unpaid work for the employer, can be misinterpreted as good organizational citizenship behaviour. In fact, it may be anything but that and may be indicative of subtle workplace bullying. It may also lead to staff dissatisfaction and attrition, and is probably detrimental to good customer service.

Measuring success by customer satisfaction levels

Mahesh (1988) considers the argument that the true worth of an organization in tourism, hospitality and leisure must be measured in terms of levels of customer satisfaction. He considers the role of traditional productivity measures within the service sector, an analysis that has particular applicability within the tourism, hospitality and leisure sector. Any measures to enhance employee output and increase efficiency must be weighed against consequences for the level of customer satisfaction, thus moving the discussion away from objective productivity criteria into a rather more subjective arena. Certainly, productivity criteria can be utilized in order to set work targets in certain areas of the industry – house assistants can be given a specific number of bedrooms to service within a set time and airlines can set a seats-to-cabin-staff ratio for their aircraft. However, such targets have to be weighted against variable and sometimes unpredictable yield and therefore may create considerable pressure when the hotel or aircraft is operating to full capacity. In such situations, customer satisfaction may suffer as a result, with guests having to wait for a room at check-in or experiencing delays with cabin service. The balance between productivity improvements on the one hand and ensuring customer satisfaction on the other is therefore a delicate one and any attempts to alter it must be supported through the introduction of enhanced technology and/or additional training. However, there is a point of some contentiousness here in that Albrecht and Zemke (1985) argue that the fewer people who are involved with the delivery of a service, the better it is likely to be for the customer.

There is no doubt, however, that major changes in employee output as measured by numbers employed have taken place within the global tourism, hospitality and leisure industry. Major airlines, for example, have downsized considerably in staffing terms while at the same time retaining a significant proportion of their route and flight density. This is a process which commenced in the 1980s, particularly in Europe where the privatization of previously state-owned assets triggered significant downsizing. The process was given further energy, globally, as a result of the 9/11 events in New York and Washington. Airlines used this catalyst to further rationalize their structures and to outsource a significant range of traditional activities. This has resulted in a noticeable diminution of traditional tangible service levels in airlines. Low-cost carriers, by contrast, have adopted a low staffing model, with relatively few core employees and a focus on staff who fly rather than on high back-up staffing levels on the ground.

Of course, such changes cannot be solely attributed to organizational and personnel restructuring. Enhanced technology within the reservations and other support systems also plays its part. Most European airlines have changed dramatically with or without privatization. The European hotel industry has also enhanced productivity and reduced its rooms-to-staff ratio significantly in response to demography and labour shortages in some countries, as well as through reorganization, the use of technology and changes in the hotel product concept, especially in the budget sector. One of the most traumatic aspects of change in Eastern Europe during the 1990s was the need to restructure the workplace so as to be competitive in international terms. Romanian hotels, for example, faced with government requirements to seek foreign partners in the private sector, had to reduce staff levels by 50 per cent as well as greatly improving rather than reducing the range and quality of services available to the customer.

Ultimately, this debate comes down to recognizing the importance of customer satisfaction as the overriding imperative within a successful tourism and hospitality company. Without such satisfaction, business success and profitability cannot be achieved. This demands a fundamental reorientation on the part of many companies in the sector.

Vulnerability to union pressure

Mahesh (1988) argues that the characteristics of service industries, especially the inability to stockpile, mean that the sector is particularly vulnerable to union pressure. The logic of this argument is clear. During major industrial action in the coal or motor car industry, for example, companies are able to draw on reserve stock and thus, in the short term, lessen the impact of the action. Likewise, industrial action within the distribution system, such as the railways, means that manufacturing companies can maintain production for a period of time and stockpile their wares for later distribution and sale. Neither of these options is available to businesses in the tourism and hospitality sector. Business lost for whatever reason cannot be recouped and therefore industrial action in an airline, hotel or food service company means totally lost revenue to the company. Likewise, industrial action within the tourism distribution system, such as airlines or ferries, has major immediate and longer-term consequences for providers at the destination, notably hotels, retailers and ground transport companies, who are unable to secure alternative business at short notice.

This argument has a compelling force of logic to it but is undermined by the very patchy level of union representation within the industry in Europe. We shall discuss some of the reasons for this in greater detail in Chapter 5. Some sectors are highly unionized, notably airlines and hotel workers in some urban areas. A strike by Dublin bar workers in 1994 was able to close 70 per cent of public houses in the city to coincide with the football World Cup. However, in rural areas such action would have been totally ineffective. Furthermore, if we accept Riley's (1996) analysis of labour markets within the major sub-sectors of the tourism and hospitality industry, it is unlikely that unionization of the industry will have the force and impact that Mahesh suggests. Riley's model of the weak internal labour market, as we have already seen in Chapter 3, includes the attributes of weak workplace customs, unspecified hiring standards, multiple ports of entry and low skills specificity, and these all act to counter the potential impact of unionization. The small-business structure of much of the industry also counters the potential for union impact. So does specific employer exploitation of these attributes, through which use of seasonal, part-time, youth and female labour in some sub-sectors of the industry has acted to counter any potential for strengthening within the internal labour market. There are exceptions to this situation. In part because of the strength of the apprenticeship training system in Germany's hospitality sector, some stronger internal labour market characteristics are in evidence and the role of trade unions as active partners in the education and training process has much greater weight.

Thus we have a situation in the tourism and hospitality industries of Western Europe where the potential for union power is considerable but where the reality is somewhat removed from meeting this potential. The situation in Eastern Europe is one where, under the old command economies, theoretical union membership levels were high but the exercise of industrial power was minimal. The period of transition, with generally high levels of unemployment in all sectors, will probably see a weakening of the position of organized labour so that similarities with the rest of Europe will increase.

Business structure in tourism, hospitality and leisure

Mahesh (1988) finally argues for the downsizing of companies as a major implication of service sector characteristics, primarily because of simultaneous production and consumption and also because of the need to be responsive to individual customer needs. The notion of empowerment, which we have already considered, points strongly to an emphasis on local decision-making. This allows front-line staff to provide service that is geared to meeting the specific and immediate needs of guests rather than offering a standard, centralized response to such concerns. The logic of empowerment, furthermore, extends beyond the immediate front line to unit and area management within large companies, allowing them the autonomy and authority to develop their businesses in response to local needs.

The reality of the international tourism, hospitality and leisure industry is that the need for the sector to be 'adaptive, decentralized and downsized' (Mahesh 1988, p.10) is already largely met because of the small-business structure of the industry in most countries. Hotels, other accommodation areas, restaurants, fitness clubs, retail outlets and attractions are all dominated by small to medium-sized enterprises, frequently family or privately owned and managed, and thus fully integrated into their local communities and sensitive to the needs of visitors to these areas.

However, the reality of trends within tourism, hospitality and leisure is such that large, multinational companies are growing in importance in all countries, although the level of market penetration in Europe and Asia by these businesses has not reached that in North America. Deregulation, the impact of the internet on distribution and privatization in the airline industry all mean that many countries are moving to a situation where dominant control is exercised by a small number of mega-carriers and alliances (such as Star, oneworld) with a global presence, linked to small, regional carriers through ownership, franchising and other marketing alliances. The hotel sector is some way behind the airlines in experiencing the impact of domination by larger companies but the trends are pointing strongly in a similar direction, especially within the rapidly expanding budget sector of the market. Budget hotel multiples are threatening the competitiveness of the traditional small hotel sector in many parts of the developed world. Budget hotels have all the characteristics of branded products and meet none of the locally focused criteria which Mahesh has advocated. This is true of branding within the middle segment of the hotel market as well, and the growing importance of this trend is strongly supported by central computer reservations systems which are frequently inaccessible to the small operator. A similar picture can be painted with respect to travel agents and tour operators in many countries, particularly since the advent of e-travel agents such as Expedia.

Ownership of the tourism, hospitality and leisure sector by major international companies is not necessarily incompatible with the service-focused approach to business which Mahesh advocates. Ownership by a major company does not necessarily rule out locally sensitive management, marketing and the empowerment of staff to respond individually to local needs. However, the principle of branding, which features increasingly within developments by the multiples, most certainly does eliminate the ability of managers and staff to provide such locally attuned service as the ethos of the product is shifted increasingly towards that of manufacturing production. In many ways, what we have here is a critical human resource dilemma. Locally focused management and staff, responsive and attuned to customer needs, are fully within our notion of sustainable human resource management within tourism and hospitality, but this places considerable emphasis on the requirements of staff selection, training, development, managerial style and general working conditions. Branded tourism and hospitality products, in many but not all respects, fit much more within the traditional human resource management paradigm which, by its nature, reduces the need for training and related support activity by placing an emphasis on the development, implementation and management of systems which are centrally determined and universally applied. The characteristics of what Ritzer (2004) and the 'McDonaldization of society' are efficiency, calculability, predictability and control. These features, borrowed and developed from manufacturing operations principles, are making an increasing impact on all sectors concerned with service delivery, but tourism and hospitality in many respects have led the way in their implementation through companies such as

McDonald's and Holiday Inn. The role of people working within this model is very different from that outlined in terms of empowerment and managerial support. There is an inherent tension and incompatibility between the move towards standardization and branding on the one hand, and demands for more locally delivered and quality services on the other, and it is not really clear at this point what shape the outcome will take. This managerial paradox is one of a number that in many ways confront the practice of modern business, and the pressures that they pose are part of the concluding discussion in this book in Chapter 10.

In this chapter we have considered the characteristics of the service sector in general and how they impact on the tourism, hospitality and leisure industry in particular. We have engaged in a detailed analysis of the implications of these characteristics, especially in terms of what they mean for the management of human resources. It is evident from this discussion that achieving quality service in the tourism, hospitality leisure industries is a business imperative and is one which will increasingly be the yardstick by which consumers differentiate between airlines, hotels and other facilities which in most other respects will not differ greatly in terms of physical product quality characteristics. Capitalizing on the benefits of the service imperative requires a major human resource focus and one that adopts the features of the sustainable human resource management paradigm.

Review and discussion questions

1. Identify company strategies that would fit into the description of relationship marketing. These may be from the tourism and hospitality industry or from other sectors.

2. What are the implications of relationship marketing for the organization, management and marketing of:

   (a) a small mountain hotel in Switzerland;
   (b) a start-up low-cost airline in India;
   (c) a large airport hotel in Hong Kong;
   (d) one of the big three tour operators in the UK;
   (e) a museum commemorating the slave trade in Ghana;
   (f) a cruise liner operating out of Singapore;
   (g) a fast-food restaurant, part of a multinational chain, located in Miami, Florida;
   (h) a bed-and-breakfast establishment in the west of Ireland;
   (i) a beach bar in Thailand;
   (j) a nightclub in Mombasa, Kenya.

3. Summarize the characteristics of services that distinguish them from manufactured products. What implications do these characteristics have for the management of human resources?

4. What is meant by a 'moment of truth'?

5. Identify the 'moments of truth' that you encountered during a recent visit to a hotel, restaurant, cinema or other service location. To what extent were these 'moments of truth' supervised by management of the establishment?

6. How can a major tour operator control the 'moments of truth' encountered by their clients in contact with various travel intermediaries during their vacation?

7. What do you understand by the term 'empowerment'? What are its constituent parts?

8. What management strategies will be needed in order to empower front-line staff in the tourism and hospitality industry?

9. What are the management implications of inverting the service triangle?

10. What are the main differences between empowerment and organizational citizenship behaviour?

11. Can there be common ground between McDonaldization and the aspiration for quality service delivery in the tourism, hospitality and leisure industry?

A dark side to the coin?

Introduction

One of the challenges which any discussion of human resources in international tourism, hospitality and leisure presents is how to resolve the many contradictions that are evident within the industry. In Chapter 3, reference was made to the high level of instability in the workforce within many sectors of the tourism, hospitality and leisure industry and this was linked to Riley's weak internal labour-market characteristics. In interpreting Riley's analysis, do we conclude that the transitory nature of much tourism and hospitality employment is a contributory factor in the creation of a weak internal labour market? Or, alternatively, do we argue that because the internal labour market is weak, conditions are created which lead to short-term and casual relationships between employers and employees? To resort to the use of clichés, this is a classic 'chicken and egg' situation. In Chapter 4 we considered the seemingly contradictory tensions between, on the one hand, the demand for greater customization of tourism, hospitality and leisure products and services, enabled in part by the process of empowerment, and, on the other, pressure towards standardization and de-skilling in the delivery of tourism and hospitality products and services, i.e. the notion of McDonaldization. We will face more in linking

Chapter 9, which considers training and development issues, to Chap..
4 and, indeed, this chapter. One example of such a dilemma linking these chapters goes something like this:

- Quality service requires skilled and well-trained service staff.
- Training and development is an expensive investment in employees.
- The characteristics of the tourism and hospitality internal labour market are
  conducive to high labour turnover, especially among those staff in customer
  contact zones.
- – If a staff member is going to leave anyway, it does not make sense to
     invest heavily in their training and development.
  - Why give staff enhanced skills which will only go to make them more
     attractive to other employers and encourage them to leave? Any
     investment in training will go to benefit the competition.
- – Training and development are strong motivators and can contribute to
     reducing attrition rates.
  - Taking pride in the job and being 'empowered' to deliver quality service
     to the customer makes it more likely that employees will be happy in the
     place of work and this will reduce turnover.

Such arguments are irreconcilable and the debate can go on and on without
clear resolution. As with many other areas of social policy and practice, one of
the roots of this dilemma is how the individual employer and employee behave
in the face of wider employment structures and trends, in other words the relationship between the individual (person or company) and society or the wider
industry context. If the positive elements of the above analysis are accepted, can
an employer afford, or afford not to, go against the macro picture and risk
investing in his or her staff, thereby increasing costs and threatening competitiveness by doing so, while faced by the possibility that staff attrition will continue? We could go on and identify a host of further issues to which similar
inconclusive analysis could be applied.

In this chapter, we will explore some of the concerns that can be associated
with McJobs (jobs associated with McDonaldized workplaces) and, indeed,
wider tourism, hospitality and tourism work. Given that service work is the
fastest growing area of employment in most developed and developing countries, Shaw and Williams' (1994) rather brutal description of tourism, hospitality
and leisure employees as 'uneducated, unmotivated, untrained, unskilled and
unproductive' (p.142) and Westwood's (2002) description of work in this area as
'a low-pay, low-prestige, low-dignity, low-benefit, no-future job' (p.3) both
require careful examination. Westwood's assertion needs to be balanced against
Hoque's (2000) analysis of the hotel sector in the UK which concludes that
hotels 'may no longer be deserving of their image as "bad employers"' (p.154)

This chapter may not directly resolve any of these problems. What it aims to
do, however, is to address a range of what Wood (1997) calls the 'issues and controversies' of working in international tourism, hospitality and leisure. The
range of 'issues and controversies' here do not precisely match those of Wood
but there is considerable convergence. Inevitably, the 'menu' of issues and
controversies that will be addressed may not be exhaustive. However, what

discussion of some of the main themes in this area will allow is an attempt at the conclusion to this chapter to synthesize their main implications in the context of the book's underlying theme of sustainability. This analysis will in turn act as a precursor to aspects of the discussion in the final chapter of this book.

Issues and controversies in relation to employment in tourism, hospitality and leisure are by no means new. As we saw in Chapter 2, the origin of work in this sector lies firmly in the post-feudal master–servant relationship, bound up with issues of social class and status and a general acceptance of the Malthusian thesis that the hierarchy of social relationships are fixed and permanent. Thus the notion of servitude in the service relationship has its origins in an unquestioning era, at a time when neither partner within the social contract that, for example, bound the English aristocrat and his retinue undertaking the Grand Tour of Europe would have dreamed of debating the rights or wrongs of their relationship. This dimension of the development of tourism, hospitality and leisure is generally ignored in both the writing of the time and in subsequent literature. Samuel Johnson, in writing about his travels in Scotland during the seventeenth century, makes little or no reference to those who acted as travel facilitators on his behalf or looked to his comfort *en route*. In more modern times, Turner and Ash (1975), in their wide-ranging and historically detailed discussion of the origins of mass tourism and what they call the 'pleasure periphery' in the latter half of the twentieth century, only arrive at a consideration of employment when discussing the economic impact of modern tourism development. The romanticized picture of the Grand Tour and travel into the nineteenth century as described by the above authors as well as Buzzard (1993), Steinecke (1993) and Towner (1985) does not recognize the work and the delivery of service required.

Saunders (1981), however, gives us a picture of conditions in service during the nineteenth century.

> Although conditions of Elizabethan times, when servants slept on prickling straw, had now passed, it was still customary in most great houses to sleep men in the cellars and women in the attics, often in a long, single dormitory. This practice of 'living in' has later been adopted by hotels, in order to maintain staff requirements in times of acute shortage. Only towards the end of the nineteenth century has the idea that 'anything is good enough for servants' given way to meeting the need of the new scarcity; nor was it usual until that time to give days off or annual holidays, it being considered quite enough to get the occasional afternoon to themselves and to have the opportunity to attend church on Sunday. (Saunders 1981, p.61)

Saunders continues by drawing on further historical links between domestic work and that in the tourism and hospitality industry.

> It will not have escaped attention that some of the practices that have grown up in this century such as living in and tipping, were carried over into some of the service industries, particularly hotel and catering. Servants suffered also the disadvantage of the scattered nature of their employment, which made it difficult for them to form associations, even at a time when the nineteenth century trade union movements showed how effective combination could become accepted

and recognized as part of the social structure. The scattered nature of catering establishments today has been one of the principal reasons why organization for the protection of common interest has proved so difficult to obtain. (Saunders 1981, p.62)

Saunders' concerns are, interestingly, echoed in an analysis of present-day domestic work (The Work Foundation 2004) which raises a range of concerns about the context and security of such work, including the comment that:

> Most domestic relationships are in the informal economy. Whilst this can work well for both sides, we are storing up longer term problems as this sector expands. Those paid cash in hand for household tasks will not be getting National Insurance payments, and are likely to be storing up pension problems – particularly as they are predominantly women, who are already more likely to be in poverty in retirement. (p.2)

Thus, while the theme of the discussion has clearly moved on from Victorian issues, it is interesting that concern still exists about the sustainability of work that constitutes the origin of much employment in the hospitality sub-sector of tourism, hospitality and leisure.

Perhaps the first in-depth picture of aspects of tourism, hospitality and leisure work comes from the 1930s and the writing of George Orwell (1933). His description of the work of the *plongeur* within the working hierarchy of Paris hotels is as perceptive as it is moving and, in many ways, provides a benchmark against which much subsequent sociological discussion of conditions in the tourism and, particularly, hospitality industry can be assessed. Fuller (1971) describes in some detail the sort of work that Orwell would have carried out.

> Work in the *plonge* was hardly an attractive task and labour not easy to obtain, and there was usually a substantial turnover of operatives working in the *plonge*. The '*plongeur*' (literally one who plunges) is the kitchen porter who has the important task of cleaning the pots and pans. For copper pots, traditional procedure was to have two deep sinks, one fitted with a steam jet to heat water in which the pans were placed, adding soda. The *plongeur* had a long fish hook to fish out the pans from the hot water and clean them with pickle made from one third salt, one third silver sand and one third flour, mixed with vinegar to paste. Traditionally he did this either with bare hands or with the skins of used lemons, rubbing all over the pan inside and out to bring a shine and effectively removing particles of food. Pans are then rinsed, wiped dry and placed on racks in order of size, each group together and handle pointing all one way. (This operation is still carried out in many *plonges* today.) (Fuller, 1971, in Saunders, 1981, p.71)

Orwell's approach is to describe his own experiences of working in Paris hotels and his relationship with colleagues and superiors from the perspective of the foreigner and the 'down and out'. Orwell's objective is to expose the extremes of social deprivation during the depression of the 1930s and, as such, is one of extreme pessimism. He considers the work of the *plongeur* in its social context.

When one comes to think of it, it is strange that thousands of people in a great, modern city should spend their waking hours swabbing dishes in hot dens underground. The question I am raising is why this life goes on – what purpose it serves, and who wants it to continue, and why I am not taking a more rebellious attitude. I am trying to consider the social significance of the *plongeur's* life. I think I should start by saying that the *plongeur* is one of the slaves of the modern world ... he is no freer than if he were bought and sold. His work is servile and without art; he is paid just enough to keep him alive; his only holiday is the sack. He is cut off from marriage or, if he marries his wife must work too. Except by a lucky chance, he has no escape from his life, save into prison ... if *plongeurs* thought at all, they would long ago have formed a union and gone on strike for better treatment. But they do not think because they have no leisure for it; their life has made slaves of them people have a way of taking for granted that all work is done for a sound purpose ... some people must feed in restaurants, and so other people must swab dishes for 80 hours a week. It is the work of civilisation and therefore unquestionable. This point is worth considering. (Orwell 1933, p.122)

Work in supposedly higher status positions in hotels was not necessarily any easier. Page and Kingsford (1971) consider the work of the chef:

The cook worked sometimes for fourteen hours or more. The heat from the stoves was immense, and the fumes and smoke drifted round the kitchen, creeping into lungs and eyes of everyone there. The life of those who worked in such kitchens was a hard one. Because of the great heat, the cooks perspired freely and to counteract the thirst this produced, they drank heavily. Beer was always ready at hand, and the more work the cook did, the more he drank, and the more he drank, the less capable he was of doing good work, the more cruel and vulgar he became. Heat and sweat, drunkenness and vulgarity, ill temper through lack of sleep, and constant noise, these were the conditions which caused the young cooks sometimes to be brutally treated by their superiors. The general atmosphere was one of chaos and disorder. The cook had the well-earned reputation of being no better than a vulgar drunkard, who stank most of the time of food, burning fuel, beer and sweat. (Page and Kingsford 1971, in Saunders 1981, p.71)

Much of what has been written, historically, about the working conditions of workers in the tourism, hospitality and leisure industry, notably hotels, is anecdotal and has little by way of empirical corroboration. However, in many respects, the tough reality that is presented in descriptive form as well as the influence of Orwell's analysis can be seen in more recent studies of the industry, which focus on negative aspects of tourism and hospitality work in a comparative social context (Dronfield and Soto 1982; Byrne 1986; Gabriel 1988). The other side of the coin, equally precise and from the same period as Orwell are the accounts written between 1937 and 1942 in some five books by Ludwig Bemelmans. However, in complete contrast to Orwell, Bemelmans is the supreme optimist and describes hotel work from the point of view of someone climbing to a senior position in a luxury New York hotel (for example, Bemelmans, 1942). The airline sector has also, historically, been held up as the glamorous side of work in tourism, hospitality and leisure, particularly in the 1950s and 1960s, one of the 'blue ribbon' sectors for employment within personal services. In contrast with comparable work areas such as hospitality, in the airline industry, issues of recruitment, labour turnover, job status and workplace recognition, among others, have been of relatively limited contention in terms of work involving direct service delivery (cabin attendants, ground handling). Indeed, during the 30-year period up to airline deregulation in the United States (1979) and Europe (early 1990s), it is fair to say that employment in the airline sector, especially within major national flag carriers, had many of the attributes of public sector work and its attendant benefits combined with high levels of trade union participation while, at the same time, offering perceived glamour and a 'fun' image (Eaton 2001). Calder (2002) describes this in terms of 'A job in aviation – glamorous, secure, well-paid employment' (p.236). This positive perspective remains in certain areas of work as, for example, a pilot or cabin crew with one of the more traditional airlines. However, as the case study at the end of this chapter suggests, not all airline work today is perceived to be so glamorous and the operating culture of low-cost airlines, with very rapid turn around, multi-tasking and a pressure to sell products and services to passengers *en route*, certainly provides a very different perspective of work in this sector.

We are thus already faced with a hint of one of the compelling debates that will be encountered in most analyses of work and its environment in the tourism, hospitality and leisure industry, particularly those located in a developed country context. On the one side, there is a very upbeat perspective, stressing challenge, opportunity, variety, mobility and a strong people dimension. This is the image that industry employers and education providers are keen to present. It is a picture that is embellished by the argument that the tourism, hospitality and leisure industry provides a broad and heterogeneous working environment, with opportunities and a place for most members of society whether they are disadvantaged on the basis of race, immigrant status or physical disability. On the other hand, there is a picture of drudgery, low pay, anti-social conditions, lack of job security, poor treatment from employers, contempt from customers and the like. Much empirical work, especially into employment at a semi-skilled or unskilled level, has produced conclusions with a focus on these latter issues in the developed world. What is lacking is serious research studies into the nature of work in tourism, hospitality and leisure in developing countries. Zhang *et al.* (2005) hint at some of the issues relating to hotel work in China, particularly in relation to the status of such work, but their work does not really constitute detailed empirical evidence. As an illustration of some of the problems faced in developing countries in relation to tourism work, UNEP (undated) note the following:

> In developing countries especially, many jobs occupied by local people in the tourist industry are at a lower level, such as housemaids, waiters, gardeners and other practical work, while higher-paying and more prestigious managerial jobs go to foreigners or 'urbanized' nationals. Due to a lack of professional training, as well as to the influence of hotel or restaurant chains at the destination, people with the know-how needed to perform higher level jobs are often attracted from other countries. This may cause friction and irritation and increases the gap

between the cultures ... many jobs in the tourism sector have working and employment conditions that leave much to be desired: long hours, unstable employment, low pay, little training and poor chances for qualification. In addition, recent developments in the travel and tourism trade (liberalization, competition, concentration, drop in travel fares, growth of subcontracting) and introduction of new technologies seem to reinforce the trend towards more precarious, flexible employment conditions. For many such jobs young children are recruited, as they are cheap and flexible employees.

In many respects, there is a realistic prospect that both sides of the argument with respect to tourism, hospitality and leisure work represent aspects of the truth. International tourism, hospitality and leisure is as diverse as it is large, and this in itself means that categorical generalizations about it will be dangerous. The industry, as has already been amply demonstrated, consists of an amalgam of sub-sectors whose work environment and other characteristics are very diverse, melded together only by the common ground of striving to meet the needs of clients, who themselves are seeking an ideal experience which is 'seamless' in the way that service is delivered from travel agent to airport to airline to tour guide to hotel to restaurant to wind surfing instructor to theme park to museum to opera time and time again.

Furthermore an additional dimension is provided by the diverse nature of the international tourism, hospitality and leisure, as we have seen, this is a variety born of historical, social, cultural, economic and political factors. Thus the nature of work and its relationship to the society in which it exists is not the same in all countries at a regional level (for example in Europe), let alone in global terms. Professional and technical status and all that these concepts imply, for example, are widely claimed to have very different historical and contemporary meanings in Germany, France and Switzerland compared to the United Kingdom and the United States. Whether this holds true today or is just another myth about work in hospitality, tourism and leisure is difficult to ascertain. Certainly, the fact that the vast majority of low-level service workers in Switzerland and a high proportion of those in Germany and France are drawn from immigrant communities suggests that such work is hardly perceived as 'noble and professional', as is widely claimed by those bemoaning the lack of status for such work in Anglo-Saxon countries.

The status of work, in turn, can affect the nature of education and training as well as status and standing in the workplace. If we then extend our discussion to incorporate work in the volatile and rapidly changing environment of countries such as Russia, further complications are immediately in evidence. Sources of security and status in employment which existed under the old regimes may now be despised, undervalued or too costly for the new system to maintain. At the same time, success is much more likely to be measured in conspicuous material terms, frequently the result of entrepreneurial activity on the grey, if not black, market. These represent generic work themes and issues common to all industry sectors many countries, developed and developing, but form a backcloth to any consideration of work, its context and consequences, within the tourism and hospitality industry.

The purpose of this chapter is to investigate the polarized positions with respect to some of the main 'issues and controversies' and to determine the extent to which they reflect a truly Europe-wide perspective as well as one representative of tourism, hospitality and leisure as a whole. The themes that will be addressed in this chapter are by no means exhaustive. Nor are they mutually exclusive. Indeed, it is arguable that any classification of the issues that affect employment in tourism, hospitality and leisure is arbitrary and does not reflect the integration of work within the industry. Such arguments reflect much good common sense. Nevertheless, from an organizational point of view, it is proposed to address themes as follows:

- remuneration for work
- conditions of work
- industrial relations and trade unionism in tourism and hospitality work
- the status of work
- the nature of skills in the sector
- professionalism and the managerial function
- the image of work in the tourism and hospitality industry
- the future of work in the tourism and hospitality industry.

This agenda accords closely with the key features of an analysis by Keep and Mayhew (1999) of the characteristics of tourism, hospitality and leisure work as having:

- a tendency to low wages, except where skills shortages act to counter this;
- a prevalence of unsocial hours and family-unfriendly shift patterns;
- a rare incidence of equal opportunities policies and the domination of higher level, better paid work by males;
- poor or non-existent career structures;
- informal recruitment practices;
- failed to adopt formalized 'good practice' models of human resource management and development;
- a lack of any significant trade union presence;
- high levels of labour turnover;
- difficulties in recruitment and retention.

Remuneration for work

The popular perception of tourism, hospitality and leisure in many developed countries is that of relatively poor pay or, as Wood puts it, 'most commentators (but few employers) are agreed that the hotel and catering industry is character-ized by poor pay' (Wood 1997, p.46). This is a reflection of a number of factors:

- Popular perceptions of the tourism, hospitality and leisure industry as synonymous with its largest and, in employment terms, highest-profile sub-sector, that of hotel and catering.

- The low skills intensity within some sub-sectors, particularly hotel and catering, where, as we have already noted, a high proportion of the workforce in both developed and developing countries fall into the operative or semi-skilled and unskilled category.

- Weak internal labour-market characteristics, as we have already discussed in Chapter 3, apply within many sub-sectors of the industry in developed countries.

- Traditions of high levels of seasonal, part-time, casual and female labour in the industry in many countries, all of which serve to depress remuneration.

- Traditions of tipping and other forms of ex-gratia or unofficial benefit in kind in some sub-sectors of the tourism, hospitality and leisure industry, which serve to hold down official levels of remuneration.

- Trends towards de-skilling and technology substitution within the industry, previously discussed in Chapter 3, have an overall effect of depressing remuneration levels. The process of de-skilling is perhaps less in evidence in those countries where stronger traditions of professionalism exist, such as Switzerland and France. In the relatively cheap labour environments of most developing and transition economies, de-skilling and technology substitution have not had the same impact, except in the case of some foreign-owned businesses.

- Associated with the above, the process of standardization or McDonaldization has created McJobs that offer little challenge and demand few specialist or professional skills. Because these are jobs that anyone can do, the price payable for them in open labour-market terms has, relatively speaking, declined. Baum and Odgers (2001) depict the situation in hotel front offices where work that previously demanded a specialist college education is widely undertaken by those with a minimum of on-the-job training for its specialist skills requirements.

- Sectors of tourism, hospitality and leisure fall readily within the working experiences of a high proportion of the population in many developed countries, especially work at an operative level. Much of this work is part-time, casual and seasonal, undertaken when people are school or college students. This exposure to work in the sector is increasing with each generation, as companies such as McDonald's build their human resource policies upon transitory and young staff. Many people, therefore, have a frame of comparison for tourism and hospitality that does not exist with respect to other industries. This lack of social distance is one of the features of tourism, hospitality and leisure in many developed countries. However, because this experience was of work at the most junior and unskilled level, there is a tendency to extrapolate more generally to the whole industry on the basis of this experience.

- Public perceptions of tourism, hospitality and leisure as a sector of low pay which, in turn, becomes a self-fulfilling prophecy. Lindsay and McQuaid (2004), for example, note that 'the low pay associated with entry-level service work emerges as one of the most important factors discouraging many job seekers from considering these jobs' (p.309).

Tourism, hospitality and leisure are by no means unique in exhibiting these characteristics in terms of business structure, the skills component and dependence on other than full-time labour. These have similar consequences for pay with respect to other high-contact service industries such as the retail sector.

Initial evidence with respect to developed economies supports the contention that hotel and catering work, if not the full tourism and hospitality industry, employs its unskilled and semi-skilled employees at rates that are lower than those prevailing in other industries. As far back as 1976, a Low Pay Unit study noted that the hotel and catering industry in the United Kingdom had the highest concentration of workers earning poverty wages among all 26 major industrial groups (Low Pay Unit 1976, p.1). Taylor, Airey and Kotas (1983), in a review of evidence, find in support of the view that pay in this sector consistently falls behind that of other industries. Likewise, Byrne (1986) estimated that in 1985 the average wage in the sector fell some £60 per week behind the national average and subsequent reports affirm this situation. This situation has not substantially changed as Figure 5.1 indicates with respect to the UK. Hospitality is identified as the second most significant sector for low-paid employment in the labour market.

It is important to recognize that any comparative assessment of the pay levels of an industry sector must be set alongside an analysis of the skills that are necessary to undertake the work. As we shall see later in this chapter, assessing the skills levels of work in tourism, hospitality and leisure is not necessarily straightforward. Sturman's (2001) study in the United States argues that it is only justified in identifying a sector as low paid if is compared to other sectors with a comparable skills profile. He concludes that hospitality workers, in particular, are paid particularly poorly in relation the technical skills that the work requires. The ILO (2001) support the contention of remuneration that is generally below average in developed countries. They report that across the then-15 country European Union:

Figure 5.1

Breakdown of jobs in low-paying sectors in the UK (in thousands), September 2004

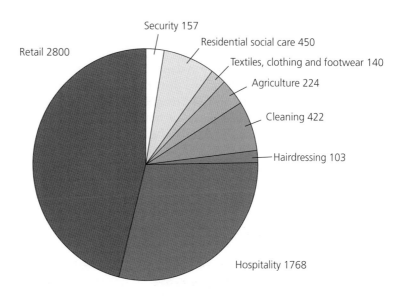

Source: Reproduced with kind permission of Low Pay Commission (2005).

Working conditions within the industry included a number of potentially problematic areas, such as irregular working hours, frequent work on Sundays, wages without a fixed basic element in 25 per cent of cases, widespread absence of overtime payments and wage levels generally 20 per cent below the European Union average. (p.4)

The ILO elaborate on this generalization with reference to Switzerland (a non-EU country) where hotel, catering and tourism workers earned about 66 per cent of average monthly pay in 1999 and the United Kingdom where a similar proportion was reported for 1998.

However, low pay is not confined to unskilled work in the industry. Wood (1997) notes that managers in catering earn some 27 per cent below average non-manual wages and non-manual employees earn 28 per cent less than the average for manual workers. In the UK, only agriculture has lower average full-time earnings than hotel and catering.

Estimates of pay levels tend to focus on basic pay as a relative indicator possibly, but by no means always, with overtime payments included. Mars and Mitchell (1976), however, point to the considerable range of additional components which need to be taken into consideration in calculating true earnings. These include additional elements within the remuneration package such as subsidized lodging, subsidized food, tips or service charges, 'fiddles' and 'knock offs', described as the total reward system. The legends within the hotel and catering sector regarding some of these 'grey' sources of supplementary earnings are fantastic but, generally, are not supported by publishable evidence. Other sub-sectors of the tourism and hospitality industry may benefit from similar additional components, notably airline cabin crew, taxi drivers in many countries and tour guides. These components can be considered in terms of the formal rewards (pay, subsidized food and lodging) which are generally accountable for tax purposes, and informal rewards which have traditionally been outside official scrutiny although, in the case of tips and service charges, this situation is changing. Tipping and 'grey economy' benefits are strongly culture-bound. In the United States, for example, tipping is accepted as a normal additional cost by most service consumers and remuneration for tipping zone positions is an anticipated component of most remuneration packages. By contrast, in many Asian countries, notably Singapore, tipping is a total taboo so much so that taxi drivers and others will be affronted at the offer of a tip. Lynn, Zinkhan and Harris (1993) note significant differences in the levels of tipping and expectations of both tippers and servers across different countries while Dirks and Rice (2004) and Lynn (2004) both point to clear differences in tipping practice across different ethnic groups in the United States and go some way to explaining this variation, based on socio-economic factors.

Lynn et al. (1993) suggest a number of reasons why consumers in tourism, hospitality and leisure tip staff for the services they receive. These include:

- desire for good service in the future
- desire for social approval
- desire to compensate servers equitably for their work and to reward effort in the service process
- desire for status and power.

Lynn *et al.* go further by suggesting that tip size is directly related to a number of factors, some of which are directly related to the people who deliver the service and their characteristics. The influencers of tip size are

- bill size
- server friendliness
- service quality
- server attractiveness – this suggests links to aesthetic and emotional labour qualities in the leverage of good tips for service
- customer gender
- dining party size
- patronage frequency
- payment method.

Both Lynn (1996) and Conlin, Lynn and Donoghue (2003) further point to the role that service staff can play in order to increase their levels of remuneration through tipping. Actions include:

- server introduction
- squatting next to table
- smiling at customers
- touching customers
- credit-card insignia on tip trays
- writing 'Thank You' on bills
- drawing a happy face on bills.

This identification of ways to increase the level of tips points to a number of things in relation to what could be seen as a servile role of front-line staff in tourism, hospitality and leisure. It suggests that ultimate levels of remuneration are linked to the ability of staff to act for or 'pander' to guests in a way that could be deemed demeaning or even humiliating in some situations and cultures. It also places considerable pressure and stress on staff in executing their role and striving to increase their pay levels. There is also the potential for role conflict in that employees may experience tension between the need to represent their organization, in their boundary-spanning role, while at the same time striving to maximize their financial benefits. Dirks and Rice (2004) look at server behaviour as a result of tipping expectations and note clear evidence of overt and covert racism by white employees when serving black guests, largely driven by perceptions and prejudices associated with their tipping behaviour. As a consequence, Friedman (2002) advocates the benefits of fixed tipping rules, as is common in some European countries through the service charge system, as a means of eliminating some of the ambiguity that can exist between customer and server and reduce the pressure on the latter to act out of their natural role.

Wood (1997) argues that there are three key concepts behind the complex system and levels of rewards that exist within tourism, hospitality and leisure. The first is the response to unpredictable demand, resulting in an inability to control the work environment in a systematic manner and consequently a tendency towards a culture of authoritarianism by management as a means of creating the necessary flexibility to cope with the variable demand. The second concept is a response to the first, the forming of individual contracts with key staff governing all aspects of the rewards system. Such contracts operate on a private basis and provide differentiation in remuneration based on local management assessment of the importance of individuals. This leads in turn to the third concept, that of core and periphery workers, which we have already addressed in Chapter 3. In many respects, core workers, especially the operative core, are those staff who benefit substantially from such individual contracts and are seen as key to the effectiveness of the operation. In part, flexible contracts are designed to counter the flexibility and autonomy that is implicit in Wood's analysis of the rewards system. However, in considering this analysis, we must also be drawn back to Riley and the weak internal labour market which is an ideal bedding ground for such practice.

While much of the published work on low pay in the tourism and hospitality industry has focused on the hotel and catering sub-sector, other areas of employment can be subjected to similar analysis. Travel agency, airline and tour operations staff, primarily young and female in profile, are frequently offered relatively poor remuneration in return for perceived attractive additional benefits, notably travel opportunities, uniforms and, generally, a pleasant working environment. This situation exists despite the relatively demanding professional and personal qualities which are required for entry. The travel sector is one of considerable disparity in terms of remuneration. Established and larger European airlines, for example, with origins or current status in state ownership, have frequently been subject to formal pay negotiations and remuneration in line with public sector norms in their respective countries. By contrast, the growing private sector airlines in Europe, generally much smaller in total size and in the type of aircraft they employ, are much more market-competitive in what they offer by way of remuneration, perhaps using perceived glamour as one means by which to depress wages, offer less security and demand more flexible working practices. Some, such as Ryanair, do not recognize trade unions for purposes of pay and other bargaining. At the same time, it should not be forgotten that the airline industry includes personnel who are among the highest-paid operational staff in the tourism and hospitality industry, namely flight crew, especially those responsible for long-haul operations and employed by major national carriers.

It is impossible to generalize about the issue of remuneration in other sub-sectors of the international tourism, hospitality and leisure industry. Some are subject to similar depressing forces to those we have discussed above, notably in the retail, leisure and entertainments areas where enterprises are frequently small in scale and subject to seasonality and similar factors. Public sector involvement in areas such as cultural and heritage tourism (for example, museums, historic sites and monuments) as well as tourism facilitation (tourist information and marketing) can have a more positive effect on pay levels, but the overall scenario is one where the majority of low skills areas are, in relative terms, poorly remunerated by contrast to the small number of highly skilled technical and administrative support staff who are employed. It is also important to recognize the role of unpaid volunteers within tourism, hospitality and leisure (see Chapter 7) who are driven not by considerations of financial remuneration but by their interest in the culture, heritage or nature that is at the heart of the organization with whom they volunteer.

As in other respects, the situation with respect to pay in developing countries cannot be analysed in exactly the same terms as have been applied to developed economies. In some countries, the majority of employment in tourism, hospitality and leisure operates on behalf of state or quasi-public enterprises and remuneration is tied to public sector norms, often relatively poor. Within the private sector of many developing countries, employment in tourism, hospitality and leisure is largely unregulated and operates within micro, often family businesses and little information is available about actual pay levels. Often a major contrast exists between employment in the local private sector and that available within foreign companies which have established as a result of the encouragement of foreign investment. The Hyatt Regency Hotel in Bishkek, Kyrgyzstan, offers pay rates that are in the order of 50 to 75 per cent higher than comparable jobs within the local private sector. As a result, they are able to attract personnel with educational and professional backgrounds who would not normally work within the sector.

The evidence with respect to pay levels in the international tourism, hospitality and leisure industry therefore is inconclusive. In some sub-sectors there is little doubt that average pay at unskilled and semi-skilled levels is below that in comparable industrial sectors. Devine and Baum (2005), for example, found that hotel front-office workers (88 per cent of whom were female) were, on average, paid just over the national minimum wage and well below the regional average across all industrial sectors. The challenge of a minimum wage in many tourism, hospitality and leisure businesses is that the setting of minimum levels of remuneration is seen purely as the 'going rate' for entry-level positions (Harris 2003). This ensures that a substantial number of workers in the sector are among the poorest paid in the community within which they live.

At the same time, remuneration is clearly linked to the level of professional tradition that exists in the industry. For example, there is a long-held view that aspects of hotel and catering work in Switzerland and France have traditions and status which are totally absent in the United Kingdom and that this is reflected in the relative remuneration of these jobs. This assessment is probably true for local, Swiss employees but does not necessarily apply with respect to the large number of migrant workers who are employed in tourism, hospitality and leisure in these countries.

Levels of pay are clearly linked to market demand for the skills on offer and, as Riley's weak internal labour market suggests, the skills required for many tourism and hospitality jobs are relatively easily and cheaply accessible in the marketplace. At the same time, skills shortages in some areas mean that remuneration is highly competitive and attractive, and we should not forget the minority in the industry who are paid at levels which are on a par with or in excess of those available in many other industrial sectors. Change, with regard to the low pay status of much work in tourism, hospitality and leisure, is, in theory, forced upon employers as a result of market forces rather than altruism. Lindsay and McQuaid (2004) rightly conclude that:

> Where job seekers' reluctance to consider working in services instead reflects a more basic concern regarding levels of pay (concerns that are quite justified in

many areas of the service economy) employers may eventually have to address their strategies in this area, if they wish to be able to draw labour from the deepest possible pool. (p.310)

Low pay will remain an issue in tourism, hospitality and leisure in developed countries as the sector has been successful in circumventing the impact of demographic change and the pressures of a tight labour market through the importation of a significant migrant workforce. Poor pay is hardly conducive to fostering a working environment which is customer focused and which supports organizational citizenship and empowerment in the sense that we discussed in Chapter 4. Whether customer demand for enhanced product and service quality will impose the need for increased service skills on the industry remains to be seen. This represents another conundrum for which there is no immediate resolution.

Conditions in the tourism, hospitality and leisure workplace

Discussion of remuneration in the context of tourism, hospitality and leisure work cannot take place in isolation from the conditions within which such pay is earned. By conditions we mean a wide-ranging array of factors which contribute to the overall working environment and, therefore, to the motivation or demotivation of employees. Thus a discussion of conditions in relation to the international tourism, hospitality and leisure industry includes consideration of factors such as the physical working environment and its safety, the physical and mental demands of the job, job security, holiday and other leave entitlements, other rights, entitlements and benefits, hours of work, the nature of work shifts, and the social contribution of work. In most countries, aspects of these conditions are regulated by legislation at a national level and, within the European Union, on the basis of EU law. Such areas normally include paid holiday entitlements, physical working conditions, health and safety matters, maternity rights and equal opportunities. Generally speaking, such conditions operate at a different level, if at all, for part-time, temporary/seasonal and casual employees than is applicable with respect to full-time staff. This differentiation in the levels of entitlement and protection is of particular importance within the tourism, hospitality and leisure industry because of the high and increasing incidence of working patterns other than full-time and permanent. A consideration of conditions, therefore, includes a range of factors which affect work and its appeal and status, as well as the legal framework within which such factors are permitted or restricted.

Popular perception of work in tourism and hospitality is undoubtedly influenced, again, by the situation that pertains in hotels and catering businesses. The main drawbacks, in the eyes of those working in the sector are:

- long and difficult hours
- many jobs are dirty
- it's very hard work
- monotonous, boring work
- on feet a lot.

Orwell's account of aspects of hotel work during the 1930s certainly paints a picture of hard, dirty and poorly paid toil undertaken by casual employees with few rights and no security, and subject to the whims and bullying of the permanent employees. Seventy years later, Schlosser's (2001) description of the work undertaken by a 16-year-old girl employed by McDonald's in the United States has more features that are in common with Orwell than are different. Likewise, Adler and Adler (2004) talk about the work expected of relatively unskilled hotel workers in the resort 'paradise' of Hawaii and conclude that much of what operative staff are expected to undertake is heavy, dirty, repetitive and poorly paid, notwithstanding the wonderful surroundings experienced by their guests.

In common with remuneration, conditions of work are, undoubtedly, influenced by industry characteristics and labour-market factors, and there are certainly tendencies in some sectors to respond to this environment by extracting the maximum by way of productivity from the workforce, while giving the minimum in terms of added benefits. The ILO's (1989) assessment of this situation is as follows:

> It would not be appropriate to characterize the entire hotel, catering and tourism sector as subject to precarious work arrangements. Many enterprises offer excellent conditions and have been able to find ways to reconcile their needs for flexibility with stable and well-protected forms of employment. There are, however, strong pressures which affect many if not most employers and workers. (ILO 1989, p.3)

However, despite the existence of minimum pay regulations in many countries, there is also pressure in many countries to maintain a degree of deregulation with respect to the work environment, in view of the pressures of variable demand and business structure. Legislation in developed countries concerning conditions of work dates back to child employment regulation in the nineteenth century and has been extended to include a range of entitlements and benefits which are largely unquestioned, in principle, in the working environment of most developed countries, although they are matters of concern and exploitation in some developing nations. Where debate and dispute does arise is in relation to the extent of such entitlements and benefits as well as their range and coverage (e.g. whether to include part-time and casual staff).

Certain sectors of tourism, hospitality and leisure are subject to the very stringent enforcement of regulations that are specific to the industry, for example working hours per shift and per day. Airline pilots are a good example, although such regulation is born, primarily, out of consideration for passenger safety. Other transportation sectors are subject to similar, if perhaps not so stringent, regulation; although such control may be widely abused as it has been with long-distance coach drivers for whom restrictions were only introduced in response to a number of fatal accidents involving tourists. Likewise, the demands of specific hygiene legislation affects the working environment and conditions of work of all food workers in the tourism, hospitality and leisure industry, although the level of enforcement varies greatly between different countries. The main focus of regulation, in both of these areas, is not generally on the enhancement of the working lives of those employed in the tourism and hospitality industry but on the health and safety of the consumer. However, the counter-experience can be cited with respect to the ban on smoking in restaurants and bars in Ireland where the legislation was introduced in order to protect those working in the industry from the injurious effects of passive smoking (Hearns 2004; McNabb and Hearns 2005).

Other aspects affecting conditions of work are subject to general legislative control, for example employment rights which protect employees from race or sexual discrimination, an area of considerable variance between different countries. In many developing countries, such legislation does not exist or is widely ignored. Likewise, maternity rights, sick pay entitlements and retirement benefits apply as they would in other industrial sectors. However, the regulation of the working environment beyond that affecting health and safety, especially of the consumer, is a highly contentious issue and the subject of dispute.

On the one hand, there are those subscribing to the liberal tradition emanating from authorities such as the nineteenth-century writer Adam Smith, who argue that deregulation of work, in all possible areas, is conducive to more effective competition in the marketplace and will, therefore, force companies to enhance the working environment as a competitive strategy to attract and retain the skills they require in order to carry out work. The liberal argument sees regulation beyond the very minimum necessary to ensure health and safety as restrictive on competitive trade. In the context of tourism, hospitality and leisure, in the European Union, for example, provisions of the Social Chapter which address such regulation, will, according to this argument, have the effect of increasing the cost of products and services so that they are no longer price-competitive with those provided by destinations outside of the EU, such as North Africa, Turkey and further afield in the Far East and the Caribbean. Alternatively, companies will seek to remain competitive and respond to what are seen as the increased costs of regulation by limiting the numbers that are employed, thus threatening product and service standards and, in turn, international competitiveness.

On the other hand, the counter, social reformist argument seeks to limit exploitation in the workplace, especially of those least able to protect themselves – the least educated, lowest skilled and poorest paid members of the workforce. Given the employment structure of some sub-sectors of international tourism, hospitality and leisure, such protection has direct implications for the working environment. The social reformist argument is founded, primarily, on concerns for social justice and a reduction of what is seen as exploitation in the workplace. Poor management is frequently blamed for failing to develop creative alternatives to the worst excesses of long and unsocial hours, repetitive and unrewarding work routines and related problems. Liberals argue for better conditions in the workplace, certainly, but in their view the impetus for change must be driven by the private sector's recognition of the benefits of good employment practices which in turn will reap rewards through enhanced productivity, quality and competitiveness.

Social reformists question the will or ability of, in particular, labour-intensive and low-skills industries such as many sectors of tourism and hospitality to self-regulate and doubt that the workings of the market can provide real workplace solutions. They argue that government regulation is the only means by which to achieve uniform minimum good practice and, eventually, real change. In some countries of Europe, a key aspect of transnational legislation relating to the working environment has been the object of the most focused opposition by lobbyists representing tourism, hospitality and leisure. The first of these relates to working time, in particular the total working week which is proposed at 48 hours per week, and restrictions on unsocial working hours, especially at night. The argument against such provision is that, given demand fluctuation, it is impossible to operate within tourism and hospitality on the basis of such categorical restriction. In highly seasonal tourist destination areas of, for example, northern Norway, the west of Ireland and some Greek islands, the cycle of business is such that over 80 per cent of turnover may be generated in two to three summer months and it is not realistic or cost effective to guarantee a maximum working week during the short peak period. Increased hours at these times are compensated for by slack periods at other times during the season. Likewise, a tourism, hospitality and leisure business needs the facilities to respond to unexpected demand, for example an unplanned coach party staying in a hotel, and to utilize its staff resources to cater for the group accordingly. Such arguments are sustainable but there is evidence that the industry does not always meet its side of the bargain and that, for example, consequent overtime commitments are not met in full. One response by the tourism and hospitality industry to the threat of regulation in this area has been to increase dependence on part-time labour, who are less affected by the 'upper ceiling' restriction of 48 hours, although this trend is also motivated by cost factors.

> The employment of part-time, temporary and casual workers, far from being peripheral to productivity, was central to it. Part-time, temporary and casual workers allowed employers to specify labour demands aligned more closely to product demands within the organization than to pressures arising from the external labour market. In this way, labour can be purchased almost on an 'as-needed' or 'just-in-time' basis. (Walsh 1991, p.113)

Casual work largely remains outside some of the provisions of employment protection measures. Much of such work is on what appears to be a self-employed basis but, in fact, may reflect casual, commission-based arrangements. A variety of working activities, all of which service tourists, can fall into this category, including street and beach vendors, timeshare salespersons and unlicensed taxi operatives as well as entertainers and prostitutes. In many countries, these 'grey' sub-sectors of the tourism, hospitality and leisure economy are of considerable significance in both value and employment terms but people working in these areas are frequently subject to exploitation and do not have any employment rights or protection in legal terms.

Legislation only addresses matters relating to part of the overall macro working environment in the tourism, hospitality and leisure industry although the impact is felt at shop-floor level. Working conditions are also affected by a range of formal and informal arrangements within the workplace and many of these stem from the fundamental attitude and commitment of management and owners to the staff that work with them. In Chapter 4, we introduced the concept of internal marketing and addressed the link between using people as a valued resource and the achievement of quality products and excellence in service delivery. If staff are perceived to be assets as opposed to taking the traditional view that they are costs, it should follow that the working environment should be designed to facilitate their needs and requirements in so far as this is compatible with maximizing customer satisfaction and achieving general business objectives. Thus working hours and shifts, for example, can be designed to acknowledge personal and lifestyle requirements of staff rather than, as has traditionally been the case, reflecting solely employer needs. Restaurants and other facilities for the internal customer can be designed using the same principles as those which would apply to facilities for the external customer, rather than the practice which is frequently found in the industry. Long-term commitment to staff can be demonstrated by share and profit participation and similar involvement measures.

The issue of conditions in the workplace within international tourism, hospitality and leisure is also one where generalizations are difficult to make given the diverse range of traditions and practice at national levels, as well as the wide variety between sub-sectors. Some areas of work in the industry offer conditions that would be deemed attractive in comparison with many alternative occupational environments, for example providing travel and related benefits that would generally be perceived as compensating for other negative aspects of work. Other jobs are, undoubtedly, repetitive and physically demanding, required at unsocial times and providing little by way of security or opportunity. In considering conditions of work, as with many issues in the human resource arena, we need to avoid sweeping generalizations because of this diversity. However, it is also important to recognize that existing and potential employees in the tourism, hospitality and leisure industry have increasing expectations of the workplace in terms of its rewards and benefits in the widest sense and the industry will need to recognize these expectations in order to compete successfully for labour. Sub-standard staff accommodation, poor meals, split shifts and dislocated social lives are examples of tangible and intangible manifestations of poor conditions which many businesses in the tourism and hospitality industry need to address. In terms of the underlying theme of this book, acceptance and perpetuation of such poor conditions represent the traditional or non-sustainable human resource management model. The needs and expectations of employees, especially young people, will only be met through human resource practices which are in accord with the sustainable paradigm.

There is little doubt that, today, employees are much more aware of their rights and entitlements in tourism, hospitality and leisure than might have been the case in the past. At the same time, they are more likely to seek a balance between working and non-working life. Staff expect better pay and conditions of service as their lifestyle and standard of living expectations are influenced by societal patterns and trends. These sources of expectation have in common the need to devise systems and methods which will facilitate improvements in productivity. The enabling mechanism for productivity improvements is a well-motivated workforce. This means that the employee expects the employer to provide a working environment that is pleasant and to offer opportunities to grow and develop, to be trained and to be promoted within the organization.

If such conditions do not prevail, employees in developed economies, especially those where choice exists in the workplace, are likely to vote with their feet. There is considerable evidence that the tourism, hospitality and leisure workplace is subject to high levels of turnover and that retention is perceived to be a problem in some sectors of the industry. The ILO (2001) describe turnover rates in some countries and regions as 'alarming' (p.5) and quote 1997 figures for the United States of 51.7 per cent for front-line employees, 11.9 per cent for supervisors and 13.5 per cent for managers. In the United Kingdom, the turnover rate of 42 per cent is second only to retail within the national economy. Figures noted by Asia are in the region of 30 per cent, rising to more than 50 per cent in Hong Kong. The ILO consider the causes of employee turnover and note that:

> Employers' representatives generally consider that turnover in the industry should be attributed to the essentially transient nature of part of the workforce, namely students, young mothers and young people as a whole, as well as the general difficulty in retaining staff. Employees, on the other hand, frequently cite low pay as a reason for changing employment, although lack of a career structure and benefits would appear to be of even greater importance. (ILO 2001, p.6)

High levels of employee turnover are widely cited as a problem in tourism, hospitality and leisure. This is clearly not always the case as there are circumstances, such as in the use of high-energy, well-educated student labour, when inevitable turnover is acceptable. Likewise, seasonal demand variation does impose considerable pressures on the sustainability of employment offered, although this may not be a problem as many working on a seasonal basis may not be looking for longer-term opportunities because they will be returning to school of college at the end of the season. High turnover, however, does have implications for the sustained quality of product and service that can be offered to customers and the training programmes that are in place to ensure consistency in spite of labour turnover. The use of technology in support of training through in-house or in-store interactive training programmes in pizza making, room servicing or customer care can assist in reducing the impact of high turnover in some workplaces. Generally, high labour turnover has added to pressures to standardize or McDonaldize production and service processes and to eliminate opportunity for the use of high-end skills and innovation.

Workplace relations in tourism, hospitality and leisure

In part, the industrial relations climate in the international tourism, hospitality and leisure industry is governed by the legislative framework within which it operates. Thus laws relating to health and safety, the employment of children, the physical working environment and, increasingly, other areas as well, provide the framework within which many of the relationships between companies, management and their employees are formalized and in most developed countries are not overtly abused. However, even this framework is subject to extreme pressure in some tourism, hospitality and leisure businesses, especially those of a highly seasonal nature operating to tight profit margins and, particularly, those in developing countries.

The counterweight in industrial relations to the effects of poor pay and conditions in the tourism, hospitality and leisure industry is frequently the role played by trade unions. As in other areas within the human resource environment in tourism, hospitality and leisure, it is difficult to generalize when discussing the level of trade union membership and the impact that such organization has on an international or cross-sectoral basis. Certainly in the tourism industry in the United Kingdom in general, and in the hotel industry in particular, trade union membership is put at as low as 6 per cent of the total workforce (Wood 1997). A number of other sectors are not unionized to any significant degree at all, notably fast food and non-hotel accommodation. By contrast, the hotel industry in Germany has a much stronger tradition of union membership and the relationship between employers and unions, especially in their partnership in support of education and training, is testimony to this. Likewise, airlines and other transport staff from what remains or used to be within the public sector have a much stronger tradition of union representation. Staff in Great Southern Hotels in Ireland, a state-owned company, have operated with reasonable protection from trends that have impacted on the workforces of other operations, in part because of the recognition of their trade union. However, the major downsizing of airlines in Europe and the United States since 2001 has seen trade unions largely powerless to resist major redundancies or diminution of pay and conditions in the face of economic pressures and a desire to avoid the total collapse of the carriers in question.

There are a number of reasons why trade union membership is, relatively speaking, low in the tourism, hospitality and leisure sectors of developed countries. These are substantially drawn from weak labour-market characteristics and the operating features of the sector, both of which we have addressed earlier. They can be summarized to include:

- the geographical dispersement and fragmentation of the sector, which makes organization difficult;
- the importance of part-time, casual and seasonal labour in the industry, groupings of the workforce which traditionally have been of little interest to trade unions and whose conditions probably demand the most urgent address;
- the high level of female employment in the industry, a group that has traditionally not been active in trade unions;
- the importance of ethnic minority and immigrant groups to the industry, especially at low or unskilled levels. These groups are low in union participation but may also be under some pressure regarding their status and thus be reluctant to 'get involved' in protecting rights and enhancing conditions;
- employee conservatism and a consequent reluctance to join trade unions which, in part, reflects historic workplace relationships in the sector, linked to a notion that service may be incompatible with the ethos of traditional trade unionism;
- high labour turnover which means that few workers remain in a job long enough to join;
- the frequently active hostility of employers and managers to union membership; and
- the historical isolation of employees in the sector from the mainstream of the labour movement. At the root of this distinction is the notion of servitude

and the implicit devaluation of personal worth that is attached to it, or what Riley (1985, p.101) calls 'the distance of serfdom'.

Within this environment, trade unionism has had major problems in making significant headway in terms of membership or support in many areas of the tourism, hospitality and leisure industry. At the same time, a general erosion of trade union influence in many developed countries since the early 1980s has not been a good backcloth against which to alter this situation. It is reasonable speculation to suggest that in those areas of the international tourism, hospitality and leisure industry where trade unions remain relatively strong, this strength is likely to be challenged as a result of globalization, privatization and competition from migrant labour.

The status of work in tourism, hospitality and leisure

The status of work in tourism, hospitality and leisure is clearly linked to the social composition of employment within the sector. In this, some sub-sectors of the industry have much in common with other, highly labour-intensive and low-skills areas of the service economy. In many respects, we are once again faced with an unbroken circle. The perceived low status of work in the industry in many developed countries means that employers fail to attract the level of skills and ambition that they desire and, as we have seen, employ workers from social groupings that are frequently perceived to be low status and marginalized within that society. This employee profile in turn fuels external perceptions of the status of work within the industry as an environment of poor conditions, remuneration and limited opportunity. We must, of course, treat this generalization with some caution because there are areas of work in tourism and hospitality that carry perceptions of high status in relation to professional and skills criteria as well as in terms of glamour and excitement. In addition, perceptions are by no means homogeneous across all countries.

Status is affected both by the sub-sector of the industry in which work is undertaken and by the nature of the responsibilities held. The airline business, *per se*, has higher employment status attributes than restaurant or retail work, and this differentiation applies to the relative status of comparable roles and skill areas between the various sub-sectors. For example, airline cabin crew generally have higher status in terms of general public perception than service staff on trains, long-distance coaches or in family-style restaurants, although arguably a substantial proportion of their work requires very similar technical and social skills. Admittedly, there are what are seen as glamour attributes and attendant benefits attached to airline work which is denied to the other groupings but this alone cannot account for the relative gap in perceived status.

Wood (1993) considers relative status within the hotel and catering industry and provides a typological classification which is useful in considering the determinants of status or lack of status within the tourism and hospitality industry in general. Wood's typology identifies three 'status markers', which place work activities in categories according to their perceived status.

First, symbolic status markers include such considerations as whether workers were uniformed, which normally accorded lower status. Or were engaged in 'dirty work', which also conferred lower status ... Second, locational status markers include whether workers were, by virtue of their job, in a position to gain direct access to clients. This position was important in procuring informal rewards such as tips, or determining whether workers occupy positions that gave them the chances to obtain other illicit rewards by petty theft of monies and commodities. The degree of access to such rewards was likely to influence status; the higher the access or reward, the higher the status ... Finally, there were skill status markers. Jobs perceived as entailing low levels of technical skills were generally accorded lower status – a commonplace social phenomenon made curious in the hospitality industry context by the fact that the corollary (i.e. that comparatively more highly skilled jobs attracted higher status) appeared to be true only when considered relative to the wider occupational structure. (Wood 1993, p.9)

This final point about skill status markers requires some further elaboration. It is worth noting the traditional higher status of skilled employees who have transferable and generic skills, such as front-office staff, to those with industry-specific technical skills, such as serving staff or chefs. It is, therefore, possible to subdivide the skill status marker category into general skill markers and industry-specific skill markers. This principle probably extends to other sectors of the tourism, hospitality and leisure industry. Engineers with generic and transferable skills will attract higher status than those whose skills are specific to aircraft maintenance alone.

The status of employment in different sub-sectors of the tourism, hospitality and leisure industry, as well as the relative status of specific jobs within sub-sectors, varies between cultures and countries. Such variation is related to a number of factors, including:

- the importance of tourism, hospitality and leisure to the overall economy of the country or region and the consequent significance of the industry's employment generating capacity. Where such dependence is high, as it is in countries of the Mediterranean or in Thailand, for example, and alternative employment opportunities are limited, relative status to that of other economic sectors is likely to be enhanced;

- the extent to which the personal service nature of much tourism, hospitality and leisure work is associated with the issue of servility in a particular culture will also impact upon its status;

- the degree to which particular work areas have succeeded in 'professionalizing' their image in also important. The rise of the personal trainer in the fitness industry, for example, is an example where image has been elevated beyond that of their counterparts in the wider fitness industry who do not have the attribute of individual, professional association with their clients;

- tourism, hospitality and leisure work may also attract higher status in societies where participation levels by males are high and those of women, minorities and migrant labour are low;

- the participation rate in post-compulsory education is also a factor that can impact upon the status of work in tourism, hospitality and leisure. Where such participation is high, the perceived low-skills demands of much employment in the industry are such that for a significant proportion of young people they see themselves as over-qualified for such work and this contributes to the overall perception of status. Where post-compulsory education participation rates are lower, a significantly higher proportion of the school-leaving population will see tourism, hospitality and leisure as a career option and thus the relative status of the industry will be higher;

- perceived skills levels are a further influencing factor. In countries and localities where traditional and frequently labour-intensive skills are still practised to their full, the status of employment in areas such as the hotel kitchen is likely to remain higher than it is in environments where the process of de-skilling has reduced the technical and creative demands and, as a consequence, the status of such work;

- status is also influenced by the extent to which regulation is imposed upon access to work in the industry. Switzerland, for example, requires specific qualifications in order to work in certain management and skills areas in the hotel industry and this contributes to the status of such work; and

- traditions and culture are also important status determinants. The rise of the media chef in many countries with celebrity status may have the effect of enhancing the status of some work areas in the sector.

These status markers in many respects accord with Riley's differentiation of strong and weak internal labour markets which we introduced in Chapter 3. High status, therefore, can in part be associated with the relative strength of the internal labour market, whereas any measures or trends which weaken the internal labour market will in turn serve to reduce the status of the work area in question.

A low skills sector?

Much tourism, hospitality and leisure work is widely characterized in both the popular press and in research-based academic sources as dominated by a low-skills profile (Shaw and Williams 1994; Westwood 2002). Bradley *et al.* (2000) apply this epithet to the wider service or new economy in questioning assumptions about a skills revolution in Britain, noting that 'jobs commonly retain a low-skill character, especially in the fastest-growing sectors' (p.129). These descriptors for the sector are used in a broad-brush manner, without consideration of the diversity of employment that exists across what we have already seen is anything but a homogeneous sector. Consideration of the work of museum curators, signature chefs, airline pilots and sports physiologists points to some of the areas of work which are frequently ignored in generalized blandishments about tourism, hospitality and leisure.

Burns (1997) questions the basis for categorizing such employment into 'skilled' and 'unskilled' categories, arguing the postmodernist case that this separation is something of a social construct. This construct is rooted in, first, manpower planning paradigms for the manufacturing sector and, second, in the traditional power of trade unions to control entry into the workplace through lengthy apprenticeships. Burns bases this argument on a useful consideration of the definition of skills in hospitality, noting that:

> the different sectors that comprise tourism-as-industry take different approaches to their human resources, and that some of these difference ... are due to whether or not the employees have a history of being 'organised' (either in terms of trade unions or staff associations with formalised communication procedures) (p.240)

This strong internal labour-market analysis leads Burns to argue that skills within 'organized' sectors such as airlines and hotel companies with clearly defined staff relationship structures, such as Sheraton, are recognized and valued. By contrast, catering and fast food 'operate within a business culture where labour is seen in terms of costs which must be kept at the lowest possible level' (p.240) and where skills, therefore, are not valued or developed. Burns's definition of hospitality skills seeks to go beyond the purely technical capabilities that those using 'unskilled' or 'low skills' descriptors assume. He draws upon Ritzer's drama analogy for the service workplace to argue that:

> Working in such an environment requires more than an ability to operate a cash register; emotional demands are made of employees to constantly be in a positive, joyful and even playful mood. An ability to cope with such demands must be recognised as a 'skill' *par excellence.* (p.240)

This case is also argued by Poon (1993) who notes that new employees in hospitality 'Must be trained to be loyal, flexible, tolerant, amiable and responsible ... at every successful tourism establishment, it is the employees that stand out ... Technology cannot substitute for welcoming employees' (p.262).

Burns's emphasis on 'emotional demands' as an additional dimension of hospitality skills has been developed in the work of Seymour (2000). Her work builds upon the seminal earlier work of Hochschild (1983) who introduced the concept of emotional work within the services economy. Hochschild argues that service employees are required to manage their emotions for the benefit of customers and are, in part, paid to do this. Likewise, Seymour considers the contribution of what she calls 'emotional labour' makes to work in fast food and traditional areas of service work and concludes that both areas demand considerable emotional elements in addition to overt technical skills. Bryman (2004) defines 'emotional labour' as relating to:

> Employment situations in which workers as part of their work roles need to convey emotions and preferably to appear as though those emotions are deeply held ... [emotions] that are supposed to make the recipient of the emotional labour feel good about the worker and the organization for which he or she works. (p.104)

The expectations of emotional labour add significantly to the skills demands of work in tourism, hospitality and leisure. There are few areas of front-line or boundary-spanning work in tourism, hospitality and leisure that do not have a very evident and, in some cases, all-important emotional dimension. In many respects, as Bryman notes with respect to Disney, employees are expected to give the appearance of enjoying their work as much as visitors are enjoying their time in the theme park. Maintaining this emotional façade in working conditions that are, often, anything but conducive to such behaviour takes its toll and requires skill and extensive training in order to be maintained. The farewell from airline crew at the end of a 12-hour flight is expected to be every bit as cheery and interested as the initial greeting at departure. Blythman (2004) discusses the problems that such demands present in the context of supermarket work:

> After several hours at a time, any urge to be cheery or pleasant was overtaken by an all-pervasive, mind-numbing blankness. I began to feel spaced out, as though dulled by drugs. Any energy I might feel at the start of a shift soon ebbed away ... Even if you wanted to try to be pleasant with people, after only so long it was impossible to keep it up. (p.131)

Bryman (2004) specifically refers to the problems of delivering emotional labour in the hotel sector where front-line staff (generally female) are expected to remain friendly and provide assistance to guests (frequently male) who, at the same time, may be acting in an obnoxious manner. In any other working context, these staff would probably be protected by rules and laws designed to prevent sexual harassment.

To the requirements of emotional labour in tourism, hospitality and leisure can be added the skills demands of what Warhurst *et al.* (2000) describe as aesthetic labour, the skills required to look, sound and behave in a manner that is compatible with the requirements of the job and with the expectations of your customers. In many cases, aesthetic labour involves staff demonstrating the ability to respond to fashion and trend imperatives in the consumer marketplace in a way that is socially exclusive of many groups and cultures within society. Aesthetic labour is about appearance but can also be underpinned by cultural cache, the ability of front-line staff to understand and engage culturally with their customers on terms dictated by the latter. Thus, service staff in some tourism, hospitality and leisure contexts (luxury hotels, premium airline cabins, fitness centres, one-to-one golf or other sports tuition) need to be able to make informed conversation with their guests or clients about politics, music, sport and almost any other imaginable topic, often from an international perspective. This requirement presupposes a certain level of prior education and cultural exposure as well as a commitment to remain up to date in these areas.

Therefore, Burns is right to argue that the low-skills perspective of tourism, hospitality and leisure is context-specific and is drawn from a Western-centric view of hospitality work. He cites the inappropriateness of these assumptions when applied to environments such as the Soloman Islands, Sri Lanka and the Cook Islands. Likewise, this author has questioned (Baum 1996a; 2002a) the validity of claims that hospitality is a work area of low skills. This argument is based on the cultural assumptions that lie behind employment in Westernized, international hospitality work whereby technical skills are defined in terms of a relatively seamless progression from domestic and consumer life into the hospitality workplace. In the developing world, such assumptions cannot be made as employees join hospitality businesses without Western acculturation, without knowledge of the implements and ingredients of Western cookery, for example. Learning at a technical level, therefore is considerably more demanding than it might be in Western communities. Social and interpersonal skills also demand considerably more by way of prior learning, whether this pertains to language skills (the ability to speak English is a widespread prerequisite for hospitality work in countries such as Thailand) or wider cultural communications. On the basis of this argument, it is contended that work that may be unskilled in the Europe and the USA requires significant investment in terms of education and training elsewhere and cannot, therefore, be universally described as 'low skilled'. This issue is one that is beginning to assume significance in Western Europe as a combination of service sector labour shortages and growing immigration from countries of Eastern Europe and elsewhere means that skills assumptions in hospitality can no longer be taken for granted. The current hospitality labour market in the Republic of Ireland illustrates this situation where service standards are under challenge as the industry recruits staff from a wide range of former Eastern Bloc countries. A government-sponsored response has been to organize special training programmes of three months' duration for new workers from Poland and Russia.

An important feature of skills within tourism, hospitality and leisure is the range of capabilities that a diverse sector can accommodate. The sector is one that provides opportunities that range from senior global business management through to work that is within the capability of people with a range of physical and learning disabilities (Baum 1995). This is a theme upon which we will elaborate in Chapter 7.

It is also useful, in summary of this section of the debate, to consider tourism, hospitality and leisure work in the light of the work of Noon and Blyton (1995). Their approach is to consider skills in terms of personal attributes, job requirements and the setting of work. This approach, with a focus on the context of work, from both an individual and an organizational point of view, is much more sympathetic to the realities of diversity within hospitality work, as argued above by Burns and Baum. Noon and Blyton appear to accept that what is skilled work in one context may be less so in another, influenced by both the cultural context of the work and also by the availability and application of technology. It is argued, therefore, that a simple labelling of hospitality work as 'unskilled' is both unhelpful and unjustifiable.

Professionalism and the managerial function in tourism, hospitality and leisure

The notion of professionalism in the international tourism, hospitality and leisure industry is one that is closely allied to that of status. The term 'professional' in most uses implies a certain status association, although in some uses such as in sport it may also have somewhat pejorative connotations. In this regard, then, the extent to which work is deemed professional' will be linked to Riley's labour market characteristics – a strong internal labour market such as that found in medicine is likely to have definite associations with high professional status. This in turn has links to issues of remuneration, conditions of employment and the nature of the work carried out and also to the ability of the industry to compete for scarce skills at a managerial and senior technical level. In the United States, the National Labor Relations Board defines a 'professional employee' as:

> any employee engaged in work (i) predominantly intellectual and varied in character as opposed to routine mental, manual, mechanical or physical work; (ii) involving the consistent exercise of discretion and judgement in its performance; (iii) of such character that the output produced or the result accomplished cannot be standardized in relation to a given period of time; (iv) requiring knowledge of an advanced type in a field of science or learning customarily acquired by a long course of specialized intellectual instruction and study in an institution of higher learning or a hospital, as distinguished from a general academic education or from an apprenticeship or from training in their performance of routine mental, manual, or physical processes. (Keiser and Swinton 1988, p.24)

In the context of tourism, hospitality and leisure in other countries, notably in Europe, professionalism goes further than the issue of status. At the level of management and skilled technicians, it includes consideration of a wide range of associated matters such as aspirations and career progression, training and development opportunities, adherence to collective norms and codes of behaviour, and role and attitudes in relation to front-line and operative staff. Thus professionalism can be taken to include personal attributes, attributes of the grouping of employees in the collective sense, and behavioural factors in the way that managers in particular relate to others. In what appears to be one of the few detailed studies of professionalism across the tourism, hospitality and leisure industry, Sheldon (1989, p.494) identifies 12 dimensions of professionalism based on a review of published literature sources, primarily US in origin. These dimensions focus mainly on the personal and collective aspects of professionalism although behavioural considerations may be implicit in them. In the order of importance, based on literature references, they are:

- long training/education (university, college);
- code of ethics (for those within the professional grouping);
- organized (through a professional association such as the Hotel and Catering International Management Association (HCIMA) or the Tourism Society in the United Kingdom);
- complex occupation (the level and range of tasks required);
- altruistic service (focused on customer service needs);
- body or corpus of knowledge (such as that prepared by the HCIMA for hotel management);
- people orientated (in terms of job descriptions and other overt manifestations of people as opposed to product orientation);
- licensed (requirement to obtain a specific licence to practise);
- high prestige (the most obvious link to status);
- competence tested (formal skills and competence testing as a requirement for practice or for promotion);

- self-employed;
- high income (relative to other professional occupations) (Sheldon 1989).

These dimensions reflect attributes which are close to Riley's strong internal labour market features and, as a consequence, absence of professionalism can be linked to a weak internal labour market. On this basis, professionalism could be added as a further dimension to the labour-market model. Sheldon's analysis of professionalism takes a perspective which includes all positions or jobs within the various sub-sectors of tourism, hospitality and leisure. While it may be meaningful to discuss the professional execution of work at the operative, semi-skilled and unskilled levels in the industry, and even at skilled craft level, in reality her criteria are more likely to have application at management and senior technical/master craftsperson level. The professional execution of work at other levels is not generally associated with the institutional framework for professionalism which features in the 12 dimensions. Thus, this notion of professionalism has relevance in terms of various management areas within tourism, hospitality and leisure as well as with respect to such areas as airline pilots, chefs, sommeliers and museum curators. The formal vestiges of professionalism vary from area to area and by country, and in most cases active commitment to the implications of professionalism is a matter for a minority of those eligible for involvement. The various associations which represent groupings of those employed in the industry are generally speaking limited in impact. In this respect, the attributes and consequences of the weak labour market operate against effective collective, professional identity. A lack of formally recognized professionalism in many sub-sectors of the industry in turn serves to perpetuate the recruitment difficulties that the industry experiences in competition with opportunities in other professions.

One possible dimension of professionalism which Sheldon does not consider and which appears to have relevance in the context of tourism, hospitality and leisure management in many countries relates to the extent to which managers perceive their role overlapping with operational functions and how they allocate time to their work in reflection of this. This is an aspect of functional flexibility but also has links to traditions in some sub-sectors of the industry, notably hotels and restaurants, whereby the education, training and early career paths of managers have included considerable exposure to craft and operational work. Wood (1997) describes this process as a form of 'pre-entry socialization into the occupation of hotel management', which is justified 'in terms of the need for managers in the hospitality industry to possess vital technical skills, particularly in the field of food and beverage management, that allows them the opportunity to control other powerful work groups such as chefs' (pp.106–107).

The traditions of hotel and restaurant management education and training in France, Germany and Switzerland, among other European countries, also demonstrate the importance accorded to the development of practical skills. This is a model that has been substantially replicated in many developing countries, as a result of development aid projects that have sought to replicate what is common practice in the developed world uncritically in recipient locations. There is also a tendency for managers to seek solace in the operational aspects of work. In a study of hotel managers in Ireland, Baum (1989a, 1989b) found that many of the sample placed considerable emphasis on both their visibility and 'mine host' responsibilities and on their ability to pull their weight in areas such as the kitchen, banqueting room or front desk as required. Likewise, Keating and Harrington (2005), in a study of hotel middle managers in Ireland, talk about the role conflict this group face when expected to implement strategic change (in this case, service quality initiatives) while, at the same time, perceiving their roles primarily in terms of the operational needs of their functional departments. The small-business nature of much work in tourism, hospitality and leisure is such that management, in many operations, must be eclectic and multi-functional, and the attraction of the practical is, in part, a reflection of this. In terms of professionalism, the facility for seamless movement between operational and managerial functions reflects weak internal labour-market characteristics. The absence of such functional mobility as well as clear job demarcation between operational and managerial tasks are much more akin to the strong internal labour market.

However, execution of practical skills is not now a priority competence for hotels recruiting newly qualified graduates, at least not among larger establishments. Baum and Odgers (2001) show these priority competencies to be in the area of what might be called 'soft competencies', or generic, transferable skills relating to areas such as guest and employee relations, communications and ICT. These findings are significant in the context of a widespread argument that higher status is given to those with transferable as opposed to specific skills. This therefore suggests that there are greater professional tendencies among managers in larger businesses and this generalization would appear to be applicable across the wider tourism, hospitality and leisure industry.

A number of trends may contribute to the undermining of what professionalism does exist in the tourism, hospitality and leisure industry of the future. In Chapter 3, we considered the impact of de-skilling and standardization upon work in the sector. These are closely allied trends which are likely to contribute to further weakening of the internal labour market at skilled technical and management levels in the industry, which in turn will weaken the professional attributes of such work. Both processes reduce the educational and training requirements for such work in the sector and allow companies to recruit from a much wider labour market base in order to fill vacancies. Branding, as a response to standardization, can reduce the range and level of decision-making involved in work at a technical and management level. Although many hotel companies, for example, have delegated aspects of greater authority to the unit and departmental level, branding and standardization act to define and 'ring fence' this authority to an increasing extent. These trends are tourism and hospitality specific. In a wider sense, there are clear moves towards a weakening of a number of professional labour markets such as law and medicine.

The image of work in tourism, hospitality and leisure

The image of work in tourism, hospitality and leisure is of considerable importance to the management of people within the sector in its attempts to recruit new entrants at all levels and to retain those that are already employed. Image and reality are not necessarily the same thing and while the real situation may reflect diversity in working conditions, remuneration, status and professionalism, the image that is projected of employment in the industry may well be based upon the lowest denominator, the worst-case employer or area of work.

It is clear that the image of work in tourism and hospitality within subsectors, between sectors and in different countries is varied. Popular perception in many countries might place e-travel companies and airlines at the top in terms of their desirability for employment and fast food and coach/bus transportation as the least attractive. It might be reasonable to suppose that those with experience of working in the area would be more positive about such employment than those without such first-hand knowledge. The evidence relating to this, however, is not conclusive. O'Driscoll and O'Connell (2005) point to a marked decline in perceptions of a long-term commitment to a hospitality career between those without and those with working experience in the industry. The gap in attitude is widest in the case of hotel and restaurant management and work in the historic/heritage and attractions sub-sector. In the case of the former, hotel and restaurant management, the gap is likely to be linked to a merging of work at operational and management level in the minds of respondents. Most studies in this area point to possible disparity between image and reality but also emphasize the possible value of exposure to the industry as a key means to overcome negative perceptions that may be held about the sector. At the same, it is that very exposure to which students on industrial placement are subjected that may be a contributory cause of the high level of drop-out from the industry after graduation.

The image of work in international tourism, hospitality and leisure is generated by the reality of the pay, conditions, social structure, status and level of professionalism within each sector and within the industry as a whole. The relative position of tourism, hospitality and leisure measured against these criteria, along with other labour-intensive service sectors, is generally unfavourable in developed countries and this results in a broadly poor image. Prior to political and economic change, tourism and hospitality was also viewed unfavourably in comparison to productive industries in Eastern Europe. However, in economies in transition in Europe and Central Asia change over the past two decades has undermined the primacy of what are now seen as inefficient and uncompetitive manufacturing and agricultural sectors and service work has risen in status. It is also one of the few areas of growth, and the creation of new employment in these countries means that such work is now seen in rather different terms. Thus new hotels and restaurants in these countries frequently attract applications from job seekers with a wide variety of professional and technical qualifications and experience (Vikhanski and Puffer 1993). In a similar vein, many of the economic migrants who find themselves working in tourism, hospitality and leisure in Western Europe do so with academic and professional qualifications and experience that far exceed the demands of the job.

In addition to countering the effect of contemporary image problems relating to the range of factors addressed in this chapter, the tourism, hospitality and leisure industry is also faced with dealing with perceptions derived from the historical relationship between the guest and the server. We have already considered this in relation to the origin and nature of work in the tourism and hospitality industry in Chapter 2. At the root of this problem in contemporary society is the relationship between service and servility. Service in many developed countries originated in a relationship that was based on servility on the part of those serving to their better-off social, economic and political masters. By contrast, in France, for example, the notion of service has a more honourable tradition, perhaps reflecting the earlier effects of the idea that all people are equal in their social and political rights. The democratization of travel and the utilization of tourism and hospitality products and services have all but eliminated the outward manifestations of this servility relationship in Western, developed countries. Emergent developing countries such as Malaysia are, in some ways, experiencing the emergence of a narrowing gap between the status and economic resources of foreign guests, on the one hand, and those serving them on the other. At the same time, social distance remains a major issue in the industry of most poorer countries. The shadow of servility remains at the root of the image that work, especially in the hotel and restaurant sector, has in the minds of potential employees and their families. This acts as a barrier to many as they evaluate, in particular, longer-term career and education/training options. Interestingly it is reasonable to speculate that those work areas which are of relatively recent origin in tourism – hospitality and leisure, notably fitness centres, airlines, tour operators and travel agents – do not face the same problems with image, and, consequently, in their recruitment and staff turnover levels, in part because their large-scale origins post-date the era of servility.

From a human resource perspective, the public perception or image that the tourism, hospitality and leisure industry projects is critical. The image can represent a problem which, at times of labour shortage, leads to the industry competing, unsuccessfully, with other industries for scarce labour resources. It also means that many university and college entrants and graduates look to tourism, hospitality and leisure as a low priority option, to be considered if other, better image areas of work fail to deliver desired opportunities. Finally, it can also mean that those studying for and working in the industry look elsewhere and use their transferable skills in other service and related industries. Tourism, hospitality and leisure's weak internal labour market, while beneficial to employers in many respects, can act to the detriment of the industry in relation to these issues. There is considerable awareness of these problems but few realistic and collective attempts to act in order to enhance poor image perceptions. As long

Case Study

I think that middle class people have more natural abilities that make them better suited to university, whereas working class people tend to be better performing menial tasks in the service sector (Letter to *Metro*, 26 April 2005)

Case discussion questions

1. How widespread are the views expressed in this letter in the country where you are studying?

2. What arguments can you form in support of the sentiment in the letter?

3. What arguments can you form against the sentiment in the letter?

as there are employers, even a small minority, who are happy to perpetuate the reality of poor pay, conditions and related problems, the poor image will remain.

Ultimately, perceptions of work in the tourism, hospitality and leisure sector are influenced by the motivation and levels of job satisfaction of those working in the area. High levels of job satisfaction will rub off on friends and family and create a positive image of the industry, Isles (2004) points to real problems for the work sectors covered in this book.

> Two thirds of UK workers seem to be enjoying the good life being satisfied or very satisfied with their work. But over 4 million workers, 15 per cent of the total workforce, are dissatisfied or very dissatisfied with their jobs. These people tend to work in low skill parts of the economy often with little or no control over when and where they work and with little say in how they work. (p.3)

Biting the hand that feeds you – employee misbehaviour in tourism, hospitality and leisure

This chapter, in part, paints a fairly bleak picture of aspects of work in tourism, hospitality and leisure. It is not the intention to imply that all work in the sector reflects this level of negativity and that there are not many excellent working opportunities in the sector. That said, are those employees who are subject to less than ideal rewards powerless to assert their rights and obtain better conditions and remuneration?

Tourism, hospitality and leisure is a sector where both the formal and informal trappings of authority and hierarchy are clearly evident, although this does vary considerably from country to country. It is a sector where uniforms are common in the workplace, particularly in transport (airlines, buses, trains, ships) and hotels but also in museums and theatres among other areas. Such uniforms are frequently quasi-military in appearance and the form of address to those in charge of aircraft and ships (Captain, First Officer) underpins this dimension. The language of communication to guests is frequently also formal (use of the address forms, 'Sir' and 'Madam') and internal relations within organizations are also hierarchical – in many airlines, the notion of seniority is important in the allocation of preferred work opportunities (routes, shifts).

Traditional notions of servility within the service transaction also contributes to an authority-led environment within the workplace. Servility implies social and economic inferiority and power by the guest over those serving him or her. As we have seen, the practice of tipping can be seen in terms of servile dependence upon the whims of the guest and can also influence the behaviour of both parties significantly.

Authority and authoritarianism in the tourism, hospitality and leisure workplace is frequently justified on the basis that staff in hotels and elsewhere are intrinsically dishonest and will seek to cheat both guests and their employers if given a chance. Anecdotal evidence appears to support this concern to some extent. Theft has historically been commonplace in airlines and hotels, for example, largely because of the ease of access to alcohol and food for so many staff. Thus, cabin staff in the past would remove quantities of miniature spirits and wines at the end of flights for their own consumption or re-sale. Kitchen and service staff, likewise, might take food home at the end of a shift or work in cooperation with suppliers in order to substitute poorer quality meat for that ordered in order to share the profits within such a transaction. Night porters in small hotels would provide drinks to guests after hours from their own private stock and ensure payment in cash so as to avoid the hotel's accounting system. Tour guides would work with retailers to ensure that unsuspecting guests were sold goods at inflated prices to the benefit of both parties. Bar staff could readily short-measure guests or substitute inferior (and cheaper) products for those ordered. 'White collar' pilferage is also widespread in tourism, hospitality and leisure as it is in others sectors of the economy and relates to a range of behaviours by managers that formally or informally transgress their entitlements – for example, the use of telephones for personal purposes or flexible interpretation of expense entitlements.

Mars (1973) studied pilferage in hotels and noted that the casual nature of much work in the sector fostered a breakdown of loyalty to both employers and customers. He also argued that there was tacit acceptance by employers and colleagues of what appears to have been institutionalized pilferage provided that the 'victim' was the guest and not anyone else in the organization. Indeed, this notion of complicity is important in understanding theft and dishonesty in the tourism, hospitality and leisure workforce. Orwell (1933) suggests that the knowledge of theft was widespread among supervisory and middle management staff in the Parisian hotel where he worked and that opportunity to gain from such transactions was tightly controlled on the basis of where you were on the hierarchy. Ditton (1977) considered the presence of fiddles in a bakery and concluded that such behaviour was certainly known to supervisors and rarely sanctioned. Fiddles and pilferage, therefore, can be seen to be tacitly accepted within tourism, hospitality and leisure as part of the overall remuneration package and, arguably, as a justification for suppressing formal and taxable pay. The black or grey benefits market was accepted as part of the returns that workers could expect from this type of job alongside tips and formal, hourly pay. Such practices have by no means disappeared from the tourism, hospitality and leisure workplace but technological controls make some aspects of these practices more difficult. Also, far more experienced and aware consumers are more conscious of what to expect from the tourism, hospitality and leisure transaction and are less likely to be taken in by cheating in the service transaction.

Theft and pilferage, therefore, can be seen to some extent as sanctioned behaviour in tourism, leisure and hospitality, especially but not exclusively within less organized and more informal sectors. Opportunities to participate in such behaviour, therefore, can become part of the informal (but implicit) remuneration package of workers in the sector. It can also be seen as a response by poorly paid workers to their situation, as an attempt to make up for inadequate formal remuneration through theft.

Ackroyd and Thompson (1999) consider theft and pilferage as one dimension of a wider phenomenon that they describe as 'organizational misbehaviour', a range of activities that take place in workplaces at all levels that are either tacitly accepted by management or cannot be controlled by them. Such behaviour also includes sabotage, recalcitrance, placing limitations on the work that is undertaken in terms of 'capping' productivity, time wasting, absenteeism and the use of humour. Beyond pilferage, there is a wide range of behaviours undertaken in the tourism, hospitality and leisure workplace that could not be formally sanctioned by employers but can be seen as part of coping strategies by employees in challenging and pressurized situations. The use of humour at the expense of guests and management, for example, can represent an attempt to break out of the increasingly standardized and McDonaldized work routines that front-line staff face. It can also be seen as a reaction against some of the responsibility implicit in boundary-spanning work, for example in representing a company's untenable position in the face of a large number of dissatisfied airline passengers, denied the flight they thought they had booked.

Clowning is also an aspect of organizational misbehaviour to which Ackroyd and Thompson refer and, in the context of tourism, hospitality and leisure, this can relate from innocent pranks to life-threatening actions – the example of two commercial airline pilots in the United States who fatally crashed their regional jet aircraft in 2004 after testing it beyond its safety limits is an extreme example (CBS News, 2005). Clowning and humour are interesting phenomena in the context of tourism, hospitality and leisure because such behaviour, when controlled and sanctioned, can very much be part of the role expectation of front-line employees. Animation or acting is part of the role and script expected of workers in some restaurants, in theme parks such as Disney, in historic sites such as Williamsburg in Virginia and Stirling Goal in Scotland where workers are expected to re-enact historical roles for the public, and in cultural shows and representations. It does not take much by way of deviancy to move marginally out of role in any of these situations and move into the realm of unapproved humour or clowning. Some companies sanction apparent deviancy in an attempt to reduce some of the pressures on their staff. EasyJet, the UK-based low-cost airline, allows cabin staff to stray from script in their cabin announcements and to use individualized lines, often humorous, within their communications to customers, provided that such behaviour does not threaten safety in any way.

Misbehaviour can be explained from a number of different perspectives, both individual and organisational and can be seen as an attempt by employees to exert a level of control over their working environment and/or their economic situation. Explanations relating to tourism, hospitality and leisure could relate to the routine and, in some situations, dehumanized work roles that people in the sector may be asked to perform. Boredom can also be another factor. In the case of the 2004 airliner crash in the United States (CBS News, 2005), commentary on the crash enquiry from the president of the Air Travelers Association included the statement that:

> This is more a story of pilots having time on their hands and playing with things in the cockpit that they shouldn't ... Flying ... is as boring as truck driving most of the time ... This was boredom and experimentation, these guys experimenting with things they had no business doing. (p.2)

Ackroyd and Thompson note the widespread failure of management and organizations to control such behaviour and, as we have already stated, complicity in it in some situations. The majority of research and discussion about behaviour that transgresses normal organisational rules is located within developed and Western economies. There is little evidence as to its prevalence or otherwise in developed Asian economies such as Japan or within the developing world and this is certainly a gap in the knowledge that is available.

In terms of our discussions in this book, organizational misbehaviour raises challenging issues with respect to themes that underpin this book. In Chapter 4, we examined the notion of empowerment and organizational citizenship behaviour, both of which imply a high level of commitment by the individual to the organization, its goals and its customers. Both can make important contributions to the delivery of good service to the customer and to the ultimate profitability of the organization. At the same time, we have introduced notions of organizational misbehaviour that operate contrary to organizational citizenship and empowerment, that suggest that employees can become largely alienated from their organizations and their customers. Such contrary behaviours can conceivably take place at the same time and in the same place, in what might be called 'parallel universes of service'.

Looking to the future of work in tourism, hospitality and leisure

The title of this chapter poses the question as to whether, in areas of pay, conditions, social composition, status, professionalism and overall image, the tourism, hospitality and leisure industry represents the 'dark side' of the employment coin. It is clear from the preceding discussion that the evidence is mixed and any conclusions cannot be other than tentative. In some geographical and economic contexts, tourism, hospitality and leisure provides an attractive, high-status working environment with competitive pay and conditions, which is in high demand in the labour force and benefits from low staff turnover. The image of the industry, consequently, is good. The other side of the coin is one of poor conditions, low pay, high staff turnover, problems in recruiting skills in a number of key areas, a high level of labour drawn from socially disadvantaged groups, poor status and the virtual absence of professionalism. Where this environment is manifest, the industry suffers from a poor image, with all its attendant problems. Both pictures represent a widespread reality and this leaves the case 'not proven' either way.

In Chapter 4, we considered the delivery of quality service in the tourism, hospitality and leisure industry and the contribution that effective human resource management can make towards its attainment. The idea of empowerment, which is central to this argument, demands employees who are committed in the long term to the objectives of the organization through effective internal marketing and who are able to deliver quality service to customers without close and constant supervision and control. This environment is only achievable in a climate where the front-line workforce is highly motivated and is supported by technical and management staff who recognize their enabling role in the provision of good service. This environment can only be achieved when both the reality and the perception of pay, conditions and related factors are consistent with the expectations that the organization has of its employees. In short, it is unrealistic to expect quality service from employees who perceive their pay, conditions and status to be poor.

As we have discussed earlier, perhaps the most compelling pressure against notions of empowered work where employees exhibit organizational citizenship is the movement towards standardization or McDonaldization, to use Ritzer's rather more broad-ranging term. It is also a process that, while generally providing a perfectly adequate physical working environment, tends to be equated with pressures towards low pay, part-time employment, low status, limited professionalism and an image that depicts the industry as a poor career option. Deskilling and technological substitution are at the heart of McDonaldization and the logic of future developments, in this respect, is that there will be further movements in these directions.

Case Study *Ryanair's latest cut on costs: staff banned from charging phones by Andrew Clark*

To most office workers, recharging a mobile phone barely registers among the perks of nine-to-five life. But the Irish low-cost airline Ryanair has sealed its reputation for parsimony by banning its staff from using chargers on the grounds that they amount to theft of its electricity.

The edict, which has infuriated employees and trade unions, will save the airline an estimated 1.4p for each charge. But even if all its 2,600 staff plugged in their phones at once, the bill of £28.60 would scarcely dent the company's annual profits of euros 226m (£154m).

Cheap, brash and no-fuss, Ryanair has transformed Europe's aviation industry since it was founded with a single 15-seat plane operating from Waterford to Gatwick in 1985. The Dublin-based carrier now carries 24 million passengers annually to destinations as far afield as Finland and Poland, using a fleet of 86 mainly brand-new Boeing 737s.

Its success has been masterminded by a belligerent, rugby-loving chief executive, Michael O'Leary, who has a taste for profanity and a mission to make air travel available to the masses, rather than merely to 'rich fuckers'. He once summed up his business philosophy by claiming that with air fares as low as 99p, passengers had little right to complain.

Ryanair's growth has been built on a 'no-frills' culture taken to such extremes that unions have dubbed it the world's stingiest company.

The ban on mobile phone chargers, which was communicated to staff in a memo, is just the latest in a string of controversial cutbacks. Staff are also expected to pay for their own uniforms, crew meals and training courses.

A Ryanair spokesman said: 'It's all just general cost control, which is very important to us. It's the same as taking out reclinable seats and head covers on our planes.'

Using the internet at Ryanair's head office is strongly discouraged, which is not surprising because a rash of Ryanair websites has spread across the internet for staff to write anonymously about their discontent.

The bitterness and vitriol expressed by staff online has concerned the company so much that it has applied for a high court injunction to unmask the identities of employees posting messages on one such site.

Shay Cody, the deputy general secretary of the Irish trade union Impact, said: 'Ryanair are absolutely on their own – they're unique. They are extremely hostile to the workforce and to any attempt to organise the workforce. It's a very, very oppressive regime there and they have extremely high staff turnover, particularly among junior pilots and cabin crew.'

Such is the concern about working conditions that the International Transport Workers' Federation has urged air travellers to think hard about Ryanair's employment policies before booking tickets.

A source at one pilots' association said: 'Essentially, when you look at Ryanair you've got to forget about conventional business models and think about the nature of what a "cost" is. You've got to stop thinking about employees as people who have rights – they're a resource which flows through the organisation and when you're done with them, you get rid of them.'

Top of the list of concerns is the way Ryanair recruits. It encourages young cabin crew with offers of hefty wages, but requires them to pay as much as £2700 upfront for training.

The pool of willing Irish workers is drying up, so the company is recruiting contract labour from agencies as far away as the Baltic states and Poland.

Pilots were recently told that in order to graduate from older planes to newer aircraft, they would have to stump up for their own retraining, leaving some complaining of 'constructive dismissal', pointing out that ageing aircraft were rapidly being phased out.

Ryanair's spokesman, Peter Sherrard, dismissed staff complaints as sour grapes: 'If I decide I want to be a barrister or a solicitor, I can't just walk up to the bar and say, "Can I have a law degree please?"'

Ryanair's supporters point out that an airline which has made such successful inroads against established players such as British Airways, Air France and Lufthansa is bound to have enemies who are keen to stress its faults.

Published in the *Guardian*, 23 April 2005. Copyright Guardian Newspapers Limited 2005.

Case discussion questions

1. How do you interpret Ryanair's attitude to its staff from this report?

2. Is Michael O'Leary justified in claiming that 'with air fares as low as 99p, passengers had little right to complain'?

3. What are the consequences of this attitude for Ryanair staff?

Review and discussion questions

1. Consider the dilemma posed at the start of the chapter. As an aspiring manager in the tourism, hospitality and leisure industry, how would you respond to it?

2. Why have writers about the history of tourism, hospitality and leisure largely ignored work and working conditions?

3. How does use of Riley's labour-market model assist in understanding pay and conditions in the tourism, hospitality and leisure industry?

4. Based on your own working experience what is your assessment of the level of pay and the nature of conditions in the tourism, hospitality and leisure industry?

5. Is tipping a good thing?

6. What are the origins of the popular perception of work in the tourism, hospitality and leisure industry?

7. What are the opposing positions taken by liberal and social reformist traditions with respect to working conditions in the tourism, hospitality and leisure industry?

8. Why has the level of part-time work increased in the tourism, hospitality and leisure industry?

9. Why is the level of trade unionism so low in many sub-sectors of the tourism, hospitality and leisure industry?

10. Is the tourism, hospitality and leisure industry really a young people's industry?

11. Is there a resolution to the customization/empowerment–McDonaldization debate? What is likely to be the long-term outcome?

12. How can we reconcile organizational misbehaviour with desired customer service standards in tourism, hospitality and leisure?

6 Cultural diversity in tourism, hospitality and leisure

Chapter objectives

This chapter is the first of two addressing the management of diversity within international tourism, hospitality and leisure. The objectives of this chapter are:

- to address the complex nature of cultural diversity within international tourism, hospitality and leisure in terms of customers, employees, management and ownership;

- to consider the extent to which migration has impacted upon the workforce of tourism, hospitality and leisure;

- to consider the contribution of theory to an understanding of cultural diversity;

- to consider the advantages and challenges of multiculturalism in the tourism, hospitality and leisure workforce;

- to address management issues relating to the management of cultural diversity in tourism, hospitality and leisure.

Introduction

This chapter considers the implications of providing for, on the one hand, demand created as a result of the multinational and varied cultural origins of the international tourism, hospitality and leisure marketplace and, on the other, managing a workforce that needs the skills and knowledge to respond to this customer diversity and that, in itself, reflects heterogeneity in its composition and origins. Diversity, of course, is not only concerned with ethnicity and culture and we shall consider other diversity themes in the next chapter. However, cultural diversity has come to the forefront of awareness in many countries in recent years as a result of high levels of mobility between and across continents, impacting upon lives in both an employment and wider social sense. Furthermore, events over the past five years have heightened awareness of the symbols and practices of diversity in a way that perhaps was not so clear in the past. Symbols of Islam, for example, in the form of traditional head-dress, have aroused controversy and debate in both France and the United States. In some countries, such symbolism has been discouraged from overt presentation within tourism. Din (2005), for example, talks in the context of Malaysia and points out the absence of traditional Malay head-dresses among hotel staff despite the Malay majority in the workforce. In this chapter, we will address some of these emerging socio-cultural themes and consider the implications of managing a diverse or multicultural environment, guest and employee, from a broad and wide-ranging perspective.

'Diversity', in the context that we are using the term here, may be defined as the presence of differences among members of a social unit (Jackson, May and Whitney 1995). Gröschl and Doherty (1999) note that 'the basic concept of managing diversity accepts that the workforce consists of a diverse population of people' (p.262). Diversity can be seen in terms of visible and non-visible differences and it is founded on the premise that harnessing these differences will create a productive environment in which everybody feels valued, where their talents are being fully utilized and in which organizational goals are met (Kandola and Fullerton 1994, p.8). Diversity is an increasingly important factor in working life as tourism, hospitality and leisure organizations, worldwide, become more diverse in terms of the gender, race, ethnicity, age, national origin and other personal characteristics of their members (Shaw and Barrett-Power 1998). As a management concern, working effectively in the diverse environment is particularly important because, as D'Netto and Sohal (1999) comment, management of workforce diversity is only 'mediocre'. In particular, they note inadequate diversity management practices in the areas of recruitment and selection and training and development.

In addressing the twin dimensions of cultural diversity (markets and workforce) in the tourism, hospitality and leisure industry, it is important to consider them as dependent variables. They do not operate in isolation of each other. It is the immediacy and directness of interaction between multicultural markets and a multicultural workforce which places the tourism, hospitality and leisure industry in a relatively unique position and presents managers with challenges that they might not face in other industries. We can present these two dimensions in the form of a matrix and then plot businesses with high or low levels of multiculturalism on either or both axes. High and low should not be taken to imply 100 per cent or 0 per cent – the model is not based on precise quantification. Figure 6.1 represents this two-dimensional model, and provides examples of business contexts plotted against it.

It is possible to extend this model so that it operates at a three-dimensional level by incorporating the extent of cultural distance between the parent corporation and the local community in which the hotel, travel agent or restaurant is located. The model and its three-dimensional extension provide the basis for assessing the extent to which management needs to incorporate the implications of multiculturalism into its guest and human resource management policies, practices and systems. Before this is undertaken, it is important to understand the origins and nature of cultural, national and ethnic diversity in the markets and workforce of the international tourism, hospitality and leisure industry.

A multicultural marketplace

It is almost axiomatic to say that the international tourism, hospitality and leisure industry caters for diversity in its clientele, whether such variation reflects different circumstances, interests, economic resources or cultural and national traditions. Such variety is reflected in differing tourism products, whether hotels which range from the budget to the luxury or in the range of sporting, leisure and entertainment options that is available to visitors in most tourist destinations. Traditional product-development and marketing strategies sought to cater for the variety in visitor interests by gradually extending the menu of facilities provided and thus aiming to cater for as wide a range of potential visitors as possible. However, such change and responsiveness was, largely, slow and reactive rather than proactive, avoiding change in so far as was possible and employing the Fordian axiom that, for example, the guesthouse visitor can have dinner at any time, provided that it is between 6.00 and 6.30 pm. Thus, evolving English resorts such as Blackpool, Bournemouth and Brighton developed facilities and attractions from the mid-nineteenth century onwards in response to the demands of a widening market base and without any specific and targeted market focus to direct such growth.

In common with more general marketing trends which have increasingly recognized the segmented nature of demand for most products and services, this 'catch-all' approach has been replaced by much more focused niche development and marketing, a strategy which recognizes that an attraction, museum, hotel or destination cannot cater for all types of potential visitors and is likely to be much more effective if it targets well-defined groups and designs facilities

Figure 6.1

Multiculturalism in tourism, hospitality and leisure

Key
A – European 'flag carrier' international airline (Olympic, Tarom)
B – Cultural show for tourists – Greece, Ireland or Spain
C – Blackpool guesthouse
D – German internal airline (Deutsche BA)
E – EuroDisney
F – Large four-star hotel in London
G – Middle Eastern Airline (Gulf, Emirates, Royal Jordanian)

to meet their identified needs. The outcome of niche development and marketing has been a considerable sharpening of the focus and image projected by individual businesses within tourism, hospitality and leisure, as well as by resorts, regions and, to some extent, countries as well.

The consequences of this change include increasingly sophisticated packaging of products and attendant marketing on the basis of demographic or lifestyle factors – vacations for the 18–30s or over 55s (Saga Holidays); resorts for these specific markets (Club Med); golf, tennis and other sporting hotels; couples-only resorts; family-focused facilities; eco-tourism products; bridge or educational cruises; female-only fitness clubs and a wide range of other examples. In the transportation arena, some airlines have targeted their product and pricing at specific markets in contrast to the more widespread approach in international aviation which seeks to cater for a wide range of market needs within the one schedule and system. Low-cost airlines in North America, Europe and Asia are specifically designed to cater for the budget-conscious traveller, whether motivated by leisure or business travel needs. On a larger scale, while the market focus of a region is largely dictated by the range of natural, historic and related attractions available (mountains, sea, monuments), specific destinations have developed and promoted reputations that reflect the management of the main focus of their products – for example, Ibiza as a location for young visitors seeking extensive night-life options.

Such segmentation is relatively self-evident and can be identified through a wide range of examples within tourism, hospitality and leisure. Segmentation and product service design in order to cater for cultural and national differentiation is also a strategy that is employed but is not as clearly identifiable as part of conscious marketing or product development approaches. The relative homogeneity of developed-country markets in tourism, hospitality and leisure terms means that many companies and destinations have played down the dimension of national diversity and concentrated on demographic and lifestyle considerations. There are obvious exceptions. Specialist coach-tour packaging and products for US, Japanese and Chinese visitors are commonplace. Beach resorts in Thailand, Spain and Greece have developed facilities in response to main market demands and the consequence is a range of restaurants, bars and shops which cater, primarily, for British, German or Scandinavian visitors. This process may be self-perpetuating as the presence of such facilities acts as a magnet to increase visitor numbers from the specific national markets.

Probably the most sophisticated packaging of tourism, hospitality and leisure products and services at destination and individual business level has been in response to cultural and national expectations and demands from the Middle Eastern and Far-East Asian markets. Hotels in many major tourist centres have responded to the specific culinary and accommodation needs of groups and individuals from these parts of the world through the development of new restaurant facilities or the provision of dedicated menu items. Some London hotels respond to the large-scale exodus of wealthy families from the Middle East during July and August by reorganizing their room service and related facilities in response to a family market that makes relatively little use of public restaurants. Published information is widely provided on a multilingual basis. Chang (2005), similarly, discusses the restaurant requirements of the out-bound

Chinese market in Australia and demonstrates their clear preferences for familiar food. Likewise, airlines make specific provision for the requirements of these markets, through menu options, alternative movies or soundtracks and multilingual information and publication services.

Product and marketing response is important in catering for this diversity but probably of even greater significance is the ability of the company's personnel to respond flexibly and with understanding to the diversity of needs displayed by customers from different cultures and nations. This provides a major human resource and, in particular, training challenge for tourism, hospitality and leisure companies seeking to operate effectively in the multicultural marketplace. The requirements go beyond language skills, although of course these are important, to a close understanding of the culture and expectations of different groups and an ability to empathize with the perspective of guests, whatever their cultural origins.

Responses to this particular challenge are diverse among tourism, hospitality and leisure companies. At a minimum level, limited language competencies are sought among as many customer-contact or front-line staff as is possible in order to cater for key market requirements, generally in major European languages such as English, French, German and Italian. In relatively monolingual countries, even achieving a limited level of provision presents considerable problems to tourism and hospitality companies and, in addition to recruiting staff with language capabilities locally, there is an increasing tendency, among major firms such as British Airways, to seek multilingual staff from outside the country. Indeed, English-speaking countries pose a particular challenge with respect to languages skills and some studies have suggested that employers, in practice, give relatively little weight to such skills when recruiting new staff for work in areas such as front office (Baum and Odgers 2001). Practices similar to those in British Airways are adopted with respect to other, major overseas markets and the presence of, for example, Japanese staff among cabin crew of airlines serving the Far East as well as in the hotels of major cities in Europe exemplifies this. In addition to providing language proficiency, this approach is designed to ensure the presence of at least a minimum core staff who have understanding for and empathy with the expectations and demands of customers from these countries. As well as providing services directly to the guests, such expatriate staff have an important role to play in the training of their colleagues to enable them to provide a better and more customized service in response to particular cultural demands.

This latter point, the training of a wider staff to understand and respond to the needs of particular cultural, ethnic and national visitor groups, is a very important human resource requirement in a Europe in which the guest profile is becoming increasingly diverse. While domestic and other European markets remain very important to most countries and regions, new growth is, largely, coming from emerging markets in Asia and elsewhere. Out-bound international travel from countries such as China, Korea, Malaysia, Singapore and Taiwan continues to grow at rates that far outstrip growth from other markets and, although much of such travel is inter-regional, the concentric expansion of the horizons of travel, which were discussed in Chapter 2, means that an increasing proportion of travellers from these markets will include overseas destinations on their itinerary. The demand for travel from these originating markets, particularly China, and from other countries in the region means that this trend is likely to remain a major influence on the international tourism, hospitality and leisure industry for the foreseeable future. While 'honey pot' destinations such as London, Paris and Venice will remain the prime objectives for many of these new visitors, considerable dispersal is also likely, with the result that the impact of the new markets may well be felt in the periphery tourist regions of Europe as well as at the core. As a result, there is a strong case to be made that all tourism and hospitality staff in Europe would benefit from greater understanding of the practical implications of cultural and ethnic diversity in the context of the need for greater guest sensitivity in general. In Chapter 4 we considered the role of human resources in the provision of enhanced service quality, especially through empowerment. A key to this process is a keen understanding of guest demands. If staff are without insight and understanding of the guest's background and culture, empowerment and enhanced service quality become somewhat elusive objectives.

Expectations on the basis of cultural variation among European guests are not perceived to show the same level of diversity that is exhibited between European and Asian visitors. Therefore, once language considerations have been addressed, few tourism, hospitality and leisure businesses address this matter in product terms or undertake any dedicated staff development or familiarization in response to the needs of specific European markets. There is a case to be made that such implicit assumptions about homogeneity in culture and expectations within Europe, as well as between Europe and North America and Australia/New Zealand, are misguided. In product terms, Accor appeared to have assumed that French and British market expectations were similar when they, unsuccessfully, introduced the Formulae 1 budget hotel product into the UK. As a result, the standard arrangement of shared bathroom facilities between four rooms was included on the basis that low price would create demand. However, this was quickly revoked when customer non-acceptance and dissatisfaction became evident. Likewise, Disney made broad assumptions about common eating patterns in the United States and Europe and designed their food and beverage facilities at Disneyland Paris on the basis of such assumptions. In Disney's properties in the US, consumption of food and drinks is continuous with no dramatic peak at any one particular point in the day. Thus excessive queuing is avoided because consumption is staggered. European eating habits were found, in practice, to be very different, with a strong midday concentration and a demand for 'proper' meals as opposed to snacks. As a result, in the initial period after opening, guests at Disneyland were initially faced with extensive peak-period waiting at food and beverage outlets and provision had to be rapidly reviewed. This change, in turn, had significant implications for the utilization and rostering of human resources and led to major operational compromises in order to accommodate local market needs. Similar steps were taken with respect to Disney's operations in Tokyo and Hong Kong, the most recently opened theme parks.

This far, we have illustrated some of the issues that are raised in relation to the tourism and hospitality industry's multicultural marketplace. In many ways, this ground is not entirely new, although the management and human resource implications of this dimension of multiculturalism are not widely addressed in personnel and human resource management texts. Similar cultural 'gaps' faced the tourism, hospitality and leisure industry in the post-1945 period, as the number of visitors from, in particular, the United States grew very rapidly. Many of these visitors had personal or historical motivations to visit some of the more remote parts of Europe, such as Connemara in Ireland, Calabria in Italy or the Scottish islands, as well as the main 'honey pot' destinations. The provision of tourism and hospitality services in these areas was considerably at variance with experience engendered at home and even with expectations modified in response to the popular, media-induced image of the regions in question. Visitor expectations of Ireland, for example, were greatly influenced by images presented in films such as *The Quiet Man* and, subsequently, *Ryan's Daughter*. Likewise, *Braveheart* provided a template for perceptions of Scotland, both natural and cultural, but the reality of an actual visit is generally at variance with movie images. At the same time, those providing the services in the post-war period had little basis from which to comprehend the needs and expectations, as well as the social and cultural norms, of their guests from overseas. Problems of this kind in Europe but also elsewhere in the world have gradually diminished over time, as familiarity between two cultures has grown. US visitors grew more tolerant of services and facilities but, at the same time, investment in familiar brands (McDonald's, Hilton) provided visitors with a feeling of familiarity wherever they travelled around the world. Tourists from Europe and Asia, likewise, travelled more extensively themselves and, even in relatively peripheral regions, were able to develop facilities and levels of service to international standards. The globalization of the tourism, hospitality and leisure product has made a significant contribution to this process but the change has not been without some cost to the authenticity and uniqueness of local communities and cultures in many parts of the world.

Where the situation today differs from that in the 1950s and 1960s is in the scale and speed of change. Tourism, hospitality and leisure businesses today cannot afford the 25–30-year 'honeymoon' or 'incubation' period which has closed the gap, in part, between European and North American perceptions. Market growth and change is much more rapid and many of the new markets have no intrinsic loyalty to one destination in the way traditionally exhibited by 'returning Yanks'. If the expectations and needs of the traveller of the future, especially from the affluent Asia-Pacific Rim, are not met, they will exercise their portable loyalty and go elsewhere, maybe in Europe but probably to other parts of the world. On this basis, effective management in the multicultural marketplace becomes an imperative in a wider sense, not least of which is the human resource considerations. We will return to this theme at a later point in this chapter.

A multicultural workforce

Cultural, national and ethnic diversity has long been a feature of the workforce in the international tourism, hospitality and leisure industry. As early as the thirteenth century, some of the first commercial hotels in Europe, licensed by the city of Florence in Italy, were run by expatriate Germans. In the eighteenth century, travelling participants in the Grand Tour of Europe took their own servants with them and, as this tour became popularized and placed on a more commercial footing, those catering for the needs of travellers in France, Germany and Italy frequently included staff drawn from the country of origin of the visitors, particularly Britain. In relation to the nineteenth century, Berry (1992) considers the growth and nature of British tourism to the French and Italian Rivieras and notes the significant number of expatiate-run businesses and services which emerged in order to cater for the visitors.

As we have previously discussed in some detail (in Chapters 3 and 5), the nature of work in many areas of tourism, hospitality and leisure is perceived to be low skilled and low status and frequently on the margins of the formal and regularized labour market, and thus includes work which is not in great demand among local populations in more affluent countries. These attributes allowed George Orwell, an Englishman, to work as a casual in the Parisian hotel industry of the early 1930s. Likewise, these conditions, combined with seasonality and related demand factors, also facilitated considerable labour mobility within the international tourism, hospitality and leisure sector, even prior to the institution of freer labour movement, for example within the European Union.

In Europe as an example, general labour mobility has certain features which are broadly reproduced within the tourism, hospitality and leisure industry. Key within this is a general movement from the external regions to the centre. On this basis, it is possible to suggest a typology of intra-union labour exchanges, from which five particular migratory situations can be identified. These are:

- longer-standing EU member states which, historically, have been preponderantly countries of departure: Ireland, Italy, Portugal, Greece, Spain;
- longer-standing EU member states which are preponderantly countries of reception (host countries): Luxembourg, France, Germany, Belgium, United Kingdom;
- EU member states (both longer standing and new accession) with balanced exchanges: the Netherlands, Denmark, Cyprus, Malta;
- newer accession states to the EU which are today's main countries of departure: Czech Republic, Estonia, Hungary, Latvia, Lithuania, Poland, Slovakia, Slovenia;
- aspirant accession states to the EU, increasingly countries of departure, from which people seek economic migration to Western Europe: Romania, Bulgaria, Ukraine and others.

In addition to European migration, a very significant level of global migration has and continues to take place, linked to historic and economic ties associated with colonialism. As a result, the populations of the major host countries in Europe are increasingly heterogeneous, a diversity strongly reflected in their tourism, hospitality and leisure sectors. The extent to which such diversity exists in Europe is difficult to estimate but Münz and Fassmann (2004) analysed all published national and EU data for the 15 pre-accession states of the EU and estimate that there are a total of 32–34 million legal migrants born outside their country of residence, within a total population of 381 million. Within this total, some 44 per cent come from other EU states and the balance from a wide range of countries, of which the most important are the Balkans and Central and Eastern Europe, Turkey, North Africa, the Middle East, sub-Saharan Africa and Asia (in particular South Asia). Similar migratory patterns can be seen with respect to other developed regions of the world, notably North America and Australia/New Zealand.

Münz and Fassmann (2004) analyse the occupational and educational backgrounds of migrants to the European Union. They note that:

> The skills profile of the foreign-born population is markedly different from that of the total EU population. Both people with low skills (immigrants: 52%; EU 15 average: 48%) and with high skills (immigrants: 20%; EU 15 average: 17%) are overrepresented among immigrants. People with medium skills are underrepresented (immigrants: 28%; EU 15 average: 39%). This is mainly a result of labour markets creating demand for high and low skilled migrants. Immigrants from southern Europe living in another EU country as well as from Turkey, North Africa/Middle East and sub-Saharan Africa have relatively high proportions of people with low skills. In contrast immigrants from northwestern Europe living in another EU country and in particular immigrants from other industrialized world regions (North America, Australia/New Zealand) have higher proportions of highly skilled people. (p.9)

Münz and Fassmann note, in particular, that migrants to the EU from outside the Union (excepting those from other industrialized countries) are disproportionately likely to be either unemployed or to work in skilled and unskilled manual occupations. Within these areas of work, they specifically identify hotels and restaurants as a dominant sector for employment. A total of 9.9 per cent of employed migrants to the EU work in this sector, compared to an average within the wider population of 4.4 per cent. Within Asian (22 per cent) and Latin American (20 per cent) communities in Europe, participation in hotel and restaurant work is, proportionately, much higher. The ILO (2001) report that the labour force in the Swiss hotel and restaurant sector included over 50 per cent who were foreign nationals and that the comparable figure for Germany was in the region of 30 per cent.

Baum (1993) parallels this analysis and considers the specific mobility of tourism, hospitality and leisure labour in terms of 'core' and 'peripheral' regions of Western Europe. The 'core' regions include the industrial and economic heart of the region, notably Germany, the Netherlands, Belgium, northern France, the south-east of England, Switzerland, Austria and northern Italy, where shortages, especially in low-skills areas, create a 'vacuum' which draws in labour from the periphery, traditionally the countries of Southern Europe (Greece, southern France, southern Italy, Spain, Portugal, Cyprus) as well as the western margins of Europe (Brittany, northern and western regions of England, Ireland, Scotland and Wales) but increasingly now from outside the core 15 EU member states. These 'peripheral' areas have tourism and hospitality industries with somewhat different structural characteristics to those at the 'core', notably more pronounced seasonality, small businesses and lower impact of major multinational investment in the industry. As a consequence, traditional labour movements have seen tourism and hospitality labour move from the 'periphery' to the 'core' in search of work, at the same time creating a mixed, multicultural workforce not found in other industrial sectors. Examples of 'periphery' to 'core' movements which have had considerable impact on the character of the tourism and hospitality industries in some areas include Irish immigration to London and the movement of Italian, Spanish and Portuguese workers to London as well as major cities in France and Germany. Some of this movement has been of a seasonal nature but the large number of Italian-owned hospitality enterprises (restaurants, fish-and-chip shops and ice-cream manufacturers and distributors) in Britain, for example, also points to the greater permanence of some migration. The majority of European immigrant workers in the industry have worked at the lowest skills levels and largely continue to do so. At the same time, it is possible to point to Lord Forte as, perhaps, the most visible success story of an Italian immigrant in the British tourism and hospitality industry. Overall, the contribution of immigration to the food culture of the host country cannot be underestimated. BBC (2005) clearly illustrates the manner in which Italian immigration to Scotland from about 1900 onwards shaped the tastes and eating habits of both large cities and small communities throughout the country. The irony of the 'periphery' to 'core' movement of labour within Western Europe is that it is in precisely the reverse direction to that of the main tourism flows, from north to south and to the western fringes. Overall south–north labour migration within Europe in its recent main phase was considerable. Between 1955 and 1974, an estimated 730 000 Greeks, 3.8 million Italians, one million Yugoslavs, one million Portuguese and approximately two million Spaniards emigrated to the north-west of Europe in order to find employment, mainly in service sectors and manufacturing industries.

As we have seen, trans-European labour mobility within the tourism, hospitality and leisure industry preceded and in some cases paralleled the large-scale immigration of, generally, low-skilled labour from the colonies and former colonies of a number of European countries. Key migration routes have been to Belgium from Central Africa; to Britain from, in particular, the Caribbean, Hong Kong and South Asia (India, Pakistan and, latterly, Bangladesh); to France from the Caribbean, West and North Africa and Indo-China; to the Netherlands from Caribbean colonies (Aruba, Bonaire, Curacao, St Eustacius, St Martaan and Saba), Indonesia and Surinam; and to Portugal from Angola, Macao, Mozambique and Goa. Münz and Fassmann (2004) report data which illustrates the continuing impact of such links. Within the core European union (pre-2004), some 65 per cent of all Asian-born migrants to the EU reside in the UK; 68 per cent of all African migrants live in France and 69 per cent of all Latin American migrants live in Portugal and Spain. In the case of Portugal and some other countries, such as France, the process of decolonization led to a return of a substantial number of settlers, frequently with little in common with the Europe that their ancestors left. Thus in a very real sense they can be described as immigrants, although their ethnic origins may be common with the majority of the receiving population. Other European countries without the colonial tradition looked to other parts of the world in order to meet labour shortages, Germany being a notable case, attracting a large number of migrant workers or *Gastarbeiter* from Turkey and the former Yugoslavia who work on a 'permanent temporary' basis with no citizenship rights. In addition to these 'main' sources of migrant workers, political and economic refugee status has permitted a significant number of immigrants from a wide variety of countries to settle in

Scandinavian countries and elsewhere in Western Europe. Over the past decade, the flow of migrants from Eastern Europe and beyond to Western Europe has also been very significant, both on a legal and illegal basis.

The reasons for such large-scale migration within and to developed countries can be summarized into 'push' and 'pull' factors. 'Push' factors reflect economic, social and political conditions in the home country or region which 'push' people to leave. In many cases, these were countries of the developing world undergoing slow reconstruction, offering limited employment or economic opportunities. Thus the chance to work at whatever level in industrialized countries was seen to be much more attractive than remaining at home. This remains a major factor, especially in the continuing legal and illegal movement of people from, for example, North Africa, states of the former Soviet Union and China to Western Europe and from Latin America to the United States. 'Pull' factors refer to conditions in the receiving country, frequently rapid growth, with a consequent shortage of relatively cheap, generally unskilled labour in certain sectors of the economy. Britain in the 1950s faced this growth situation and turned to the new Commonwealth countries of the Caribbean and South Asia in order to fill employment vacancies in transport and the Health Service as well the hospitality sector.

The consequence of the various levels of migration between and to developed countries has been the creation of multicultural and multi-ethnic societies, especially in larger urban, industrialized centres. This reality is not accepted by all political persuasions and right-wing racist reaction has been strong in a number of countries in attempts to undermine the position of ethnic minority groups within the wider community. Estimates of the total number of non-nationals living within member states of the European Union are subject to considerable unreliability because of the considerable level of illegal residence in some countries. Although the 'official' number of foreigners living in Italy was 926 000 in 2002, other estimates put this figure at close 1.65 million and growing when illegal immigration is taken into consideration. As long ago as 1991, King referred to the employment impact of tourism and hospitality in Italy and notes 'illegally hired hotel and restaurant workers, many from Third World countries such as Ethiopia and the Philippines (these clandestine immigrants are particularly important in Rome and other big cities)' (p.137). A similar issue of illegal immigration can be found in other Southern European states, notably Spain, Greece and Portugal, primarily from other Mediterranean countries but increasingly from further a field as well. Eironline (undated b) state that:

> A considerable number of people enter or stay within the EU illegally and carry out undeclared work, often in sectors and regions where the 'underground' economy is more developed. According to the European Commission: 'both illegal and legal immigrants are more vulnerable than national workers; they are often ready to make concessions concerning their wage and other work-related rights.' (p.4)

The ILO (2001) note that:

> The hotel, restaurant and catering sector remains an area in which use is frequently made of undeclared labour. In some countries, this may involve the clandestine employment of illegal foreigners who are willing to accept less

advantageous conditions of employment than nationals. It may also take the form of employees being declared as working for a certain limited number of hours while actually working longer hours and receiving supplementary payments in cash, thus enabling both employer and employee to avoid payment of a proportion of social insurance contributions. Undeclared labour is employed mainly in small enterprises where cash is available outside the official accounts. (p.22)

The total numbers of documented non-nationals living in a range of European Union and other countries is presented in Table 6.1.

Such figures give a sense but little more of the extent of the cultural, national and ethnic mix in Europe today. Even with the assistance of figures relating to non-national presence in the population, it is almost impossible to put an accurate figure on the level of cultural mix within any one country, largely because definitions of ethnic groupings are somewhat restrictive and the information collected is subject to considerable error. Non-nationals data, for example, give no indication of the ethnic or cultural mix of the national population. In Switzerland, for example, approximately 18.3 per cent of positions in the total workforce are held by non-Swiss nationals, but because of severe restrictions to the taking-out of Swiss citizenship, this figure incorporates many long-time residents of a wide variety of ethnic, national and cultural origins. Gilg (1991) notes that, in the tourism and hospitality industry:

Table 6.1		Foreign labour force	
	Country	% of total labour force	Total (n)
Foreign labour force in selected European countries in 2000	Austria	10.5	398 622
	Belgium	8.9	378 243
	Czech Republic	2.0	115 431
	Denmark	3.4	100 076
	Finland	1.5	39 109
	France	6.0	1 603 185
	Germany	8.8	3 599 877
	Hungary	0.9	43 645
	Ireland	3.7	59 619
	Italy	3.6	926 271
	Luxembourg	57.3	107 091
	The Netherlands	3.4	248 452
	Norway	4.9	114 431
	Portugal	2.0	101 681
	Slovak Republic	0.2	5 864
	Spain	1.2	211 736
	Sweden	5.0	239 951
	Switzerland	18.3	707 294
	United Kingdom	4.4	1 293 649

Adapted from R. Münz and H. Fassmann (2004) *Migrants in Europe and their economic position*, p.28.

> Foreign workers account for one worker in three in the hotel and restaurant
> sectors. This is largely because few Swiss want to work in jobs which are seen as
> poorly paid and offering poor career status, and also because Switzerland has a
> very low unemployment rate. (p.141)

Gilg also points to consistent increases in the number of foreign workers
employed in the tourism, hospitality and leisure industry in Switzerland, especially among those holding permanent jobs. The impact of migrant workers,
however, must also be taken to include a substantial number of students, in
work as part of their training programmes.

While migrant labour does bring benefits to receiving countries and,
arguably, to those who seek work outside their own country, such migration is
not without problems. Migrant has clear benefits but can also raise issues within the labour market which hosts incoming workers. Eironline (undated b) note
that:

> Migration is of course closely connected to the labour market, with many people
> migrating for purposes of work. It can play a role in meeting employers' needs
> for labour, in the light of demographic change or skills shortages, while at the
> same time raising questions such as the relationship between migrant workers
> and nationals who are unemployed, or the fair treatment of migrant workers in
> employment, both on grounds of equity and related to concerns about 'social
> dumping' in the form of a pool of migrant workers employed on a low level pay
> and conditions, or willing to accept employment on such terms. In this context, it
> can be expected that migration will have major effects on industrial relations
> systems and become an issue for the social partners and in dialogue and
> bargaining between them, as well as a theme in government employment policy
> and legislation. (p.2)

Refugee status is also frequently a passport to disadvantage and, notwithstanding opportunity in weak labour market sectors of the service economy, many
migrants fail to access meaningful work. Sergeant and Forna (2001) report high
levels of unemployment (over 50 per cent) among the UK's refugee population
despite the fact that close to 90 per cent of adult refugees were in employment
in their native countries before being forced to leave.

In Britain, perhaps 4 per cent of economically active persons of working age
are from ethnic minority groups. There is considerable geographical variation in
the distribution of the non-white population in Britain, including figures of 21.7
per cent for Leicester, 21 per cent for Slough, 19 for inner London, 15.2 per cent
for Birmingham, 11.2 per cent for Bradford, and, within other urban centres, 1.6
per cent for Edinburgh and 2.1 per cent for Glasgow. The implication is that the
presence of ethnic minorities in rural and 'peripheral' regions of the United
Kingdom is very limited. With respect to the tourism, hospitality and leisure
industry, there is evidence of considerable geographical variation in the proportions of workers employed from ethnic minority.

It is noticeable that tourism growth in some regions has not been matched by
the creation of employment opportunities for the local population. Williams and
Shaw (1991) note cases in the French Alps and the Algarve where tourism development has either confined the local community to lower-skills employment or,

because of its scale, drawn in additional labour from outside of the locality. While these examples point in all probability to labour mobility that is intra-national, the socio-cultural impact of this form of migration to the character and management of the workplace cannot be ignored. The Republic of Ireland represents a country where rapid economic growth in all sectors of the economy but particularly within tourism, hospitality and leisure has been combined with demographic impacts of fewer school leavers. As a result, there has been large-scale recourse to the employment of migrant labour in the sector, drawing on workers from the EU accession states, Romania and Russia as well as elsewhere.

The practice of attracting international employees, of course, has major human resource management implications in terms of our discussions in Chapter 4 in that tourism, hospitality and leisure businesses may well be providing services to customers with a front-line team who speak the languages of neither their guests nor their management.

Migrant labour, while generally associated with developed countries, is by no means exclusive to such locations. In Malaysia, for example, about 10 per cent of the total workforce is from other countries, notably Thailand and Indonesia, and the majority of these employees work in agriculture, construction and other areas that are widely seen as unskilled, including tourism, hospitality and leisure. It is also important not to forget internal migration, particularly in developing countries, in this discussion of mobility. One of the major migratory trends is that from rural life to an existence of squalor in major urban centres. As a result, major cities in countries such as China, India and Iran have grown dramatically in the past few years, primarily through domestic migration away from the difficulties of rural life. As with transnational migration, many of those moving to major cities find work in tourism, hospitality and leisure as a first stop on the road to the affluence to which they aspire.

One aspect of tourism, hospitality and leisure labour mobility that has not, traditionally, been associated with developed countries on a significant scale is that at a management and senior technical level. The use of expatriate labour in tourism, hospitality and leisure is an issue of considerable political, social and economic significance in many parts of the developing world. For example, in Jamaica, under the Manley Government of the 1970s, the issue became one of considerable political and subsequently economic significance when the government required hotel companies to replace overseas managers with local expertise. This policy created considerable problems because of the lack of lead time and the sector suffered considerably as a result. Limited movement of expatriate labour has a long-standing tradition in Europe, with French chefs as well as German and Swiss chefs and managers featuring in the London hotel industry since the early years of the last century. The growth of multinational companies has further developed this trend. However, perhaps the most significant trend in this respect at the present time and one that is likely to continue relates to the development of the tourism, hospitality and leisure industry in developing countries. Much development investment and operational control is foreign and this brings – understandable – requirements for the protection of that investment and reputation through the employment of Western European and North American expertise in key positions. This expertise, represented on the ground by significant numbers of managers, chefs and other personnel, is further supported by the importation of management and working cultures which are largely alien to the experience of the local working population. The practice of expatriatism is probably only justified and will only be sustainable in the long term provided that local staff are trained and given the opportunity to progress to positions of senior responsibility in the companies in question. The experience of many developing countries is that the development of such practice is by no means universal.

To conclude this section, the international tourism, hospitality and leisure industry is by no means unique in operating within a multicultural, multinational and multi-ethnic working environment. Where the industry does differ from the environment found in other sectors is in the extent to which this diversity in the workplace interacts with the high level of variety within the customer base in situations of high contact and association. The potential for situations of misunderstanding but also for enlightenment is considerable. Our next task is to consider the implications of the work of key theorists in understanding cultural diversity.

Case Study *Diversity in Irish tourism*

Ireland has a long tradition of multiculturalism in its tourism and hospitality workforce but in forms and numbers that mitigated against any major impact on recruitment, training and management within organizations. Ireland has long attracted tourism staff from other EU member states in specialist areas such as food and beverage and accommodation. There has also been a long tradition of international entrepreneurship in the small tourism business sector, notably restaurants, retail and similar operations. In some cases, for example ethnic restaurants, businesses attracted employees with the skills and cultural profile to enable them to assimilate relatively easily into the business environment within which they worked. Historically, however, the numerical impact of multiculturalism has been small.

In recent years, this situation has changed. According to the Central Statistics Office there were just under 20 000 international workers employed in hotels, restaurants and bars at the end of May 2004. Of these, just 6500 were from the European Union, 3000 are from non-EU European countries and the remainder, just under 8500, were from the

rest of the world. These figures, reflecting multiculturalism in the sector, do not include employees from minority communities in Ireland who are citizens or permanent residents here. Never before have Irish businesses and their customers encountered such a multicultural workforce and as the industry becomes more dependent on a culturally diverse workforce the necessity to develop successful integration models becomes more acute.

Diversity among Irish tourism workers includes a wide range of groups, including:

- Irish nationals or permanent residents, either by birth or naturalization, who are from ethnic, cultural or religious minority groups and who may be attracted to work in tourism through traditional recruitment methods (schools, agencies). People in this category may or may not avail themselves of formal tourism-training opportunities prior to or while working in the industry.

- Members of communities in Ireland who have been granted refugee status and who are seeking economic independence through employment. They may be

▶

attracted to work in tourism through traditional recruitment methods (schools, agencies). People in this category may or may not avail themselves of formal tourism-training opportunities prior to or while working in the industry.

- Tourism staff recruited overseas by employers or agencies specifically to work in the sector. If from non-EU countries, this group are subject to work permit restrictions in terms of the location of their work and the duration of their stay in Ireland.

- Trained tourism staff, primarily from other EU or EEA (European Economic Area) countries who choose to seek tourism employment in Ireland and do so through the same recruitment and job-searching processes as local staff.

- International staff who choose to come to Ireland for a variety of personal reasons (for example, to improve their English) on a temporary basis and elect to work in tourism because of the availability of jobs

or their previous skills and training. In this situation, tourism work may be incidental to their decision to come to Ireland.

- International students on internships or placements in Ireland, either from colleges in this country or from overseas. Such placements are time constrained (generally up to a maximum of 12 months).

Edited extract from Fáilte Ireland (2005a) and reproduced with permission.

Case discussion questions

1. To what extent and in which of the above ways is the tourism, hospitality and leisure sector in the country where you are studying culturally diverse?

2. How might tourism, hospitality and leisure staff identified in the case study groupings differ in their workplace expectations and training needs?

3. What are the benefits and drawbacks of employing staff within each of the above categories?

The contribution of theory to an understanding of cultural diversity

An understanding of cultural diversity is clearly important to managers and employees in the international tourism, hospitality and leisure industry in the context of both a workforce and a customer marketplace that is multicultural, multinational and multi-ethnic in origin. Understanding of culture and its variation is provided in the main by the work of anthropologists and sociologists, and a brief consideration of some of these theoretical sources can be of value to a discussion of the management implications of working within a multicultural environment. Leeds, Kirkbride and Duncan (1994) provide a clear analysis of a number of these theories, all of which contribute different cultural dimensions or aspects to our understanding. This leads these authors to propose a typology of culture clusters for Europe. In this discussion, we will follow and develop their analysis by focusing on three of the main theoretical models that are used in formulating their typology. The other research models are also of relevance but will not be dealt with in any detail here.

Perhaps the best-known researcher in this field is Geert Hofstede who, through his work based on factor analysis of data from a major empirical study was able to identify four major dimensions as the key to cultural differences

(Hofstede 2001). Hofstede applied his dimensions to some 40 countries world-wide, with a strong concentration in Europe. The five dimensions are as follows:

- *Power distance*, defined as 'the extent to which the members of a society accept that power in institutions and organizations is distributed unequally' (Hofstede 1985, p.347), is a measure of the interpersonal power or influence between two people, as perceived by the less powerful of the two. Power distance in Hofstede's studies was found to be small in Northern European countries and, relatively speaking, higher in Southern Europe and the Arab world. Attributes of organizations with a high power distance include steep hierarchies; autocratic, directive or paternalistic management; special status symbols and privileges for senior staff; and ambivalent attitudes of employees to management. High power distance in many respects reflects traditional management–subordinate relationships in the tourism, hospitality and leisure industry, especially hotel and catering. It is difficult, however, to reconcile this with the concept of empowerment which we considered in Chapter 4, although cultural acceptance of a high power distance relationship by both parties may make this somewhat easier. Power distance measurement is also an interesting tool by which to compare the cultural climates of different industries across national boundaries. Hofstede found that lower-education, lower-status occupations tend to produce high power distance values while higher-education, higher-status occupations tend to produce low power distance values, with education the dominant factor in determining this split. This, in part, may account for the traditions of authoritarian management and its acceptance in lower-skills sub-sectors of tourism, hospitality and leisure, notably hotel and catering.
- *Uncertainty avoidance* reflects a society's fear of the unknown and the extent to which uncertainty generates comfort or discomfort in its members and is thus important to avoid. Low uncertainty avoidance societies include Denmark, the Netherlands, Ireland and the United Kingdom, which are characterized by tolerance of diverse views, informality, limited impact of experts, few formal rules and emotional self-control. By contrast, high uncertainty avoidance is characteristic in Japan, Germany, all Southern European countries and the Middle East; these cultures feature an emphasis on laws and rules to cover all contingencies, maintaining careers within the same organization over a long time span and a focus on formal procedures at work and in leisure. High uncertainty avoidance places greater stress on intellectual and reflective approaches to problem-solving as opposed to the pragmatic and action-focused strategies adopted in low uncertainty avoidance societies. The nature of many tourism, hospitality and leisure businesses, with highly fluctuating demand cycles and propensity for change in the product and market environment, demands management that is relatively low in uncertainty avoidance. However, Hofstede found no specific occupational links with uncertainty avoidance tendencies.
- *Individualism/collectivism* is Hofstede's third dimension. Individualistic societies (the United States, Australia, the United Kingdom) are those in which ties are loose, where all members of society are expected to care for themselves and their immediate family only, and where emphasis is placed

on individual achievement, identity and decision-making. Managers prefer to maintain social and professional distance from their subordinates. By contrast, collectivist societies (in South America, for example) reflect close and extended family units and, in the work situation, the need to form strong groups through alliances, seeking harmony at work, consensus at meetings, face-saving strategies and group decision-making. In Hofstede's research, only Portugal and Greece among European countries were identified as collectivist in focus. Given the teamwork emphasis of much activity within the tourism and hospitality industry, an extreme individualistic culture may be problematic and not in the interests of customers. Again, however, Hofstede found no occupational correlations within his individualism data.

- *Masculinity–feminity* is Hofstede's final dimension, although the use of these terms is open to criticism in that they appear to assume innate gender characteristics against which to plot national cultures. An alternative spectrum might be assertive–nurturing. In masculine countries, characteristics include those of male stereotypes such as competitiveness, individual advancement, materialism, profit, assertiveness, strength, action focus and considerable distance between male and female roles in society. Countries representing these traits include Germany, Greece, Italy, Spain and the UK. By contrast, feminine attributes include cooperation, warm relationships, caring and nurturing, life-quality factors and a merging of male and female roles in society. Feminine countries are Denmark, Finland, Norway, Portugal and Sweden. Hofstede links the masculinity or femininity of an occupation to the level of female work participation in that sector and their influence in the industry. In this sense, the tourism, hospitality and leisure sector exhibits some tendency towards female values and the caring culture of the guest–employee relationship in many situations would seem to bear this out. It is hardly surprising, therefore, that some hotels in Russia are seeking to employ former care workers as the most suited to hospitality work. In some respects, however, traditional management demands in tourism and hospitality, especially the hotel industry, focus on masculine traits and this is supported by the dominance of males in positions of authority and power within the industry, despite their minority status.

- *Long-term orientation* is a dimension that addresses the business and, indeed, personal perspective of cultures in terms of their goal achievement. Typically, Asian cultures such as those of China and Japan and as well as those of Southern Europe (Greece, Portugal) appear to exhibit a greater willingness to invest over time in order to achieve their objectives. By contrast, Northern Europe and North America include countries where short-term objectives and achievement are valued. In the management of people, such distinctions are important and are reflected in matters such as career commitment, seeking promotion opportunities (within and external to an organization) and participation in external development programmes.

As with any analysis of this kind, Hofstede's theoretical model must be treated with some caution as an analytical framework and not as a precise programme for the management of staff from different countries.

The second theoretical position to be considered is that of context and time. The work in this field is associated with Hall, who identified and drew attention to what he described as high- and low-context societies (Hall and Hall 1990). 'Context' is a communicational concept, indicating the extent to which the message, given by a person, is explicit, as in the form of specific instructions or computer programs (low context) or is coded in the sense that little is actually written down or said but much is implied in what is said (high context).

Hall's concept of high or low context has significant implications for the conduct of business and other forms of negotiation. Low-context people tend to be specifically focused on the requirements of the current item on the agenda and to avoid any merging of issues and concerns. They move straight into the reason for the meeting or negotiations while high-context people may well have a number of explicit and implicit agenda items in mind and are happy to merge these into the same meeting or series of encounters. Time to get to know each other is important to negotiations in the high-context culture and problems and deadlocks will not be sorted out unless interpersonal relationships are permitted to develop. Therefore work and social topics, in particular, are permitted to merge and are not kept separate as in the low-context society.

Differences are also evident with respect to an understanding of time and punctuality in particular. Low-context people tend to be very precise about things like punctuality. Time for low-context people is defined in very short 'chunks' and lateness, therefore, applies in a matter of a few minutes. High-context people, by contrast, are much more relaxed about time and define lateness in terms of much longer time spans. The Swiss and German railways represent the precision of a low-context culture and are legendary in this respect, but it is also interesting to note the precision of US airline timetabling, where flights are due to arrive and depart at, for example, 7.03 am or 5.24 pm, suggesting a predictive accuracy which other parts of the world do not attempt.

Hall mapped levels of context and, in Europe, placed Northern European countries such as Germany, the Netherlands and Scandinavia in the low-context camp and Southern Europeans as high-context countries. Britain and France are placed in an intermediate position between the two. The Irish would certainly appear to be higher context than their British neighbours and, here, the influence of dominant religion may play some part. Most religions in general, but the symbolism of Catholicism in particular, exude a strong sense of high context and this may well provide a link between countries such as Ireland, Italy, Spain, southern Germany and Austria as well as Poland to the east.

The potential for misunderstanding between high- and low-context people is considerable at a business and social level. High-context people will not necessarily divulge information in an entirely explicit manner and may assume that an agreement contains rather more than is stated on paper. Low-context people will see the formal contract or written document as the totality of the agreement and will not expect to move outside what is in black and white. They will give and expect quick decisions and will see delay as suggesting a lack of interest while the reverse will be in the case in the high-context society. The US way of doing business, which has considerable influence within the globalization of tourism and hospitality, is clearly low context while, by contrast, that of the Japanese is high context.

Hall's context framework, which has been tested empirically on a number of occasions, has considerable implications for the management of businesses and people in the tourism and hospitality industry, especially where the two meet. For example, the nature of the distribution of tourism movements is such that tour operators from low-context countries in Northern Europe are required to negotiate contracts for services with colleagues from southern countries in Europe and the potential for misunderstanding is considerable. Likewise, the high-context Japanese, Koreans and Taiwanese are increasingly important markets for low-context Northern Europe. The critical requirement to understand the needs of customers from these countries discussed earlier is, perhaps, made clearer by considering it in terms of Hall's framework.

The migratory trends of labour in tourism, hospitality and leisure, as we have also seen, have brought peoples from high-context countries to work in subservient positions in the tourism and hospitality industries of low-context countries. Low-context managers, therefore, are dealing with a higher-context workforce and this dichotomy has the potential to create considerable misunderstanding unless both parties, but especially management, are sensitive to the differences. Providing written instructions or notification on how to do a job or on new approaches to customer service may make eminent sense and is a very efficient form of communication to a low-context manager but may be seen as remote and threatening by workers who operate by high-context codes. Considering empowerment in the context of Hall's framework is also interesting in that true empowerment can only be achieved within a workforce that is known and fully trusted by management and where front-line staff in particular also feel that they are viewed with a sense of trust and worth by their managers. Such relationships may be much more achievable in the high-context, informal society. However, if we reintroduce Hofstede here, we find that many high-context societies in Europe are also masculine in character and rate high on uncertainty avoidance, dimensions that are incompatible with empowerment. Hall's framework also has considerable implications for important supervisory and management functions such as coaching, correction and censure. Such measures can be relatively explicit and direct in the low-context environment, where they will be compartmentalized and have few consequences for relationships beyond the specific situation to which they relate. By contrast, the interrelationship of a diversity of agenda items, business and social, in high-context societies means that it may be difficult to isolate the circumstances of one correction or censure from the wider relationship environment of the individuals or groups concerned.

Hall's work is also interesting in terms of the comparative cultural norms of specific industries although such work has not been undertaken with respect to the tourism, hospitality and leisure sector. Certain structural and traditional factors within the industry may influence its positioning on the continuum of high–low context. Small businesses (which dominate tourism, hospitality and leisure in many countries) are more informal in the way that they operate than larger organizations and thus aspects of high-context practice may be more prevalent as a result. The demand cycle and attributes of the industry which we have already considered may also predispose towards high-context relationships, in that the management of hotels, for example, is often seen as a reactive, multifunctional, verbal and non-paper activity.

Leeds *et al.* (1994) introduce what they call the 'systematic–organic dimen-sion' as the third approach to understanding cultural variation and link this to leadership style in order to create a matrix in which to place different cultures. The systematic–organic dimension relates to the extent to which people believe that rational or systematic order should be applied regarding human behaviour and organizations. Rationality and systems lead to the view that the organiza-tion is rather like a machine and loyalty is to the organization rather than to its individual members. Consequent behaviour has many similarities to Hall's low-context dimension – careful planning, keeping to schedules and agendas and precise job definitions. Managerial authority is largely derived from competence and professionalism within a particular field of responsibility. By contrast, the organic situation is much more high context in that the organization is seen in social terms and operates to rather more informal and unwritten behaviour codes. Features include vague job definitions, informal communication and management behaviour, implicit group relationships based on loyalty and trust to the group and the minimization of red tape.

> In 'organic' societies order and control tends to be based on personal influence and power, the latter coming less from a person's competence or role, but from his position in the hierarchy. Managers have a high standing in society and it is accepted that they might offer advice outside their particular function. People are status conscious, use power for personal ends and compete through outmanoeuvring others. (Leeds *et al.* 1994, p.17)

Mole (1990) adds the concept of leadership to this dimension in order to create what he calls a cultural map of Europe.

> The leadership dimension is based on the extent to which it is believed that power is given by groups to individuals. This form of words was carefully chosen to reflect that a leader's authority, at least in a European business organization, can only be exercised with the consent of the people who are being managed. The values associated with followship are identical to those associated with leadership. The spectrum of belief about leadership ranges from individual to group. (Mole 1990, p.167)

On this basis, Leeds *et al.* describe individual leadership as authoritarian, direc-tive, top-down and autocratic, with power perceived as a right to be directed by superiors at their subordinates. By contrast, group leadership is egalitarian, par-ticipative, bottom-up and democratic in style, with all employees having a right to be heard and to make a valued contribution to their work unit or to the organization. Using the systematic–organic and the leadership dimensions, Mole created a cultural map of Europe, as represented in Figure 6.2. Again, a north–south divide becomes evident in European terms, with the former more inclined towards the systematic and the south to the informal. The individ-ual–group leadership dimension, however, cuts across the other dimension and thus two-dimensionality provides a rather more culturally sensitive instrument than that provided by Hall. Again, it would be interesting to consider an indus-try sector analysis on the basis of Mole's map.

It is easy to criticize any of the models that we have considered here because they attempt to impose generalizations upon diverse and heterogeneous national, cultural and business environments. The typologies can be faulted in that they fail to accommodate French-speaking Switzerland as well as common characteristics found at the Celtic fringe. They also neglect Eastern Europe and this is a deficiency that will need to be addressed by further studies. The prime focus is within mainstream, developed-country cultures. However, what the typology as well as the specific theoretical models from which it is derived does allow is assistance in identifying some sense of the requirements and sensitivities that are necessary for multicultural market and workforce management within tourism, hospitality and leisure. This is the focus of the final section in this chapter.

Management in a multicultural environment

It is important to recognize that cultural diversity in the workplace is complex and reflects a range of historical, political, economic and practical business factors. Few developed countries now have the homogeneous population that they might once have done. In addition, employees from the diverse backgrounds that characterize many tourism, hospitality and leisure sectors are, themselves, heterogeneous, both in terms of their backgrounds and their motivations for working in the sector within the host country.

So far in this chapter we have given consideration to the multicultural background of the tourism, hospitality and leisure marketplace as well as to the diverse origins of the industry's workforce. We have complemented these diversities with an introduction to some of the theoretical classifications or typologies that have been developed as a means of explaining cultural differences, particularly from a business and working environment point of view. However, the work of Hall, Hofstede and Mole may also be of assistance in an understanding of guest needs and priorities and this is, perhaps, a neglected aspect in the consideration of these theories. For example, an understanding of Hall's time dimension within low- and high-context societies is of considerable importance in managing a hotel's services in support of a conference attended by delegates

Figure 6.2

The Mole map of Europe

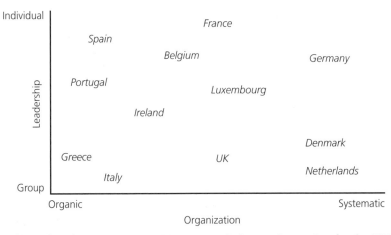

Source: Kirkbride (1994) *Human Resource Management in Europe: Perspectives for the 1990s* (eds) Leeds *et al.* (1994) p.18 with permission

from one particular country or representing a multinational mix. A predominantly low-context group is likely to expect services at times precisely agreed on the programme while the hotel may need to be much more flexible in its time response for a high-context group.

It is important to emphasize that the generalizations which are derived from any classifications and typologies must be treated with extreme caution in order to avoid their use in support of stereotyping and, ultimately, the promotion of racist attitudes. This is especially true in the classification of cultures. They provide guidelines and identify the fact of cultural variation in the way that groups and people behave and respond to different situations. However, each guest and employee/colleague is, first and foremost, an individual who may or may not fit into the general attributes identified for his or her cultural, national or ethnic group. The management of these dimensions of diversity in the tourism and hospitality industry must at all times be sensitive to individual behaviour and needs as well as to the norms of a group.

Fáilte Ireland (2005a) identifies the advantages and disadvantages of operating within a multicultural workforce environment. Advantages include:

- Improved innovation based on the concept that differences will provide new and different ideas. Problem-solving is aided by staff with different perspectives, backgrounds and training. The more ideas on the table, the more likely the big winner is to emerge.
- Different perspectives offered by a workforce that is more representative of global demographics. These perspectives are better able to support the development of new and varying product offerings for a diverse client base.
- Improved staff retention and the ability to attract and recruit the best staff. Employees will give of their best and are more in tune with the customer base. Problem-solving, creativity and innovation among employees will be enhanced. Other benefits can include competitive edge, better public image, increased productivity, job satisfaction and morale, as well as improved inter-staff relations and a satisfying work environment. It is also possible to point to other, rather more intangible benefits which include improved quality and better customer service.
- Drawing from the full talent pool, both domestic and international. A diverse workforce means that employers are recruiting from as wide a talent pool as possible and enhancing their prospects of recruiting the best employee for each available position, particularly when traditional labour pools are unable to deliver the required skills and numbers.

The challenges posed by a cultural diverse workforce include:

- *Increased training costs.* For example, a multicultural workforce may require language and cultural-awareness training to facilitate integration into the workplace and local society.
- *Increased incidents of conflict.* Conflicts arise when two or more individuals differ or disagree on a particular situation. In diverse workplaces, the most common conflicts arise from feelings of superiority, ignorance or fear, and result in derogatory comments or gestures. If management ignores such incidents, productivity suffers.

- *Mismanaged diversity*, which can cause employee dissatisfaction and affect productivity, leading to lower job performance.
- *The need to accommodate a variety of religious and cultural expectations* such as holy days and dietary needs.
- *Reverse discrimination*. Reverse discrimination is a claim by a member of the majority that a member of a minority received preferential treatment because of their minority status and not their ability or qualification.

From the point of view of a manager in the tourism, hospitality and leisure industry, multiculturalism, multinationalism and multi-ethnicity present different challenges, depending upon the context in which they occur. The multiculturalism model that we discussed earlier in this chapter (Figure 6.1) illustrates the diversity of interrelationships that can be found when the two main dimensions are brought together. There are arguments that diversity in the workplace can create competitive advantage for tourism, hospitality and leisure organizations (Mok 2002).

As we have seen, there are arguments identifying the specific benefits of multiculturalism in the workplace. Managers working in an environment of cultural diversity need to be cognizant of both the benefits and challenges of diversity within the workforce. In addition, there are a number of common situations where practical awareness is important of the influence that an individual or group's origins and background can have on the way that they perceive a situation and behave in response to it. These include the following:

- where a business in the tourism, hospitality and leisure industry receives guests from countries, cultures and ethnic backgrounds that are different from that of the dominant culture in which the business is located, for example Japanese visitors staying in an Australian hotel or a Thai school party visiting Disneyland in Hong Kong;
- where guests are from different cultures, nationalities or ethnic origins to those of the workforce, for example in a Chinese restaurant staffed by immigrant Chinese staff and catering for local demand in, say, Bucharest, Windhoek or Sydney;
- where a varying proportion of the workforce in a business or department are of different cultural, national or ethnic origins to that of the dominant local culture. This is a very common situation in certain departments in the hotel industry in Europe and North America. In some situations, ethnic diversity may mean that people from a wide range of nationalities and cultures are employed. In others, cultural diversity is reflected in one, or perhaps two, major cultural, national or ethnic groups – the strong presence of Irish employees in the hotels of the Channel Islands or of the Vietnamese in housekeeping in many London hotels are examples of this. In both types of situation, it would be common for management staff, especially at senior levels, to be drawn from the dominant local cultural, national or ethnic groups. As we have seen in Chapter 5, migrant workers and ethnic minorities are generally under-represented at supervisory and management grades in the tourism and hospitality industry;

- where the management of the tourism, hospitality and leisure business represents a different culture or ethnic background to that of the majority of the workforce. This is a common model where expatriate management is used and is applicable in the case of the hotel industry in many parts of the world, particularly Asia and the Caribbean. It is also a model widely employed by airlines, where local station management tend to be expatriates. Disneyland in Paris, at start-up, employed US management and expertise in a number of key posts but the objective of these postings was always short term and, it could be argued, was important in order to ensure the transfer of what are essentially US culture and systems to Europe;

- where the corporate culture of the tourism, hospitality and leisure business is significantly different to that normally prevailing in the country or community in which it is based. In human resource terms, this may mean that although there is little or no distance between the management and operational staff in terms of their original culture, corporate norms create new divides which must be addressed.

Any of these situations as well as variants of them has the potential to produce misunderstanding, conflict and discriminatory behaviour in the relationships between managers, staff and, indeed, guests. Such tensions, whether overt or part of a hidden agenda, can only undermine guest and working environment within the tourism and hospitality business and, ultimately, detrimentally affect the quality of service that is delivered to guests. Anticipating potential problems in the interrelationships of different customer and employee groups and instituting positive measures to avoid their occurrence is called 'multicultural management'. The term normally applies to the management of human resources within an organization, but is a concept that is equally applicable to the management of the wider guest and employee environment.

The management of cultural diversity, then, is the application of general human resource management principles and strategies within the context of the ethnic and cultural diversity found in a tourism, hospitality and leisure operation. This approach to human resource management operates on the premise that the ethnic identities and cultural orientations of employees at all levels together with their backgrounds and experiences are important influences that affect how everyone acts in the workplace. Managing diversity recognizes that work habits and attitudes are influenced by culture. Thus, cultural considerations are of importance when seeking to manage a team that is ethnically and culturally diverse. Managers of tourism, hospitality and leisure operations are increasingly expected to manage cultural diversity, for it is a part of the daily life both of their role functions in tourism, hospitality and leisure, and of the industry itself.

Working and managing in a multicultural, multinational and multi-ethnic environment does not necessarily require skills and capabilities that are intrinsically different from those demanded of work in monocultural environments, with the possible exception of additional languages capabilities. There are, however, a number of critical issues to do with cultural, national and ethnic heterogeneity which those working in the tourism, hospitality and leisure industry at all levels will benefit from addressing. These include the following:

- The need to recognize and respect diversity within the guest and workforce populations and thus to avoid imposing dominant values and practices upon either group. In guest terms, the tendency to impose rules which determine, for example, what, where and when they eat is much less pronounced in many countries than it was in the past and this change permits hotels greater flexibility in meeting specific cultural or ethnic requirements. It also means reviewing a range of guest-handling procedures and systems in order to ensure that they are not designed on the basis of implicit assumptions about the dominant (generally local) culture. For example, different cultures have different ways in expressing dissatisfaction with service and it may be fair to assume that some groups of guests will utilize guest comment cards or address problems directly to staff or management while others will be more reluctant to do so. Lack of complaints via this route from Japanese tourists does not necessarily mean total guest satisfaction but may imply discomfort with direct or confrontational methods of expressing complaints or other comments. In relation to the workforce, the recognition of diversity and its potential implications for a variety of workplace practices is also of considerable importance and both the explicit dimensions of the working culture (rules, regulations, etc.) and those which are implicit but not formally stated need to be reviewed in the light of the cultural, national and ethnic composition of those employed or those who may potentially join the workforce.

- Recognition and respect, however, are only part of the process. The next and critical step is one of learning and understanding, and this involves far greater investment. Language is an important aspect of this but is rarely sufficient in itself. The ability to communicate with guests in their own language is widely recognized as important in the tourism and hospitality industry and both major and small companies have taken significant steps to enhance employee capabilities in this direction, both by employing staff with multilingual skills and by instituting specific language-training programmes for their front-line staff. Rarely, however, is the importance of intra-staff communication recognized to the extent that language skills are provided in order to enhance communication within the operational workforce or between staff and management. Front-line staff are, generally, not employed unless they speak the main language of the locality and in other generally low-skills areas, such as cleaning in airports or housekeeping in hotels, inability to communicate in the local language is overcome by the employment of bilingual supervisors. Thus it is quite frequent for managers to have no direct means of communicating with their staff except through an intermediary. The 'normal' assumption is that it is the responsibility of the possibly poorly educated and low-skilled staff concerned to learn English, French or German. An alternative viewpoint is that managers and supervisors, personnel with higher educational levels, should be the ones to learn at least the rudiments of the main languages which their colleagues and staff employ, whether it is Spanish, Bengali or Turkish. Recognition of this alternative is quite widespread in the United States where Spanish classes and self-study texts for the hospitality industry are widely available for monolingual, non-Hispanic managers.

- Mention has already been made of the employment of, for example, Japanese and Indian staff by major airlines to service routes to and from those countries. This is an important step in ensuring that guest needs and expectations are understood by key front-line personnel and it is likely that aspects of the approach adopted by these staff will 'rub off' on their working colleagues, thus enhancing the wider sense of understanding of cultural needs. A similar principle can be effective in relation to a workforce that is multicultural or multi-ethnic. Token steps have already been mentioned such as providing interpretive intermediaries to overcome language barriers. However, it is far more effective to invest in the training and development of staff from cultural, national or ethnic minority groups. We have already noted significant under-representation of ethnic minorities in positions of responsibility in tourism, hospitality and leisure. Policies which are designed to support and facilitate the promotion aspirations of staff from minority groups so that, eventually, they can take responsibilities as supervisors and managers is, probably, the most effective strategy for overcoming cultural and ethnic divisions and a lack of mutual understanding and respect.

- Explicit as well as less overt forms of racism are widespread in many societies and examples of the extreme and violent expression of such attitudes has been seen in a number of countries in recent years. Some countries, such as Britain, have specific legislation which is designed to outlaw discriminatory practice on grounds of race in the workplace and in other areas of society. Such legislation is by no means universal nor is its application entirely effective where it is in place. However, it is an important principle for employers to view their human resources in a way which allows them to maximize the potential and actual capabilities of each and every member of staff and also to recruit those who will be able to offer the most to the organization. This is an essential step in seeking to offer quality service to guests and in the application of the principles of empowerment within the workforce. Discriminatory practice, at any level, patently does not meet these objectives. Companies benefit in this regard if they have clear statements of policy with respect to equal opportunities, supported by a programme of action to ensure general awareness and specific training in relation to its implications. Colleges and universities, offering tourism, hospitality and leisure programmes, can readily support learning in this area by providing greater focus within their curricula to legal and other aspects of multiculturalism and multi-ethnicity.

  Racial discrimination in the tourism, hospitality and leisure workplace may exist in what can be called 'institutionalized' form, whereby traditions and practices are in place that ensures the division of responsibilities and opportunities is based on essentially ethnic or racial criteria. Adler and Adler (2004) describe the working environment of resort hotels in Hawaii and conclude forcibly that the allocation of roles and rewards is ethnically stratified. Adler and Adler identify a number of distinct groups within the resort workforce – new immigrants, locals, mainlanders and management – all of whom have distinct motivations, aspirations, commitment to the area of work and functions within the work environment.

The economic structures and their segregated racial base represents a strong bastion of institutionalized racism and explicitly stratified inequality. New immigrant workers were slotted into (and gladly accepted) the lowest strata of work. Their status as the relatively newest arrivals puts them at the bottom of the hospitality pecking order, and the resorts gladly exploited their labor and dedicated service at low wages and poor conditions. Even so, the situation of these workers compared favorably to that of even newer immigrant groups from Micronesia and other places, whose only choices involved toiling outdoors in the agricultural industry. Newer immigrants could not even manage the clean, presentable appearance that the Filipino, Tongan, Chinese and other resort employees had attained. Locals gladly ceded the jobs occupied by new immigrants to these groups, seeking employment in departments where their language skills and acculturation enabled them to work with haole (white) co-workers ... and in better-paying houseman work that was still heavy but not as dirty. Here they interacted with guests occasionally, were in view of guests frequently, but dealt mainly with one another. Haoles, at the top of the pyramid, still performed temporally shifting and somewhat physically demanding labor, but their efforts were more highly remunerated. (pp.166–7).

The principles of this division are not significantly different to that described by Orwell in the 1930s in relation to Parisian hotels. The structure that Adler and Adler represent does not necessarily represent conscious and planned racism by any one individual within the tourism, hospitality and leisure sector in Hawaii. However, it is indicative of practices and customs that ensure work is ethnically allocated and, thus, represents institutional racism in action. For example, recruitment is frequently by word of mouth within the communities which dominate the work area in question. Therefore, it is virtually impossible for someone outside that community to access such jobs. There is also tacit acceptance of customer prejudices in that certain ethnic groups are more acceptable in direct service roles than others to a significant proportion of the hotels' mainly white, mainland customer base.

- Implicit racist attitudes and behaviour are much more difficult to legislate against than direct discriminatory practice and, therefore, are rather more insidious. They are also a major problem in some societies and, consequently, in the tourism, hospitality and leisure industry. This form of racism can operate at a number of levels:
  - from guests/customers to employees;
  - from guests/customers to other guests/customers;
  - from employees to guests/customers;
  - from employees to other employees;
  - from management to employees.

The manifestation of racist attitudes from guests to other guests and from guests to employees has, of necessity, to be treated with some care and caution. In extreme form, neither behaviour can and should be tolerated and should be sanctioned in the same way as any other form of abuse or disruptive action by guests or customers. At other levels, complaints by fellow guests cannot be ignored and discreet action may be required by senior management. In relation to employees, it is an important principle to protect and support members of staff against abuse and mistreatment of any kind, whether from guests or fellow employees. Racism may well become part of wider problems of service and servility and these needs to be addressed in the context of wider empowerment development. However, in situations where the guests are predominantly from one cultural or ethnic group and those serving them are from another, there is a clear danger that assumptions about status and the superiority of one group over another may be drawn from these respective roles. The responsibility lies with management to ensure that such perceptions are not perpetuated, either explicitly or implicitly, and do not detract from the level and quality of service that is provided to guests.

Racism, in any form, in the way in which employees relate to their guests must be totally unacceptable to tourism, hospitality and leisure businesses in any sector. Such racism may manifest itself in the form of apparent humour out of the sight, hearing or language comprehension of guests but may also show in favoured or differential treatment of one group of guests over others. It is a management responsibility to demonstrate clearly that such behaviour is totally unacceptable. Punitive measures alone, however, are insufficient to deal with problems of this nature. Training and development programmes, designed to enhance understanding and tolerance of cultural and ethnic diversity, may also be necessary.

Such training programmes can also contribute to overcoming racial tensions within the staff body. Given the cultural and ethnic diversity of the workforce of many tourism and hospitality businesses, there is considerable potential for inter-group rivalry on the basis of culture or ethnic origin. At times of contracting employment, for example due to recession, the Weberian term of 'group closure' may take place, with the dominant group excluding and even scapegoating minorities in order to protect their own position. Racist behaviour, whether perpetuated by groups or individuals, must be treated with all seriousness and action taken early in order to avoid the development of overt and possibly violent responses.

Finally, the manifestation of racist attitudes or behaviour by managers to their staff cannot be acceptable within a reputable tourism, hospitality and leisure business. Training, again, can make some contribution to overcoming tendencies in this direction but the most effective strategy lies in managers becoming familiar with their subordinates as individuals in order to enhance understanding of their background and needs in the workplace.

- Racism, prejudice and intolerance of customs and practices other than the 'norm' are often the result of ignorance and a lack of contact with people from different cultural or ethnic origins. Given the diversity both in the origins of guests/customers and the workforce of the industry worldwide, the college and university education and training of those aspiring to work in tourism, hospitality and leisure at all levels will be enhanced through formal consideration of the implications of this diversity. It is a theme which can be introduced into the curriculum in a number of ways, within, for example, a consideration of marketing, human resource management and the tourism and hospitality industry structure. The theme can be reinforced through discussion and analysis prior to and following work placements. Among the most effective means of breaking down barriers and assisting students to enter the tourism and hospitality industry with an open mind and without the baggage of prejudicial ignorance is to include a period of study or work within a different cultural, national or ethnic environment. Programmes that specifically include periods of study or working placements in other countries can make a major contribution to overcoming the barriers of ignorance and prejudice. Many courses, at a variety of levels, include such components and in time this practice may also spread more widely.

Bringing together the cultural, national and ethnic diversity of the global tourism, hospitality and leisure industry in terms of its markets and its workforce has the potential to be one of its prime strengths. The intensity of the relationship between customers and front-line staff is such that effective management, training and development in the area of multiculturalism can make a significant contribution in the area of relationship marketing and provide a real competitive advantage to companies. Likewise, recognizing and addressing the issue of multiculturalism in the workforce has the potential to offer opportunities for effective team-building and can contribute to enhanced customer service quality by improving staff commitment and facilitating real empowerment.

At the same time, mismanagement of a multicultural, multinational and ethnically diverse environment in the tourism, hospitality and leisure industry has the potential to be very destructive. Tensions derived from this source are difficult to defuse or control and can lead to a situation where all management decisions are assessed and questioned against cultural and ethnic criteria.

Case Study *The youngsters changing the face of Aviemore by David Ross*

Once it was known as the carbuncle on the face of the Cairngorms, now it is looking to revolutionise the tourism industry in Scotland.

Aviemore, the town ridiculed for turning tourists off with its concrete monstrosities, has undergone a renaissance to become an international centre of tourism excellence – importing bright, keen students from Croatia, Poland, China and South America.

The redeveloped resort will soon unveil a partnership with a hotel school in Croatia which will allow an exchange of hospitality students between the Adriatic and Badenoch.

The first Croatian students, who arrive next month, will study at a new hospitality and catering training college, said to be the first of its kind in the UK, which is part of an £80m redevelopment of Aviemore.

There they will join a multi-ethnic community of tourism professionals already employed by the resort.

A consortium led by Macdonald Hotels, Bank of Scotland and the Tulloch Construction Group has already funded a leisure centre and spa, a conference centre, woodland lodges and the refurbishment of the Macdonald Highlands and Academy hotels.

This is where the Croatian students will train for six months. Reciprocal placements for Scottish students in Istria will follow.

Alan Jones, training director at the Aviemore Academy, said:

'This exchange agreement is with the prestigious Caesar Ritz College in Croatia, which bears the name of the man who opened the Ritz hotels in Paris and London. It has been in the planning stages since I met representatives of the College at a recruitment fair in Switzerland.'

That is where he also found highly motivated employees for Aviemore, such as Sylvia Castillo.

The 32-year-old from Colombia said: 'My mother is Peruvian and my father Spanish. I was born in Peru but raised in Colombia. When I finished school, I went to study modern languages in Madrid.

'Then I wanted to do a masters degree in hotel management at the Caesar Ritz at Brig in Switzerland. That's where I met Alan Jones who made us all fall in love with Aviemore and made us want to come and work here to help build the resort.

'I just got here in January and have been working as a receptionist in the leisure centre.

'I find the Scottish people very friendly and very educated. It's good to be here.'

She had heard suggestions that some Scots were lazy, which amused her: 'I don't think you are lazy, but I am from South America.'

Marta Lubiejewska, 25, from Rudmik in southern Poland, however, thinks the description is sometimes accurate: 'I find the Scottish people very friendly, very helpful. But some can be lazy. Many people come here to work from Europe to make money, so do their best.

'I don't think all Scottish people do that. In Poland, everyone wants things done yesterday. Here tomorrow will do.'

That is not her approach. An MSc in environmental engineering, she is now studying for a qualification from the Chartered Institute of Management.

She heard about Aviemore from her brother and caught a bus from Poland, arriving in June. She started working at the Dalfaber timeshare resort and then the Macdonald hotels, where she was waitress, trainee supervisor, supervisor and is now a trainee manager in charge of housekeeping in the lodges. She will soon start working on the resort's environmental policies, her commitment to the place growing.

'I am enjoying myself, a new place, new people. I love the mountains, the fresh air. It is a good environment, and nobody seems to resent us being here,' she said.

Shivakumar Kandaswamy, 33, agrees, although it is too cold for him to spend much time outside at present. A Rangers supporter from Bangalore, he is in charge of the four-star Aspects restaurant. He had been working on the P&O cruise ship *Oriana* when one of the passengers asked him to work for him in a small hotel in East Lothian.

He said: 'A year later, I saw the advert for Aviemore and learned of the huge investment.

'So I came up last June. I especially liked the idea of getting in at the start and working with so many different nationalities.

'They are like one big family to me, very warm.

'I also find the Scottish people the most friendly in the UK, but laidback. I can't get over how everything still comes to a grinding halt for two days on a Friday night. In my country, we are open 24 hours a day seven days a week.'

He is frustrated by Scottish perceptions of his chosen profession. He said: 'There is a lot of potential for hospitality in this country and it is growing.

'We need more people coming into it, but people don't apply for the jobs.

'People here don't take jobs in the hospitality industry seriously. I decided to make it my life. In my family, most are doctors or computer software engineers. I was the only one to go into hospitality and they weren't happy.'

▶

His ambition is to open a truly upmarket Indian restaurant in Scotland, but until then he is happy to be working in Aviemore. His friend and colleague Jasmine Lin Mei, 25, from Beijing, has a similar perspective.

She has a degree in business management from Singapore; a diploma in hotel management from Switzerland; and an MSc in international hospitality from Strathclyde University, where her dissertation was on job satisfaction among housekeeping employees in budget hotels in Glasgow.

'I had been offered a job at a ski resort in America and another one on a cruise ship.

'But I wanted to come here because the resort was just starting presenting a lot of opportunities. Scottish people don't seem to think that work such as housekeeping is a proper job. Because unemployment is really quite low, they see hotel work as temporary and the job satisfaction is not very high. But I think it is good both for us and for the Scottish people, that we are here.'

Mr Jones agrees: 'Roughly 45-per cent of the resort's workforce is local. We would like more.

'But unemployment in the valley is low, about 2-per cent while something like 40-per cent of the population is over 70. That's the challenge.'

Published in *The Herald*, Glasgow, 7 March 2005. Reproduced by permission of The Herald (Glasgow, Scotland).

Case discussion questions

1. What are the benefits to tourism, hospitality and leisure companies in establishing a dedicated, company-based training school?

2. The article implies that some nationalities may be harder-working while others are lazier than others. What is your assessment of this view, what are the arguments in favour and against such claims and how should managers handle perceptions of this nature?

3. What are the management benefits and challenges in employing staff from a diversity of linguistic, ethnic and cultural backgrounds within a business?

Review and discussion questions

1. Consider a range of additional situations that could be added to the multicultural matrix (Figure 6.1).

2. Consider situations that you might have experienced where tourism, hospitality and leisure businesses have provided specialist services for particular cultural, ethnic or national market segments.

3. What steps might a traveller take in order to prepare him- or herself for a visit to an unfamiliar culture or country?

4. Why do tourists seek out products and services that are familiar when they are away from home? What might host countries do in order to encourage greater patronage of local and authentic tourism and hospitality products and services?

5. What are the main benefits of working in a new environment, in a different culture or country?

6. How can the level of migration within the tourism, hospitality and leisure industry be explained?

7. Why does the tourism, hospitality and leisure industry attract a significant level of illegal immigrant labour?

8. How can tourism, hospitality and leisure managers make use of the theories of multiculturalism addressed in this chapter?

9. What are the potential dangers in classifying cultural, ethnic and national groups according to broad characteristics?

7 The social composition of employment in tourism, hospitality and leisure: diversity beyond culture

Chapter objectives

This is the second chapter on diversity themes. The objectives of the chapter are:

- to review a range of diversity themes in relation to tourism, hospitality and leisure, including gender, age, ability, social inclusion and motivation/choice;

- to consider the key issues in relation to each of the above diversity areas;

- to identify the benefits and disadvantages of diversity (other than cultural) in the tourism, hospitality and leisure workplace.

Introduction

In the previous chapter, we considered diversity in terms of the cultural and ethnic composition of the tourism, hospitality and leisure workforce, and we have looked at diversity issues in terms of guests and clients in a similar vein. Clearly, an interpretation of workplace diversity does not need to be constrained by cultural or ethnic considerations. Of equal importance is consideration of diversity against a range of other criteria, including:

- gender
- ability and disability
- age
- social inclusion
- motivation and choice.

We have already considered the breadth of tourism, hospitality and leisure in relation to the types of employment opportunities that are available and the differing skills that these positions demand. The context within which these opportunities are located is of equal importance. Thus, a front-office position in a busy city centre hotel, while ostensibly carrying the same job title as that of a small country-hotel business, is in fact a totally different job, so that the two positions have pressures, skills demands and responsibilities that bear little relationship to each other. This diversity is represented throughout tourism, hospitality and leisure so that it is very difficult to prepare universal job specifications that have applicability to all situations and contexts. From a positive perspective, the diversity of work roles in tourism, hospitality and leisure creates opportunity for people of differing capabilities and backgrounds. At the same time, in some countries access to some areas of work is restricted for reasons of tradition, culture, gender or image.

The tourism, hospitality and leisure industry is frequently portrayed as an industry for the young, beautiful and super-fit, and this projection is used to create the image of vibrancy, energy and fun. Companies such as TGIF (Thank God It's Friday) restaurants, Club 18–30 resorts and Carnival Cruises specifically focus on this image in their recruitment and look for employees, male and female, who match the environment they seek to project, that of youth and fun. They are also seeking to match their staff image to that of the client profile of the restaurants or resorts and, by doing so, to reduce the social distance between guest and employee. This represents the use of what Nickson *et al.* (2003) describe as 'aesthetic labour criteria' in the selection of employees – people who match both the physical and the cultural ideals of their clientele.

Other tourism and hospitality companies also seek to project an aesthetic image but in a different context than that of energy and fun, the 'adrenalin factor', which drives some of the above examples. The history of the changing role of flight attendants in the USA points to the early years of work in the airline sector as elitist and essentially middle class. 'Sky girls … were required to retire at the age of 32, remain single, and adhere to strict weight, height and appearance requirements' (Association of Flight Attendants, undated) so that as recently as 1968, the average career of a flight attendant lasted just 18 months. Williams (1988) adds an aesthetic dimension to the age requirement. Women attendants as a group are subject to a set of appearance criteria from which men are exempt. Williams concludes by arguing that female airline attendants are viewed as a vital 'part of the packaging of the product' (p.96), on the basis of their appearance. Singapore Airlines also use the image of the 'Singapore Girl' in order to project quality, caring and, to some extent, sensuous service. The image, of course, is gender-specific but the client will find that in reality the airline's services are provided by a mixed gender cabin crew. To a large extent, however, youth is the image of fun and frivolity in the tourism, hospitality and leisure industry. Where employment legislation and social attitudes permit, this image is perpetuated by the termination of employment contracts when female staff reach a certain age – in the case of some Asian airlines this is in the early 30s. The end to marriage bans, whereby women were required to give up employment on marriage, is only a thing of the relatively recent past in many European airlines. However, when an image is required to convey issues of safety, security and, in general, confidence, a more mature model is portrayed. Thus the airline pilot or hotel manager in advertising and promotion tends to be portrayed by a slightly greying, more mature male – with the obligatory good looks!

Internationally, the employment composition of the tourism, hospitality and leisure industry does confirm the image of youth, but it is possible to identify other specific groups within society beyond those just defined by age, both in work areas that have a strong glamour appeal and in the more routine and humdrum aspects of employment in the industry. The demographic structure of many developed countries is already a major force for change in the social composition of the sector's workforce. The decline in the youth population means that the tourism and hospitality industry's traditional source of relatively cheap and flexible unskilled labour is declining in size. The competition for labour is intense in many developed countries and the response is, generally, to seek new sources of labour from abroad. Other than this, relatively few businesses have really taken the implications of demographic change aboard and acted as a consequence of them by raising the wage levels and benefits payable to young recruits or by looking to alternative sources of labour. There are strategies which can be used to focus on the recruitment process and, subsequently, on how employees are treated at work in order to attract young people in a competitive and shrinking labour market. Fáilte Ireland (2005c) address a range of recruitment strategies that are targeted at both traditional school leavers and wider sources of labour, including women returning to work and older workers seeking new opportunities.

Adler and Adler's (2004) work, located in Hawaii, points to clear stratification of employment within hospitality on a variety of grounds including gender, ethnicity and vocational motivation. Their anthropological analysis of the various groupings in resort hotels notes clear differentiation in the roles played by the various groups of employees, specifically native Pacific islanders, local Hawaiian and mainland white American.

Gender

In purely numerical terms, tourism, hospitality and leisure is a sector that has been dominated by young and female labour in many parts of the world. For example, the ILO (2001) report that women account for 52 per cent of restaurant workers in the United States; 58 per cent of hospitality employees in Australia; between 60 per cent and 70 per cent of all hotel, catering and tourism employees in Austria; and 62 per cent of hospitality workers in Denmark. However, particularly in relation to gender roles, the situation is very different in cultures where a strong male presence in all service or customer contact areas is much more common. This is the situation in parts of Southern Europe, the Middle East and other parts of Asia. In Spain, ILO figures point to 42.5 per cent female employees but this figure is rising (ILO 2001). This structure is also strongly linked to the hierarchy in the industry in that there is under-representation not only of youth (not surprisingly) but also of women, ethnic minorities and non-nationals diminishes significantly at supervisory and management levels in most sectors of the industry. In developed countries women dominate numerically in all sectors of tourism, hospitality and leisure where there is customer contact, including front-office and dining-room personnel, airline staff, tourist-office personnel and tour guides. However, when it comes to the more senior positions in these same areas, where the jobs have less customer contact but a greater management and decision-making role, the situation is usually reversed. Employers in these situations either announce that women operate so well at their existing levels that it is impossible to replace them or else cite the perceived negative traits of women such as their inability to gain authority and respect, their timidity and their indecisiveness as barriers to promotion.

In most developed countries, tourism, hospitality and leisure is, numerically, a sector that is dominated by female employment. As a weak labour-market sector, women hold a majority of the lower-skills and routine customer-contact positions in a range of business in the sector, including hotels, airlines, travel agencies, tour operations and cultural organizations. At the same time, most of the technical and senior roles in organizations within these sectors are held by men. In developed economies, this reflects deep-rooted role divisions within the labour force and also draws upon issues such as workplace flexibility, low pay and work status. In the United States, Diaz and Umbreit (1995) note relative neutrality in terms of gender balance at lower and middle management within the hospitality sector, but senior management participation by women is less than 1 per cent of the total number of positions. A similar imbalance was reported in the UK tourism sector by Jordan (1997). Specifically within leisure, Aitchison, Jordan and Brackenridge (1999) report that women experience both structural and cultural constraints in attempting to secure management careers in the sector but that there are grounds for optimism with respect to future change.

Women's position within the labour market of most developed countries is changing significantly. While they dominate low-skills work in tourism, hospitality and leisure, their overall level of participation in the workforce of most countries is considerably less then that of men. Table 7.1 illustrates this position in the case of Spain relative to that of the wider European Union and demonstrates the significant level of change that occurred during the period 1995–2003.

There is also a dimension to gender division in tourism, hospitality and leisure that draws upon the notion of aesthetic labour (Warhurst *et al.* 2000; Nickson *et al.* 2003) and perpetuates the employment of women as cabin attendants in airlines and representatives for tour operators. Adkins (1995) points to the varying demands that gender imposes with respect to recruitment in tourism, hospitality and leisure. She notes that:

Table 7.1								
Female participation in the labour force in Spain								
	1995	2000	2001	2002	2003	Increase 1995–2002 (% points)	EU core 15 average	EU objectives for 2010
Overall employment rate, people aged 16–64	45.9	57.1	58.7	59.5	59.3	+13.4	63.9	70
Female employment rate, people aged 16–64	31.2	42.0	43.8	44.9	48.7	+17.5	54.8	60

Source: Eironline (undated), with permission, http://www.eiroeurofound.cu.int

What was clear was that women workers were subject to a set of criteria relating to appearance regardless of occupation, while men were not. These criteria can be said to exist regardless of occupation in two senses. First they existed not because of the occupation 'needed' its workers to possess these qualities – you do not have to be pretty to make sandwiches – but because women workers were constructed as somehow needing these appearance qualities to be workers ... The second way in which these criteria can be said to exist regardless of occupation [is because]) women also became operatives precisely because of the existence of appearance criteria. (pp.107–108)

Adkins continues by arguing that, in tourism, hospitality and leisure,

For women to have access to employment, most have no choice but to occupy the position of sexual subjects. To get a job, most women (regardless of their occupation) were required to fulfil conditions which related to the production of an 'attractive' female workforce. These conditions meant ... that the primary work of women was the work of being a sexual commodity, and they did this on top of serving drinks or making sandwiches or washing up. (p.145)

Gender roles in the tourism, hospitality and leisure industries of developing countries reflect both differing cultural and economic considerations compared to more affluent settings. In some situations such as that in Saudi Arabia, the participation of women in the workforce in any capacity is restricted and does not extend to guest-contact positions on the front line. In Iran, by contrast, the recent growth in tourism means that women play an increasing role in front-line positions in some sectors of the industry, notably as cabin attendants and in the rooms division (front office and housekeeping) in privately owned hotels. In countries and regions where economic pressures mean that people value access to work that, in other contexts, would not be highly rated, male participation rates in the tourism, hospitality and leisure sector is likely to be much higher. Thus, food and beverage service and front-office staff in Kenyan hotels are predominantly (but by no means exclusively) male and also represent a much more mature age profile than would be the case with their counterparts in developed countries. Where women feature in the tourism, hospitality and leisure labour market in developing countries, they do so, according to Chant (1997), on the basis of:

Male constructed and male-biased gender stereotypes [which] place women in occupations which in many respects crystallize and intensify their subordinate positions in society, whether through their assignation to low-level, behind-the-scenes domestic work as laundrywomen or chambermaids, or to jobs where their physical attributes are used to attract men or to gratify male sexual needs, as in front-line hotel, commercial and restaurant posts and in entertainment establishments. (p.161).

There is a dimension to tourism, hospitality and leisure work that, while not wholly gendered, is dominated by female participation of both adults and children. This relates to what is variously called 'sex work' or 'sex tourism', depending on the context and the profile of the clientele. It is a phenomenon that exists widely in both developed and developing countries. In the developed world, the link between sex work and tourism is not necessarily apparent although, as Muroi and Sasaki (1997) point out, a significant proportion of female in-migration to Japan is for economic reasons associated with prostitution and is linked to demand created by the experiences of Japanese men in South-East Asia. It is, however, subject to the highest level of scrutiny in developing countries, notably in Asia, on grounds of the exploitation of both women and children in countries such as India, Thailand and Vietnam (Rao 1999; Ryan and Hall 2001). Indeed, it is a theme where the economic and moral debates can be found in fiction (Houellebecq 2003) as well as in academic writing. Although there have been high-profile cases where tourists from developed countries have appeared before courts facing charges of paedophile sex with minors in a number of Asian countries, little coverage is given to wider health, people-trafficking and exploitation issues that are stimulated by this form of tourism across much of the developing world. It is one dimension of tourism's employment creation that most governments are keen to downplay. With respect to child sex tourism, the ILO (2001) points to the scale of such exploitation, both in terms of children and women.

> The sexual exploitation of children of both sexes, as practised through child prostitution and child pornography, forms a somewhat hidden part of the overall commercial sex sector. Although a worldwide phenomenon, it is more prevalent in Asia than elsewhere ... Certain holiday destinations are now frequented by paedophiles. At a national level, pimps, taxi drivers, tour operators (by organizing package sex tours), hotel staff, brothel owners and entertainment establishments all work together to satisfy foreign tourists' demand for prostitutes. At the international level, agents disseminate information about particular resorts where such practices are commonplace. (p.20)

Case Study 'There's suggestion, but the thong stays on' by James Morgan

During last week's media frenzy over Glasgow's lap dancing clubs, the city council crowed that its new report showed that the clubs are covers for prostitution and should, therefore, all be classed as sex shops.

I find that idea insulting to my intelligence and the people I work with. We dancers haven't been given any opportunity to have our say. I want to confirm that much of the alleged damning evidence and press coverage relating to my job is insultingly inaccurate. It has angered me to read it.

Believe it or not, what I do is generally no raunchier than what people see on an MTV rap video; sometimes less raunchy. We're dancing for men but it's strictly non-contact. We're there to be female fantasies, but we're not providing a sexual service. It's entertainment and nowadays most female entertainers have to meet standards of sexual perfection. I'm not saying that's right or wrong, but it is everywhere in our culture.

My job is an interesting and admittedly unconventional one, not to every woman's taste. It has good and bad points, which I am prepared to face because I choose to. I arrive at work at 9 pm and get ready. I'm self-employed, so I pay a house fee, £12, do my make-up with the other girls and maybe have a drink. Then I go downstairs to the club,

▶

relax and start talking to the clientele. There are bouncers circulating all the time, there are no private rooms, just a curtained area where there can be as many as 10 dances going on and, even there, there's CCTV.

I enjoy performing, as do most of the girls there. I wouldn't say that I love attention. What I like is dancing: moving and exercising to the music. Sure there's sexual suggestion – it's a topless bar, but the thong stays on. Like any job involving the public and alcohol, you do get people being rude. They might say: 'Oh I like my breasts a bit bigger, love,' but I just reply: 'You're not my type, either.' Then I get the bouncer. The girls take no crap – we give as good as we get.

Personally, I have found my past jobs far more degrading and exploiting. I suffered more disrespect from men while working in call centres, as a secretary, a receptionist, a waitress, or a bar maid.

The public outrage seems to me to be based on a very negative, even outdated, kind of feminist thought, one where women are poor defenceless victims of male oppression. But I don't know any 'victims' in the club where I work. I don't know any single mother who's struggling, anyone who's addicted to drugs, any victims of managers or victims of men. These are all very strong women, women like me who have chosen to work here. Shouldn't equality be about the right to choose? Closing the clubs would be taking away that choice for many women, women whose job in a clean, pleasant, closely super-vised and safe club is being slandered. There are many women who've been making a good living over a number of years and are managing their money. They have account-ants and they declare their taxes. We do our job with pride and success, because we are settled here, and because it's a job like any other. Academic, politician, whoever – if you want to tell me that what I do is degrading and I don't feel degraded, does that make me a fool?

But if the authorities don't like what they see, they should try looking at all angles – positive and negative, and should thus be supportive and pro-active, not damning and destructive.

Do they really think that slapping a sex shop licence on a clean club is going to help? I think that it would just encourage the good clubs to live up to their outrageous stereo-types.

I agree with stricter policing of clubs, espe-cially if it stops them charging their dancers too much. At the moment there's no union for dancers and I think that would help.

Some people will always call my club seedy, but I think that's quite a humorous term. It's harmless fun and we're in control. But if Glasgow City Council wants to clean up the city's image, it should promote tolerance and de-stigmatise good clubs, not set out to whip up a storm.

Published in *The Herald*, Glasgow, 27 August 2004. Reproduced by permission of The Herald (Glasgow, Scotland).

Case discussion questions

1. What are the arguments for and against allowing women to work in lap-dancing clubs?

2. Is lap-dancing more degrading to women than restaurant or bar work?

3. Is it the responsibility of governments to control work opportunities in the sex industry?

Ability and disability

The tourism and hospitality sector can be described as one that offers opportunity to members of a society across much of its ability and disability range. It is a sector (and the same is true for areas of leisure) that can accommodate the expectations and abilities of those with exceptional talent (in culture, entertainment, sports, technology, entrepreneurship as examples) as well as the majority of most communities which may include those who face challenges of a different sort in terms of physical or intellectual ability. In this sense, the weak labour-market characteristics of the sector facilitate access in that the requirement for formal qualifications and pre-entry skills is limited, particularly in economies such as Singapore and the UK where the service sector faces major employee shortages. Tourism, hospitality and leisure include a wide range of employment areas that are predominantly routine in their technical demands and where the lack of skills requirements provides opportunities for those who might otherwise find regular employment difficult to achieve. In many countries, the sector has an excellent record in offering work opportunity and experience to those with varying degrees of intellectual disability. In the UK, legal provisions, under the Disability Discrimination Act, require employers to include a certain number of staff members who are registered as disabled in their workforce; it also requires them to make appropriate provision to enable such staff to work effectively. This can be in terms of providing access for those with physical disability and technology modifications for those with sight or hearing disability. Small businesses, which predominate in tourism, hospitality and leisure, are exempt from this employment requirement although they probably provide the environment most conducive to the accommodation of diversity on the basis of ability. There is no provision to ensure working opportunity for those with intellectual disability. However, there is evidence that participation in constructive and rewarding work and enterprise can contribute significantly to alleviating some forms of mental health problem (Mind/Social Firms UK 2004).

While opportunity to include employees with a wide variety of abilities represents a positive dimension of the tourism, hospitality and leisure sectors, such opportunity must be tempered with the need to protect vulnerable members of society from exploitation in the workplace. There is potential danger that unscrupulous or ill-informed employers will exploit members of the disabled community who may be unable to ensure their own rights in terms of payment, conditions and opportunities.

We have already noted the role that emotional and aesthetic labour play in the delivery of services in some sectors of tourism, hospitality and leisure. The requirement to conform to employer and customer expectations in terms of dimensions, such as emotional engagement, style and appearance, physical attainment attributes and specialist interests, among others, may act against the participation of some disabled people in the sector's workplaces. As a result, disabled people's participation in tourism, hospitality and leisure work is in danger of being 'ghettoized' into low-style, routine and lower-status areas of employment.

Case Study *SMART Buffet, London*

SMART is a social enterprise located in London. SMART seeks to promote mental health through purposeful activities by offering work, training and social opportunities to people with serious and enduring mental illness. The organization aims to create a supportive environment, which gives members the opportunity to benefit from joining a social network, to re-discover and develop talents and skills, and, for some, to move towards more independent living.

The cafe project is at the heart of SMART and is perhaps the most vibrant project within the organization which also includes workshops and horticulture. The cafe is used not only by members but is also open to the general public, so the operation can be very busy. For people wishing to get back to work this is an excellent project to start on the road to independent employment. There are only five people at any one time working in the cafe project. These members therefore have to be able to work as part of a team, be reliable, good timekeepers and be able to cope with a little bit of pressure when working over the lunchtime rush.

There are various different jobs that people can become involved in, when working for the cafe. Front-of-house members can get involved in working on the service side of things. They get taught customer care skills. Members interested in getting involved in food preparation will get trained in basic food hygiene and catering skills.

SMART supports its members in seeking further skills through training and by placing them in selected external employment opportunities. The long-term aim is to develop a pool of local employers who understand the challenges faced by SMART members and will provide a supportive, transitional working environment. Two of current members of SMART started off in the cafe a year ago and with a little encouragement have also started to attend the local catering college, doing a professional chefs qualification. They will be supported further in transition to full-time work in the local community.

SMART is an example of a variety of schemes that are aimed at potential employees with disability or a background of mental illness. Their work illustrates the potential for some participants to make a useful transition to tourism employment, provided that the appropriate support systems remain in place as long as they are required. Supporting those socially excluded in the direction of useful employment is a challenge within the context of social and skills training. SMART is one very small-scale initiative, targeting a particular group of people in need. In many respects the challenge is not so much within the social organizations which provide the bridging, it is with potential employers in the tourism sector itself.

SMART go beyond training to providing working experience in an outlet and supporting the further training of participants. The real challenge is to educate those local employers who can offer an appropriate work environment to the value of recruiting from those with disability in the labour market.

Case prepared by the author for Fáilte Ireland from publicly accessible websites. Reproduced with permission.

Case discussion questions

1. To what extent could the SMART training model transfer to other cultures and industry contexts?

2. What are the potential benefits to the tourism, hospitality and leisure sector in supporting projects such as SMART?

3. What are the potential dangers in extending the SMART training model?

4. Why does the case suggest that 'the real challenge is to educate those local employers who can offer an appropriate work environment to the value of recruiting from those with disability in the labour market'?

Age

A widespread marketing image of tourism, hospitality and leisure is that of young people interacting with each other as consumers and delivering services to their guests. This represents an image which, until relatively recently, depicted a reasonably accurate reflection of reality in most developed countries. The effect of the 'baby boom' of the 1960s and 1970s was that there were large number of young people seeking employment and tourism, hospitality and leisure offered wide-ranging opportunities for school and college leavers. As a result, the industry could readily project itself as a young people's environment. Consumer trends also supported this image, with the focus of much product development and marketing on family vacations. In employment terms, the structure of the industry has, historically, been very much one tilted towards youth and, while this is changing, it remains a dominant feature. The ILO (2001) report that, in the United States, restaurant sector employees consist of a group of whom 25 per cent are aged between 16 and 19 years, 19 per cent between 20 and 24 years and a further 25 per cent between 25 and 34 years. In Austria, 14.5 per cent of all hotel, catering and tourism workers are below 20 years of age while in the Netherlands the average age of sector employees is 23 years. In Spain, over 50 per cent of all hospitality employees are under 30 years. Labour-market deregulation in many countries means that much of the work that is undertaken by younger people in the tourism, hospitality and leisure sector is characterized by 'increased income insecurity, wage polarization and deteriorating conditions of employment. Full-time permanent employment is being replaced by part-time and casual work' (ILO 2001, p.18).

This 'young' world of tourism, hospitality and leisure, while not disappearing, has certainly modified since the mid-1980s. Demographic shifts and advances in medical care mean that the fastest-growing group in terms of leisure participation in developed countries is the over-60s who stay fitter, live longer and have more disposable income than their preceding generations. As a result, they travel extensively and take part in a wide range of leisure activities, both sporting and cultural, at ages when, in the past, such participation would have been deemed beyond them. At the same time, the same communities have experienced severe declines in the birth rate so that the school and college leaving population, the traditional source of fresh labour for tourism, hospitality and leisure businesses, is far smaller than it was in the past. This is a major factor behind skills shortages in the sector. One redress is the import of labour from other countries, a response that we have already considered. Another approach is to recruit older workers to work in tourism, hospitality and leisure, in part to compensate for the shortage of younger employees but also to develop an employee profile that is more in tune with the guest profile of many operations. In Canada, this change means that 25 per cent of the accommodation workforce is over 44 years old (ILO 2001). In addition to providing companies with a source of labour that is socially and culturally more in tune with a significant proportion of its older clients, older workers can bring different skills into the workplace. In the case study presented below, B&Q are able to employ older workers who have a passionate interest in aspects of DIY as a leisure activity or may have previously worked as a painter and decorator, electrician or plumber. Thus they bring a level of expertise into the job that will probably be lacking in more traditional and younger retail workers. The B&Q case study refers to paid work. There are many older workers, however, who opt for unpaid, volunteer positions, particularly in tourism and aspects of leisure. Typically, such workers work with heritage sites, in museums, as local guides and as volunteer information sources at airports and other transport termini, available to give directions to arriving travellers. In the UK, organizations such as the National Trust, as custodian of many historic properties, would be unable to meet its commitment to provide access to visitors without the support of, generally, older volunteer workers.

In some situations, however, there may be perceptions that older people are unsuited to the work demands of tourism, hospitality and leisure operations. In the late 1980s, McDonald's in Singapore sought to overcome recruitment problems by employing older workers for some of their front-line positions. They faced problems as a result because of the desire of such workers to engage in conversation with customers for periods that exceed the service model in place within a fast-food restaurant and their reluctance to work with the level of intensity characteristic expected in this model.

In developing countries, where the population structure is biased far more in favour of youth, a major social need is frequently the challenge of unemployment among the population who are under 25. In this situation, the pressure to achieve age balance in the workforce is less evident. However, lack of employment opportunities in the labour market means that attrition rates can be very low. As a result, people working in tourism, hospitality and leisure are likely to have been in the same organization and, probably, the same post for an extended period and, literally, will have grown old in the job. In Iran, for example, many hotel workers obtained their positions in the immediate aftermath of the 1979 Islamic Revolution and have remained in post for over 25 years with no opportunity for development or promotion within the job. Such situations present very different challenges with respect to age diversity within the workforce.

Historically, the high proportion of young people within the workforce has linked but independent causes. The truth is that the social structure of the industry in developed countries reflects a complex amalgam of social, economic, cultural and historical factors, many of which are closely interrelated. These include the following:

- the skills structure of many sub-sectors, with a preponderance of positions at operative, unskilled or semi-skilled levels;
- the nature of the labour market in many tourism and hospitality sub-sectors (see Chapter 3), which enables flexible access and attrition, in particular to operative positions, by those with varied or no formal qualifications or experience;
- de-skilling in some sub-sectors, especially food production and service, which allows much more general access to positions previously protected by specific skills requirements;
- variable demand, especially seasonality, which reduces the security and permanence of employment in many areas. One response to this is the active promotion of, in particular, seasonal work, for example of positions as tour

operator representatives in Mediterranean resorts to the young. The low skill demands of many jobs in the industry also attract young people to make use of the consequent flexibility of access and departure in order to support travel and mobility within Europe and beyond. A high proportion of young Australians and New Zealanders in Europe for perhaps a year work in a number of tourism- and hospitality-related jobs for this reason;

- contraction of core employment opportunities and the growth in peripheral part-time and casual work, especially in north-western Europe;
- recruitment strategies and conditions in some companies which are designed to attract those interested in short- and medium-term commitments only and do not appeal to those seeking permanent and long-term employment or career opportunities;
- levels of pay and conditions in some sub-sectors of the industry which are only acceptable to immigrant or otherwise marginalized members of society;
- restructuring of tourism-, hospitality- and leisure-related employment in transition economies includes growing levels of foreign investment, frequently through major international hotel groups, restaurants and airlines. Employment policies frequently focus on the recruitment of young school and college leavers with no previous experience. At the same time, established local businesses are having to downsize their labour forces of older workers significantly in order to survive and compete in the new marketplace.

The issue of the age structure of the tourism, hospitality and leisure sector has wider social implications in both developed but particularly developing countries. Child labour within the tourism, hospitality and leisure industry is common in both developing and developed countries, particularly within smaller family businesses. The ILO (2001) estimate that between 13 and 19 million children aged under the age of 18 (10–15 per cent of all employees in the sector) are employed in the industry worldwide. Plüss (1999) provides a detailed classification of the work undertaken by children and young people in the tourism, hospitality and leisure sector and this is reproduced here as Table 7.2.

Table 7.2	*Sectors*	*Workplace*	*Occupations*
Occupations of children and young people in tourism	Accommodation	Hotels Holiday resorts Boarding houses Guesthouses Bed-and-breakfasts Rooms in private homes Laundries Cleaning companies	Receptionists Baggage attendants Bell-boys Lift-boys Chambermaids Room-boys Domestic servants Grooms Porters Garden hands Laundry workers Cleaners

▶

Table 7.2

continued

Sectors	Workplace	Occupations
Catering, food and beverage	Restaurants Cafes Teashops Snack bars Beer gardens Pubs Bars Beach snack outlets Street stands Mobile vending stalls	Kitchen helpers Dishwashers Water carriers Cleaners Waiters(tresses) Delivery boys Vendors of fruit Vendors of ice-cream
Excursions, recreational activities, entertainment	Excursion sites Sightseeing locations Sports and beach activities Fitness centres Animal shows Circuses Folklore performances Casinos Nightclubs Lap-dancing parlours Massage salons Brothels	Tour guides Postcard vendors Ticket vendors Flower girls Photo models Shoeshine boys Beggars Beach cleaners Caddies Umbrella girls Surf school helpers Pony ride helpers 'Thai boxers' Animal exhibitors Acrobats Divers for pennies Beach boys 'Hospitality girls' 'Guest relations officers' Dancers Masseuses Prostitutes Procurers
Tour operating and transport	Travel agencies Airports Train stations Bus and taxi firms Excursion boats	Handling agents Errand-boys Baggage attendants Bus attendants Car guards Car cleaners Ship boys Deckhands Trekking porters

Souvenir production	Wood carving	Manufacturers of souvenirs
	Plastic processing	
	Textile industry	
	Sewing shops	
	Straw/palm-leaf weaving	
	Shell, coral, mother of pearl processing	
	Leather production	
	Gem/stone mining	
Selling of souvenirs	Shops	Souvenir vendors
	Hotel boutiques	
	Stands	
	Itinerant sales on beach	

Adapted from Plüss (1999) *Quick money–Easy money?–a report on child labour in tourism*, SDC.

It would be erroneous to see all the activities listed in Table 7.2 as exploitative of children and young people. However, many of these activities are undertaken by children less than 12 years old who are vulnerable to abuse, exploitation and the loss of key benefits of childhood, including education, health and the freedom to enjoy life.

Case Study *B&Q DIY stores*

B&Q is owned by the Kingfisher Group and operates two different kinds of stores, the larger B&Q Warehouses that target the typical "DIY'er" and B&Q Supercentres which are suitable for less specialist shopper. The retail company employs over 36 000 people in more than 320 stores across the UK. The DIY retail market supports one of the largest areas of leisure activity in the UK and other developed economies.

This case reports on how B&Q committed itself to employing a mixed age workforce. In the late 1980s, B&Q anticipated the effects of demographic changes and started recognizing the advantages of employing older employees. Since a successful initiative, whereby it opened a store in Macclesfield with all employees aged over 50, the company aims to ensure its recruitment policy prevents discrimination on the ground of age.

B&Q's recruitment policy invites older people from the local community to apply for jobs every time it opens a store. To do so the retailer makes it clear it recruits people of all ages, young and old. One of them is Reg Hill who celebrated his 90th birthday at B&Q in June 2004, after working for 13 years at B&Q since he joined the company at 77 years of age. Such a recruitment policy recognizes the benefits of using the skills and life experience of older employees. It also acknowledges that a mixed aged workforce combines new ways of thinking and a whole range of experiences. That is why B&Q focuses on the aptitudes and abilities of candidates regardless of their age. As Bill Whiting, B&Q's chief executive recognises, 'Our aim is to recruit people of all ages because we want the best person for the job'. B&Q also benefits from employing older people because of the very nature of its activity. As a DIY retailer, the company values the hands-on experience of older employees, who have acquired a basic knowledge of DIY throughout their lives. At the same time, customers also feel reassured to ask advice of older employees whom they believe have DIY knowledge. As Bill Whiting comments, 'we actively recruit older workers as their knowledge and attitude contributes to the quality of service we can offer our customers'.

Today, almost one in five of B&Q's workforce, representing 6300 employees, are aged 50 or over, a number which keeps increasing. This is the result of a recruitment policy that has proved beneficial for employees, customers and the community as a whole. It is widely acknowledged in B&Q stores that the staffing by mixed aged employees benefits all groups of workers. Older employees enjoy working with younger people and the latter group learn from the skills and experience of mature colleagues. B&Q has also reaped the benefit of employing such a mixed workforce, enjoying a combination of new ideas and expertise. In addition, customers' positive feedback reflects their ability to talk to both young or older employees depending on their needs. Last but not least, the larger community may also find B&Q's initiative highly valuable. As Bill Whiting says, 'UK employers need to realize that economic drivers are changing the shape of Britain's workforce ... Older workers nowadays both need to and want to work, so it's about time that they were given the opportunities to do so.'

Older workers represent a relatively untapped labour market for most tourism, hospitality and leisure businesses in developed countries. Where more mature workers are found in organizations, this is generally because they are long-serving personnel rather than new recruits. B&Q have created the conditions within which older workers can thrive by, on the one hand, recognizing the contribution they can make and, secondly, operating with sufficient flexibility to meet their personal circumstances. There is no reason why similar models could not work across different businesses in the sector, including within seasonal operations and, indeed, may suit older workers' lifestyle requirements in this regard. Training support would be required in a manner similar to that required for any untrained group. At a policy level, the implications of mature workers' pension entitlements and tax situation may need to be addressed by the tourism sector and government.

Case prepared by the Scottish Centre for Employment Research for Fáilte Ireland. Reproduced with permission.

Case discussion questions

1. What are the benefits of employing a diverse workforce for B&Q?

2. What were the main incentives for B&Q to recruit a proportion of their workforce from the over 50s?

3. What are the possible drawbacks in recruiting older workers?

Social inclusion

The tourism, hospitality and leisure industry has the capacity to be socially inclusive in its employment creation. By 'social inclusion' here, we refer to the capacity of the sector to offer opportunity to all segments of society and, in particular, to those faced with particular social or cultural disadvantage. We have already addressed issues of social inclusion or exclusion in terms of ethnicity or culture, ability or disability and age. A further dimension addresses social inclusion in relation to economic participation in society and is an issue that has relevance, albeit in varying forms, in both developed and developing countries.

One of the challenges facing tourism, hospitality and leisure in many locations is a shortage of skilled labour or potential employees with the required blend of technical and generic skills required for the jobs that are on offer. The sector faces such shortages in cities as diverse as Dublin, Glasgow, Hong Kong, Mumbai and San Francisco. Vacancies cover a wide range of levels and skills areas and range from work that requires limited on-the-job training in, for example, hotel housekeeping to positions demanding extensive and expensive training for work as airline pilots. As an example of apparent contradiction, such vacancies exist alongside endemic and long-term unemployment within communities in both cities and in rural areas. The aesthetic demands of the industry (Warhurst *et al.* 2000; Nickson *et al.* 2003) may provide a partial answer to this dilemma in that some sectors of tourism, hospitality and leisure impose implicit or overt entry barriers, based on appearance, cultural cache and education, upon those seeking work and many of those from socially excluded communities do not meet such criteria. In developing countries, the barriers are also likely to be primarily educational in that the sector, catering for the international visitor market in particular, imposes educational barriers in terms of language ability and culturally based skills (knowledge of Western food and beverages as an example) upon entrants that exclude most aspirants from poorer family backgrounds (Baum 2002a).

There is a real challenge in terms of overcoming social exclusion in the tourism, hospitality and leisure workplace so that the sector can meet its staffing shortages from such relatively untapped labour pools. At the same time, work in the sector, once attained, can provide opportunity that goes beyond the immediate job and creates chances for wider development for participating individuals. The Juma case outlined below illustrates this point.

Case Study *Juma Ventures and Ben and Jerry's, San Francisco*

Juma Ventures (originally known as LBV) provides supported employment to high-risk youth living in San Francisco. The organization is a spin-off of Larkin Street Youth Center (LSYC), a 12-year-old organization dedicated to helping homeless youth find lasting alternatives to street life. Each year LSYC provides a continuum of services to over 1000 young people in San Francisco, including outreach, a drop-in centre, counselling, medical care, education and housing. Over the course of its history, LSYC has enjoyed tremendous support from all sectors of the San Francisco community and beyond.

It is widely recognized both in the United States and abroad for its pioneering work with homeless youth.

Creating valuable, valued and sustainable employment opportunities for socially excluded groups is a real challenge. This case provides an example of where a creative project was able to link with a socially responsible corporation to meet this challenge. This is an example of creating employment opportunities which are more likely to be esteemed by those participating in the work than is frequently the case with social employment initiatives.

▶

Juma worked with Ben & Jerry's for several years developing plans for a 'Partnershop'. As part of its social commitment, Ben & Jerry's waived its standard $25 000 franchise fee. Start-up costs for each franchise can total an additional $200 000, not including pre-development and planning expenses. In the case of Juma, the majority of these costs were covered through an enterprise development grant from The Roberts Foundation, which was augmented by additional grants from other foundations. Juma is the sixth non-profit in the United States with whom Ben & Jerry's has partnered in the development of a scoop-shop franchise.

On 27 April 1995, Juma opened its first Ben & Jerry's scoop-shop franchise located at 2146 Chestnut Street in San Francisco's marina district. The shop has a prime location directly across from a busy movie theatre and near many popular restaurants and retailers. The store's atmosphere is fun and entertaining, offering customers high-quality ice cream and service. The shop, run by a strong adult management team, involves youth employees in virtually all facets of business operations including customer service, marketing, inventory, management and bookkeeping. Young people begin their work as 'scoopers' and may be promoted to shift supervisor positions upon achieving a higher level of knowledge and skill.

Ben & Jerry's has a successful track record of working with not-for-profit organizations and communities; its image and values are such that employees could wear tie-dyed T-shirts as their uniform, and Ben & Jerry's well-known social action activities could provide the youth with a channel for positive community involvement.

To date, the first scoop shop has created 14 part-time positions – nine for more than 20 hours per week and five for less than 20 hours per week. Of those, six are supervisory positions. This was the first of a number of collaborative ventures between Juma and Ben & Jerry's, all of which have been highly successful in creating both initial employment opportunities and subsequent promotion to supervisory positions. During Juma's first year of operating its ventures, a total of 55 young people participated in the training programme, which consisted of pre-employment training and on-the-job training. Of those 55, a total of 23 were trained for and/or worked in the scoop shop and 35 were trained and/or worked at the Candlestick Park concession. Three individuals crossed over and worked in both enterprises. Juma has conducted some follow-up of the original trainees for both businesses to assess individual outcomes of the young people involved with its ventures. For the scoop shop's first round of trainees, Juma has demonstrated remarkable success. Of the 11 young people who participated in the first training round of the scoop shop, nine completed the pre-employment training and two did not. Of the nine who completed and went on to work at the scoop shop, five continue to be employed at the shop and four have made positive transitions to other employment, working for software companies, for retail clothing establishments or in the food service industry. Moreover, four of the five still employed at the scoop shop have been promoted to supervisory positions.

Case prepared by the author for Fáilte Ireland from publicly accessible websites. Reproduced with permission.

Case discussion questions

1. In what ways does work in tourism, hospitality and leisure offer opportunities to those members of the community who otherwise might remain socially excluded?

2. What are the potential difficulties for companies following the Ben & Jerry's example of creating socially inclusive work?

3. How could this case model be extended to offer opportunity to other socially excluded groups?

Motivation and choice

A final dimension to our discussion of the composition of the tourism, hospitality and leisure workforce looks at people who contribute to the sector for motivational reasons that are not so much born of their innate characteristics and abilities but rather reflect specific choices that they have made. They constitute two distinct groups, both of which are prevalent in sectors of tourism, hospitality and leisure, and can be styled 'volunteers' and 'lifestyle employees'.

As Jago and Deery (2002) note, volunteering is an important part of the social life of many cultures. Volunteering covers a wide range of activities, frequently in the social services and is seen as part of civic duty in countries such as Singapore. It is also common in areas that contribute to tourism, hospitality and leisure across a wide range of activities. Notable among them are maritime safety – the Royal National Lifeboat Institution in the UK and Ireland is a good example of an organization that depends heavily on volunteers as crew members and fundraisers – and search and rescue in mountainous and other difficult terrain. In both instances, tourists and leisure consumers are major beneficiaries of the services provided by such organizations. Likewise, major international (but also more localized) cultural and sporting events depend significantly on the contribution that volunteers make to their smooth operation. Kemp (2002) discusses what she calls the 'hidden workforce' that supported the Olympic Games in Lillehammar in 1994 and Sydney in 2000, noting that the role of those volunteering at both venues was 'critical to the staging of both ... games events because they provided the substantial amount of unpaid additional labour that was needed' (p.110). Kemp's findings point to a wide range of factors as motivating volunteer participation, including 'to be part of a unique event and the celebratory atmosphere; job skills; social skills such as learning about themselves; feeling valued; increased feelings of self-worth; new confidence; cooperation; learning about people; welfare issues; and job characteristics' (p.116). Olympic games volunteering is an example of what Shin and Kleiner (2003) call 'spot volunteering', casual, short-term participation in a specific event or to meet a short-term need. They also discuss more formally-based volunteer work (such as rescue work or a regular commitment within the heritage sector) and voluntary work which is the result of employer pressure or requirement.

Clearly, Kemp's wide-ranging motivational factors and benefits cannot be derived from all volunteering activity in tourism, hospitality and leisure but many of them are likely to apply in the context of work volunteers undertake in museums, historic houses and battlefield sites. The social dimension involved in both meeting guests and engaging with colleagues is identified as a major motivating factor by those opening their gardens to the public (Ryan and Bates 1995). The wish to continue to use existing skills, whether technical, social or administrative, influences the participation of older, often retired, volunteers who choose to work in the heritage sector. Frequently, volunteers work alongside their remunerated colleagues and the potential for divergent perceptions of priorities with regard, for example, to business outcomes and customer service can create problems. Indeed, issues relating to the management of volunteers and volunteer relations are areas that receive considerable attention in the literature (du Boulay 1996; Deery and Jago 2001; Shin and Kleiner 2003). Because of their volunteer status and varied motivations, volunteers cannot, necessarily, be subject to the same management regime as their paid colleagues and this can create challenges when seeking to institute change at both an operational and a strategic level. However, contemporary volunteer management programmes recognize the importance of working with them on a professional basis and ensuring that they are not peripheral to key aspects of the organization's operations and development. As an example of this, the Volunteer Development Working Group of the Scottish Museums Council formulated the following Mission Statement:

> The Scottish Museums Council works to support and develop the role of volunteering within Scottish museums and galleries, using SMC resources and staff expertise.
>
> Aims:
>
> - To promote the vital contribution that volunteers make to museum life
> - To encourage equal access to training and development opportunities
> - To enable museums to successfully recruit and retain a wide range of volunteers
> - To enable museums to realise their potential through effective volunteer management
> - To encourage museums to make effective use of resources
>
> (Scottish Museums Council 2003)

Similarly, the London Canals Museum (undated) provides a highly professional listing of current vacancies, stressing clearly that the positions in question, including technical, administrative and service work, are all unpaid but that the expectations of post-holders are every bit as demanding as if they were remunerated. Organizations in tourism, hospitality and leisure also recognize the contribution that volunteers bring, particularly that way in which volunteers can bring a richness to the composition of the workforce. The presence of volunteers can also enable otherwise uneconomic operations to maintain a significant level of paid employment.

The second category of those with somewhat unorthodox motivations is the category of the sector's workforce who are predominantly driven by lifestyle considerations in electing to work or establish a business in tourism, hospitality and leisure. Adler and Adler (2004) discuss a number of their respondents, working in beach hotels in Hawaii, who are essentially there in order to meet their desire to surf during their free time. These same employees are transitory in their commitment to their hotels and, indeed, to Hawaii, moving on when better surfing opportunities arise elsewhere or for a winter season working and playing on the ski slopes of the Rockies or Europe. Working in tourism, hospitality and leisure as a means of accessing lifestyle benefits is widespread but unquantified. It is a feature of many tourism destinations in Europe, North America and parts of Asia, where the motivation may be climate or culture. Arguably, for many Northern Europeans working as tour reps in the Mediterranean and elsewhere, such work does not represent a serious long-term career option but is a means to access good weather and lifestyle benefits while being paid to do so. This motivation, arguably, allows employers to pay low salaries to their reps because the demand for such opportunities far outweighs available positions. Another source of motivation for working temporarily in tourism, hospitality and leisure, is the opportunity to learn a new language while located in a different country. Because of the weak labour-market characteristics of front-line employment in tourism, hospitality and leisure, as well as the high level of customer and colleague contact that can be expected, access to work in the sector for transient staff is relatively easy.

The second dimension to lifestyle work in tourism, hospitality and leisure relates to people who select the sector in order to establish small businesses, often after a successful career in another sector of the economy, located in a major business centre. Such entrepreneurs, establishing accommodation, restaurant, activity or retail operations, do not necessarily adopt business objectives that fit conventional models with respect to profit and growth (Andrew, Baum and Morrison 2001). As Getz, Carlsen and Morrison (2004) point out, 'Not all businesses are started for growth, profit maximization, or even for permanence – many are established or purchased with the needs and preferences of the owners and their families being paramount' (Getz *et al.* 2004, p.1). Businesses operating within this motivational paradigm do not necessarily see phenomena such as seasonality as a 'problem', rather seasonality provides an opportunity to wind down for the winter and enjoy lifestyle benefits elsewhere.

Review and discussion questions

1. What are the reasons for the under-representation of women in managerial positions in the tourism, hospitality and leisure businesses of most developed and developing countries?

2. Are there 'women's jobs' and 'men's jobs' in tourism, hospitality and leisure?

3. To what extent are age considerations with respect to employees important for the image of a successful tourism, hospitality and leisure business?

4. What benefits do (a) young employees and (b) older employees bring to a successful tourism, hospitality and leisure workplace?

5. What challenges do (a) young employees and (b) older employees bring to a successful tourism, hospitality and leisure workplace?

6. What managerial qualities are of value in working with employees who are registered as disabled?

7. What contribution can staff who have physical or intellectual disabilities bring to a tourism, hospitality and leisure business?

8. Should social inclusion be a consideration for a tourism, hospitality and leisure organization in preparing its staff recruitment plans?

9. Are lifestyle aspirations and sound business objectives compatible in tourism, hospitality and leisure?

8 Education, training and development

Chapter objectives

This chapter focuses on issues relating to education and training in tourism, hospitality and leisure. The objectives of the chapter are:

- to place education, training and development in context within tourism, hospitality and leisure;

- to explore different interpretations of education, training and development;

- to outline the main factors that underpin the provision of education, training and development within tourism, hospitality and leisure;

- to address key curricular and organizational issues relating to education, training and development within the sector.

Introduction

The education, training and development of employees of all levels within tourism, hospitality and leisure are vital in maintaining the industry's competitiveness in the international arena. In essence, education, training and development are the means by which a number of the key outcomes which we have considered in preceding chapters can be achieved.

These include the following:

- The attainment of optimal service quality should be the aim within tourism, hospitality and leisure businesses. This is a function of effective education and training practices both within the companies themselves but also within the preparatory educational experience of those recruited.

- Moves towards enabling all staff, particularly those in boundary-spanning roles, to undertake the complex nature of their responsibilities can only be achieved in the context of well-trained and, indeed, educated staff at all levels.

- Effective relationship marketing, a key feature of a service-focused company, depends heavily upon enabling boundary-spanning employees to undertake their work with confidence and competence, requiring them to receive effective education and training.

- The nature of the tourism, hospitality and leisure labour markets needs to be recognized together with the implications of Riley's weak labour-market attributes for education and training within the sector. It must, however, be understood that there is no identifiable and unitary tourism, hospitality and leisure labour market but rather an amalgam of a number of sub-sectoral markets. That said, Riley's concept of the weak internal-labour market and its consequences for vocational education and training is of particular relevance to our discussion here. This issue will be further considered during the course of this chapter.

- Achieving harmony and effective cooperation and teamwork within a multicultural and, frequently, a multilingual workforce depends on effective training of the team themselves as well as of their supervisors and managers.

- College students and employees within international tourism, hospitality and leisure have the opportunity for global vocational mobility, either in support of personal aspirations or of company requirements. Some countries have invested more in this than others and the very differing language skills of the Dutch, on the one hand, and the British on the other, bear testimony to this. Education and training have a major part to play in this preparatory process.

- The upgrading of tourism, hospitality and leisure operating standards, especially in service delivery, requires sound education and training principles if it is to succeed but, even before that, creating recognition of the need for educational and training input is required.

- Addressing some of the worst excesses in terms of conditions, rewards and benefits, within international tourism, hospitality and leisure has a major educational component at its heart, focused primarily on a willingness by those in authority within the industry to learn from their enlightened peers.

As well as drawing on the concepts of previous chapters of this book, our consideration of education and training for tourism, hospitality and leisure will also act as a precursor for the final two chapters. These address issues of macro planning, development, sustainability and social responsibility with respect to human resource development for tourism, hospitality and leisure. Clearly, education and training form a major component within this framework.

In is important to remember the context within which the development history of tourism, hospitality and leisure education operates and the impact that this has on what takes places in different countries and systems. As we saw in Chapter 1, the specific attributes of a destination determine the nature of the industry in that location, the character of the sponsoring institution and the educational and tourism industry framework within which it is located. In many countries, tourism, hospitality and leisure education has developed from training at the practitioner level, designed to meet the skills needs of the local hotel and restaurant industries through a process of academic and professional evolution whereby new and higher tiers have been added to existing provision in response to both industry and student demand. Thus, both the Dublin College of Catering in Ireland and Westminster College in London started as professional culinary schools in the early years of the twentieth century. Both have maintained this tradition but have extended their range of courses in both horizontal and vertical terms, offering a range of allied programmes in tourism and leisure at operational through to management degree levels. Similar patterns can be found in the development of a number of Asian schools, notably Singapore Hotels Association Technical Education Centre (SHATEC) and the National Khaosiung Hospitality College in Taiwan. In a minority of instances, programmes were established with a focus on higher-level management education from their foundation: what might be styled the Cornell University model. The Scottish Hotel School at the University of Strathclyde in Glasgow was established as a specialist management college in 1944 as the oldest university provider of tourism, hospitality and leisure education in Europe and the first to offer both degree and postgraduate courses in this area.

Tourism, hospitality and leisure education programme diversity is, in many respects, one of the real strengths of provision at an international level. This strength comes from the manner in which programmes are able to respond flexibly to industry needs at a local level or in terms of the specialist sub-sectors that they aspire to support. There has been ongoing debate about the extent to which such diversity is, indeed, a virtue (Baum, 1997). Attempts to achieve harmonization of training and qualifications in tourism, within countries and at a transnational level, have been relatively unsuccessful despite support from international organizations such as The European Centre for the Development of Vocational Training (CEDEFOP) and EURHODIP in Europe. Recognizing the influences that exist as stimulants for diversity alongside global pressures for standardization is important for our understanding of the ways in which education and training operate in international tourism, hospitality and leisure.

Education and training – the concepts

The exact distinction between education and training has taxed philosophers and thinkers for centuries. Notable contributions include those by Whitehead and Dewey. John Dewey, the American philosopher, writing in 1916, defines education thus:

> It is that reconstruction or reorganization of experience which adds to the meaning of experience, and which increases ability to direct the course of subsequent experience. (Dewey 1916, pp.89–90)

Bertrand Russell (1926) entered the education and training debate by considering the contrast between that which is 'ornamental' in education – in his terms this refers to a classical education – and that which is 'useful' – which includes the sciences and applied vocational areas, some of which may well fall into rather more contemporary definitions of training. He disposes of the issue of utility in fairly strong terms:

> Nevertheless, I believe the whole controversy to be unreal. As soon as the terms are defined, it melts away. If we interpret 'useful' broadly and 'ornamental' narrowly, the one side has it; in the contrary interpretations, the other side has it. In the widest and most correct sense of the word, an activity is 'useful' when it

has good results. And these results must be good in some other sense than merely 'useful', or else we have no true definition. We cannot say that a useful activity is one that has useful results. The essence of what is 'useful' is that it ministers to some result which is not merely useful. Sometimes a long chain of results is necessary before the final result is reached which can be called simply 'good'. A plough is useful because it breaks up the ground. But breaking up the ground is not good on its own account; it is in turn merely useful because it enables seed to be sown. This is useful because it produces grain, which is useful because it produces bread, which is useful because it preserves life. (Russell 1926, pp.15–16)

Such a debate may appear to be primarily semantic and Russell certainly develops the discussion considerably further in order to demonstrate that the ornamental and utilitarian have little useful distinction when the logic of their definitions is dissected and analysed. On this basis, it is sufficient to say, as we do conclude here, that the distinction between education and training is spurious and unhelpful in the context of human resource management for tourism, hospitality and leisure.

However, some of the definitions that have emerged from very extensive discussion of the distinction have tended to polarize the two concepts. In addition, a veneer of relative status and a class dimension is frequently introduced when separating the two terms, in that education is perceived to be that which is of a general and developmental nature while training is deemed to be vocationally specific and often the precursor of trade or craft positions. So, for example, with regard to law in England, students are educated within the university context but frequently complete their vocational training for careers as solicitors in an entirely different, specialist college. Likewise, the learning of foreign languages is frequently the educational concern of universities while the application of this learning, for example in preparation for a bilingual secretarial career, is a training matter for different institutes.

Such absolutist distinctions are not really helpful in understanding the role of either education and training in the context of the tourism, hospitality and leisure industry. The nature of much technical skills development within the sector is that it requires a contribution from a number of sections of what is more appropriately thought of as a continuum between, on the one hand, Pavlovian response training and very specific, limited skills development and, on the other, the extremes of philosophical, mathematical and creative speculation processes without evident application. As we have already noted, the general trend in meeting the skills requirements of tourism, hospitality and leisure is a move away from technical and specific skills to a range of generic skills encompassing communications, interpersonal attributes, ICT and emotional and aesthetic dimensions (Baum 2002a).

In tourism, hospitality and leisure there is a widespread acceptance that entrants at all levels require inputs of both an educational and a training kind, although traditional practice tends to focus primarily on the latter in preparing students and employees for what are perceived to be the lower-skills positions in the industry, particularly within hotel and catering. Even here, skills training builds upon a number of years of education within the school system and many formal programmes, primarily training in focus, include what might be deemed a broader educational dimension within the curriculum.

In considering the respective roles of education and training (if it is of value and meaning to separate them) we are faced, once more, with the consequences of operating within a very diffuse and variegated sector. There are few generalizations that can be made with respect to the sector as a whole. The labour-market characteristics, the initial education and training requirements, the cost of this training and its subsequent updating, the levels of remuneration and reward, as well as vocational and social status, vary dramatically between a hotel kitchen porter and a beach vendor on the one hand, and a senior Boeing 747 pilot or director of a national tourism office on the other. The only common denominator is that they all work within tourism and that as a result the tourist in some part depends on their skills and knowledge for the enjoyment of her or his vacation experience.

Training is for skills and education is for life?

Any conscious separation of education and training as distinct processes has strong historical origins. It is a popular misrepresentation, simplification and throw-away distinction to argue that training is for a skill and education is for life. However, historically, this distinction has a degree of validity. In pre-Industrial Revolution times, when training for a craft took place in an environment where the requirements and traditions of those skills did not change significantly over long periods of time, training really was designed to equip the apprentice with skills which he would use throughout his working career. Master status within the context of the trade guilds in England, for example, implied that the craftsman (and, historically, we are only talking about men in this context) had acquired all the necessary skills and knowledge for the independent execution of his craft. There was no more to learn and, while the skill may have been honed with experience, there was no expectation that the demands of the job would alter during the working life of that craftsman. Thus the cup of skills, empty at the start of the training process, was now full with everything that was available by way of skills in that society to the master carpenter's physician, lawyer, stonemason, baker or goldsmith.

The concept of education at this time, by contrast, was rather more fluid. While the rudiments of European education in Medieval society had many features in common with skills training within the crafts, in that students were taught the fundamental skills necessary to internalize classical and religious orthodoxy, the assumption was that the process would continue throughout life as part of a search for increased wisdom, provided that the rules and obligations of prevailing orthodoxy were observed. Of course, it is important to emphasize that the benefits of both models, skills training and learning as part of education, were accessible to but a very small minority of the population in Europe. Education was, by and large, a carefully guarded prerogative of the Church until the time of the Reformation while access to the skills of the guilds was equally jealously protected and controlled. Likewise, learning in this educational sense in the great Asian traditions in China and India was privileged and the right of a small minority in society.

To say that the fixed skills model, the filling of the cup, altered as a result of the Industrial Revolution is only partially accurate. What the industrialization process did was to divide and simplify the work in many craft areas, so that in partial form tasks could now be performed by less skilled workers at much lower cost and using the machinery of a factory rather than in the workshop of the craftsman. This is a process which has, in many respects been carried forward through mass production industrialization with Henry Ford and others to contemporary de-skilling processes in the service workplace, or McDonaldization (Ritzer 2004).

The profit motive of industrial capitalism, the division of labour upon which it depended and, above all, the technology that it employed created a further and entirely new factor within the workplace, that of ongoing and incessant change. From the certainty and stability of the craft guilds, where skills, literally, remained the same from generation to generation, the working world, at least within the industrial sector, was rapidly plunged into a constant process of change, with machinery rapidly becoming redundant and newer technology replacing both earlier generations of machines as well as the age-old craft skills. Ironically, the world of education was much slower to respond to this process of change sparked off by the Industrial Revolution. Classical study models in Europe, China, India and the Middle East, derived over thousands of years and refined through the influence of religion over that same time period, remained the dominant educational model, largely impervious to the impact of science and technology until the twentieth century. The classical model was deemed to be a suitable education by which to prepare entrants for careers in government, the military, the arts and the professions and no compromise to the needs of vocationalism were made except, possibly, in the specific cases of medicine and law.

The process of change has remained the one constant in the world of work since the mid-eighteenth century and has accelerated with each succeeding generation. As a result, the currency of skills taught by technical institutes and in the workplace has become shorter and shorter with the consequent need either to retrain staff or to replace them with newer generations of employees. The impact of change was, perhaps, not fully recognized within each generation of workers until the post-1945 period but comparison between generations, between mother and daughter and father and son, would have highlighted changes in the machinery employed and the procedures followed. Up to this point, the only incentive to change in the individual was to meet the requirements of promotion and greater responsibility, and even that change was readily assimilated and finite in its demands. The advent of computer-based and, latterly, microprocessor-based information and communications technology has reduced the life cycle of some jobs to within the working career of most employees. The punch card operator, so important to computer operations during the 1960s and early 1970s, probably only existed as a significant employment designation for 15 to 20 years before tape, disk and chip technology made the skills and the jobs obsolete.

The process of change in other non-industrial sectors of the economy has, apparently, been much slower. Agriculture was for a long time immune to the level of changes which were taking place within the industrial sector but the introduction of technology and chemical fertilizers as well as work and management systems has revolutionized work in even this sector. The numbers employed on the land in most developed countries is just a fraction of what it was 40 years ago but at the same time total agricultural output has increased to levels of surplus. Likewise in the service sector, for example banking, the impact of change in the workplace has taken time to be felt but now has taken hold in a major way as technology replaces human skills and financial institutions dispense with old routines and procedures in the workplace.

What has this potted history of work to do with the mass tourism, hospitality and leisure industry which, after all, was only in its infancy at the dawn of the computer age? In the context of some work areas in tourism, hospitality and leisure, the answer is quite clear. For example, the skills and knowledge requirements for airline pilots has gone through massive change in the past 40 years, as aviation moved from using the relatively straightforward technology of the DC3, with its high dependence on pilot skill and judgement, to the high-technology sophistication of the new generation fly-by-wire, computer-controlled Airbus 380 and Boeing 787 airliners. Likewise, the impact of developments with respect to both technology and markets have significantly changed the work routines of museum curators, travel agency employees, airline check-in clerks, hotel receptionists, and food and beverage operatives in fast-food restaurants and a host of other areas.

However, it is possible to argue that the technical components of many, lower-status, customer-contact positions in the tourism, hospitality and leisure industry remain the same as they were 40 years ago and, on the face of it, may continue to do so for the foreseeable future. On the basis of this argument, therefore, change is not as significant a factor in many parts of the tourism and hospitality workplace as it is in other business sectors. As a consequence, according to this analysis, skills once learnt should be adequate to meet the needs of the tourism, hospitality and leisure working environment without further enhancement during an employee's career. Such beliefs remain implicitly prevalent within many sectors of the industry in many countries, particularly hotels and catering. A good, but by no means unique, example of this attitude was expressed by the general manager of a large hotel in Iran. Noting that all his staff had, substantially, been working in the same positions in the hotel for the past 20 years and that none had left in the interim, he stated that the hotel had no need to implement training programmes as 'all the staff are fully trained' – a good example of what has earlier been described as the 'full cup' concept of training. Even if this analysis was to be accepted on technical grounds (and this would be a highly contentious conclusion), it is fundamentally flawed for two further reasons.

First, while change may not impact on the specific technical tasks undertaken by many tourism, hospitality and leisure employees, the social and market context in which they are working has altered dramatically over the time frame in question and continues to change inexorably. In Chapter 2, we considered the way in which the social context of work in the tourism, hospitality and leisure industry has altered in response to mass participation and the democratization of the industry. In Chapter 4, discussion focused on the ever-changing expectations of the marketplace and how this impacts on the role of employees in responding to what Balmer and Baum (1993) described as the true motivating factor for tourists, service quality, as opposed to those aspects which are increasingly taken for granted, the physical product 'hygiene factors'. Thus, tourism, hospitality and leisure employees are working in a customer environment which is constantly changing and, unless they themselves are able to comprehend these changes and respond to them, their skills will be as redundant as if they were coopers operating in an age of aluminium barrels or the flag carriers who walked ahead of early locomotives in the era of the TGV and Bullet train.

The second problem which an analysis which seeks to separate tourism, hospitality and leisure skills from those in other sectors faces is related precisely to the fact that the industry cannot exist in isolation or in a vacuum, insulated from the wider world of work. Lashley and Morrison (2000) explore whether hospitality can be seen as having unique attributes alongside wider business and service disciplines, but their arguments do not extend to the total isolation of the sector from areas such as marketing and finance. The technical and generic skills debate is particularly focused with respect to tourism, hospitality and leisure. As we have seen, historically, skills in tourism, hospitality and leisure were seen almost exclusively in terms of their technical requirements and this formed the basis of the training agenda pursued by colleges in Europe and, subsequently, almost worldwide in the developing world through funded aid programmes, for much of the twentieth century. Jobs in hospitality, likewise, were constructed on the basis of an accumulation of skills required for specific technical tasks (ILO 1979). Changes in the nature of work, the impact of technology and customer expectations have forced a fundamental re-evaluation of the relative roles of technical and generic skills in hospitality work.

Skills shortages in tourism, hospitality and leisure are increasingly seen in terms of generic rather than specific technical competencies. Studies of employer expectations of graduates (Tas 1988; Baum 1990; Eaton and Christou 1997; Christou 1999, 2001; Christou and Eaton 2000; Whitelaw 2005) note demand for communications, people management and problem-solving as the priority in both the US and a number of European countries. However, the priority given to various skills and competencies within five studies across time and place does show significant variation. Whitelaw (2005) summarizes these in Table 8.1.

Competencies required for management in tourism, hospitality and leisure, therefore, are clearly influenced by the context within which they are required and cannot be seen in terms of a series of general and internationally transferable traits. D'Annunzo-Green (2002), in a discussion of the competencies required by expatriate hotel managers in Russia, comments that:

> A general consensus among the hotel expatriates was the need to be patient, listen and accept that the adaptation process will take time. The expatriates stressed the need to start off slowly by giving the local staff evidence of their professionalism and technical competence. (p.83)

She goes on to identify the following competencies as core requirements for work in the Russian environment:

- an ability to build trust and be patient
- an ability to manage change
- an ability to manage relationships
- flexibility of managerial style.

| Table 8.1 | Top 10 graduate competencies across five studies |

Competencies	Rank order and scores on a five-point Likert scale of five studies				
	Whitelaw (2005) Ireland	Christou (1999) Greece	Christou and Eaton (2000) Greece	Baum (1990) UK	Tas (1988) USA
Motivates employees to achieve desired performance	1: 4.60	9: 4.57	7: 4.58	8: 4.52	8: 4.44
Develops positive customer relations	2: 4.55	2: 4.76	3: 4.72	6: 4.55	5: 4.60
Displays innovative approaches to problem-solving	3: 4.51				
Possesses needed leadership qualities to achieve organizational objectives	4: 4.50	8: 4.59	5: 4.60	9: 4.40	7: 4.48
Demonstrates professional appearance and poise	5: 4.50	3: 4.73	2: 4.83	5: 4.56	3: 4.61
Strives to achieve positive working relationships with employees	6: 4.49	5: 4.66	4: 4.63	4: 4.57	6: 4.52
Communicates effectively both written and orally	7: 4.49	4: 4.70	9: 4.52	3: 4.61	3: 4.61
Follows hygiene and safety regulations to ensure compliance by organization	8: 4.49	11: 4.50	13: 4.38	2: 4.71	13: 3.99
Follows legal responsibilities associated with business operations	9: 4.45	10: 4.54	11: 4.50	7: 4.54	14: 3.90
Manages guests with understanding and sensitivity	10: 4.44	1: 4.89	1: 4.89	1: 4.81	1: 4.80
Maintains professional and ethical standards in the work environment	12: 4.37	7: 4.60	6: 4.58	9: 4.40	2: 4.69
Identifies operational problems	18: 4.31	6: 4.63	8: 4.54	13: 4.24	12: 4.00
Delegates responsibility and authority to personnel according to departmental objectives	25: 4.19	17: 4.30	14: 4.36	7: 4.14	16: 3.84
Effectively disciplines staff when appropriate	26: 4.18	18: 4.27	18: 4.20	19: 3.97	10: 4.15
Assists in the development and control of departmental productivity	30: 4.09	12: 4.45	10: 4.52	23: 3.87	19: 3.75
Follows established personnel management procedures in supervision of employees	32: 4.04	14: 4.38	19: 4.11	14: 4.23	9: 4.33

Source: Whitelaw (2005), pp.391–2 with permission

None of these, interestingly, feature directly as core requirements in the earlier studies addressed above.

The nature of skills that are required for effective work is an issue that informs debate across the wider service sector – see for example, Tesco (1999) as well as within the wider economy (FEFC 1998; QCA 2000) with their development of core or key skills. QCA identifies key skills as:

- communications
- application of number
- information technology
- working with others
- improving one's own learning and performance.

These key skills represent capabilities that have, traditionally, been integrated as 'normal' expectations within tourism, hospitality and leisure curricula at operational and management levels and a specific focus on the development of these skills, outwith main curriculum delivery objectives, may be questionable in the context of this sector.

However, HtF (2000a) also report employer demands for improved generic skills as a priority. These skills include communications, showing initiative, delivering customer service and demonstrating a willingness to learn. Recommendations to tackle the generic skills gap include:

- building generic skills development into full-time education programmes
- funding for training providers to deliver key skills and develop appropriate aptitudes and attitudes within young people
- ensuring providers are developed to be able to deliver key skills
- ensuring that recruitment practices encompass generic skills requirements.

HtF's (2000b) delphi study of skills requirements in tourism, hospitality and leisure also reports that the skills gaps, as seen by the industry, focus on what can be styled the generic agenda – communications, problem-solving and customer service in addition to job-specific skills. Tomkins (2004) notes that employers wanted self-assured, independent thinkers who could communicate effectively with a range of stakeholders but instead got graduates who were under-confident in their first jobs.

Empirical evidence from a study of front-office work and skills requirements across a number of European countries (Baum and Odgers 2001; Odgers and Baum 2001) shows clearly that this focus operates in practice. Hotels in all quality categories in seven European countries recruit on the basis of generic employability rather than specific skills and experience. Odgers and Baum (p.9) note that even five-star hotels 'accept the reality of the marketplace and are willing to recruit staff without Front Office experience provided they have good general education and a willingness to learn'. The same report also comments that:

> A key evolving change in Front Office work is the integration of technical and interpersonal skills in all aspects of work. This is the result of a growing emphasis

on the latter while technology has developed as a support for the delivery of service rather than as an objective in itself. In a technical sense, technology will continue to reduce the skills demands of Front Office work as systems become more user friendly and share their basic operating features with widely used office and domestic computer software. (p.18)

Odgers and Baum further note the weakening of traditional workplace hierarchies in front office, with a decline in the position of junior or assistant receptionist so that given 'the virtual elimination of traditional, routine office-related tasks such as basic typing, filing and photocopying, it is, in any case, difficult to distinguish between the job content' of various levels of work within the area (pp.19–20). They conclude that 'in the absence of experienced, qualified staff, many hotels will increasingly look to generic, non-technical competencies (communication, problem solving, customer service and IT) in recruiting new personnel and build in extended on-the-job-training within the induction phase' (p.21). In addition to these generic skills considerations, the work of Warhurst *et al.* (2000) suggests that aesthetic criteria also feature in the recruitment of front-line staff for hospitality work. Indeed, ongoing studies in Glasgow suggest that recruitment criteria employed within the hospitality sector increasingly recognize the triangular nature of skills – technical, generic and aesthetic. The priority accorded to each of these depends on the nature of the job and the type of business that is involved.

As a result of this generic skills focus, vocational training and preparation for the world of work, in general, places significant emphasis on preparing young people for working lives that will not be single track, in the one job and with the same employer, over a 40-year period. Expectations are, increasingly, built around mobility and change and the anticipation that an individual may move between companies and sectors at a number of points within his or her working life. Each of these stages will, in all probability, require training and the acquisition of additional qualifications. As a result, the labour market brings expectations to the workplace that emphasize the opportunity to change and to face new challenges, through rotation between different functional areas but also through enhancement and promotion. The tourism, hospitality and leisure industry is not isolated from this environment and cannot pretend that such aspirations do not and should not exist within it. Thus training has a role to play at all levels within the tourism, hospitality and leisure workforce, as an ongoing and continuous process designed to enable employees to meet changes in their working environment but also, and of equal importance, to cater for their own personal and career needs and aspirations.

Where does this discussion take consideration of education and training, one as a finite and terminal activity and the other as an ongoing, non-terminal process? What it certainly does do is to blur and confuse any absolute distinction between the two concepts, or at least confound the notion that there is any value in perceiving the two as independent processes, carried out with respect to different cadres of people and in separate learning and training institutions. So much of the preparatory process that young people undergo in anticipation of a working career fuses the specific and the generic in a way that is impossible to separate and this process is not exclusive to the formal school, college or training centre environment. It can hold true of work-based learning as well.

Vikhanski and Puffer (1993) point to this in the context of McDonald's and the foundation for working life that even part-time working exposure to the yellow arches provides for many young people:

> In the United States, McDonald's is often the first job that young people take, and the company's training practices are a solid foundation that can serve a person well in any type of employment. Many American employers value prospective candidates who have excelled at McDonald's because they recognize that these people have acquired good work habits. (Vikhanski and Puffer 1993, p.105)

The reality is that, within the contemporary working environment in many tourism, hospitality and leisure enterprises, most employees at all levels have a need for attributes that, on the basis of traditional distinctions, could be described as both educational and training in nature. Managers require the skills that are developed as a result of training in accounting and finance and may even need the ability to demonstrate the benefits of training in specific technical skills – in small hotels, for example, managers will frequently substitute for the absent breakfast chef or function waiter if required. Likewise, as was argued in Chapter 4, front-line staff in all tourism sectors require the confidence of empowerment and a real understanding of marketing and their customers in addition to the technical attributes of their jobs, and such understanding can only be derived from exposure to educational as well as training processes. It is, perhaps, because of this overlap and the evident lack of clear-cut distinctions between the separate concepts of education and training that a unifying term, 'development', is frequently employed.

'Development' has the advantage of being a term which has equal applicability to skills and knowledge and is one which is more generally understood. It is also a term which does not have terminal or absolute connotations but can be seen to have a role to play at all stages of a person's formal development (while at school, college or university), their vocational development (at vocational school, training centre or in the workplace) and their informal development (in any of the above situations as well as at home and during social and leisure situations). The three types of development are also not mutually exclusive in that the same context can contribute to more than one. In a management development programme which is set in an outward-bound context, we may learn about our ability as leaders in a way that has applicability in the workplace but, at the same time, may also develop in a personal sense in our relationships with colleagues and friends. Likewise, a work placement from college in another country may help us develop skills with respect to the preparation of French, Russian or Cantonese cuisine but, in all probability, it will also assist in the development of personal resilience in our ability to cope away from home and will contribute to our understanding of other cultures and traditions.

Furthermore, there are no time constraints or problems of sequencing inherent in the concept of development. It is a process of which any component can occur at any time and in any order during a person's working or nonworking life. Individuals can, within certain constraints, respond to changing personal, vocational or other requirements by availing themselves of any form of development at any point of their lives. Recognizing an individual's infinite potential for development throughout his or her life is a critical responsibility for managers in all sectors of the economy but has particular relevance within tourism, hospitality and leisure. What this implies is that all people have the potential to learn new things at all stages in their lives and negative assumptions about their interest or capacity to learn should not be made by others on their behalf. As we have seen, the tourism industry is characterized by its breadth in terms of sub-sectors, its labour intensity, its small business structure in many countries and its geographical dispersion (it is truly an industry of every parish). As a result, tourism and hospitality can provide working opportunities for an incredibly wide range of people in terms of their ability, their interests, their aspirations and their availability – career-focused professionals, craftspeople, technicians, housewives/husbands seeking flexible employment opportunities, students seeking temporary employment and school pupils seeking their first jobs, as well as those who, for a variety of social and physical reasons, cannot find employment in other areas, in particular the physically disabled or the intellectually disabled. Given this diversity in its workforce, it is easy to make assumptions about an individual's capability and potential based on the tasks and responsibilities that they currently have and, thus, to deny some the opportunity to avail themselves of development chances. Furthermore, given the change factor which is inherent within tourism, hospitality and leisure today, employers require a workforce that can adapt to new technologies, systems and markets and it is far more cost and socially effective as well as sustainable to invest in this change through internal development rather than to replace labour already employed with new staff. To do so requires recognizing both the potential and the limitations of the whole workforce.

The context of development

It is implicit in the above discussion that development is a process which can take place at any time and is not constrained by formal parameters at specified points within an individual's childhood, adolescence or working life. The same flexibility applies to other contextual dimensions such as the reasons/motivation for the development, location of development, its duration and timing, how it is carried out, its assessment and the recognition accorded to the outcome. Development is not something that is confined to the classroom, laboratory or training room nor is it, in situational terms, restricted to planned and formalized group sessions in college or the workplace. Development activities may consist of a brief half-hour session or a full year's programme and they may or may not be assessed in academic or practical terms. The outcomes may lead to formal recognition through certification, promotion within the company, enhanced remuneration or none of these. It is important to recognize the potential for such diversity within development and here we are only talking about what might be described as planned or structured development.

In the vocational context of tourism, hospitality and leisure, development needs to be considered as a planned process. Therefore, it is necessary to put to one side unplanned and unstructured learning which we have included implicitly in our discussion up to this point. Planned and structured development is a process over which management, as well as the individual, has control and

| Table 8.2 | The context of education and training |

Time	Place
Macro	School/college/university/training centre
Compulsory education age	Classroom
Optional schooling	Lecture theatre
Post-secondary school	Seminar room
Postgraduate	Tutor's office
Post-experience/mid-career	Laboratory (science, kitchen)
Return to education/new career	The web
Post-redundancy	Simulated work environment (kitchen, restaurant,
Pre-retirement	travel agency)
Post-retirement	Real work environment (kitchen for public
Lifelong learning	restaurant, travel shop)
Virtual learning	ICT laboratory
	Language laboratory
Micro	Library
During 'normal' school/college hours	Audio room
Evenings	Field trip/site visit
Weekends	Independent learning suite
Day release	At home (online, open learning, homework,
Block release	assignments)
During 'normal' working hours	On bus, train, in cafe, etc.
During 'normal' leisure time	
Summer schools	Workplace
	Classroom/training suite
	Seminar room
	Manager's/supervisor's office
	Simulated work environment (flight simulator,
	restaurant)
	Real work environment (no customers)
	Real work environment (customers)
	Company training centre
	Site visit
	Open learning facilities
	At home (open learning, assignments, practice)
	On bus, train, in cafe, etc.

Provider	Reason/motivation	
	Personally motivated	Employer-motivated
School	Career opportunity	Enable promotion
College (real/virtual)	Career enhancement	Fills skills gap
University (real, virtual)	Career change	Keep employee
Specialist training provider	Advance in pay/benefits	Personal development
Employer	Job protection	Reward performance
Professional association	Updating of skills	
Trade union	Personal development	
	Interest in subject	
	To re-enter workforce	

| Table 8.2 | *continued* |

Meeting the costs	Method
State	Lecture
Individual	Seminar
Individual's family	Tutorial (face to face, online)
Employer	Discussion
Potential employer	Demonstration
Trust/foundation	Laboratory practical
Shared between any of above	Simulated real situation practical
	Controlled real situation practical
	Sit-by-Neil/Nellie
	Simulation
	Case study
	Group activity/project
	Individual project
	Research project
	Online project
	Field trip/visit
	Counselling

Measurement of outcomes	Recognition of outcomes
Type	Award of diploma/degree
Closed-book examination	Professional guild accreditation
Open-book examination	Certificate of attendance/participation
Paper assignments/project	Increased/changed responsibilities
Thesis	Promotion opportunities
Multiple-choice type test	Career opportunities with new company
Online test	Career opportunities in new area
Practical text	Enhanced pay/benefits
Practical project	Commendation from supervisors/peers
Simulated real situation	Enhanced self-esteem
Observed real situation	
Progress in the workplace	
Management/authority for assessment	
Public authority (education ministry)	
Private agency	
Professional body	
School/college/university	
Employer/company	
Manager/supervisor	
Training/personnel department	

where both parties may anticipate what will occur, prepare for the occasion and evaluate the outcomes. Therefore it is possible to identify the main contexts in which such development takes place in relation to the tourism, hospitality and leisure industry:

- time
- place
- provider
- reason/motivation
- meeting the costs
- method
- measurement of outcomes and
- recognition of outcomes.

The elements of this contextual map are by no means mutually exclusive or, for that matter, entirely comprehensive as the purpose of developing such a contextual map is to demonstrate the wide range of situations in which development within tourism, hospitality and leisure can take place. Table 8.2 (on p.215) elaborates further on the dimensions of this contextual map.

Placing development activities in their appropriate context is an important activity for both the individuals concerned and for tourism and hospitality industry employers. It can, for example, assist in determining the respective roles of both parties if they are involved, who pays the costs and what are the terms of such payment, and how the outcomes are to be evaluated and acted upon.

It is important to recognize, however, that any contextual combination from Table 8.2 represents legitimate development activities for the individual, the employer or society, and all combinations do in all probability take place within tourism, hospitality and leisure at some point.

Case Study *Advanced Certificate in Tourism with Business*

PROGRAMME PHILOSOPHY, AIM, OBJECTIVES AND LEARNING OUTCOMES

Aim

The philosophy guiding the development of this programme focuses on providing learners with the knowledge, skills and competencies necessary for effective work within the tourism sector while affording them the opportunity of access and progression to a wide range of alternative employments and further educational choices.

On completion of the programme learners can expect to work in a position of responsibility in a range of different tourism-related businesses as identified within an underpinning research study. Graduates with suitable post qualification experience may reasonably expect to work as

Travel Advisors

Tourist Information Officers

Guides in Visitor Attractions and Heritage Centres

▶

Administrative positions in tourist-related businesses and the wider services sector

Customer contact and front desk positions across the tourism sector

Sales and marketing executives including telesales

Airline ground crew and reservations personnel

Cabin crew

Tour representatives

Tourism retail assistants

Customer relations

A fundamental aim of this programme is to meet the needs of the various sub-sectors of the tourism industry at local and national levels.

Objectives

1. To foster the intellectual ability of learners in a manner which enables them to make a meaningful contribution in their personal and professional lives.

2. To develop critical thinking skills and a questioning, creative and innovative approach to their studies.

3. To introduce learners to the scope and economic and social potential of the tourism industry.

4. To facilitate learners' interaction with industry through a mandatory work placement programme.

5. To facilitate learners to explore the determinants, implementation and subsequent measurement of best practice within the tourism industry.

6. To enable learners to develop competence and confidence for successful work in the tourism sector by the acquisition of the necessary business, technological, social and communication skills.

7. To develop in learners the skills and knowledge necessary to implement and evaluate the application of information technology and e-commerce as a

significant component of tourism operations.

8. To foster creativity, innovation and a spirit of enterprise in learners.

9. To enable suitably qualified and motivated learners to progress to higher level studies.

Learning outcomes

Learners graduating from this programme with an Advanced Certificate will be able to:

1. Operate effectively and innovatively in a position of responsibility within the tourism sector.

2. Draw independent conclusions based on a systematic approach to problem identification, analysis and solution.

3. Make decisions in a clear, coherent and structured manner so as to adapt to changing business environments.

4. Demonstrate a clear understanding of the tourism industry in Ireland and internationally and to appreciate the significance of the sector to the Irish economy.

5. Demonstrate a thorough knowledge of the operation of organisations and their context within tourism.

6. Understand and effectively apply the principles and practice of customer care and quality service, anticipating, meeting and exceeding customer expectations.

7. Demonstrate competence in the use of information and communications technology and e-commerce as applied in the tourism sector.

8. Demonstrate an understanding of the key business functions and procedures associated with effectiveness and profitability in the tourism sector.

9. Operate effectively within a diverse environment.

10. Communicate effectively in a European language.

Reproduced with permission from Fáilte Ireland.

Education, training and development and the tourism, hospitality and leisure labour market

Chapter 3 addressed the structure of the labour market with respect to tourism, hospitality and leisure. It was difficult to reach generalized conclusions about tourism labour markets primarily because of the heterogeneous nature of the industry. The discussion drew quite heavily on the work of Riley (1993 and 1996) but his model, while suitable to some of the main sub-sectors – notably hotels and catering, retail and aspects of attractions work – does not have universal application. The internal labour markets with respect to, for example, travel management, transportation (notably in the airline sector), and culture and heritage management, among other areas, have characteristics which make them much 'stronger'. They do exhibit many of the structural features which Riley associates with a strong internal labour market, such as specified hiring standards, single or limited ports of entry, high skills specificity, continuous on-the-job training, fixed promotion and transfer criteria, strong workplace customs and fixed pay differentials.

Thus applying labour market models to a consideration of vocational education in tourism, hospitality and leisure, as Riley does, has certain inherent problems. However, given the size and importance of the weak internal labour-market sectors within tourism as a whole, it is useful to consider Riley's analysis in some detail here. His analysis of the contrasting internal labour market leads to the presentation of a model which attempts to describe the relationship between type of work, labour markets and mode of human resource management. This model is reproduced in Figure 8.1.

This model is dynamic in that it proposes a two-way influence of labour market characteristics, mode of human resource management and qualitative demands that are made upon vocational education. This model leads Riley to certain propositions with respect to vocational education. These are discussed in Table 8.3 along with analysis in italic of their applicability, as well as illustrative examples.

Riley's labour market model provides us with a useful tool with which to analyse the relationship between companies in the tourism, hospitality and leisure sector and the providers of vocational education and training. It also points to the situations within which education, training and development are likely to occur with respect to the various sectors of the tourism, hospitality and

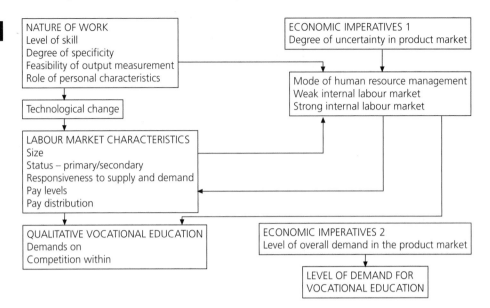

Figure 8.1

A model of the relationship between type of work, labour markets and mode of human resource management

Source: Riley (1993) p.50, with permission from Elsevier.

Exhibit 8.1 Relationship of weak and strong internal labour markets to vocational education

The weaker the internal labour markets . . .

. . .the lower pay levels will be and the attraction of specific, preparatory vocational education will be reduced as a result

This analysis is certainly born out by experience where no-cost pre-entry training programmes for entry-level careers in food and beverage service and accommodation services/housekeeping in some countries regularly fail to attract sufficient applicants because, on the one hand, work in these areas is perceived to be low status and, on the other, graduates of the training programmes are recruited into the same positions in industry as those without the formal training.

. . . the greater will be the dependence of the industry on vocational education to provide skills

This is because resources allocated to in-house training will be limited as a result of high labour turnover, creating an inherent contradiction between low demand for vocational education and great dependence upon its services.

. . . the greater will be the range of skills required from vocational education

This characteristic has a certain logic to it in that skills demands from industry are likely to be very specific, designed to fill clearly identified gaps or needs in

the workforce – i.e. for a coffee shop station waiter or junior travel agency clerk – because establishments do not wish to or do not have the capability to invest in their own specific training. However, there are some indicators within vocational training which run contrary to this analysis and others which support it. Specific job-related vocational training is, in some instances, being replaced by the development of more general and transferable skills. General National Vocational Qualifications (GNVQ) in England, Wales and Northern Ireland provide a broad-based introduction to the skills needed in the workplace. At the same time, very specific, competency-based training towards National Vocational Qualifications (NVQ) are also offered but have fewer prospects of providing educational and vocational progression to participants. By contrast, the German dual system remains very skills-specific in its training focus but depends heavily on the industry to provide much of the training.

. . . the harder it will be to match courses with jobs and careers

If the initial skills and training demands made on vocational education by the tourism industry are highly specific, squaring these with the longer-term aspirations and ambitions of young people may prove difficult. We have already suggested that course and career choice factors are much more broadly based than was previously the case and, in providing this breadth, GNVQs, for example, were a response to student market demand. However, as a consequence, graduates of these courses cannot be slotted into precise industry positions and grades without additional training and without clear indications of career structure in front of them. In this sense, the weak internal labour market can benefit the employer in that vocational education will provide a flexible and mobile recruit, able and expecting to undertake a variety of tasks in different functional areas of the business. However, recruiting course graduates with the expectations of filling a specific slot on a permanent basis becomes rather less likely.

The stronger the internal labour markets are . . .

. . . the more specific and qualitative will be the demands on vocational education

This is clearly true with respect to the strong internal labour-market areas within tourism, hospitality and leisure in jobs such as museum curator or airline pilot. At the same time, sectors of the weak internal market industry are placing increased emphasis on specific general or generic skills – the 'soft' competencies (an apparent contradiction) – as their training priority. This suggests a strengthening of these internal labour markets but in a somewhat unusual manner.

. . . the easier it will be to match courses with jobs

This follows with respect to both types of strong internal labour market, discussed above.

After Riley (1993) p.50. Italic print indicates discussion by this author, with permission from Elsevier.

leisure industry. However, it is a model and thus does not provide a universal explanation as to how labour markets and vocational education relate within tourism, hospitality and leisure. Some of the possible areas of difficulty are elaborated within Table 8.2. The next section will consider models of education, training and development for tourism, hospitality and leisure to illustrate the various approaches that exist within this environment.

Models of education, training and development for tourism, hospitality and leisure

Essentially, the provision of educational, training and development opportunities is a partnership between the tourism, hospitality and leisure industry, primarily in the private sector, and the education and training system, mainly within the public sector. Of course, there are exceptions to this generalization. As we saw in Chapter 2, public sector interest within the international tourism, hospitality and leisure industry remains substantial, through fully or partly state-owned national airlines as well as in the hotel sector (Great Southern Hotels in Ireland, for example) and through tourism information and promotion organizations. Likewise, many countries have seen the entry of private education and training organizations into the market of providing courses for those entering the tourism industry – the Swiss hotel school sector is a good example as are private colleges in Malaysia and Singapore.

Despite Riley's assertion that the inherently weak nature of tourism labour markets inevitably creates a high level of dependence on the vocational education system for the tourism industry, there is substantial evidence that the successful and large companies of international tourism, hospitality and leisure are investing increasingly in their own training and development capabilities, especially those which are predominantly internationally focused corporations. This is, in part, a response to perceived weaknesses in the external college training system but also allows what is seen as greater focus and control within both initial training programmes and those provided as part of in-company development. It may also reflect the move towards stronger, branded images within some companies and the consequent desire to employ those trained specifically within the culture of the organization. This approach is important to companies that are placing increasing emphasis on branded and standardized products and services. Control is very important to the development ideology of a company like Disneyland, Paris, and was a major plank within the pre-opening strategy of the theme park in 1993. Major global hotel brands, including Accor, Taj, Oberoi and Sheraton, all have dedicated corporate universities, offering a range of programmes at different levels and including some that are formally accredited by major universities worldwide.

At the same time, it must be recognized that in most developed countries but also in developing countries, the dominant business structure in terms of the number of units is the small to medium-sized enterprise. It is in this sector that Riley's analysis does have currency because smaller businesses are less able to provide the infrastructure and support for in-house training and development activities and have, traditionally, depended to a great extent on the external training system. Many Swiss hotels, for example, most of which are small family businesses, have probably the highest level of dependence on students on college placement (stagiers) anywhere in the world and include the expectation of an ongoing supply of these students within their normal staffing establishments.

The training and development provided within tourism, hospitality and leisure companies is also of very variable quality and focus. There are plenty of examples from large as well as small businesses where the training is conducted on a limited and specifically 'needs must' basis in order to meet the short-term skills requirements of the company or unit. Such training rarely leads to formal recognition for the newly acquired skills and thus is not of great value to the individual within the context of his or her career development. In some situations, such an approach may be entirely justified. McDonald's, for example, recruit young people, many still at school or college, in the sure knowledge that they are providing short-term, part-time working opportunities for people who have no longer-term aspirations with the company. Thus, rapid-immersion training, designed to allow the new recruit to undertake the required tasks as quickly and as efficiently as possible, can be justified. As a general rule, however, this model of training and development is both short-sighted and ineffective.

However, tourism, hospitality and leisure businesses increasingly recognize the importance of education, training and development as components within the wider strategic development of the company and its markets. In Chapter 4, we considered the link between service quality and the attributes of the human resources which a company employs, particularly in relation to the concepts of empowerment and organizational citizenship. Staff, at all levels, do not become 'empowered' at the dictate of a senior management decision but can only move in that direction with the support, training and development of the company and as a result of total confidence in the new corporate culture.

Recognition of the place of the training and development process at a company level is strongly fostered by governments and their various agencies. Spending of companies in this area relative to turnover is carefully monitored as one means of understanding other indices of industrial (and service) output and productivity. However, such data are difficult to compare accurately on a transnational basis because of the differences in starting points relative to initial education and training, differences within the external education system, and the problems of quantifying the outputs of this investment as opposed to the inputs. It is relatively easy to identify the number of hours of formal training that each employee receives within a company, even if this quantification does neglect the impact of the wide range of informal learning opportunities that exist. However, measuring the return on this investment is much more difficult and, frequently, cannot be undertaken in a clear-cut and quantifiable manner.

Despite the problems inherent in evaluating the outcomes of specific training and development initiatives, difficulties that can be used to detract from the value and purpose of the whole notion of committing resources to this area, it is difficult to dispute the principle that investing in human resources has tangible and market competitive benefits to most companies within the tourism sector. For this reason, participation by major tourism and hospitality companies in the British Government's Investors in People (IiP) scheme is relatively high.

IiP provides a public statement that companies have satisfied national criteria as a company which invests wisely in its people, ensures each individual gets access to training and development, and links its training spend with business goals.

IiP involves companies in a thorough and public overhaul of their human resource systems and practices, not just in the development area but also covering areas such as managing employee records, ensuring widespread awareness of and access to training and development opportunities, conducting employee attitude surveys, formally evaluating each training course and seeking to assess the impact of training and development interventions over time. IiP involves external scrutiny and validation and thus ensures public accountability. Companies with IiP are making a public statement about their attitude and commitment to staff and this is utilized as a major marketing platform for those who achieve the required and demanding standards.

There is clearly a tension between the competing roles of education and industry in the formation of employees who work in the sector as well as the choices that are available to individuals and this tension is well represented in the differing collaborative models that we address below. Fáilte Ireland (2005b) explores these issues in a particularly cogent manner.

> An effective sector-wide approach to people and organisational development in tourism must maintain an appropriate balance between individual and organisational learning. To do this, the sector must be able to identify the skills it needs as well as understanding the best means of developing these skills. There is much emphasis at present on the workplace emerging as the centre of learning in the future. This makes sense where business practices require team-learning, or the transfer and dissemination of 'tacit knowledge' which is organisation specific. In other cases where fundamental or advanced skills (of a more generic nature) need to be developed, it is likely that conventional college based programmes will be suitable. The key in this respect will be the capacity to recognise the circumstances in which different approaches to learning might be suitable. (p.37)

The reality in tourism, hospitality and leisure in most countries, however, is that education, training and development are partnership processes between the tourism industry and its amalgam of public and private sector operations on the one hand, and the specialist providers of courses and development activities, again both public and private sector, on the other. There is a variety of formats through which such partnerships may operate, including official structures in Germany or Switzerland or on the basis of ad hoc arrangements in France and Britain. Thus it is a partnership that operates according to a number of different models and with differing centres of control and influence. These models include the following, although the examples are simplifications and do not necessarily apply in total within any national system.

The total separation model

In this model there are few links between the different levels of training and development. The industry depends upon the external education and training system as the main source for its new recruits but contributes nothing to the education and training process and is not consulted by education and training providers in terms of curriculum, teaching methods, etc. Historically, Romanian tourism education and training operated relatively closely to this model. The country's main providers of education and training for tourism, the National University, the National Institute for Tourism Management and Training and tourism high schools, had little formal contact with what was an exclusively publicly owned tourism and hospitality industry. The parties were so remote that the industry did not contribute to training through work experience placement, taking the view that those on formal courses did not have the skills to work in the professional environment. On graduation, students were placed in jobs within the industry, where industry found it necessary to apply its own training input, but up to that point the two parties maintained no links.

Airey (1994) noted similar problems with respect to tourism, hospitality and leisure education in Poland in the early 1990s and concluded that:

> Links with industry are poorly developed in Polish education. For example, employers are rarely involved in courses or curriculum design; few teachers have recent or any experience of industry and industrial secondment for teachers is virtually unknown; case studies based on industry rarely form part of teaching; while most courses include industrial placements for students these are rarely well integrated into the courses. (Airey 1994, p.8)

Airey also notes difficulties with respect to the other four pointers, notably inadequate and out-of-date resources; outmoded curricula, especially in business and customer-focused areas; insufficient breadth to reflect the range of the modern tourism, hospitality and leisure industry; and courses that do not challenge, especially with respect to the development of responsibility and independence in the workplace which is an essential educational precursor to work in an empowered industry environment.

Industry and education in partnership

Examples of this model are those in place in Germany within the dual system which focus on an apprenticeship model in all trade areas. Indeed, the German apprenticeship schemes which prepare school leavers for careers in the various tourism, hospitality and leisure sectors operate within a system whereby developing the specific skills requirement of the job is the task of industry working to clearly stipulated curricula and guidelines, while local colleges take responsibility for the continuing general education of the apprentices. Deissinger (1997) defines the German system as more than just a location of learning in two places: it also has an underpinning legal dimension.

> The dual system is an institutional framework which is subdivided into two 'learning venues': the company or master providing on-the-job training (the actual apprenticeship) and the part-time vocational school where the apprentice receives theoretical instruction and is taught in subjects such as German, mathematics or social studies. The two institutions underlie different legal systems as laid down in the German constitution: education in schools is the

responsibility of the federal states whereas on-the-job training policies and standards are the formal responsibility of the federal government, advised by the Federal Institute for Vocational Training (Bundesinstitut für Berufsbildung, BIBB). (p.298)

What is important in the German system is the extent to which the private sector through employers invests in both the skills and the wider vocational socialization of young people, in other words making them into good employees as well as effective technicians.

All young people leaving school at the age of 16 in Germany continue in education through a combination of training in the workplace and attendance on a part-time basis at local training colleges or *Berufsschule*. Programme content in the workplace is decided through a nationally agreed training code, determined through extensive consultation between educational, employer and trade union interests. Educational curricula are also decided nationally. Hotel and catering trades are well provided for within the German dual system but the importance of the model in the travel and leisure sectors is much less pronounced, perhaps because of the extent of formal training organized and run by that sector in its own right. The German 'dual system' apprenticeship scheme has much to commend it. It is distinguished by the extent to which it is employer led, employer controlled and in part employer delivered by staff trained and qualified to do so. However, it has the added advantage of drawing not only on those who have left school before the age of 18, but also many in their late teens and 20s, who wish to top up their formal education with vocational training for specific jobs.

A very different and smaller-scale model of cooperation between education and industry in tourism, hospitality and leisure is that which has been developed over 25 years by Kenya Utalii College in Nairobi. The college is the premier provider of tourism, hospitality and leisure education in East Africa and offers programmes at craft and management levels to students from Kenya and a range of neighbouring countries. Kenya Utalii graduates work throughout the industry in the region and this provides one of the key cornerstones of the cooperation between the college and the tourism, hospitality and leisure industry. All students undertake extended periods of work-based learning through placements that consist of meaningful jobs. Therefore, when they complete their college courses, students are well equipped for the real world of work.

Kenya Utalii College also works closely with the industry on an outreach basis. All teachers spend an extended period of college vacations running short refresher courses throughout Kenya as well as in other countries for personnel in the industry, both at basic and advanced levels. The college, therefore, is actively involved in upgrading skills to a minimum national standard. Industry personnel also play an active role in college academic life, as guest lecturers and examiners.

Models of close collaboration between educational providers and the tourism, hospitality and leisure sector are not without their challenges. Mulcahy (1999) addresses some of the tensions that exist in terms of roles and outcomes when he discusses vocational work experience in the sector:

At its simplest, the notion of work experience can be seen as a triangle incorporating three parties: the educator, the employer, and the learner. The fact that three separate components are involved (each with its own agenda and goals) signals a complex nature and it is important to view work experience from a perspective that reflects this. For example, the teacher may regard work experience in investigative terms as an opportunity to learn more about the structure of the industry, whereas the student may view it as a career opportunity, and the employer as an opportunity for cheap labour. This perspective can be viewed at many different levels in a dualistic way; examples which are obvious could include that of industry versus education; the role of being a worker (being in production) versus that of being a trainee (learning); the function of a trainer versus that of an employer. Inherent in these dualistic natures are tensions that can act in a positive or negative manner, not necessarily in concert, nor with equal power. It may be possible that the systematic management of these tensions facilitates effective work experience. (p.165)

Mulcahy's recognition of the importance of learning that takes place in the workplace is reinforced by Fáilte Ireland (2005b), who note that work-based learning:

can be very operational in focus, it sometimes involves collective learning across a team, and it can frequently involve the accumulation of tacit knowledge. In this latter case, the nature and extent of the learning can remain somewhat ambiguous, precisely because the content learned may be tacit and may remain unarticulated in any formal curriculum statement.

Notwithstanding the ambivalence that can surround such learning, this type of developmental activity is frequently the most valuable because it is closest to the immediate skills requirements and behaviours associated with the high standards of job performance. (pp.43–4)

An arm's-length model of education and industry partnership

In the UK, ad hoc and very variable links exist between individual education and training providers and the tourism, hospitality and leisure industry at a local, national and, increasingly, international level. These partnerships frequently work very effectively. On the other hand, the mainstream system is much more government-led than is the case in Germany. Traditionally apprenticeship schemes did operate, especially in the hotel and catering sector, but without the strength and organization of their German counterparts. The system collapsed owing to a lack of control and incentive to participate as well as through the impact of economic downturn during the 1980s. The model which has replaced it is unique in Europe in that it focuses on the outcomes of training, in other words the skills and competencies which employees can demonstrate regardless of where they were acquired, rather than on the formal programme designed to assist students and trainees to acquire those skills.

The UK system includes National Vocational Qualifications (NVQs) and Scottish Vocational Qualifications (SVQs) which are programmes that require study of the core skills of communications, numeracy and ICT alongside vocational skills development in both the workplace and the classroom. Tourism, hospitality and leisure education in England, Wales and Northern Ireland is offered on the basis of a five-level framework which applies both in colleges/universities and within enterprises and, indeed, learners can develop the requisite competencies in either location (EURHODIP 2003). What is interesting when this system is compared to that in Germany is the absence of specific reference to a vocational context within the descriptors for the five levels, because they are designed for application within both vocational and non-vocational learning situations.

- *Level 1* provides students with a range of competencies which involve the application of skills in the execution of a varied range of vocational activities, most of which are routine or predictable.

- *Level 2* equips students with competencies which involve the application of skills in the execution of a series of significant activities which are complex or non-routine and which require a certain level of responsibility or autonomy. Working together with others, as part of a team, for example, is a frequent requirement.

- *Levels 1 and 2* equate to qualified work status and lead to the award of a certificate.

- *Level 3* is a specialist qualification and leads to the award of a diploma. Level 3 offers students competencies which involve the application of skills in the execution of a wide range of varied professional duties, executed in a wide-ranging series of different contexts, most of which are complex and non-routine. A considerable amount of responsibility and autonomy is required, as well as frequently involving team management and supervision of other workers.

- *Level 4* provides training for the advanced specialist and leads to the award of a degree. Level 4 brings students competencies which involve the application of skills in the execution of complex, technical or professional activities, performed in a wide-ranging field of different contexts and involving a substantial level of personal responsibility and autonomy. Responsibility for the work of others and the allocation of resources are often involved.

- *Level 5* is designed for the education of senior executives through postgraduate courses for MBA and equivalent qualifications. Level 5 provides students with competencies which involve the application of a series of fundamental principles in a variety of extensive and often unpredictable contexts. A very substantial level of personal autonomy and often significant responsibility for the work performed by others, and the allocation of substantial resources, are often characteristic of work at this level. There will also be personal responsibility for the analysis, diagnosis, design and execution of planning and assessment.

The UK's NVQ/SVQ model allows experienced tourism and hospitality staff who have received no formal and certified training during their career to demonstrate and claim their competencies and offer these towards nationally recognized awards. This process is known as the Accreditation of Prior Learning. In practice, NVQs are obtained either through the college system or within a formal training context in industry. Teachers and trainers are formally recognized as verifiers, able to accredit competency in the requisite skills areas and, in turn, have their assessments monitored by external verifiers. While an element of partnership exists within this system, it is also true to say that, in part, the tourism and hospitality industry and the education/training system are now in competition within this system, competing for the right to train young people and to access public funding in order to do so. One of the main benefits in providing formal recognition for the training and skills development which occurs in the tourism, hospitality and leisure industry is that it allows those who are able to claim recognition for their skills to use the NVQs as stepping stones onto the ladder for further training and development, both within the industry and back within the formal education system. The model will also help to plug what is a very worrying training and skills deficiency within the tourism and hospitality industry in Britain, especially in certain sectors. A very high proportion of the two million plus workforce in the hotel and catering sector have received no formal training for the work they are undertaking. Clearly, the British model has the potential to cope with this problem.

The Irish model

This model also operates at two levels in that the ad hoc and informal level exists, as in Britain, between colleges and industry at local, national and international level, especially in relation to the provision of work placement opportunities. The other level is managed through a unique coordinating agency, an Irish semi-state body, responsible to the Minister of Tourism formerly known as CERT and now merged into the Tourist Board to form a new agency, Fáilte Ireland. CERT was founded in 1963 and developed its range of programmes in collaboration with the tourism, hospitality and leisure industry and public sector agencies in parallel with the growth in Irish tourism. Fáilte Ireland operates under the authority of a board which is representative of employers, trade unions, educational institutions as well as government agencies and departments. The education and training function of Fáilte Ireland is to coordinate all aspects of the planning of human resources needs within tourism at a macro level through research and the determination of training/development priorities as well as through the design and implementation of courses through the agency of its own training centres and the college system. Fáilte Ireland works with the Irish Further and Higher Education Qualifications Authority to coordinate the certification of tourism, hospitality and leisure employees trained in a variety of situations. Fáilte Ireland is also responsible for the provision of in-company and short-course training on behalf of tourism industry businesses on a commercial basis. The Irish model is unique in that it provides by far the most comprehensive approach to coordinating the inputs of education and the tourism, hospitality and leisure industry into a unified system and, through Fáilte Ireland, coordinates the identification of training and development needs at both macro and micro levels. We will consider Fáilte Ireland's role in relation to labour-market planning at a national level in Chapter 9.

Case Study *South West Trains, UK*

South West Trains (SWT) is part of the Stage-coach Group. London Waterloo is the hub for SWT business networks and is also home to London Underground and Waterloo International terminal for Eurostar services to Paris and Brussels via the Channel Tunnel. SWT run 1635 trains every weekday, serving 207 stations and employing around 5250 staff. Approximately 143 million passenger journeys a year are made on routes through Hampshire, Surrey, Dorset, Wiltshire, Berkshire, Devon, Somerset, Cornwall, East and West Sussex and Greater London, serving a mixture of commuters and longer-distance travellers. Since taking over the franchise in 1996 the company has added in excess of 12 000 additional peak seats, resulting in a 5 per cent increase in usage by the customer.

South West Trains introduced an in-house role-play course to help employees deal with all types of passengers. Although part of a wider cultural change at SWT, the course has had a positive effect on both customer and staff satisfaction levels. Customer complaints about staff behaviour have decreased. Sickness absence levels have also fallen, from an average of 12 days per person to 9.4 days, saving £1.3 million, while staff retention has risen to 94.4 per cent.

In 2000, SWT, teamed up with training provider Dynamic Solutions to teach its 3800 staff how to tailor behaviour to suit each customer. The result was Quantum Leap, a three-day in-house role-play course.

Courses are held at the Centre Stage training facility in a formerly disused building at Basingstoke station. One room has been converted into a mock station, complete with a ticket office, railway platform and seating booth. Each course begins with the actor playing an employee and a delegate portraying a particular type of customer, for example a nervous passenger unused to rail travel. The trainer periodically stops the action to discuss the actor's responses, picking up on body language, tone of voice and facial expression. This helps delegates recognise and question their own responses. Delegates then become amateur psychologists, using the Myers-Briggs Type Indicator to identify their personality types.

Next, delegates learn to identify other people's natures. The actor, this time in the passenger role, acts out four versions of a simple scenario, each time demonstrating a different personality type. A delegate takes the employee role, while the other participants suggest how they could improve their response and the actor gives feedback.

Finally, delegates divide into two teams and give each other a scenario – based on an event they have experienced – to test their new skills. With previous scenarios including everything from how to prevent a distraught dog-owner from climbing on to the track to rescue their pet, to how to cope when a passenger produces a weapon in a deserted carriage, this is often a 'challenging and emotionally charged day'.

After the programme, the trainer completes a feedback form that can be used to highlight exceptional candidates. This has resulted in people being promoted for demonstrating previously unnoticed qualities. Staff have become much more confident in general in their relationships with customers and a significant number have been promoted to supervisory and management levels as a result.

Front-line staff in tourism take on, perhaps, the most challenging roles on a daily basis in the industry. Helping them to understand individual customer needs within the constraints of professional service and company requirements is an important step in assisting to reduce the pressures and tensions which can exist in this role. Central to this process is the need to recognise the particular expectations and needs which different groups of customers may have – in the case of South

West Trains, commuters, business travellers, excursionists, tourists and others.

Prepared by Frances Devine of the University of Ulster for Fáilte Ireland, from a number of publicly accessible websites. Reproduced with permission.

Case discussion questions

1. What are the main challenges in helping tourism, hospitality and leisure employees to understand their customers' needs?

2. What factors used in the SWT training case contributed to the success of the programme?

3. How effective would be role-play training be in workplaces with which you are familiar? What might some of the barriers to the successful use of this form of training be?

Management education, training and development

Thus far, the focus of discussion on partnerships between education and training interests and the tourism, hospitality and leisure industry in various countries has, in fact if not in intent, focused on training and development at a level which is normally described as 'craft', 'skilled trade' or 'apprenticeship'. The issue of meeting the training and development needs of future and existing managers for tourism, hospitality and leisure has not been addressed except in so far as it is covered by in-company provision. The management environment also provides a diversity of approaches within and between national systems. Holloway (1993) points to a definitional problem which, while applicable at all levels, creates particular difficulties at university-level education. He notes that:

> The variety of definitions [of tourism] within Europe leads to different approaches to course curriculum design which add to the difficulties in seeking mutual recognition of qualifications between the European partners. For example, in the Netherlands recreation is seen as integral with travel and tourism, and in France, too, the terms 'leisure' and 'tourism' are used synonymously – at least, in terms of curriculum development. Germany has not yet recognized the need for vocational education or training for leisure and recreation, while (at the management level) Britain has chosen to develop distinct curricula for leisure and tourism, despite significant areas of overlap in knowledge and skills. (Holloway 1993, pp.101–102)

In many ways, these problems of definition arise through historical accident within universities and other providers of management education. The location, scope and even the existence or not of specialist provision in the tourism area is frequently linked to the origins of initiatives of this kind. In Britain, the study of tourism in a wider context has frequently originated within specialist hotel and catering studies faculties – two of the earliest examples, at the Universities of Strathclyde and Surrey, have followed this model. Leisure, by contrast, is often closely linked to sports science and sports education. This has greatly influenced programme structure and content as well as the professional as opposed to academic focus of courses. Other models have seen the study of tourism, hospitality and leisure develop rather more independently – at the Free University of Brussels in Belgium, for example. Belgian programmes in tourism are strongly influenced, in their design and emphasis, by the department in which they are located, which may be social sciences, economics or psychology. In the United States, programmes in tourism, hospitality and leisure management have a diversity of discipline origins, a good example being the links to agriculture and the land-based economy that underpins the work of Purdue University in Indiana. In many developing countries, management programmes in this field are of relatively recent origin but, likewise, have links to a variety of underpinning disciplines. In Malaysia, for example, Universiti Putra Malaysia was also originally an agricultural university and its two strands of programmes in tourism, hospitality and leisure are linked to studies of land economy and food science.

The issue, in many respects, relates to the balance between practical vocational, professional business and academic theoretical inputs into the curriculum and the confusion which use of differing nomenclature can cause. For example, the Swiss Hotel Management Diploma, offered by many private institutions after two years' study, admits students who might not qualify for university-level education elsewhere in Europe. They undertake a highly practical, vocational course with 12 months in class and 12 months on work placement in the Swiss industry, undertaking entry-level work, primarily in the food and beverage area. The compelling necessity of describing the programmes as 'management' is market-driven in that courses would not recruit if they were described otherwise. It is a term frequently used within the tourism, hospitality and leisure sector to describe education and training at a level where it would not be applicable or admissible in other economic sectors.

One of the management-level issues which forms the kernel of much debate within the tourism, hospitality and leisure industry relates to achieving the appropriate balance between the vocational and professional on the one hand and academic or intellectual on the other (Ladkin 2000). It is a debate which generates considerable passion from supporters of both extremes. On the one hand, the important concern of vocational relevance is used as a guiding benchmark within those systems which are aiming to ensure that their graduates can fit into the opportunities provided by the industry and undertake those tasks demanded of them immediately. This model has particular strength within the hotel and catering sub-sector and is at the root of the German apprenticeship scheme, which is the start of the long route to management. Swiss hotel management education also draws upon the premise that the start of a career which aspires towards the management of a hotel must be well grounded in practical, vocationally relevant and, preferably, food and beverage skills. Within these systems, more complex and less practical skills and requirements are met at a later stage in the educational and training process.

The alternative extreme places the main emphasis of preparation for a management career within the tourism, hospitality and leisure industry in the context of a general university-level education. This provides the intellectual development and training upon which the specific demands of the tourism and hospitality sector can be grafted, either through postgraduate conversion programmes in universities and colleges or within workplace training and development. This route is rather more akin to some vocational traditions in the

United States – for example, American legal training only commences when a college or university graduate enters specialist law school. It is also a view that has some support within sectors of the tourism, hospitality and leisure industry where recruitment focuses upon generic as opposed to specific skills and competencies.

The reality, given the diversity of the tourism, hospitality and leisure industry, is that the ideal model, if such a concept exists, lies somewhere between the two extremes and that there is a place and need for programmes which place greater emphasis in both directions. However, our discussion in Chapter 5 pointed to the problems of image and lack of perceived professional status which the tourism, hospitality and leisure industry faces. One contribution to overcoming this problem could lie in the nature of qualifying education that is provided at higher levels. A review of curricula, learning resources and teaching methods employed within many tourism, hospitality and leisure management education programmes suggests that the emphasis on vocationalism has important consequences for the level of academic and intellectual demands that are made on students. By comparison with colleagues studying in areas such as psychology or the sciences, the benefits of vocational relevance may be gained at a cost to conceptual demands and academic rigour. This cannot be in the long-term career interests of those participating in such programmes.

Riley's weak internal labour-market model highlights multiple ports of entry and a lack of formal progression criteria as characteristic of some sub-sectors within the tourism, hospitality and leisure industry. In practice, this means that the industry's managers have a wide range of backgrounds and training and that formal and specific academic or vocational training routes offer only one option among many to those aspiring to manage in the industry. At the same time, issues of status and professionalism as well as wider moves to place greater emphasis on formally recognized qualifications show the need to ensure that those in management can point to equivalenct status and skills in terms of their capabilities, whether gained in the workplace or in college. Thus, formally recognized progression routes for those entering the industry at whatever level and for those already working in it becomes an important issue. In the United Kingdom, this need is being addressed through NVQs (and their Scottish equivalents) which provide for recognition of skills and capabilities acquired in both the educational and workplace setting. The theory of the system is that it offers full portability between work and education and allows managers and others, as their careers progress, to acquire additional recognition for what they are doing at work or learning in college.

Portability is also the theory behind moves to establish equivalent courses and qualifications for tourism and hospitality within the European Union. With established harmonization and recognition between training routes and courses, it should be easier for tourism and hospitality sector employees to avail themselves of opportunities in different countries of the EU. The work of CEDEFOP, as the EU's vocational training agency, has been important in establishing the framework for vocational harmonization within the 12 member states. However, it is fair to say that the impact of CEDEFOP's efforts has been rather limited in an industry that, in general, does not place great credence upon formal qualifications and where, as we saw in Chapter 6, there is already a well-established tradition of mobility within Europe. At university level in

Europe, the Bologna agreement is designed to ensure a common framework for higher studies across the European Union and, at least in terms of structure and level, this is intended to enhance the portability of qualifications, including those in tourism, hospitality and leisure.

Education for tourism, hospitality and leisure, especially at management level, is going through a period of significant change. This is not only true in developed countries but is even more applicable in developing and transition economies, where major reforms are required to enable institutions and the industry to modernize the management and operation of businesses in all sub-sectors. Given the priority accorded to tourism, hospitality and leisure within the strategies for economic reform in most developing countries, it is important that such change addresses education and training as important vehicles for such reform. Lennon (2002) notes somewhat cautiously that:

> A fundamental need for any nation developing or extending its tourism appeal is the development and training of service and production employees for employment in the hotels, resorts, tourist attractions, travel and related infrastructure. However, in many developing countries, training for these sectors is often relatively unsophisticated and lacking in industry credibility. (p.147)

The main imperative for change, however, is likely to be the continuing process of globalization within the industry, and the pressure that this will apply on institutions to ensure that courses and qualifications meet the needs of both individual graduates and the major employing companies.

Alongside the pressures of globalization, fundamental changes in the labour markets of developed countries are also impacting on the nature of education and training that is available for all stakeholders in tourism, hospitality and leisure. Skills shortages in key work areas, particularly evident in this sector, has resulted in a reinterpretation of the skills that are required to perform specific jobs and, indeed, a watering down of traditional entry requirements for some work areas (Baum and Odgers 2001) so that some existing college programmes are no longer viable or suitable. Alongside this approach has been the widespread employment of migrant labour within the sector. This also has clear education and training implications in terms of both technical and cultural skills development in a sector where face-to-face contact with guests is so important.

Educational systems have also sought to re-evaluate how they make sure that maximum opportunity is available to all sections of society to participate both in education/training and in the workplace. Issues of access within education, therefore, are of paramount importance so that fewer people are excluded by virtue of educational failures within the school system and within the home. US education has long been held up as particularly successful in maximizing participation and progression, both for young people and in terms of lifelong learners, providing opportunity to people of all ages and stages within their working lives. In the UK, the introduction of foundation degrees in 2000 has been designed to:

> Allow integration of academic and work-based learning through close collaboration between employers and programme providers with the overall aim of equipping learners with the necessary skills and knowledge relevant to their

employment thereby satisfying the needs of both learners and employers.
(Quinn *et al.* 2005, p.1)

On the face of it, this appears to mirror aspirations of the German dual system. However, the main difference lies in the level of qualification involved and the progression routes that are offered. Foundation degrees in the UK can be offered either in college or in the workplace or, indeed, through a combination of both. Sponsoring providers can also be either education or industry. Completion of a foundation degree leads to the award of a formal university qualification but also provides direct access into the final years of a conventional university degree, either on a full-time or part-time basis. The focus, therefore, is much more on the merging of operational and academic learning towards higher educational outcomes than is the traditional objective of the German dual system. One outcome, it is hoped, will be to help to overcome the high level of 'vocational drift' that occurs with respect to graduates of tourism, hospitality and leisure programmes, a high proportion of whom fail to choose employment in the sector upon graduation (Jameson, Walmsley and Ball 2005).

Learning – a lifelong experience

Education and training in today's change society not longer fits into traditional life models within which the preponderance of our learning took place within the formative years between birth and the age of 20. The nature of social and working life today, particularly in developed countries, is one of constant change and with this instability comes a requirement to acquire new skills and to anticipate and adapt to changing circumstances. Learning the skills associated with information seeking and management on the internet is something that everyone who is over 30 in 2005 has had to do in adult life, after the traditional period for useful learning had been completed. Learning to send text messages is a similar new skill that many adults have had to learn after their school and college years. It is not only technology which has imposed new learning beyond the period that we would historically have associated with this activity. Changes in the workplace driven by new markets, new legislation, new opportunities and new labour-market pressures mean that ongoing learning in the workplace is now expected of many employees at all levels. People are also more likely to change direction in their lives and to seek the skills to avail themselves of new opportunities in employment areas not previously thought of. Healthier retirement allows people to learn new skills with which to enjoy the time when work no longer dominates their lives. In the developed world, this notion of ongoing participation in education and training from pre-school to post-work is known as 'lifelong learning'. Hutton and The Work Foundation (2005) define the concept as follows:

Comprehensive lifelong learning is understood as the provision of an interconnected, universal system of education and training that permits high-quality learning from the early years to retirement. It allows learners to earn recognised and clearly understood qualifications, and to build on them over their lives with credits earned in formal and informal learning settings that will promote their employability, help realise their personal potential and make them better citizens. (p.4)

Hutton and The Work Foundation elaborate upon this definition by exploring the various components of lifelong learning to include workplace learning and initiatives to meet the needs of all key groups in society. Their analysis pulls together a range of initiatives promulgated by the European Union. The components that they identify include:

- Well-developed employer-led training institutions with a strong sense of industry-wide labour-market dynamics and technological developments. Employers need to know more about their current skills base and their future needs. Training institutions should be focused on raising demand for skills as well as ensuring an appropriate supply.
- A national qualifications structure that facilitates access, encourages participation, and enjoys the confidence of employers and employees. Importantly, learning credits should be transferable between formal and informal learning, implying mutual recognition between sectors and institutions.
- An environment where both employers and workers understand the pay-offs from training – with employers committed to investment in skills and workers expressing high demand for learning. Responsibility for investment in training should be shared and co-financed between government, employers and workers.
- A clear prioritization of groups currently disadvantaged, including older workers, the disabled and single parents.
- Diversity of training supply – a mix of public and private provision, with formal and informal learning opportunities.
- Employer engagement at all levels with leadership on questions of qualifications, assessment and the quality of provision.
- Powerful mechanisms to ensure minimum standards together with the supply of able teachers/instructors.

The concept of lifelong learning means different things in different social and economic contexts. Its value is well recognized in Singapore where government policy is designed to support learning within all age groups. People build up learning credits throughout their working lives. These are credits that can be set against vocational or recreational learning at any point in the future, both short term and in the longer term, to prepare for a change of career or for retirement.

In poorer developing countries, the concept of lifelong learning is less well developed. In many such countries, priority must, of necessity, be accorded to children and young people and the state system cannot support additional learning opportunities for older people.

Tourism, hospitality and leisure is a sector that can significantly benefit from lifelong learning initiatives. As we saw in Chapter 7, it is a sector that is well suited to accommodate older workers seeking a change of direction and those seeking a return to work after an extended sabbatical in the home or elsewhere. It is also a sector subject to constant change, requiring re-skilling of existing workers. The sector is, however, one where traditions of supporting ongoing learning are limited and creating recognition of the value of such investment, both by employers and employees, is a real challenge.

Case Study *The Punch Pub Company, UK*

The Punch Pub Company is the second largest pub company in the UK and owns over 6500 pubs. Rather than managing these pubs directly, they are operated through a type of franchising arrangement in the form of tenancies and leases with the individual 'licensee' (also known confusingly as the pub 'landlord'). In effect each pub is run by a small firm-owner/manager who pays rent and is tied to buying alcoholic and non-alcoholic drinks from the pub company.

From the company's perspective, Punch owns the property, and earns revenue from both rents and supplies bought by their tenants/lessees. It is a business format which minimises risk to the company, as it always retains ownership and rents provide a major income stream which is not subject to the vagaries of fluctuating trading conditions. Also consistent with this franchising format, it is hoped that the licensee, as an independent business, has an added incentive to build the business as they profit from increased trade.

Whilst this format allows Punch to operate with minimal risks and low overheads, the company's ability to grow, other than through acquisitions, is via the business performance of the 'entrepreneurs' running their pubs. In many cases, these were found to be 'lifestyle' entrepreneurs who had low-level business objectives and limited skills in business management. In the past, courses offered on a voluntary basis by the company to improve skill levels were undersubscribed and many programmes were cancelled because of low uptake by the tenants/lessees.

Following a report commissioned by the British Institute of Innkeeping, the company recognised that their low training take-up experiences were not unique to Punch, but a consequence of the type of small firms with whom they were dealing. The company introduced two compulsory training programmes for 'licensees'. The Modern Licensed Retailer is a ten-day programme aimed at tenants/lessees who are taking on a Punch pub for the first time. All take the course as a condition of their agreement with the company, even experienced licensees who have managed pubs in the past undertake the programme. The Contemporary Licensed Retailer is a five-day programme which is compulsory for tenants/lessees who are in receipt of an investment grant from the company for property improvement.

In both cases, the Company invited external consultants to undertake an evaluation of the impact of these programmes on the subsequent business performance of participants. Despite the past history of low uptake and reluctance to train, the impact of these training interventions was remarkable. Comparing, before and after 'wet' sales, participating tenants/lessees showed an across the board sales increase of 24 per cent amongst participants compared with non-participants. Interviews with participants revealed that 68 per cent reported that sales in their pub had increased and 70 per cent reported a profit increase as a result of their attendance on the programme. Similar proportions reported increased customer satisfaction and improved customer repeats, and substantial minorities reported reductions in staff turnover and increased employee satisfaction. Over 80 per cent reported that they would recommend the course to another 'licensee'.

▶

This case study confirms the importance of ensuring 'franchises' have the skills needed to build their business. In this case, Punch recognised that just having this support available is not enough because there are a number of barriers, both intrinsic and extrinsic barriers to participation in development programmes by lifestyle entrepreneurs. Compulsory participation resulted in a win–win situation for both the individuals concerned and the company.

Meeting the training and development needs of lifestyle entrepreneurs is a major challenge for locations where this model of business growth is seeing rapid expansion, especially in more rural, more peripheral locations. At the same time, destinations become vulnerable to the vagaries of lifestyle entrepreneurship in terms of quality and sustained service delivery.

Investment in training is one answer. The Punch model works because of the control and influence which the company, as the franchisor, has over its franchisees. As a result, Punch can require participation and can demonstrate benefits, particularly to the bottom line. Dealing with independent operators, for whom profit is but one motive, is rather more challenging and points to a role for public sector training agencies to incentivise participation or require it as a part of access to marketing and other quality standards support.

Original case written by Professor Conrad Lashley of Nottingham Trent University for Fáilte Ireland. Reproduced with permission.

Case discussion questions

1. The Punch case is an example of compulsion in training. What are the benefits and drawbacks of requiring staff or franchisees to undergo specific training?

2. What are the business benefits of investment in training implied by this case?

3. Is it possible to train entrepreneurs?

Review and discussion questions

1. How important is the education versus training debate? Has it surfaced at any point in your own school, college or working career?

2. Identify jobs and tasks which have changed significantly within your own lifetime and that of your parents (not only in the tourism, hospitality and leisure industry). What development needs resulted from such changes?

3. How can providers of education and training prepare students to be responsive to change?

4. If the main needs of tourism, hospitality and leisure employers are for staff with good interpersonal, communication and guest-handling skills, should colleges and universities dispense with practical and vocational skills development and just concentrate on these areas?

5. Consider three situations where you participated in a specific training or development programme (in college, university or the workplace). Place each of these within the 'contextual map' (Table 8.1) against each of the categories specified. How could the programmes have been effectively varied through use of alternatives within the 'map'?

6. In what ways do the characteristics of the tourism, hospitality and leisure internal labour market affect the nature of vocational education and training it requires?

7. What are the main distinctions between the macro models of education and training for tourism, hospitality and leisure that are considered in this chapter?

8. How can the industry-education partnership operate more effectively in the tourism, hospitality and leisure sector?

9. How can the adoption of a comprehensive structure for lifelong learning benefit the tourism, hospitality and leisure sector?

Planning to meet the human resource needs of the international tourism, hospitality and leisure industry

Chapter objectives

This chapter considers the planning process for the effective utilization of people within tourism, hospitality and leisure. The objectives of the chapter are:

- to review the process of labour-market planning at the level of the company, the multinational organization and the destination (region, country);

- to review methods designed to estimate employment levels in tourism, hospitality and leisure in quantitative and qualitative terms;

- to review in detail a national model for human resource planning for tourism, hospitality and leisure.

Introduction

In this chapter, we return to one of the central tenets of effective human resource management and development: the need to institute effective strategic and operational planning mechanisms in order to cater for human resource requirements within tourism, hospitality and leisure at a micro and macro level. At a micro level, one of the main criticisms of the traditional human resource model within tourism and hospitality is that planning is based on contingency requirements and the attainment of short-term objectives. By contrast, macro models at the level of countries and regions tend to focus on long-term interpretation and do not necessarily permit sensitivity to a wildly fluctuating external environment.

Steele (1991) is particularly critical of human resource planning models as they have been applied in developing countries. Her perspective is that:

> Traditional manpower planning, consisting in forecasting future requirements in labor skills, is on the decline as a tool for designing human resources interventions. Instead, 'labor market analysis' is taking over. There are several reasons for the decline of manpower forecasting. Although its rationale sounds

logical ('you must have the right skills in order to produce'), at closer examination there are several problems with this approach which has proven to be non-responsive to the needs of the developing world. Standard manpower planning examines the output of the sector in question up to some year in the future, usually 10 or 20 years. Then a manpower coefficient is applied to the absolute increase in production to arrive at a forecast of the extra labor requirements by that future year. This methodology ignores substitution possibilities, ignores the cost of training one type of labor relative to another, relies on manpower input-output norms that may soon be out of date, puts undue emphasis on higher levels of training, relies heavily on the formal wage sector, is based on a narrow criterion for planning an educational or training system, and can lead to errors of a substantial order. (p.459)

This view is wholly supported by Castley (1996) who develops similar points in relation to developing countries and concludes:

Given the limited catchment area for recruiting many skills, it is highly questionable whether national plans are required for most occupations. For example most semi-skilled workers and artisan skills are recruited locally and mostly technician and sub-professional within a particular region. (pp.15–16)

Castley's arguments in favour of an approach to labour-market planning that is driven by wider social and economic policy accords closely with the Irish case that we will explore in some depth later in this chapter.

'Short-termism' at a micro level abounds within the tourism, hospitality and leisure industry. It is characteristic at unit level, where it is common to witness recruitment and redundancy closely tracking cyclical and seasonal changes in demand without any apparent sense of anticipation or planning. This was certainly true in Hong Kong during the SARS crisis and in the UK when the country was faced with foot and mouth disease. The instability and uncertainty which such policies engender impacts upon the ability of the business to deliver the product and service which the customer is entitled to expect. Such practice puts the short-term profitability of the company before the delivery of quality services to the customer, in itself a major factor in ensuring long-term competitiveness. At the corporate level, performance demands on individual business units are frequently such as to ensure the short-termist approach outlined above. There is also a danger at corporate level that human resource decisions are made without reference to the needs of the individual business unit. In some hotel companies, for example, it has been traditional practice to rotate general managers on the basis of a two-year cycle of duty and to judge their performance on, primarily, financial outcomes over that short period. The consequence at unit level of this policy is an environment in which planning becomes almost non-existent and human resource practices focus almost exclusively on tactical outcomes. To those involved, decisions are only seen to be of relevance in the context of two-year outcomes. Finally, short-termism is commonplace at the macro level of the region or the country, where planning is deficient in order to meet the long-term needs of the tourism, hospitality and leisure industry as a whole. However, probably of greater significance at this level is the absence of coordination between a plethora of government and private sector agencies within the human resource area, with an inevitable impact on the planning process.

In this chapter, we shall address human resource planning (or 'manpower planning' as it is frequently known) at these three levels. Particular emphasis will be given to the final dimension, that of the macro; and the case of one country, the Republic of Ireland, will be examined in some detail in order to illustrate planning and coordination processes at work. Consideration of the planning process has deliberately been left to the latter part of this book because of its dependence on other aspects which have been considered in earlier chapters, notably the historical antecedents, characteristics and structure of tourism, hospitality and leisure (Chapter 2), the labour markets within the sector (Chapter 3), the role of human resources in the delivery of quality service (Chapter 4) and the role of education and training (Chapter 8).

The principles of human resource planning have strong similarities at whatever level is being considered. The process is by no means new although its emergence as an identified field of activity and expertise cannot be traced much further back than the 1960s. Bramham (1983, 1994) attributes this focus to the social and economic climate of the period which increased the complexity of management. Technological and economic change imposed new constraints on management's freedom of action while labour shortages, especially in key skills areas, focused attention on the competitive nature of the labour market in a manner that had not really been experienced in the past. Subsequently, the need for a focused process of planning has been strengthened by pressure on companies to derive greater efficiency and productivity from their human resources, processes frequently accompanied by significant reduction in the number and status of staff employed. Within this changing environment, planning of human resources becomes an essential process.

A number of definitions of human resource planning exist:

The systematic analysis of human resources in the future, directed to minimize uncertainty and surprise and to eliminating mistakes and wastage. (Lester 1960, in Donald 1974, p.14)

Manpower planning aims to maintain and improve the ability of the organization to achieve corporate objectives, through the development of strategies designed to enhance the contribution of manpower at all times in the foreseeable future. (Stainer 1971, p.3)

Human resource planning (or manpower planning) may be defined as a process whereby courses of action are determined in advance and continually updated, with the aim of ensuring that

a) the organization's demand for labour to meet its projected needs is as accurately predicted as the adoption of modern forecasting techniques allow and

b) the supply of labour to the enterprise is maintained by deliberate and systematic action to mobilize it in reasonable balance with these demands.

(Bramham 1994, pp.155–6)

Two of these definitions are focused primarily on the needs of the organization; only Lester appears to go beyond that in order to imply the need to plan human resources at a macro level as well.

At a national level, Steele (1991) grapples with the distinction between manpower planning and her favoured approach of labour-market analysis in the developing country context, a distinction that is compatible with the thinking underpinning discussion in this book. She argues that:

> The focus of manpower planning is on the number of people with skills that are deemed to be necessary for producing the basket of a country's goods and services. Labor market analysis changes the focus to the labor force, a much wider concept, which includes those with no skills and the unemployed. Rather than counting the number of bodies required to fill some projected need, labor market analysts measure the wages in both the public and private sectors. There may be labor shortages in the public sector because wages offered for similar positions in the private sector are higher and/or more flexible. Manpower planning typically uses data only from the formal employment sector of the economy. This is not very relevant in developing countries where the majority of the labor force is engaged in agriculture and informal activities. Labor market analysis, on the other hand, is based on household surveys which capture the characteristics of the entire labor force, including the unemployed. (p.460)

Castley (1996) puts flesh onto this change when he identifies the key components of a move to labour market analysis at a national level, to include:

- measuring wages (as a possible cause of skill shortages);
- more emphasis on household surveys (to monitor the unemployed as well as the employed);
- tracer studies (to study the effects of training courses on the labour market);
- more emphasis on educational profiles (since many occupational categories do not translate easily into educational profiles and occupation itself is not a policy variable);
- more attention to the informal sector (where, in some countries, the majority of workers are found);
- greater concern for issues of poverty and equity;
- more emphasis on general training rather than specific vocational/technical qualifications, which is considered more cost effective in the long run;
- shifting of the cost of training from the general taxpayer to the direct beneficiaries;
- encouraging the development of private training institutions, which are considered to be more cost conscious and market responsive. (p.16)

Bramham (1982) identifies three central concerns which apply to human resource planning at whatever scale it operates:

1. What sort of information about the external and internal environment is required?
2. To what uses will such information be put, particularly with respect to planning?
3. What techniques and methods of manpower planning should be utilized?

Bramham further developed a framework for the planning process which incorporates all three areas. This provides a model at the level of the company which can be compared to that proposed for planning at the macro level later in this chapter (see Figure 9.1). However, many of the framework's components do have applicability in a wider context as well. In many ways, Bramham's framework, in its relationship to the external environment in particular, takes us back to the earlier consideration of the tourism, hospitality and leisure labour market in Chapter 3.

Human resource planning at the level of the business unit

Bramham's approach provides a useful mechanism through which to plan human resource requirements at the level of the business unit. The fragmented nature of the tourism, hospitality and leisure industry and the small-business structure of many enterprises within the sector in many countries mean that, in reality, such planning (along with many other aspects of business planning and forecasting) is comparatively infrequent and unsophisticated in its application. Much management practice – and that in the human resource area is no exception – is driven by traditional practice (i.e. staffing levels are based on custom and practice with some shedding of numbers in response to changes in performance) and a relatively crude evaluation of needs. This process may be influenced by seasonality and other cyclical factors which impact upon tourism, hospitality and leisure businesses. Thus, hotels and attractions in locations such as Rhodes in Greece, Donegal in Ireland and Newfoundland in Canada plan their staffing needs around the seasonality factor. Staff are recruited or return when the businesses reopen in the spring and are released again in the autumn when many seasonal businesses close. In terms of fluctuations in demand within the day or the week, planning revolves round the utilization of part-time or casual support staff to the main core establishment. In countries where the cost of labour remains low (in developing countries or transition economies), tight seasonal management may not be a major imperative and staff are frequently retained even if there are few guests to serve. This is a feature in tourism, hospitality and leisure operations in both rural Kyrgyzstan and Iran. By contrast, given the high cost of labour in most developed countries, this aspect of planning is one that few tourism, hospitality and leisure businesses can afford to neglect.

In the information collection or investigation stage of the human resource planning process, there are four main areas that require consideration. The first of these is the business plan, which provides detailed information on a company's projected sales and financial targets as well as objectives with respect to new products or markets. This process will apply both to the independent small business and to the single business unit within a larger company. In the latter case, a local business plan may be prepared within the context of corporate objectives and both sources will require consideration within the human resource planning process. The business plan may impact on human resource requirements in a number of ways. For example, a hotel may project increased business as a result of a new arrangement with a tour operator or may plan a special low-season promotion to increase business at that time of the year.

Likewise, an equestrian centre could target new overseas markets in Germany or Japan, supported by special multilingual promotional material. Such changes, and a wide range of others, will impact on the number of employees required at specific times of the year as well as upon the specific skills that will be needed to cater for changes in business activity. In the example above of the equestrian centre, enhancing the language skills of existing or new staff may well be a necessary response to planned activity within the business plan.

The second component in the investigation stage is that of the organization. Consideration of the existing structure and management within the business or business unit as well as in the wider corporate context will influence the level and type of human resource provision that is required. For example, the process of centralization or decentralization of functions impacts on the range of functional responsibilities that are retained within an individual unit of a company. Many tourism, hospitality and leisure companies have demonstrated both processes at the same time in recent times. While some functions such as marketing and sales have been centralized as a result of enhanced technology, a contrary move to greater unit autonomy in some companies has resulted in an increased and more complex range of tasks executed at unit level. Other organizational changes, such as moves towards the standardization of certain brands and products, also impact on both the level and skills of staffing that are required within individual units as well as corporately. Distancing strategies, such as those already discussed in Chapter 3, are also examples of organizational change which impact upon the human resources that a business unit will require in order to perform its functions – the elimination of an in-house laundry or the franchising of the restaurant are good examples from hotels, while the contracting out of maintenance or catering functions by an airline represents the same process at work in a different sub-sector of the industry. Thus, human resource planning can only be carried out in a successful manner if organizational features are fully analysed and changes since previous planning activities are recognized.

Our analysis of factors which influence the tourism, hospitality and leisure labour market in Chapter 3 pointed to a wide range of external environmental forces which influence the internal human resource climate. Likewise, the external environment must be considered when undertaking human resource planning at all levels. Legislative factors, local market trends, technology adoption by customers and suppliers, local employment features and changes in local training provision are examples of the kind of external considerations which a tourism, hospitality and leisure business must include in a preparatory analysis prior to human resource planning. The opening of competition to the beach bar, windsurfing school or heritage centre previously in a monopoly position are examples of information vital to the human resource planning process.

The final dimension of the investigation stage focuses on internal human resources, in other words an analysis of the existing staffing situation within the business unit or company. This analysis may include consideration of productivity levels, skills deficiencies and the reasons for high levels of staff turnover (collected by, for example, exit interviews). In addition, consideration of the age, gender and ethnic profile of the workforce can be important within the planning context, especially if reference is made to preparation for promotion as well as easing the responsibilities of some members of staff prior to retirement. This aspect of the information collection process requires regular attention, especially in those sub-sectors of the tourism, hospitality and leisure industry where staff turnover levels are particularly high. The information generated with respect to staff turnover in specific departments or within certain age groups can assist in the recruitment and staff retention planning process. Traditional dependence on transitory student labour, for example, may be reduced by looking at alternative sources of labour, such as mature women returning to the workforce, where turnover is not such a problem. This move, however, may require planning for changes in shifts and in the support facilities available for staff. Indeed, the gradual movement away from split shifts in the hotel sector in many countries may reflect the increasing level of part-time female employment in the industry, at lower levels.

Bramham's second consideration, that of utilizing the information collected, is at the heart of the human resource planning process. This is the stage where the range of information collected is analysed and its implications translated into planning, both specifically in human resource terms and in the wider strategic context of the business unit. Thus, human resource inputs may warrant a separate 'compartment' within the overall plan, but it is important to ensure that this compartment is not isolated from what are frequently seen as the mainstream concerns of product and marketing. There is a symbiotic relationship between all areas of the business, with a high level of mutual dependency. It is a common problem, particularly in the small-business sector of the tourism, hospitality and leisure industry, that plans for the development of new products or new markets are made in relative isolation of what these plans mean for the area of human resources. When, finally, human resources considerations are addressed, it is frequently too late to intervene in a way that allows opportunities to be met and problems to be overcome in a sustainable manner. A hotel, for example, committed to catering for a new market may well only commence language and cultural customs classes for existing personnel or seek to recruit staff with necessary language skills when the first group of guests are already in town. Such lack of foresight in planning can easily undermine the efforts put in terms of marketing and product development. Likewise, significant changes in hotel occupancy or airline load factors may stimulate a marketing response within the strategic planning process. However, reference to the human resource 'compartment' could have identified accelerating staff turnover and consequent deterioration in service as a possible contributory cause of the problem. In the summer of 2004, British Airways were forced to cancel a large number of flights in the height of the holiday season because of a shortage of trained staff. Seasonal business levels are relatively predictable so a failure to plan recruitment and training alongside marketing is difficult to understand.

Human resource planning is, broadly, utilized in four main respects. The first purpose is that of forecasting human resource requirements. In the tourism and hospitality industry, business levels can be difficult to predict because demand is cyclical and is also very vulnerable to external influence. Thus the SARS crisis in Asia reduced the level of both business and leisure travel within and to Hong Kong and other regional locations by a very large factor. This crisis could not be fully anticipated, although contingency plans could be and were implemented in order to reduce the impact of loss of traditional business sources. During the foot and mouth crisis in the UK, many hotels reacted by altering their market focus from international to domestic visitors and, at the same time, reducing their staffing levels in a fairly draconian manner.

Many businesses in tourism, hospitality and leisure claim that seasonality and cyclical demand within the week, for example, make the accurate forecasting of human resource requirements close to impossible. Provided that appropriate management information systems – especially yield management – are in place giving detailed information on the demand cycle and other factors which will influence the need for human resources in the short, medium and long term, the relatively accurate forecasting of human resource requirements is achievable.

Such forecasting is not purely a quantitative process designed to enumerate the requirement for labour within the business unit. It is a common failure to estimate the number of employees that is needed without giving consideration to factors such as the experience and skills requirements as well as the training inputs that will be necessary to meet these requirements. These qualitative aspects are of equal importance to those in the quantitative domain. It must also be recognized that forecasting beyond the short to medium term can be highly unreliable and subject to the influence of a variety of factors which cannot be predicted. Therefore, there are temporal limits to the accurate forecasting of human resource requirements. Anything beyond a two- to three-year period may be primarily indicative and responsive to major external trends, such as technological developments or the coming on stream of a new training college, rather than local factors.

For the small tourism, hospitality or leisure business, forecasting of human resource needs presents a number of problems.

- Predicting any future events at the macro or micro level is difficult and uncertain as experience of global events since 2001 have clearly shown.
- There is a temptation to extrapolate from historical data in an uncritical manner without modification in response to the present situation and anticipated future. Small and seasonal tourism, hospitality and leisure operations will generally plan human resource requirements for the new season on the basis of the number and skills profile utilized in the past.
- For many businesses, insufficient information about past workload, productivity and skills levels has been retained. Effective human resource planning is an ongoing process and the system takes a number of years of record-keeping and experience to operate to maximum effect.
- The bases for the assumptions that are essential to planning are often difficult to establish, whether they relate to market factors or the impact of changes in a company's product profile.
- There is frequently a lack of effective corporate or business planning. Discussion of the need for human resource forecasting has assumed that effective strategic and business planning takes place and that the forecasts will be inputted into this process – this is by no means always the case in the small, family-owned tourism, hospitality and leisure operations that dominate the European industry. In the absence of wider planning, it is difficult to forecast human resource needs with any accuracy or meaning.

Where such planning is in place, it is often difficult to integrate human resource forecasts into the main planning process.

- The main techniques involved in human resource forecasting are statistical and extrapolative. Such reliance on the quantitative can give a spurious impression of precision and can also readily lead to the ignoring of important qualitative considerations.

- The processes involved in making accurate and useful forecasts of human resource needs are time consuming and expensive and require skills that are not always available within the small-business context. Units that belong to a larger corporate structure may be able to seek the support and guidance of the parent company but such services are not available to the small business and these problems frequently lead to the neglect of the process altogether.

Forecasting the supply of human resources is the second purpose identified in Bramham's approach and relates to the use of information obtained within the investigation stage. The objective of effective human resource planning is to match demand with supply. Ensuring this actually occurs requires that a company has as full knowledge as possible about its internal and external sources of human resources. Thus, supply forecasting is based on the analysis of a number of sources of information, including the following:

- The profile of the existing workforce, according to age, gender, home location, skills, qualifications and related factors. This will allow planning to cater for retirement, likely attrition for other reasons, potential for promotion within the existing workforce and similar projections. Many tourism, hospitality and leisure businesses faced with high turnover rates and the effects of seasonality may feel that such effort is not really worthwhile. However, identifying demographic, skills and related characteristics of employees can be a useful starting point towards reducing staff turnover and also in establishing some annual stability within the core of the seasonal workforce. For example, balancing a predominantly student, non-local workforce with some local, more mature personnel, who can be offered work again the next year, may give the opportunity of starting the next season with some of the required skills in place, thus benefiting the product and service standards during the early part of the season. Such strategies cannot be planned or implemented without the requisite information. Many tourism, hospitality and leisure businesses depend heavily upon student and migrant labour to meet their seasonal requirements. By its nature, this supply of labour is unstable and a business will benefit from introducing some means to balance and stabilize the overall workforce, such as utilizing a local core group. The hotel industry in Switzerland operates with a very high level of temporary labour, primarily foreign students who are on six-month stage placements in the establishment and are replaced by other students when they complete their time. This approach can only work if allied to a strong and permanent supply of local operational and supervisory skills, equipped to work with the temporary employees. Operating in these conditions depends on full management knowledge of their permanent employees and their characteristics.

● An analysis of leaving rates and the reasons that staff are choosing to move to other positions is also an important step in forecasting supply requirements and will influence future recruitment practices. People can leave for a variety of reasons – voluntary resignation to move to another job or out of the workforce (for example, to college or the home) redundancy, retirement, dismissal, completion of contract (at the end of the season, for example) and death. Businesses can benefit from understanding the reasons why people leave as one step towards reducing its impact – catering for recruitment, training and development can be time consuming and expensive and it is in the company's interest to reduce but not totally eliminate staff turnover. People leaving of their own volition is the most significant cause of staff turnover and an understanding of the reasons why they leave (gained through exit interviews and similar techniques) may lead to changes within the working environment but may also result in alterations in recruitment strategies through targeting groups who are less likely to leave. Thus if a tourism, hospitality or leisure business located in a remote area consistently loses young employees because of factors such as the absence of local nightlife and homesickness, it may be beneficial to concentrate recruitment more on the local workforce and, possibly, to invest more in training and development in order to upgrade local skills, as opposed to selecting those from further away who may already have the requisite skills profile. This kind of change in recruiting cannot be undertaken effectively without forecasting and planning for its consequences.

● Strategies to influence the external labour supply environment in response to current and projected skills requirements. In particular, such strategies can focus on local and possibly national education and training provision. Thus if an analysis of existing skills requirements and of those offered by education and training providers shows significant gaps or disparity, managers and owners of tourism, hospitality and leisure businesses may attempt to influence change at the level of the providers or to look to alternative sources of skilled labour, either through in-house training or turning to providers elsewhere. Colleges and universities in many countries actively involve local tourism and hospitality representatives in an advisory capacity, and this is one legitimate strategy through which to address any such problems.

The third way in which understanding the human resource environment in which a company is located can make use of forecasting needs is with respect to skills, management development and career planning. Planning to meet these needs, both from a company and an individual point of view, is the logical consequence of forecasting. This process depends on careful identification of both company and individual skills and other needs and the ability to match the requirements of the organization with those of the individual. This is by no means always possible, especially within small and family-owned tourism, hospitality and leisure operations. Whatever the potential of a young employee, there are times when opportunities for promotion and enhancement do not exist within the organization, often because other individuals have been in post for a long time or because certain responsibilities are earmarked for family members. The options in this situation include recognition that it is possible to outgrow a company and to assist that person to move elsewhere with good grace.

Alternatively, it may be possible to take a longer view and to anticipate opportunities in the future. A number of hoteliers in Ireland, for example, have developed the practice of encouraging promising young employees to take positions in Switzerland, Germany and the United States in order to further their experience and skills in a way that would not be possible in the 'home' hotel and have assisted them to find appropriate positions. Such placements are designed to tie into anticipated opportunities in the original company when the employee returns. Of course, they may never return but that is a risk to be taken.

Developing an effective career planning structure within a small company is never easy and, clearly, business units that are part of a larger national or multinational group have the distinct advantage of being able to link into the wider corporate environment, both to provide opportunities for their own staff and to recruit talent from elsewhere in the organization. However, small businesses cannot afford to neglect the needs and aspirations of their staff because they are likely to become disgruntled and to work with less commitment and interest, thus adversely affecting the quality of product and service on offer. They will also, probably, leave in any case but on a sour and negative note. Those who do not have ambitions or aspirations for promotion are likely to remain behind and be unresponsive to customer needs and, in all probability, a liability as a result. Thus, close monitoring of individual staff performance, ambitions and needs is an important contribution to ensuring continued motivation and commitment.

Managing skills and career development has a company as well as an individual focus. Planning development needs in response to or anticipation of identified skills shortages (due to growth in demand or anticipated retirement, for example) or changes in product or a service requirement ensures the smooth passage of change rather than major disruption and dislocation. Thus a business can derive considerable benefit from investing in training and development well in advance of the expected need so that transition or change can be as seamless as possible in so far as customers and fellow employees are concerned.

The final input that human resource planning can make is to the wider company policy formulation and planning process. At a budgeting level, forecasts with respect to the costs of recruitment, training and development and expected remuneration packages are central to both short- and longer-term cost management and will impact on the ability of the company to develop in other areas, notably on the product and marketing sides. However, the contribution of human resource planning goes beyond solely budgetary considerations. An underlying thesis of this book, most clearly represented in Chapter 4 but evident throughout, is that people within a tourism, hospitality and leisure organization are crucial to its success. Without good boundary-spanning staff, quality in terms of product and service cannot be delivered, and without quality, business levels and consequently profitability will decline. Acceptance of this position places human resource planning at the forefront of the wider company planning process and not as a peripheral agenda item.

Human resource planning for the tourism, hospitality and leisure industry is more than the sum of the information that is collected and the use to which such data are put. Human resource planning is a frame of mind within the company environment, and thus in its most effective form integrates consideration of all aspects of the management of human resources into the company's planning process. Planning is the recognition that human resources cannot be seen as a purely short-term, immediate concern but require similar forethought to any other aspect of the operation of the business. In this context, it is also worth reflecting on the impact of Riley's concept of the weak internal labour market (discussed in Chapter 3) upon human resource planning within tourism, hospitality and leisure. Such reflection may lead to the conclusion that a number of the problems which such planning faces and the barriers to its effective implementation can be directly attributed to the characteristics of the labour market within which the industry exists. Clearly these considerations apply beyond the level of the individual business unit at corporate and macro levels as well.

Human resource planning in the corporate context

In essence, human resource planning at the corporate level where a company trades through multiple outlets and in a number of locations (national and international) is the same process and operates to the same constraints as that applicable in the context of the individual business. While clearly the scale is likely to be much larger, the objectives and process are largely the same. However, there are a number of factors which need to be taken into consideration at the corporate level which represent a difference in emphasis to that of the small company or individual business unit. Some of the factors make the process of human resource planning easier while others require additional skills and responses. These differences do not all necessarily exist between small and multi-location businesses in the manufacturing sector. They are in part influenced by the characteristics of the tourism, hospitality and leisure industry as part of the service sector which we have already considered in Chapter 4. These factors include the following:

- The fragmented nature of business units within the organization, whether they are hotels, travel agents, restaurants or airline stations in a large number of locations, may result in wide dispersion not only within a country but also on a global basis. As a consequence, companies may opt to plan on a national or regional basis but this, in itself, has certain drawbacks in maximizing the full benefits of planning in that important information may not be shared corporately as a result.

- This fragmentation impacts on the techniques of data collection that are employed at the investigation stage. There is likely to be greater emphasis on quantitative techniques in response to scale, and more qualitative assessments of needs and resources may be neglected as a result. Considerable care is required in assembling information at a corporate level so as not to lose important local dimensions and requirements.

- Fragmentation also means that individual units may well be operating in different customer and demand cycle (seasonality) environments. Responding to different customer expectations may require variation in the human resource provision, both in terms of numbers and skills, which are in place within units. Thus universal formulae for staffing levels may be totally inappropriate within all units of a company and the planning process needs to acknowledge this. One response to different market requirements has been branding within the hotel industry. This seeks to match broad customer requirements with respect to price, facilities and service to general specifications which are applied throughout the brand. Examples within the Accor group, for example, include their Formulae 1, Ibis, Novotel, Mercure and Sofitel products. Branding is designed to standardize customer expectations so that an educated marketplace will know what to expect from a particular hotel type and, therefore, will not be disappointed at what is on offer. Between each brand, different human resource planning criteria will apply, although common practice will normally operate universally within the brand. However, even within the parameters provided by branding, it may be difficult to respond fully to the range of customer requirements across a large number of outlets and to provide staffing levels and skills to meet these demands. As we have already seen in Chapter 3, it is argued that the process of labour globalization will see companies harmonizing human resource policies and practices on a global in addition to national basis, with the notion of a single set of workplace standards inevitable as companies seek to standardize both production and delivery of goods and services. Branding is one step in this direction but the counter-argument, which is much more compatible with the sustainability model, is set out below.

- Despite this argument, fragmentation further implies that individual units operate within diverse labour markets and human resource planning must be sensitive to these variations. Differences in labour-market characteristics can be found between operations within the same city as well as on a larger national or international plane. Such variety is the result of cultural, social, economic and political factors and will impact on a range of human resource concerns, including:

  - the application of employment legislation;
  - the effects of competition within the labour market from other tourism, hospitality and leisure operators as well as from other sectors of the economy;
  - the impact of local attitudes to employment within tourism and hospitality;
  - remuneration rates which are paid locally;
  - recruitment strategies that will be necessary;
  - training and development requirements;
  - the framework of conditions, benefits and services applied to staff (relating to areas such as shift work, provision of meals, housing and crèche facilities).

- Scale, however, provides companies with the facility to overcome some of the problems which small businesses face in planning human resource requirements. By operating a number of units, companies can adopt a level of flexibility between them in order to cater for variation in demand and the timing of demand between different business units. Thus key staff can be deployed to seasonal businesses as demand requires and then withdrawn to units with less seasonality when they are no longer needed. Likewise, companies can operate effective promotion and development strategies at a corporate level, moving staff between units in order to fill vacancies or to meet the identified needs of individual staff members.

- Linking to the above, companies are able to offer genuine career ladders within technical and managerial fields and thus are more likely to retain good staff than independent businesses. Companies can also plan the career paths and promotion opportunities of key personnel, based on complete information about impending vacancies and changes in skills requirements, and so prepare individuals for their next move within the company. This process is known as 'succession planning' and in some organizations operates with the assistance of a company-wide computerized database.

Sparrow, Brewster and Harris (2004) argue that globalization requires consideration of human resource planning in a holistic and wider business context, through what they describe as 'enterprise modelling', a process that is derived from the notion of enterprise resource planning.

> Enterprise Resource Planning (ERP) systems have so far served to integrate accounting, finance, sales, distribution, materials management, human resources and other business functions to a common architecture that links the firm to its customers and suppliers ... Enterprise modelling is a natural extension of this process thinking combined with knowledge of management interests. It is defined as the process of building models of the whole or part of an enterprise from knowledge about the enterprise (p.80)

The key here is the generation, management and analysis of useful information about the organization in a way that links rather than isolates key functional areas, in order to identify and model the implications of both internally and externally driven change.

Clearly, planning human resource requirements on a global stage places demands on organisations that are very different from those faced by organizations that operate within a more homogeneous and familiar local or national labour market. The balance to be struck between the recruitment and employment of local staff, familiar with the contextual environment as opposed to importing the technical knowledge and tacit knowledge of the company that expatriate staff can offer, is a difficult and, at times, sensitive issue. Both routes pose a range of challenges. Dowling and Welch (2004) consider some of the issues associated with the assumption that the use of expatriate staff within a global enterprise can be based on the idea that the world of management, within the 'bubble' of corporate culture and the familiar brand, can defy the impact of the local environment. They talk about the myths of the global manager, identified in terms of statements, all of which they proceed to rebut.

1. There is a universal approach to management.
2. All people can acquire multicultural adaptability and behaviours.
3. There are common characteristics shared by successful international managers.
4. There are no impediments to mobility.

Dowling and Welch go on to discuss some of the causes of expatriate failure, which are substantially driven by the failure to recognize the fallacies implicit in each of the above myths. Both Adler (1993) and Harris (1995) develop these themes within the specific context of women and their opportunities in international management and point to a range of additional challenges that they face, both within organizations and in the diverse host cultures within which they are expected to work.

It is clear that effective human resource planning is essential at the global corporate level as it is in smaller businesses. There is a need for guiding principles at a macro level combined with local flexibility within this planning and its application. Such flexibility has not always been a priority among major tourism, hospitality and leisure companies which are attracted by the benefits of increasing standardization in product, service and working environment, or McDonaldization (Ritzer 2004). The combination of local sensitivity and global awareness or 'glocalization' provides what is probably the most effective response to inherent tensions in this area.

Human resource planning at the community, regional, national and transnational level

The final approach to human resource planning for tourism, hospitality and leisure, and the one most neglected in the literature, is that at the macro level, whether involving a community, region, country or at a transnational level. The principles and parameters involved have much in common with small business and corporate planning but a number of factors differentiate the macro process from that within a single company. These factors include the following:

- The scale of operation is frequently much larger than that within a company although – given the size of some multinational tourism, hospitality and leisure companies – this is not a necessary distinction.
- The multi-sector nature of the industry is also a consideration which impacts on the process of planning at this level.
- There is a substantial involvement of public sector interests, both as employers within tourism, hospitality and leisure and as contributing partners within the human resource management process.
- Many companies and organizations are involved both in the public and private sectors, and therefore there are attendant problems of obtaining data from such a range of sources within the investigation stage.

- There is a frequent lack of a single coordinating authority at local, regional, national or transnational level with responsibility for the planning of human resource matters within tourism, hospitality and leisure. At the same time, the management and development of human resources for the sector may fall within the remit of a wide range of public and private sector companies and agencies. Examples of bodies whose brief may include a significant human resource component with respect to tourism, hospitality and leisure include:
  - local, regional and national tourism organizations;
  - government ministries with specific responsibility for tourism;
  - other ministries and agencies responsible for the delivery of aspects of the tourism product (for example, ministries of agriculture, the environment, culture);
  - security and home affairs ministries with responsibility for police, immigration and customs, all of whom may have significant visitor contact;
  - local authorities responsible for the provision of leisure facilities (museums, entertainment complexes, sports centres) within a community;
  - national agencies responsible for the promotion of arts, culture and sports (such as the Arts Council in the UK);
  - national or regional education ministries, perhaps with a divide between responsibility for tertiary, vocational and university-level provision;
  - labour/employment/manpower ministries;
  - economic development agencies;
  - schools, colleges and universities in both the public and private sector;
  - public sector bodies responsible for the funding of education and training within the school/college system and in industry;
  - specialist tourism, hospitality and leisure training agencies and consultancies;
  - public and private sector tourism enterprises and companies;
  - tourism and hospitality industry representative associations; and
  - transnational public organizations within the European Union and other geographical regions (Baum 1994).

All these bodies may have a legitimate interest in the planning process for human resources in tourism, hospitality and leisure on whatever scale is involved. Such planning cannot operate effectively without the cooperation and input of these interests. There are few examples worldwide of really inclusive and effective human resource planning within one industry sector at the scale implied here. The model that, perhaps, comes closest to this is that which operates in the Republic of Ireland and we shall consider that in greater detail later in this chapter. It is interesting to note that the World Tourism Organization's comprehensive guide to national and regional tourism planning (WTO 1994b) includes only the briefest of references to human resource requirements in this field and the argument for an integrated approach – and one that includes human resources as a mainstream consideration in wider tourism planning – is all but neglected. The focus of the WTO's discussion is almost exclusively on policy and strategic development with respect to structure, sustainability, economic and cultural considerations, implementation and control, monitoring and market planning.

In order to undertake effective human resource planning for tourism, hospitality and leisure at a macro level, it is necessary to pursue a process comparable to that proposed by Bramham, especially in addressing the information gathering or investigation stage. A conceptual framework which is designed to contribute to the development of an integrated human resource environment for tourism and hospitality at a macro level is proposed by Baum (1993a). This framework is designed as a flexible and responsive approach to human resource planning in the context we have been discussing and is:

- *comprehensive*, in that it includes all sectors of the tourism, hospitality and leisure industry, all relevant aspects of human resource development and all levels of training and development, and is sustainable in that it reflects the demands of local cultures, traditions and tourism and hospitality markets;
- *integrated*, in that all components in the framework have clear and identifiable links to other elements and contribute to, or are beneficiaries of, other parts of the framework; and
- *cohesive*, in that the total framework, the overall outcome of the process, has a logic and applicability in its own right almost independent of its individual parts.

The framework is intended as a mechanism to support the coordination of human resource policy formulation and planning for tourism, hospitality and leisure at a macro level. It has the benefit of breadth in that the approach is designed to incorporate as many as possible of the diverse influences and considerations which affect effective human resource planning on this scale. It is non-evaluatory in that no assessment is implied of the relative importance of the various components. The framework focuses on five main areas, which substantially consists of the investigation stage in Bramham's terms in relation to whatever is being addressed (local, regional, national or transnational).

1. The tourism, hospitality and leisure industry environment, its features and products, structure, markets and the impact of tourism in economic, social, cultural and political terms.
2. The tourism, hospitality and leisure industry and the labour market, relating to considerations such as features of the wider labour market, public employment and labour-market-related policy, education and training policies, the application of official occupational classification schemes to tourism and hospitality occupations and available statistical information about the labour market in tourism and hospitality and competing industrial sectors.
3. Tourism, hospitality and leisure and the community, giving focus to matters such as public attitudes to tourism and tourists, awareness of the industry and its economic/employment significance and related perceptual awareness considerations.

4. Tourism, hospitality and leisure and the education system, covering the administration and funding of public and private education for tourism and hospitality, assessment and quality management, tourism and hospitality studies within the school curriculum at vocational and management levels, the education of teachers for tourism and hospitality, the outcomes of education programmes (destination of graduates, attrition from the industry) and tourism and hospitality industry attitudes and commitment to education and its providers.

5. Human resource development in the tourism, hospitality and leisure industry, giving consideration to matters such as in-company training policies and practices, financing and investment in human resource development from private and public sources (tax concessions, levy schemes), the role of industry in the education and training process (apprenticeship schemes, work placement/stages) and recognition of training and skills development towards national qualifications and by the education system.

This conceptual framework is shown in summary diagrammatic form in Figure 9.1 (see p.259). A more detailed breakdown of each of the main elements within the framework can be found in Baum (1993a).

The framework provides the information base from which competent authorities in the public or private sector can develop policies and specific plans with respect to human resources in tourism, hospitality and leisure. It does not, of course, address what or who such competent authorities are and this question is not as readily answered as it might be at the individual business or corporate level. At national level, for example, few countries allocate responsibility for the development and implementation of human resource policies for tourism and hospitality to a unitary body. Rather, inputs are fragmented and may be duplicated between government ministries, national tourism organizations, and education and training providers, as well as the public sector itself. At transnational level, such coordination becomes even more fragmented as experience in Europe indicates.

Case Study *The context of tourism planning in Ireland*

Tourism in Ireland employs a core workforce of 145 000 people across 16 500 separate businesses. When part-time and casual workers are taken into account, it is estimated that the tourism workforce exceeds 200 000. In 2004, 6.5 million overseas visitors came to Ireland generating export earnings of €4.2 billion. In the same year domestic tourism grew by 10 per cent giving rise to total tourism earnings of €5.2 billion, and representing some 4.2 per cent of GNP last year.

Despite its size and significance, tourism is a fragmented industry, and at an operational level it can be considered as 'an industry of every parish'. It is difficult at times therefore for individual enterprises to take a step back and make a more holistic assessment of the sector. In broad terms, the outlook for Irish tourism is reasonably benign and the industry is currently working towards meeting a number of demanding targets that will see overseas visitor numbers reach 10 million by 2012

▶

with an associated rise in export earnings to €6.0 billion.

Reaching the growth targets set for the industry will require an expansion in the tourism workforce over a period of time when the economy is expected to remain near full employment, when the school-leaving age cohort is expected to decline by 15 per cent, and where labour force partici-pation by women has already exceeded the EU average.

Increasingly therefore employment expan-sion in tourism will be sustained by non-national workers. Tourism will also have to compete with adjacent economic sectors to attract workers into the industry, and this reality will drive further improvements in work practices and conditions. Tourism has tradi-tionally struggled with negative perceptions of employment practices and conditions, and this continues to be the subject of consider-able comment. Looking forward however, measures which have recently been taken to improve this image will be intensified as the industry builds the skills and know-how required to sustain the anticipated growth in the sector.

In terms of developing these skills, tourism depends significantly upon providers of fur-ther and higher education. The education sec-tor itself can appear a somewhat congested space with a significant number of overlap-ping courses and service providers. In 2003, almost 5000 students received a tourism related education award. Some 56 per cent of

these were awards made to students taking Post Leaving Certificate courses through the VEC college system. A further 36 per cent of awards were made to graduates of the Institutes of Technology and the Dublin Institute of Technology (DIT). Because of the nature of the courses taken, these latter graduates represent the most important labour pipeline into the tourism industry. Tourism depends substantially upon the craft skills of its workforce – it is the quality and range of these craft skills that will determine whether the tourism workforce will emerge as a key source of sustainable competitive advantage. It is important therefore that the relationship between industry and the Institutes of Technology and DIT is carefully maintained, so as to ensure that tourism workers continue to receive the further edu-cation and training they need, and have the opportunity to progress to programmes of higher education as appropriate.

Extract from Fáilte Ireland (2005b). Reproduced with permission.

Case discussion questions

1. Identify the implications of the information provided in the case for human resource planning within Irish tourism.

2. Can you identify gaps in the analysis where you might require further information?

3. Write a similar analysis, based on data for the country where you are studying.

In human resource planning terms, one of the most significant sources of information to assist with the process is accurate statistical data about the quan-tity of employment and the attendant skills profile of the tourism, hospitality and leisure industry, as well as the means to estimate and project future employment and skills trends. Such information is not readily available in a form that is designed specifically for application within tourism and hospitality. In the United Kingdom, for example, it is necessary to combine data from a number of categories within the Standard Occupational Classification in order to aggregate total tourism, hospitality and leisure employment, and even this is by no means inclusive – a number of occupational areas are omitted as they are included within broader, non-tourism/hospitality categories and cannot be isolated. Similar problems are found when employing the international Standard Classification of Occupations. Definitional problems are further compounded by the overlap in terms of demand and consumption between tourists and non-tourists of many goods and services and the problems inherent in isolating the employment impact of one from the other.

Essentially, there are four basic approaches to the quantitative measurement of tourism, hospitality and leisure employment, although only one of them gives any depth of qualitative information. These are:

1. input–output analysis;
2. direct survey of the tourism industry;

Figure 9.1

An integrated human resource development framework for tourism and hospitality

A *The tourism environment*
- Features and products of tourism
- Structure of the industry
- Tourism industry markets
- The impact of tourism

B *Tourism and the labour market*
- The national and/or local labour-market environment
- Public labour-market/ employment/industrial relations policies
- Educational and training policies
- Quantitative and qualitative information about human resources in tourism

C *Tourism in the community*
- National commitment to tourism
- Public attitudes to/awareness of tourism
- Attitudes to and awareness of tourism as an employer
- Tourism within education
- Tourism and the media
- Careers awareness

THE HUMAN RESOURCES ENVIRONMENT IN TOURISM

D *Tourism and education*
- The administration and management of public sector tourism education
- The funding of public sector tourism education
- Quality standards and qualifications equivalences in tourism education
- National assessment, examinations and awards
- Education for tourism at secondary school level
- Vocational skills education for tourism at craft level
- Supervisory and management education for tourism
- Centres of excellence in tourism education
- National recruitment and selection of entrants to programmes of study in tourism
- Teacher training for tourism
- Curriculum development centre for tourism

E *Human resource development in the tourism industry*
- Financing and investment in human resource development
- In-company training policies and practices
- Recognition of industry-based training within local and national education and training provision
- Role of industry in education

Source: Baum (1993a) p.241

3. the proportional method; and
4. the application of macro-economic methods.

Input–output analysis

This method makes use of the multiplier concept in order to derive estimates of aggregate employment within the tourism sector. According to Fletcher:

> The multiplier concept is based upon the nature of production and the purchase of intermediate goods and services within the production process. Each sector of the economy will, to varying degrees, employ labour in order to produce its output. If the number of persons employed by a firm is divided by the total output of that firm, labour/output coefficients (or ratios) can be calculated which show a crude relationship between the level of output and the number of people that would have to be employed in order to produce that output. (Fletcher 1993, p.78)

The multiplier effect can be extrapolated to a macro scale so that estimates of employment at community, regional, national and transnational levels can be derived. Input–output analysis produces estimates of employment at three levels. These are direct employment derived from actual tourism expenditure and its employment creation impact; the indirect effect relating to the employment impact of secondary purchases by, for example, hotels and airlines which are necessary in order to cater for their customers, as well as building work, provision of electricity and a host of other goods and services; and, finally, the induced effect relating to employment which is generated because tourism, hospitality and leisure employees spend part of their own wages on goods and services and this expenditure, in turn, generates further employment.

Input analysis can derive the employment effect of these three forms of multipliers through analysis of 'out-of-state' tourist expenditure based on the normal assumptions on which such calculating tables are constructed. The analysis is based on a 'transactions' matrix which summarizes the entire structure of the economy and allows a complete analysis of the relationships between its various sectors. In other words, we can look at the way each sector engages in transactions with other sectors and with final demand.

Although allowing a rigorous analysis to be made of the economy, the technique is not without weaknesses. There are basic difficulties in dealing with domestic tourism by this method and, in many countries; this is a severe delimiter as the domestic tourism economies of countries such as France, Malaysia, the UK and the USA make a major contribution to the overall level of activity within the sector. Also, the length of time taken to develop input–output tables limits their usefulness. A lack of currency is a major drawback and is one that does not allow this method to make a serious contribution to pragmatic human resource planning within the tourism, hospitality and leisure industry.

The direct survey method

If conducted on anything like a significant scale, this method is the most expensive information collection technique but is likely to give relatively comprehensive direct employment statistics, the method's contribution with respect to indirect employment is, of course, minimal. The approach normally involves conducting a survey of a sample of businesses involved in tourism, hospitality and leisure activity. Respondents may be asked to give details of their total employment figures and to estimate the proportion of these associated directly with tourism *per se*.

As well as its limitations with respect to indirect employment, this method is vulnerable to allegations of subjectivity, especially in the allocation of business activity to tourism or non-tourism sources. However, the undoubted merits of the approach lie in the quality, depth and variety of data that can be collected within a survey. The impact of changes in employment structure, training opportunities, sub-sectoral variance and seasonality, to identify but a few significant factors, may all be estimated, albeit with the same caveat for subjectivity.

In the context of this discussion, perhaps the most significant benefit of this approach lies in its predictive value – this dimension can be incorporated into the survey and can be usefully employed to anticipate and plan for labour and skills changes within the industry. The direct survey method is one that can readily be updated on a regular basis – with appropriate resources, biannually is not unrealistic. Experience with this method in Ireland and Singapore, for example, suggests that there are further, extraneous benefits to be derived from the close contact and feeling of involvement/commitment within the industry which can result from participation in such studies.

The proportional method

This is the method employs a simple theoretical approach. It estimates the proportion of total expenditure in each sector which is derived from tourism, hospitality and leisure and then applies this proportion to total employment in the relevant sectors. In this way, tourism-related direct employment is estimated. Indirect tourism-related employment estimates are obtained by using the relationship of intermediate demand to total output in the economy as an indicator. For direct employment estimates, this approach has the very practical benefit that it can use current annual data such as the breakdown of personal consumer expenditure from the national accounts as well as relevant employment statistics. Some predictive estimates can also be obtained.

There are a number of theoretical difficulties with this approach and estimates with respect to factors such as regional variation and job/skills differentiation are only as good as the source segmentation that is available. Thus the practical value of this approach to those planning the labour and skills needs of the tourism, hospitality and leisure industry may be limited. That said, the method provides a feasible basis for annual estimation of sectoral employment and one that can form the basis for selected in-depth studies.

Macro-economic methods

The three above methods provide point estimates of tourism employment. The use of a macro-economic model in the area of tourism, hospitality and leisure employment is designed to assess the marginal effect of increments in out-of-state tourism revenue. This is an attempt to use a behavioural model incorporating supply-side constraints to predict the employment effect of marginal changes in revenue.

As with all econometric models, a considerable degree of simplification is inherent in this approach and thus results have to be treated with some considerable caution. Judgement is required in deciding when to override the model where necessary and a mere mechanical application could well result in erroneous conclusions.

The advantages of this approach lie in its conceptual neutrality which is lacking in varying degrees with respect to the other methods. Furthermore, it benefits from being a theoretical model in that it allows for the approximate prediction of the consequences of policy or environmental changes on employment. However, the local and fragmented nature of the tourism, hospitality and leisure industry cannot readily be acknowledged within this model and its value in planning and implementing local, regional and, in some cases, even national initiatives is severely limited.

One assumption that is implicit in three of the above methodologies (the direct survey method being the exception) is that employment and tourism, hospitality and leisure expenditure and growth have a fixed association which is universally applicable to the whole industry. This may well not be the case as tangible evidence of growth, say through the building of a new hotel or the purchase of new aircraft, may well have very different employment effects relative to investment. The impact of similar developments will also vary greatly between different countries and companies. These variations are outlined in a WTO report:

> In broad terms, a four- or five-star hotel directly employs one person for every room. But, in addition, employment is created in other sectors of the tourism industry and it is estimated that this amounts to a further one and a half jobs for each hotel room. An investment of $95,000 for a hotel room therefore creates two and a half new jobs.
>
> The calculation of job creation in airline operations is more complicated and subject to substantial variations depending on the type of operation (long-haul or short-haul) and the efficiency and productivity of the airline concerned ... It can therefore be concluded that an investment of $150 million in a B747 will give employment to 400 people whereas an equal investment in hotels would give direct employment to over 1,500 people and total employment to 3,750 people. This is a major factor which governments must take into account when judging the merits of alternative policies. (WTO 1994a, pp.58–9)

What the WTO report fails to address within this conclusion is the issue of job quality and remuneration, concerns that we considered in some depth in Chapter 5. Considerable disparity regarding these factors between various industry sectors will partially reduce the gap in terms of the value of employment generated.

This methodological review is by no means exhaustive nor does it do full justice to the approaches described, either from a theoretical or a practical point of view. What it does do is to point out some of the potential difficulties in attempting to link employment predictions and planning too closely to the main research and analytical models that are available. As one examination, based on the planning process used, of the Irish tourism, hospitality and leisure industry will attempt to illustrate, an industry which is so complex and fragmented does not respond readily to generalization and classification – attempts to do so in too simplistic a form may have significant consequences for the planning process in the human resource area.

The Republic of Ireland: a case environment

The Irish model, in many respects, is a good representation of Castley's (1996) policy-driven model of labour-market planning. Castley identifies a number of components within his policy cycle:

- identification
- data
- analysis
- policy formulation
- dissemination
- decision-taking
- policy implementation
- evaluation and feedback.

The scope and significance of the tourism, hospitality and leisure industry in the Republic of Ireland is well documented, the sustained growth and performance of the sector since the mid-1980s has exceeded that of any other Western European country (Deegan 2005) although recent performance has been rather more erratic. As a tourist destination, Ireland is perceived to offer attractive and unspoiled scenery, an interesting cultural heritage, a friendly people and a good quality and standard of amenities. Current investment in tourism is relatively high by comparison with previous decades, spurred in part by positive and aggressive government support and incentives. This will have the effect of upgrading the standard and variety of facilities and of providing a stronger marketing and development base through which to promote the country's attributes as a tourist destination, particularly in the outdoor leisure and culture fields. Tourism in the Republic of Ireland has been blighted by the levels of political violence in Northern Ireland during the 'Troubles' of the 1970s, 1980s and early 1990s but the instigation of the peace process, culminating in the 1998 Good Friday Agreement has radically changed the tourism landscape in both parts of Ireland and has also driven institutional change within public sector tourism in Ireland.

Membership of the European Union and the impact of the single market economy has greatly benefited Irish tourism as a result of investment through European structural, social and regional funding programmes. In terms of actual performance, the growth and performance of Irish tourism is, in no small way, due to this government support, but also reflective of more general business and financial optimism. Overall growth, in terms of foreign arrivals, domestic bed nights and total expenditure by tourists, has maintained a steady rate since the late 1980s at a level that is very impressive in European terms. Total international visitor numbers in 2003 were over six million compared to little over one million in the early 1980s.

However, this growth must be treated with some caution as we are, in part, witnessing some partial redress of a long period of under-performance during the 1960s and 1970s. Traditionally, the Republic is highly dependent upon the large British market for volume visitation and on that of the United States for high-spend tourism. After September 2001, US arrivals declined dramatically and recovery by 2005 has only been partial. Visitor numbers from other European countries is up considerably but their low level of expenditure does not fully compensate for the absence of Americans. Above all, change can be linked to government policy which has given priority to tourism development since 1987, although Deegan and Dineen (1993) portray this attention to tourism almost as an act of desperation on the part of policy makers following the failure of industrial policy in other sectors.

Before addressing the human resource issues in the Irish tourism, hospitality and leisure industry, some reference to the structure of the industry and its business environment is necessary. Tourism, hospitality and leisure in Ireland are characterized by diversity and dispersion; they form an industry 'of every parish' with particular impact on rural areas of the country where the effects of economic and social deprivation are most acute. The large number of sub-sectors that comprise tourism, hospitality and leisure cover a wide range in terms of product, role and, above all, size, reflecting many of the components that we have already considered. They include the one-person cottage industry or service as well as larger businesses of Irish tourism in the form of the major hotel and transportation companies, and include businesses in the accommodation, leisure, food and beverage, transport and information/facilitation sectors. The key point – and one that cannot be overstressed in the context of human resource planning – is, on the one hand, the diversity and, on the other, the predominantly small, family-business structure of the industry. Outside the main cities, the tourism and hospitality industry is a highly seasonal activity in Ireland, particularly in the scenic west and south-west, and while the overall upturn in business since the 1980s has led to significant season elongation, this has not impacted on all areas and tends to concentrate business in already overstretched destinations such as Dublin, Cork and Galway.

Employment within the Irish tourism and hospitality industry reflects its business structure. The average operation has five employees, probably including part-time assistance and almost certainly with a major seasonal element, and is very likely to be built around a family structure. The use of temporary, seasonal and casual staff is extensive and, in some areas, constitutes a tradition in employment patterns that would be difficult to break. The main structural phenomenon in employment in Irish tourism, hospitality and leisure over the past ten years has been the influx of migrant workers from elsewhere in Europe and beyond. Upwards of 50 per cent of all sector workers in Dublin and a significant proportion of those outside of the capital are non-nationals, a total that is estimated to be 25 000 in 2004 (Fáilte Ireland, 2005a). This development has significantly altered the character of employment in Irish tourism, hospitality and leisure and has changed the nature of labour-market planning undertaken at both micro and macro levels. Even within the larger, more sophisticated sectors of Irish tourism, the majority of concerns are very small by the standards of almost any other industry or, indeed, Western European country. Of registered hotels 80 per cent have 40 bedrooms or fewer. At the same time, the impact of major hotel groups, is increasing significantly but, notwithstanding this, the vast majority of businesses are proprietor owned and managed.

Actual numbers in direct employment in 2004 totalled approximately 145 000 (Fáilte Ireland, 2005b), broken down broadly into hotels (39 500), restaurants (39 600), bars (32 000) and tourism services and attractions (34 000), these being the 'raw' figures which have not been adjusted to reflect part-time, seasonal or non-tourism related factors which raises this figure to over 200 000. These figures also do not take into account transportation or leisure outwith tourism. This places tourism in second place within the Irish employment league, behind the declining agriculture sector and roughly on a par with manufacturing.

The reality of a tourism and hospitality environment such as that described above (and which in many of its aspects has major similarities to the industry in many other countries) is that its fragmentation and the scale of its operations act as severe constraints on the application of tourism/hospitality/leisure business – employment impact models. Particular factors which blur the validity and practical use of such models include the following.

● The extent to which staff utilization and productivity are maximized within key tourism, hospitality and leisure industry sectors. In many cases, the sector is an 'anticipation' business in which staffing levels have to be judged on the basis of expected or possible business levels which may not always materialize. Thus, especially in small outfits, existing staff can cater for quite considerable increases in business volume without the requirement for additional personnel.

● Most tourism, hospitality and leisure sectors in Ireland involve considerable specialization and job demarcation. While multi-skilling is certainly on the increase in Ireland, within a tight staff structure it is not necessarily feasible to staff up within each area to reflect business growth. Thus specialisms need to be prioritized and staff increases or restructuring may be out of line with business patterns.

● Competition, especially for skilled labour within very tight employment markets, may result in 'skills hoarding' by some employers in anticipation of business growth – this has the effect of limiting the impact of increases when they do occur and also of denying other companies access to these skilled personnel. Given the intense competition within a finite home labour pool in Ireland, such expensive practice is commonplace although the inflow of migrant labour has reduced pressure in this regard.

● Within predominantly seasonal industries such as in Ireland, the impact of growth often results in season extension rather than increasing the number of tourists in resorts already working to capacity. Thus, while actual numbers in employment may not increase, the period in work may be significantly longer. How such effects can be evaluated in terms of raw job increase targets is difficult to ascertain. The alternative to this scenario is that high-season business goes elsewhere – if this is to another region within the same country (for example Kerry to Donegal) this is acceptable at a national if not a regional level. However, if the impact is to move tourists to another country (Ireland to Wales or Scotland), no employment benefits can accrue.

- Economic or human resource planning models do not anticipate the possibility that available employment, even in areas of high unemployment, may not be taken up. There are a variety of possible reasons for this, reflecting upon industry image, remuneration, geographical factors and the draw of employment elsewhere within an open labour market, to cite but a few. In Ireland, the haemorrhaging of skilled personnel remains a major issue within the industry. Historically, Ireland has been a net exporter of tourism, hospitality and leisure labour but this situation has changed in recent years with a large number of international staff seeking opportunities in the country (Fáilte Ireland 2005a).

- Finally, key labour shortages and the areas of main demand within a growing tourism economy are frequently at a skilled level and thus offer opportunities not accessible to the untrained worker. In Ireland, for example, the key shortages are for chefs and management staff within hotels and restaurants. Thus investment in preparing these skills must parallel, indeed precede, initiatives in marketing and product development which will generate the extra tourism business.

Ireland provides an excellent example of a tourism and hospitality environment where a simple application of employment impact modelling will not necessarily provide an accurate picture of the real changes that occur in the labour market when the level of tourist arrivals increases.

The Republic of Ireland: fine-tuning the employment implications of growth in tourism, hospitality and leisure

Thus far in this discussion we have reviewed some of the problems that arise when standard macro methodologies are employed to predict the employment impact of tourism growth. The issue is not with the methods in themselves but rather in their inability to localize and sectorize with sufficient precision for the purposes of planning and development of appropriate strategies in education, training (pre-service and in-company) and other labour-market measures. In other words, we may be able to predict that the tourism, hospitality and leisure workforce will grow by x thousand within a defined period but that does not give much indication as to whether these jobs will be full- or part-time or seasonal; their level in terms of skills; whether they are 'new' jobs or extensions of existing ones; whether they represent more existing designations (as in the demand for more chefs in Ireland) or an entirely new breed of worker (as was the case in the Paris region with the opening of Disneyland); or what will be the geographical distribution of the new jobs by locality or region. In Ireland, the implementation of short- and medium-term strategies in order to cope with these factors falls within the ambit of the education and training arm of Fáilte

Ireland, the Irish Tourist Board and an organization with the strength of position to take a broad national coordinating and development view of labour issues in Irish tourism. Fáilte Ireland's approach is designed to assist the industry to provide for changes within the manpower environment in tourism, whether these changes reflect retrenchment or boom. Some of these initiatives will be described and evaluated in terms of their impact in the context of what has already been said about tourism and the tourist industry in Ireland.

Fáilte Ireland's programme of research studies is at the centre of the information-gathering stage of national human resource planning for tourism and hospitality in Ireland. It is a major support platform for the development of both policy and practical interventions within Irish tourism. These programmes range from extensive and intensive studies of human resources in the industry by main sector (and using broadly the methodology described previously as the direct survey approach) to specifically focused surveys and analytical studies which are designed to home in on particular areas of concern. The national labour-market studies are undertaken approximately every two years and, running back to the early 1980s, provide a unique record of the link between tourism policy, tourism growth and changes in the employment environment over a 25-year period. The studies go considerably beyond the basic estimation of actual employment. They focus on both the quantitative and qualitative detail relating to that employment, changes within the labour structure of businesses, the impact of labour market and training initiatives, predictions of numerical requirements, and regional and type of business variations (grade, size, etc.). The studies have direct impact on the provision of education and training places by public sector authorities as well as on priority training categories and the attendant curricula required for their preparation. Specifically focused studies concentrate on the needs of specific sectors (for example leisure within hotels) as a means of providing rapid-response training for newly identified or emerging skills needs. They also look at the impact of technology in the industry and the implications of current Irish demographic trends for tourism, hospitality and leisure into the future.

Commitment to this programme of research has ensured that Fáilte Ireland was able to respond fairly rapidly to the specific demands of government with respect to their tourism employment targets. The crucial need for skilled labour as opposed to untrained, semi- or unskilled personnel formed the main thrust of this response, which allowed the agency to map out and target human resource development priorities by category without further research. The inability of the existing education and training system to provide for these identified requirements is another issue and arguably one of the main weaknesses in overall government strategy for tourism.

Cost-effective and rapid-response training is a major platform within Fáilte Ireland's approach to meeting short- to medium-term skills requirements and has become a very significant component within the overall tourism, hospitality and leisure training strategy in Ireland, largely because of the failure of existing institutions to meet demands in terms of quantity, hampered as they are by tight financial restrictions. This strategy involves the use of temporary training facilities during the down season, generally hotels, and the provision of mainstream school-leaver courses or programmes for the long-term unemployed without extensive capital investment or commitment.

This model is one which has wide applicability in other countries. An extension of this approach is the establishment of an increasing number of permanent training centres, operated under the auspices of Fáilte Ireland but established in short-lease premises frequently within industrial estates and designed to provide 'stop-gap' training places prior to investment in more permanent facilities within the Irish third-level college system. These centres are able to offer virtually year-round training and thus their output is considerably greater than is normally the case within mainstream education, where tradition and fixed agreements result in considerable under-utilization of facilities. One potential matter of concern in the establishment of such facilities is staffing, especially given the need to employ teachers with industry skills and experience when such attributes are in limited supply. The seasonal nature of the Irish industry means that the period of temporary training coincides with the down period in employment terms and the consequence is that there is a significant pool of seasonally under-employed personnel available for teaching posts. An added benefit of this process is that the temporary instructors return to industry with considerably enhanced training skills.

The Fáilte Ireland system has responded positively to labour-market changes, in particular demand within the industry for additional international labour. Fáilte Ireland were in the lead in providing training for international workers and in organizing joint recruitment and training programmes for targeted workers from Poland and Russia from the mid-1990s onwards. Their report on the management of cultural diversity in the tourism, hospitality and leisure workforce (Fáilte Ireland 2005a) is an informed and innovative response to a national labour-market challenge.

The design and implementation of curricula and programmes originate under the same roof as the research programmes which invariably precede them. This common responsibility within Fáilte Ireland means that there is a very close association between the interpretation of research findings and their translation into new educational and training initiatives within tourism. The facility to experiment and innovate is also exercised and this allows for relatively localized or sub-sector specific programmes to be implemented. There have been a range of initiatives that have been put in place as a result of the close tie-in between research and development within education/training for Irish tourism. This direct contribution to providing a relevant and responsive menu of educational and training programmes for Irish tourism is complemented by significant support activities which also link closely to research initiatives. These include national student recruitment for tourism and hospitality craft education, allowing Fáilte Ireland to monitor and manage the categories of tourism and hospitality staff trained for the industry and to maximize the utilization of scarce training places within the system. This is complemented by the centralized placement of graduates and work experience trainees, the effect of which is to go some way to ensuring a reasonably even distribution of trained personnel throughout outlets and regions. Training within colleges, centres and the industry is also enhanced by tailor-researched and developed resource materials, prepared because of the evident unsuitability of materials from outside of the country.

Developments across tourism, hospitality and leisure together with organizational maturation within the Irish education and training sector mean that the role of Fáilte Ireland in terms of the quality management of provision has changed significantly. CERT (Fáilte Ireland's predecessor) established the National Tourism Certification Board (NTCB) in 1982 as a partnership agency with the Department of Education, providing colleges and the tourism, hospitality and leisure industry. All craft courses for the sector were designed under the auspices of the NTCB and students were assessed and gained certification through this agency. With growing independence and autonomy within the college sector and the establishment of national qualifications agencies in Ireland (FETAC and HETAC), the need for the NTCB declined and Fáilte Ireland were able to pass over much of its role to provider colleges and the new agencies. At the same time, the core role of coordinating a national perspective on labour-market needs and the design of programmes to meet these needs has remained a Fáilte Ireland responsibility (Owens 2005).

Fáilte Ireland's remit in undertaking this central coordinating role in all areas of human resource development within the Irish tourism, hospitality and leisure industry is to act in liaison with, and on behalf of, appropriate government departments to ensure the optimal use of state funds within the education and training of new entrants and experienced personnel and, at the same time, to work closely with the public and private sectors of the industry in order to ensure that training and skills development are in place to meet the specific needs of all businesses within all sectors of the industry. In many respects, the conceptual culmination of this role was the 2005 publication of a national human resource strategy for Irish tourism, the output from the 2003 national tourism policy review (Fáilte Ireland 2005b). The national human resources development strategy is embedded within the wider context of economic development and commitments to competitiveness and quality within wider Irish society. As such, it is a critical assessment of the role of people in achieving a high-quality, internationally competitive tourism, hospitality and leisure sector within which the knowledge element in the deployment of human capital is given precedence over traditional manual skills. This strategy also embeds Fáilte Ireland's long-term role in supporting the development of people within the sector and ensures that Fáilte Ireland's human resource planning role remains internationally unique. This is the model which provided the impetus to the development of the human resource management framework discussed earlier in this chapter and is also a model which, if appropriately resourced, has the potential to make a real difference in newly emerging tourism destination countries in the developing world.

Transnational perspectives

We have considered the problems that are faced by those attempting to manage the planning of human resource requirements for tourism, hospitality and leisure at a community, regional or national level. Fáilte Ireland provides a successful model by which to undertake such planning, but on the basis of highly interventionist and largely centralized public policy, which may not be politically acceptable within all European countries. Seeking an equivalent role at a trans-European level, therefore, presents even greater challenges and problems.

The tourism, hospitality and leisure industry is very diverse in its product characteristics, its traditions and origins, the markets that it serves, the role that it plays in the national economies and, above all, the labour markets within which it exists (with regard to employment traditions, education and training systems, and the status of tourism and hospitality employment, among other considerations). Given the diversity within and between national systems, achieving transnational agreement and congruence presents a real challenge.

Therefore it is not surprising that only limited contributions have been made to coordinate planning of human resource concerns on a pan-national basis. Within the European Union, the closest that any initiative has come to this is through the 1991 Action Plan to Assist Tourism (CEC 1991), which proposes some limited measures in the human resource area, all to do with education and training. These are:

- identification of professional profiles of the sector;
- encouragement of the participation of tourism businesses in existing community action programmes for training;
- support for cooperation between universities and tourism schools and tourism professionals; and
- pilot actions for specific training in the sector: rural, social, cultural, environmental.

Such actions hardly constitute a comprehensive human resource plan for the tourism and hospitality industry. Even where specific actions have been undertaken, their impact to date has been limited. Attempts to facilitate labour mobility within the Europe by identifying job and qualification equivalencies under the auspices of the EU's vocational training agency CEDEFOP have produced requisite documentation but little or no actual use within the tourism, hospitality and leisure industry of the member states although labour-market forces have generated mobility on a very large scale, largely without the assistance of international agencies. Despite the failure of human resource planning at a transnational level in Europe, there is a certain irony that the European Union has been active in supporting regional development projects in the Caribbean, South-East Asia and South Asia; projects which are designed to facilitate regional cooperation between participating countries in meeting their human resource development needs within the tourism and hospitality industry. Experience from this work suggests that some limited progress can be made towards applying the planning process beyond national boundaries.

Review and discussion questions

1. What are the main purposes of human resource planning?
2. Outline the main features of Bramham's approach to labour-market planning and consider its applicability to the tourism, hospitality and leisure industry.

3. What are the main constraints to effective human resource planning at the individual business/business unit level in the tourism, hospitality and leisure industry?
4. What are the main benefits to the small tourism, hospitality and leisure business of human resource planning?
5. How does human resource planning at the corporate level differ from that at the individual business unit level?
6. What are the main constraints to effective human resource planning at the corporate level in the tourism, hospitality and leisure industry?
7. How can the integrated human resource development framework (Figure 9.1) be used to assist human resource planning at a national level?
8. What are the uses and deficiencies of the four measures of tourism employment that are considered in this chapter?
9. What are the main barriers to effective human resource planning at the macro level?
10. How might elements of Fáilte Ireland's approach to human resource planning be utilized in another country with which you are familiar?

Sustainability and the future of work and employment in tourism, hospitality and leisure

Chapter objectives

This chapter addresses two key issues relating to one of the key themes within contemporary international tourism, hospitality and leisure. The aims of this chapter are:

- to review the changing role of people in the delivery of service through a discussion of work and employment within the sector. The chapter demonstrates how tourism work and employment are likely to develop in the future, although tourism and labour-market behaviours are both particularly difficult to predict with real accuracy;

- to consider the role of a sustainable approach to the development and management of tourism, hospitality and leisure as a key underpinning to our understanding of the role of people within tourism, hospitality and leisure.

These are themes that arise from questions that have been raised throughout this book. In many respects, these two themes are closely aligned and, its is argued in this chapter, the future of people and work in tourism, hospitality and leisure depends upon recognition of the need for sustainable practices if the sector is to have a future of value to society and to its various stakeholders, particularly those employed in its businesses.

The changing role of people

It is a much overplayed truism to describe tourism, hospitality and leisure as a 'people industry'. What does a cliché such as this mean in the context of contemporary reality? To what extent can such a clichéd descriptor remain a label within tourism, hospitality and leisure in the future and will it retain its significance as the sector develops further in a global context? The major change environment which tourism, hospitality and leisure, worldwide, constantly experiences in terms of its products, marketing and operations are widely seen to be driven by the external political and economic environment as well as by evolving consumer demand, the pressure of global competitive forces and by technological innovation. To what extent does the work and employment environment within which tourism, hospitality and leisure operates drive change within the sector rather than playing what is generally seen as a reactive role?

Notwithstanding the challenges imposed by major diversity within the international tourism, hospitality and leisure industry and, indeed, contradictions in the area of work and employment, it is possible to identify a number of underpinning themes with respect to work and employment in the sector. These themes have emerged as important but beyond the capacity of traditional approaches to the management of people within tourism, hospitality and leisure to cope with; therefore they impose challenges. They have implications beyond traditional human resources departments and create wider challenges for marketing, quality, product development, finance and operations. The purpose of this chapter is to address a number of key contemporary themes in the management of human resources within international tourism, hospitality and leisure and to consider how the sector is responding to the pressures, challenges and opportunities afforded by them.

The nature of work in tourism, hospitality and leisure

As we have already seen, tourism, hospitality and leisure work exhibits diversity in both horizontal and vertical terms. In a horizontal sense, it includes a very wide range of jobs, the extent depending upon the definition of the sector that is employed. The traditional research focus on work in the sector concentrates on areas that are located with the hospitality sub-sector and, largely, focus on food and beverage and, to a lesser extent, accommodation. Research into wider areas of tourism, hospitality and leisure work, particularly those that have emerged with the expansion of services and functions in the area (front desk, leisure, entertainment, reservation call centres) is much more poorly served. This book has drawn on a limited range of work in these areas. The 'newer' areas include functions and tasks that exhibit considerable crossover with work that fall outwith normal definitions of tourism, hospitality and leisure in food and drink manufacture, office administration, IT systems management and specialist areas of sports and culture. The characteristics and the organization of the tourism, hospitality and leisure industry are subject to ongoing restructuring and evolutionary change. There are major labour-market, employee welfare and skills implications of such change, as businesses reshape the range of services they offer or respond to fashion and trend imperatives in the consumer marketplace.

Vertical diversity in tourism, hospitality and leisure work is represented by a more traditional classification that ranges from unskilled through semi-skilled and skilled to supervisory and management. This 'traditional' perspective of work and, therefore, skills in tourism is partly described by Riley (1996) in terms that suggest that the sector is dominated by semi-skilled and unskilled employees and that knowledge-based positions are a small proportion of the total workforce. This simplification masks major business organizational diversity in tourism, hospitality and leisure, reflecting the size, location and ownership of businesses. The actual job and skills content of work is predicated upon these factors so that common job titles (e.g. restaurant manager, sous-chef) almost certainly mask a very different range of responsibilities, tasks and skills within jobs in different establishments.

The skills profile of tourism, hospitality and leisure, in turn, is influenced by the labour market that is available to it, both in direct terms and via educational and training establishments. The weak internal labour-market characteristics in themselves impose downward pressures on the skills expectations that employers have of their staff and this, in turn, influences the nature and level of training which the educational system delivers. There is an evident cycle of down-skilling, not only in response to the actual demands of work or of consumer expectations of what it can deliver, but as a result of the perceptions of potential employees and the expectations that employers may have of them.

There is a strong case to argue for the social and cultural construction of what we understand to be work and employment in tourism, hospitality and leisure. This argument is built upon recognition of the changing nature of work across services in general, the emphasis moving from technical to generic skills considerations. This discussion is part of the growing interest in the nature of service work and recognition of its complexity and variety (Korczynski 2002) and, indeed, status as suggested in Nickson and Warhurst's (2003) reference to the changing nature of work hierarchies. The move away from technical-driven definitions of work in tourism, hospitality and leisure adds concepts such as emotional labour (Hochschild 1983; Seymour 2000) and aesthetic labour (Warhurst *et al.* 2000; Nickson *et al.* 2003) to the demands of such work. The context in which these attributes feature and the combination of skills that they demand generate work attributes that are context specific. Therefore, debate about work issues, in the context of tourism, hospitality and leisure, is informed by wider, generic consideration about the nature of employment in the context of changing employment, technology and vocational education, within both developed and developing economies. The range of issues that flow from this assertion are addressed in part by authors in Warhurst *et al.* (2004), who recognize the diverse influences on work and skills across the contemporary economy. The major gap in understanding is the extent to which work which is perceived to be 'low skills' in the Western, developed context, can be described in this way in other contexts because of differing cultural, communications, linguistic and relationship assumptions which underpin such work in developing countries. Work in the tourism, hospitality and leisure sector varies greatly in both the skills base it requires and in its social status according to its location in either a developed- or developing-world context.

The impact of globalization on work and employment

The impact of globalization on the management of people in tourism, hospitality and leisure is primarily driven by three factors: technological, political and economic. Globalization makes distance a relatively insignificant factor in the establishment of long-distance economic, commercial, political and socio-cultural relations. It is more than simply a way of doing business or running financial markets – it is an ongoing process. The modern communication systems make the process easier. For example, the British and US service sectors are increasingly dealing with their customers through outsourced call centres in India. Another major manifestation of globalization is the increasing power of global business corporations, which follow a strategy of global expansion.

Globalization has definite influences on work and employment in tourism, hospitality and leisure. Changing labour markets in developed countries make low-paid jobs scarcer for the lower-educated, simultaneously creating increased demand by higher educated people for these lower-paid jobs in the absence of attractive alternatives. These trends create a mismatch between available labour and labour for which a demand exists. Job seekers with a lack of vocational training get more and more excluded from job opportunities. At the same time, because of globalization, the supply of labour from less developed countries affects the market position of all of those who have no scarce skills to offer. This results in a position where only the most competitive can retain their relative position in the labour marketplace.

The globalization of business has a number of implications for human resource management. Knowledgeable and skilled workers are increasingly becoming mobile so that their recruitment is from a global rather than a national or local pool. Employers who are unable to provide competitive packages will be confronted with an increasing 'flight' of these types of workers and an accompanying shortage.

In recruiting new employees from a global pool, employers will have to use global media rather than local or national media. The information technology capacity and the extent to which workers who possess knowledge and skills to be competitive in a global sense will be connected to new media will enhance their recruitment. Selection procedures will also increasingly be based on media using electronic information technology. Face-to-face testing and interviewing will be used less, due to long distances and possible cost factors, and will be replaced by electronically mediated selection procedures. The ability to operate on a global environment will be one of the key selection criteria. Appointments will be made on the basis of internationally acceptable contract laws and agreements and at remuneration and benefits levels, which increasingly become standardized across national boundaries.

A major consequence of globalization in tourism, hospitality and leisure is the issue of matching employee skills with changing industry requirements. The traditional practice of employees learning the majority of the skills on the job and gradually progressing to senior positions is threatened by rapid technological change and the need to respond to the changing service requirements. Employees at the operational and managerial levels are now required to be more flexible and adaptive to constant change. This is a requirement for which they may not be fully equipped (Keating and Harrington 2005). Globalization has major implications for work and employment in tourism, hospitality and leisure, and these include (Becherel and Cooper 2002) the following:

- The need for different skills and competencies in the employees to be able to deal with the widespread use of technology, especially, the internet.
- Dealing with the employment-related consequences of mergers and strategic alliances.

- Issues of relocation of employees, and social and cultural sensitivities of those working away from home.
- New forms of tourism, hospitality and leisure, utilizing natural and cultural environments, create a demand for indigenous employees, who could deliver better quality and original products and services.
- Meeting the needs of 'high-skilled tourists', who are more experienced and demand higher-quality products and service.

These pressures of globalization in tourism, hospitality and leisure have significant implications for work and employment, especially for human resource development and dealing with the cultural aspects.

The de-skilling of tourism, hospitality and leisure work

The extensive debate that surrounds the issue of 'McDonaldization' as developed by Ritzer (2004) has suggested that de-skilling is an inevitable consequence of growing standardization or routinization across the service sector. There is evidence to support this process in tourism, hospitality and leisure in the form of a growing fast-food sector, within budget accommodation; and through the growth of no-frills airlines. The growth of these sectors all point to a simplification of tasks in the workplace and the creation of McJobs, aided in part by technology substitution but also by changes in consumer demands and expectations. It is also arguable that these sectors have grown in response to new consumer demand as opposed to displacement of demand for traditional services. Therefore, while their growth may have had the global effect of 'dumbing down' average skills levels in tourism, hospitality and leisure it is difficult to argue that they have eliminated demand for higher-order skills within other sectors of the industry.

The argument that tourism, hospitality and leisure is moving towards increasingly multi-skilled models of training and work has been aired since the early 1980s (Baum 1987). The focus of this argument has been targeted towards meeting employer needs, particularly in smaller businesses where the notion of flexible rotation between, for example, different hotel departments in a way to suit the demand cycle is presented as a logical business solution. In reality, such work represents multi-tasking because the level and nature of the work in question (food service, bar service, portering, housekeeping) offers little by way of enhancing the actual skills of employees other than extending the operational context within which they are exercised.

Creating the opportunity to develop a wider range of skills within the workplace is frequently included within models of job enrichment. Multi-skilling or multi-tasking across departments, as generally practised within the tourism sector, does not offer much to employees that can be described as 'enriching'. Of probably greater value to employees is the breakdown of job demarcation within tourism, hospitality and leisure departments, such as the virtual elimination of the traditional parti system within kitchens in Britain and the merging of front-office functions (cashier, reception, concierge) in many hotels (Odgers and Baum 2001).

Technology – are people necessary?

There is little doubt that technologies across a wide range of tourism, hospitality and leisure work, including production, operations and communications technologies, have impacted greatly upon tourism work. The routinization of work in many areas (food preparation, airport handling, reservations) is due to the introduction of technologies which allow a wide range of tasks to be performed both more efficiently and, frequently, more effectively with less or, indeed, no human input. Low-cost airlines have demonstrated clearly how the introduction of technological systems and the use of creative operational approaches can significantly reduce labour costs in tourism, hospitality and leisure and, indeed, impact on employment across the wider sector (for example, on travel agencies). It is conceivable (but unlikely) that technology substitution for labour will eliminate a wide range of work within tourism except within highly standardized, low-cost areas of activity.

Labour intensity is a widely attributed feature of the tourism sector although changes with respect to product, service expectations and technology have altered this picture to some degree in recent years (Baum and Odgers 2001). With the development of various forms of support technology, the operational systems in tourism have been improved towards the development of more efficient and cost-saving practices. For example, central reservation systems in airlines and hotels, employing effective yield management, benefit the industry in terms of forecasting sales, arranging essential 'raw material' and managing good customer relationship marketing and after-sales service. Moreover, the introduction of labour-saving technology provides the industry with opportunities to improve the quality of much soul-destroying work so accurately described by writers from Orwell (1933) through to Gabriel (1988). All these new technologies make the hotel sector more efficient and responsive to customers' expectations.

However, there are some functions which cannot be substituted by technology, such as room-cleaning, table-serving, door-greeting and other personal services. The new technology brings out better 'tools' for the operations to manage, but not for them to entirely replace routine work. In a people-oriented or labour-intensive industry, labour still plays an important part in production procedures. However, as Guerrier and Adib (2001) point out, the duty of the many tourism, hospitality and leisure workers is still to manage the 'dirty' and to keep it away from the guest as far as is possible. To certain extent, staff in this sector have much in common with nurses, sharing similar working conditions in terms of difficulty, relatively poor pay, low status, shift work and feminized activity.

Employment matters as drivers of change

Traditionally, the area of employment (and human resources management in general) has been seen as an area which is reactive to changes and the demands of the wider business environment. Thus, there is a widely accepted assumption that the role of people within organizations is required to change and develop in response to developments in markets, products and technology. Most large tourism, hospitality and leisure companies operate on the basis of this assumption and this permeates into the manner in which they organize work and support human resource functions such as training and development. This model is only valid in so far as the external labour market permits employers the luxury of thinking in this way.

In situations where high-quality 'contemporary' labour, skilled in emotional, aesthetic and information management skills, is scare and in high demand, tourism, hospitality and leisure companies may need to re-engineer the way in which work is packaged for existing and potential employees. This will require new approaches to flexibility in the workplace (traditionally seen as flexibility by the employee to the benefit of the employer) (Lai and Baum 2005) so that the focus is on accommodating the life-style requirements of workers and facilitating work–life balance for all employees. This is already happening. Underlying the practice of many organizations in tourism recognized as excellent in terms of their approach to work and employment is appreciation by such companies of the need to respond to work–life balance issues within the workforce. Effective people management is designed to move out of traditional employment paradigms (40-hour week, fixed shifts) and to tailor the work environment so as to meet the needs of both employers and employees. The consequences of this approach include the creation of fluid workplaces, characterized by diversity in terms of who works there, what their motivation for work is, when they work and what they do. Organizations which fail to respond to the need for flexibility in its broadest interpretation are likely to suffer in terms of recruitment, retention, commitment and productivity. This fluidity has significant implications for training and development policy and practice, both within organizations and in the context of external training providers.

A consequence of a focus on employee work–life balance needs at a micro level, manifest at a company-wide level, is that recognition of these needs can become important drivers of an organization's approach to its markets, its products and its use of technology. Creating flexibility in the workplace in a way that suits both partners to the employment contract probably requires compromise and adjustment on the part of both parties. It also requires a sophisticated understanding of the labour market at a local, national and, in parts of the world such as Europe, international level. This understanding can then drive the shaping of the products and services that a tourism company is able to offer and will also help to identify the investment costs (in terms of training and development) that are likely to be required in order to meet the human resource demands of such decisions.

New models for careers

The tourism, hospitality and leisure sector offers many and varied opportunities for rewarding and sustainable working lives across its diverse sub-sectors and at different levels throughout the world. The industry's heterogeneity, geographical spread and stochastic demand provides both opportunity and challenge in terms of mapping these opportunities against the aspirations and expectations of those attracted into the tourism, hospitality and leisure industry, either as new entrants to the labour force or in the context of change opportunities within their working lives.

In most developed countries, traditional models of one-sector working lives, built on the notion of a logical and progressive career 'ladder', represent a reality which will face fewer and fewer entrants to the job market in the future. For many people, this is not a concern or a fear but provides the basis for challenge and opportunity, the ability to take control of aspects of their lives and to respond to changes within the external environment in a positive manner. Unlike their grandparents, today's school leavers and college graduates are more likely to think of their working lives in terms of finite segments rather than sustained and permanent careers, viewing the future in terms of what has been called, in the Australian context, 'fragmented futures' (Watson *et al.* 2003; Buchanan, Watson and Briggs 2004). Working-life segments can contain periods of commitment within different sectors of the economy, periods of study within models of lifelong learning and periods of travel sabbatical as 'the year-out experience' becomes more and more common to those in their 20s, 30s and beyond. Vocational mobility within is greatly facilitated by recognition of the underpinning 'generic' skills set which much education and working experience provides today and which permits ease of both formal (qualifications-driven) and informal (experience-driven) transition, particularly within the dominant and growing service sector.

Fragmentation, however, cannot be seen in terms of a lack of commitment or disloyalty to an employer nor does it necessarily create a sense of fear and insecurity for those operating within its various working phases. Perceptions of working lives held by younger people today are focused more on short-term wealth generation and much less on job status, security or permanence of employment than was the case with previous generations. Therefore, within the time scale allotted to work in a particular company or sector, commitment is likely to be strong despite, maybe because of, the transitory nature of the employment relationship.

At its simplest, leading businesses have already recognized the changing nature of the employment relationship and have responded by a reconfiguration of operations and service delivery at certain levels within the traditional quality spectrum. As a leader within this process, McDonald's early on accepted that they would offer, at best, transitory job opportunities for many school and college students as well as others in the workforce. Therefore, they ensured that processes could be learnt very quickly by bright people who would be productive within a short period of time. Both parties know very well that there will not be a long-term commitment to the working relationship but that, while it lasts, both sides seek to maximize respective benefits. For McDonald's and similar operators, this involves streamlining and simplifying processes and relying on the energy and enthusiasm of their workers for the delivery of their services.

Other tourism, hospitality and leisure businesses have recognized the value of this approach. In Glasgow, as an example, over half of all hospitality workers are students and this is becoming a common model throughout North America, Northern Europe and elsewhere (Canny 2002; Hofman and Steijn 2003). As a result, the industry in Glasgow is now configured to depend upon this source of labour and education providers have also had to adjust their delivery models accordingly. Trends in the cities of most developed countries are unlikely to be significantly different in this respect. For businesses, there has been some considerable dumbing down of both product and in relation to technical skills with a greater focus on 'generic skills' of communication, personality (aesthetic and emotional labour) as well as a greater use of technology. Traditional training as offered through colleges and formal courses plays a lesser role in meeting industry needs within this new model of tourism employment. The decline in relevance of and demand for technical courses in tourism, hospitality and leisure also reflects upon the marginalization of those with low qualifications in contemporary society (the traditional recruitment pool for such courses) who frequently also face social and economic disadvantage. In their place, the flexible student labour market offers employers many perceived advantages which traditional training routes do not.

Likewise, many tourism, hospitality and leisure businesses in rural areas have turned to short-term labour pools of students and others from abroad, in Ireland/UK to learn English (from countries such as Spain or Germany) or for their year out (from New Zealand or Australia) as ready-made, articulate and, in some cases, lower-cost alternatives to local labour. Lifestyles or attractive employment in Donegal, West Cork or Kerry in Ireland can be offered seasonally to workers from elsewhere in Europe at lower cost and lower hassle than would be incurred drawing on local labour markets. Training required and offered is minimal and there is hassle-free disengagement at the end of the tourist season.

An extension of this employment culture is reflected in the increasing use of other flexible labour strategies within tourism, hospitality and leisure. Part-time work models can offer opportunities to enhance service as suggested with respect to student labour. Shackleton (1998) points to the contribution of targeted part-time labour in the development of 'super-service' in food retailing. Likewise, agency staff within some areas of tourism, hospitality and leisure employment, are of increasing importance, particularly in urban centres. Hotel housekeeping and banqueting are the main work areas where agencies provide a 'just in time' model for businesses which allows for rapid response to variable demand and eliminates surplus staffing on an employer's books (Lai and Baum 2005). It also creates an environment where longer-term employment relationships and structured longitudinal training models have little relevance.

These expedient models of employment are most prevalent within the systematized, middle-quality rankings and 'fast' delivery sectors of the tourism, hospitality and leisure sector. The concept of a career within this sector for all but a minority in positions of managerial responsibility is of limited and decreasing value. The role of education and training in the context of transitory working lives, both within the external college environment and in industry itself, is to support mobility, mid-life entry and re-entry to the sector and development in relation to new technologies and products. This represents a fast-moving, ever-changing and challenging model of lifelong learning which, in the future, will play an important role in support of the 'popular' sector of the tourism, hospitality and leisure industry.

'Fragmented' and transitory employment relationships and practices may still leave problems for those 'high-end' businesses which remain within the traditional skills paradigms and which employ crafts personnel in the conventional mode (skilled chefs etc.). For them, the concept of the traditional, longitudinal career within a chosen craft area has relevance, and career management in this sense requires participation by employees themselves and their employers but also by those responsible for maintaining, managing and enhancing quality within Irish tourism. At the same time, accommodating and marketing the outcomes of such skills will necessitate premium pricing and careful management of the price–value relationship.

The policy issue for the tourism, hospitality and leisure sector, therefore, relates to the proportion of the industry which currently operates or can aspire to operate to standards which require traditional skills delivery and can, therefore, offer sustained career opportunities for crafts personnel within the industry. If this craft skills environment can legitimately be attributed to a significant proportion of the tourism sector in the country and both domestic and in-bound market demand exists for its delivery, then the maintenance of an educational and training structure in support of it remains legitimate. It is also within this model of the tourism industry that the industry can best stake its claim within the knowledge economy.

The working lives projected for today's young people bear little relationship to the linear career models aspired by their grandparents and they will be characterized by change, short-term goals and ongoing renewal. Planning for human resource development in tourism, hospitality and leisure must respond to the challenges and opportunities presented by fragmented learning and working lives.

Predicting the future?

A number of themes and issues are currently impacting upon the nature of work and employment in international tourism, hospitality and leisure. In experiencing change across a wide spectrum of areas relating to work, the tourism industry is by no means unique and a similar analysis could readily be constructed for areas such as retailing or office administration. However, the visibility of this work to the consumer, combined with our exposure, as customers, to the execution of tourism work in both developed and developing countries, does make this sector significantly different to most other parts of the service economy.

Predicting the future from an analysis of the present is hazardous but a reasonable assessment is that mega trends such as globalization, de-skilling and technology impact will continue to play major roles in shaping the tourism workplace for the foreseeable future. Less predictable in their potential impact on work are changes in consumer expectations and taste with respect to both product and service in tourism. These both have the potential to influence greatly the manner in which work is carried out in all sub-sectors of the industry. The notion of work–life balance and its impact on tourism, hospitality and leisure is also an area where prediction is hazardous. Evidence points to increasing recognition, by both employers and employees in developed countries, of the value in meeting the wider life aspirations of tourism, hospitality and leisure workers through flexibility in employment arrangements. At the same time, there is little evidence of such approaches in the developing world, where exploitation of the vulnerable within the sector's workforce (child labour or sex workers as examples) remains a major challenge. There is also evidence that employers within the developed world are looking to circumvent their moral obligations with respect to work–life balance by looking beyond their traditional, local labour pools to more vulnerable, less-demanding migrant labour sources. If this continues to be the case on a large scale into the future, the prognosis for tourism work remains relatively bleak and does not point to real progress from the time of Orwell in the 1930s.

Sustainability in contemporary tourism, leisure and hospitality and the role of people

An underpinning theme in any discussion of international tourism, hospitality and leisure is the sustainability of activities under this broad umbrella of activities. As we have already seen, an historical perspective on tourism, hospitality and leisure points to a sector of activities that is very well established in some destinations. At the same time, more recent developments internationally include examples of locations and projects that have failed to stand the test of time, for a variety of reasons. Butler's (1980) Tourism Area Life Cycle model provides a partial explanatory framework which helps to understand why some locations fail after periods of successful operation while others are able to remain at the forefront of international and domestic tourism for much longer periods. Butler refers to a stage of decline which can hit destinations unless they are able to rejuvenate their offering. This model focuses on the supply side and does acknowledge the role that changing market demand can have on the fortunes of a resort. The decline of Northern European seaside resorts in Britain and France, for example, are open to both supply- and demand-side explanations – the facilities are ageing and dated while there are the alternative opportunities to travel to newer and warmer destinations afforded to travellers through cheap airfares. In some respects, resorts such as Deauville (France), Scarborough (England), Portrush (Northern Ireland) and Largs (Scotland) have demonstrated sustainability in that their gradual decline through periods of major change has not been terminal and each has adapted to altered circumstances. It could be argued that their slow emergence as tourism destinations during the Victorian era and after has been mirrored by gradual decline and partial rejuvenation. By contrast, more recent experience in some Mediterranean, South-East Asian and Caribbean destinations is of rapid development and rapid decline, the consequence of unplanned development and fickle consumer demand which shows little destination loyalty. Lloret de Mar in Catalunia is an example of a 1960s destination (Baum 2002b), created without thoughts of physical or market sustainability for the first wave of mass tourism to Spain and now exhibiting accommodation and facilities stock that has very little appeal to tourists who can choose from a wide range of higher-quality alternatives on offer in this and other parts of the world.

The theme of sustainability in tourism focuses primarily on supply-side issues although these cannot been seen in isolation of changing demand. No discussion of the role of people in tourism in the context of contemporary international tourism would be complete without some reference to the theme of sustainability. This theme underpins the arguments developed throughout this book and will emerge explicitly at various points in the text. Therefore, it requires some contextualization at this point. The theme of sustainable tourism has, in recent years, generated a significant literature in its own right and at least one specialist publication dedicated to the area (*The Journal of Sustainable Tourism*). A useful definition of the concept of sustainable tourism is provided by Bramwell and Lane in their introduction to the first edition of that journal:

> Sustainable tourism is a positive approach intended to reduce the tensions and friction created by the complex interactions between the tourism industry, visitors, the environment and communities which are host to holidaymakers. It is an approach which involves working for the longer quality of both natural and human resources. (Bramwell and Lane 1993, p.2)

Bramwell and Lane were, at the time that they wrote, unusual in addressing the concept of sustainability specifically from the perspective of tourism. Many sources derive their definitions from a wider discussion of sustainability in economic, environmental and cultural terms. Cooper *et al.* (2005), for example, draw on the wider definition used by the World Commission on Environment and Development in 1987 (the Bruntland Report) which defines sustainability in terms of meeting the needs of the present without compromising the opportunity for future generations to meet their own needs.

One of the earliest writers to address the consequences of a sustainable approach to tourism development (without specifically mentioning sustainability as a concept) was Poon, writing in 1993. She addressed a range of issues of issues facing contemporary tourism through an analysis of new and old models of tourism. She applied these by comparing the characteristics of travel and tourism during the period up to the 1990s with those of the 1990s and into the future (Table 10.1).

What is interesting in the context of this book is Poon's reference to human resources and training within the context of wider tourism development. This is relatively unusual in discussions of sustainable tourism.

'Sustainable tourism' is recognized as a complex and multi-dimensional concept. In this, it draws from the much wider concern for sustainability in all aspects of economic and environmental care and management. There are interdependencies and, indeed, paradoxes in our understanding of sustainability in terms of environmental, economic and political issues. This is, perhaps, best illustrated by reference to the recognition of global warming as a threat to the future well-being of communities in both the developed and developing world which exists alongside unrestricted use of fossil fuels, particularly for air and car travel. A commitment to sustainable development is designed to protect and enhance the natural environment while meeting basic human needs, promoting equity and improving the quality of life for all people.

As already suggested, examples of non-sustainable development are widespread, both in a general sense and, specifically, within tourism. Unplanned and uncontrolled development along various stretches of the Mediterranean, the Black Sea and Thai coasts provide examples of building that took place in the name of tourism and its economic benefits without serious consideration of its long-term consequences of the needs of the environment, the local community or of possible changes in consumer demand and expectations. On the Romanian and Bulgarian Black Sea coasts and in ski resorts in the same countries, there are monuments to mass and uncontrolled development which are now very out of date and unsuitable for contemporary customer requirements. Mass tourism developments in locations such as these were responses to perceived immediate market demand where longer-term consequences were not considered. The problem with these developments when viewed with the benefit of 20 to 30 years' hindsight is one of renovation and reconstruction, in many cases an almost impossible challenge.

However, the issue of sustainability also relates to the suitability of large-scale resorts and structures, detached physically and culturally from the environments and communities in which they have been built. Lloret del Mar, already mentioned, is an example of intense, concentrated development in a manner which is probably irredeemable without virtually razing the location to the ground and starting again. Benidorm and Torromolinos, also in Spain, and

Table 10.1	Characteristic	Pre-1990s	Into the future
Characteristics of tourism, pre-1990 and into the future	Production concept	Mass tourism	Flexible travel and tourism options; internet driven; mass tourism from new markets
	Products	Mass, standardized and rigidly packaged holidays, mass markets	Flexible, segmented, environmentally sound holidays
	Instruments of production	Packaged tours; charter flights; franchises; holiday branding; large-scale organization; large hotels and resorts	Managed yield; specialized operators; destination competence; independent holidays; low-cost airlines and customer management of packaging process
	Organization of production	Scale economies; anticipated growth in demand for more of the same; large-scale purchase of stock	Scale and scope economies; flexibility; close to market; diagonal integration
	Manning and and training	Seasonal labour; high labour turnover; low-paid jobs; low labour flexibility	Flexible use of labour; lifestyle considerations; high levels of labour mobility
	Marketing	Mass marketing/advertising	Tailored marketing, internet distribution; customer control of distribution decisions
	Customers	Developed world, inexperienced; apparently homogeneous; sun-lust, predictable, price motivated	Developed world, experienced; developing world, inexperienced; heterogeneous; eclectic product choice; unpredictable; value motivation

Source: Poon (1993) *Tourism, Technology and Competitive Strategies*, Wallingford: CABI, with author's updates and modifications, with permission.

Constanta in Romania are other locations where over-development has left resorts with options of either catering for a low-paying, mass market or starting again from scratch.

One of the real challenges facing development of this nature is that its use, at time of development, was targeted exclusively at tourists, primarily those from overseas. There is, therefore, little co-ownership or shared sense of responsibility between visitors and the local community. From a leisure perspective, the resources developed to meet the needs of visitors can frequently exclude or marginalize the local community for reasons of cost, political ideology, location or culture. In many developing countries, resorts such as Nusa Dua in Bali were built as exclusive enclaves, from which the local community was deliberately excluded, not least on grounds of cost. In Cuba, tourist resorts are, likewise, generally all-inclusive enclaves into which the local community are not encouraged to venture and, further, those working there are forbidden to fraternize socially with visitors outside of the strict work context. As a result, facilities that could serve valuable community leisure functions are deemed off-limits for such users who also may find many of their traditional playgrounds, notably beaches, fenced off and out of bounds for their use. The physical sustainability of such resorts, therefore, becomes a real challenge that goes beyond the wear and tear of the bricks and mortar.

There are, of course, other dimensions to sustainability. The preservation of fragile natural, cultural or historic resources is of equal significance. In many cases, these are the very reasons why tourists come to the destination in the first place. This is true of coral reefs, rare wildlife, great cathedrals and mosques, unique works of fine art, renowned performances of dance or drama as well as mountain walks, cliff-top paths or Medieval cities. Unrestrained tourist access, while commercially attractive in the short term, has the effect of 'killing the goose that laid the golden egg' – in other words, it destroys the very tourist product by over-use and consumption that attracted the visitor to the location in the first place. The sheer weight of numbers during the high season detracts from the appeal of cities such as London, Venice, Oxford and Paris. In the case of Venice, the fragility of the environment is such that excessive visitor numbers are contributing to the actual destruction of parts of the city. The threat to endangered flora and fauna is also widespread, not only in the very visible context of, for example, Kenyan game parks or the rainforests of Sabah, but also in many European locations such as Zakynthos, the Greek island famous for its giant sea turtles.

At a socio-cultural level, the potentially negative impact of tourism, hospitality and leisure activities on traditional cultures has been widely discussed, especially with respect to the developing world. Examples can be found from destinations such as Bali and the Maldives but also in Europe where Falaraki in Rhodes has seen clear conflict between mass tourism and more traditional social values in the local community. Tensions have also been reported in the context of remote communities of western Ireland, the Scottish islands and Lapland. The effects of tourism, hospitality and leisure on established communities can be far reaching, involving changes to the employment structure, changes in the availability of traditional agricultural and other products, inflationary increases in the cost of commodities and land, health considerations such as the spread of AIDS and major epidemics such as SARS and Avian flu as well as changes to traditional beliefs and practices. 'Sustainability' in this context means a tourism, hospitality and leisure sector that recognizes its potential to change a community and seeks to minimize that community's perception of its most extreme effects.

One response to threats to the sustainability of tourism, hospitality and leisure is to manage access and use of facilities so as to protect their futures. Stonehenge, in England, for example, allowed virtually unrestricted access to visitors in the late 1960s when family picnics frequently made use of the large stones for seating, now carefully controls access to the site through a series of visitor management strategies, designed to protect this unique heritage site. Such rationing measures have proved insufficient in some locations. Historic sites such as the Blasket Islands off the south-west of Ireland now cannot be visited except in very limited and controlled circumstances. Price rationing is one policy to ease demand on some locations, a policy followed by major cathedrals in Britain. Another alternative is a process of attraction substitution by which tourists are offered virtual reality interpretation and mock-ups as an alternative to the real thing in order to support preservation. In the context of leisure, price rationing is the means by which, for example, scarce golf resources in Japan and other countries are managed, stimulating golf tourism from such locations to destinations where golf course congestion is not so evident and visitors can thereby combine their leisure pastimes with tourist travel.

The concept of a location or facility's carrying capacity as a measure to control access and ensure preservation is one that has gained considerable currency in contemporary tourism development. 'Carrying capacity' is defined by Mathieson and Wall (1982) as:

> the maximum number of people who can use a site without an unacceptable alternation in the physical environment and without an unacceptable decline in the quality of experience gained by visitors. (p.21)

Cooper *et al.* (2005) go beyond what is an excessively physical definition when they talk about carrying capacity as:

> that level of tourist presence which creates impacts on the host community, environment and economy that is acceptable to both tourists and hosts, and sustainable over future time periods. (p.268)

This latter approach can readily accommodate the concept of sustainable human resource development in tourism, hospitality and leisure which we address in this chapter.

The concept of sustainability in relation to tourism, hospitality and leisure can be developed and interpreted beyond the tangible impact of visitor or user numbers and their relationship to physical and socio-cultural phenomena within a location. Sustainability in tourism, hospitality and leisure can be interpreted to mean forms of activity which develop in harmony with local community aspirations, help to meet the needs of such communities in economic, social and personal terms and are thus responsive to local democracy with regard to the kind of development that is seen to be acceptable. This is clearly a controversial dimension of sustainability and impinges, for example, on local community influence on planning processes and relationships with outside investors, especially from overseas. Ultimately, a model of sustainability which incorporates this dimension includes the right of the local community to say 'no' to tourism development and tourists, although such an extreme reaction may be rare. However, it is a dimension which has significant implications for any discussion of human resources in the context of sustainable development in tourism, hospitality and leisure.

What, one may reasonably ask, has this discussion of sustainability in tourism to do with the management of human resources? Sustainability is not a term that has been widely associated with human resource policies and is only addressed in passing in the mainstream of sustainable tourism literature. Lane (1992) touches on this issue when, in his classification, he refers to non-sustainable features as including 'no career structure' and 'employees imported' as opposed to 'career structure' and 'employment according to local potential' within his sustainability paradigm. Poon (1993) also implies this distinction but such references are relatively unusual. Urry (1994), for example, in considering the social and cultural impact of tourism development in Europe and writing very much from within what might be called the 'sustainability' camp, considers what he considers to be the main changes in tourism during the 1990s. These are classified under headings of changes to companies, changes in travel patterns and changes in the types of tourism. Interestingly and significantly, no reference is made to changes in employment and the wider human resource agenda. In fact, the theme of sustainable people or human resource management within tourism, hospitality and leisure is one that was neglected in the literature until the preliminary work of Conlin and Baum (1994) and, in greater depth, that of Baum (1995). Jithendran and Baum (2000) have taken discussion of the principles of sustainability in people management a step further in their consideration of such principles at a national level in Indian tourism. Their argument centres on planning dimensions within sustainability; that integrated development across all sectors and levels of tourism, hospitality and leisure create a climate which is sustainable and developmental in culture. As we have seen in Chapter 9, these arguments also underpin Fáilte Ireland's (2005b) national human resource development plan for Irish tourism.

The notion of sustainability within the management of people in tourism, hospitality and leisure is one that underpins much subsequent discussion in this book. It is one that is worth elaboration at this point in order that its significance can be fully appreciated at later stages within this text.

It is widely claimed within the tourism, hospitality and leisure literature and, indeed, within the wider service sector, that people are the most important asset of the sector. This claim is subject to critical analysis in this book, particularly in Chapter 5, but represents a moral high ground for an industry within which some sectors, notably accommodation, catering and fitness, belie this sweeping claim in the manner that they actually treat and remunerate their staff. One of the key issues here is that, in reality, investment in employees is often not a priority for businesses that operate on the basis of short-term goals and outcomes, not an attitude that is consistent with effective asset management. Developing the people asset or human capital is frequently a short-term expedient, designed to train staff to do their current job better and little more. It is arguable that tourism, hospitality and leisure is only a people sector in so far as people are an exploitable resource, an argument that may well accord with the views of Wood

(1997) and others who have been particularly critical of the record of the sector with regard to its human resource practices. Should the unlikely opportunity arise to offer acceptable standards of product and service within tourism, hospitality and leisure without human intervention, it is likely that the industry would show few qualms in pursuing this route. Indeed, there is already considerable evidence that sectors of the industry are heading down this route through technology substitution, productivity maximization, job de-skilling and, above all, standardization or, as Ritzer (2004) and others have called it, 'McDonaldization'. Blythman (2004) clearly demonstrates the effects of self-service and standardization on retail work and this is readily mirrored in hospitality and transport. Were it not for the constraints of regulation, low-cost airlines might well seek to eliminate the majority of human interactions to complement the electronic reservations that already dominate their bookings.

However, as things currently stand, it is true that tourism, hospitality and leisure can be viewed as a people industry from three perspectives. First, tourism is about people as the guest, and the delivery of the tourism, hospitality and leisure product and service is evaluated on the basis of the frequently illogical demands and expectations of the guest. Second, the delivery of a high proportion of the tourism, hospitality and leisure product and service is by people and, while productivity in many sectors may have increased and technology substitution has had an impact on delivery, the labour intensity of much of the industry is inescapable and results in its variability, despite strenuous efforts towards standardization by many companies. Tourism, hospitality and leisure employees are also part of the tourism product, as entertainers for example. Finally, people as guests are part of the experience which fellow tourists and visitors pay for, whether as fellow customers in a busy restaurant, as part of the crowd at a concert or sporting venue, on stage in Karaoke or on the dancefloor at Butlins or Sandals.

Applying the concept of sustainability in the context of human resources in tourism, hospitality and leisure necessitates recognizing this three-dimensional people input into the transaction. Because of the human element, the delivery of most products and services in the sector defies standardization (despite the efforts of many companies) and is subject to variability and iconoclastic interpretation. In part because of this but also in order to maximize the benefits of human intervention in the delivery of tourism, hospitality and leisure in the long term, sustainable human resource development results in an approach that contrasts strongly with much traditional practice in the industry of which Wood (1997) is rightly very critical. It is characterized by, arguably, somewhat idealistic principles:

- Investment in people is a long-term commitment by both parties, employers and employees, and all actions must be guided by the recognition of this.

- Effective human resource management requires a faith in the capacity for good and the potential for enhanced achievement of each and every individual within an organization. At its most positive, this optimistic view is expressed by Mahesh (1994):

  > The question, 'Is nobility and perfection a natural quality in Man, and cruelty and pettiness an aberration, or vice versa?' is likely to be answered very soon

in favour of human nature being intrinsically capable of unfolding its potential for perfection. The reasons for such optimism lie in some significant changes that have taken place globally, which have collectively led to the phenomenon that Alvin Toffler calls the Third Wave. (p.1)

- Companies must demonstrate a faith in the capability of people in the community within which they locate and must invest in enabling these people to achieve their full potential.

- Consequently, employment of those from outside of the community, region or country should be a last resort. Parallel to this necessity should be a commitment to the training and development of local potential to fill positions taken on a temporary basis by those from outside. This may appear somewhat xenophobic, especially in the context of an integrated Europe with its commitment to full-labour mobility, but it is a necessary dictum especially in less developed regions, in order to maximize the benefits of development within the community.

- Companies must recognize the impact that they have on the character and balance of the local labour market and utilize its strengths and compensate for its deficiencies in so far as is possible.

- Training is about more than attaining finite skills in order to undertake the immediate task at hand. It is also about providing flexible and transferable capabilities over the full length of a person's working career to enable him or her to respond to changing work demands and opportunities for new responsibilities as they arise.

- The detailed planning of human resource requirements is an integral part of all tourism development planning and must take place in tandem with the preparation of the physical facilities. The lead time, in terms of recruiting and training highly skilled personnel, is arguably longer than that which applies with respect to physical product or marketing, especially at the macro level (Baum 1993a).

These principles consolidate themes that have been addressed in earlier chapters of this book. They are also principles which provide us with a framework within which we may make a comparative analysis of human resource management and development according to the 'traditional' paradigm and on the basis of practices derived from the application of principles of sustainability to the human resource environment. In many respects, this model is an attempt to provide the framework which Poon has originally suggested is missing when she suggested that 'human resource strategies for travel and tourism are not yet clear' (Poon 1993). Here we argue that greater clarity is at hand, and the outcome of this analysis is presented in Table 10.2.

The comparison in Table 10.2 provides an insight into how human resource practices which are compatible with models of sustainability within the tourism, hospitality and leisure industry can be developed. The reality is that few companies adopt policies and practices which are exclusively on one side of the divide or the other. Even within companies, the application of broad principles may result in widely diverging outcomes and, at the micro level, how human resource policies are actually implemented will depend greatly on individual managers and their commitment to principles within the right-hand column.

| **Table 10.2** | Traditional and sustainable human resource practices in tourism, hospitality and leisure |

Old human resources practice	Sustainable human resources paradigm
Recruitment and staff turnover	
Recruitment undertaken without reference to local community and its labour market	Recruitment based on careful analysis of local community and its labour market
Ad hoc, unplanned recruitment to meet immediate needs	Recruitment based on planned human resources strategy
Employees recruited on basis of immediate skills needs	Employees recruited on basis of potential for development
Recruitment/'poaching' of staff from competitor organizations	Employees recruited locally or developed within the company
Unclear skills and attribute requirements when recruiting	Clear statement of recruitment objectives and use of person specifications
Recruitment process exclusively on basis of employer needs only	Recruitment process to match needs of both employers and potential employees
Expatriate staff recruited on a long-term basis	Expatriate staff only employed to meet short-term needs to support development of local staff
High staff turnover seen as inevitable and/or desirable	High staff turnover not fostered
No measures to reduce staff turnover	Active company policies to avoid unwanted staff turnover
No concern as to why staff leave	Active exit interview policy
Promotion and career development	
Few internal opportunities for promotion and development	Career planning and tracking within company in anticipation of promotion opportunities
No career ladder/unclear criteria for promotion	Clearly defined and transparent career ladder with accessible criteria for promotion
Promotion to 'plug gaps' with no preparatory training	Planned promotion programme with preparatory training programme
Key staff imported from outside/abroad	Key staff grown/developed within company/locality
Part-time or seasonal staff excluded from training/development/promotion opportunities	Part-time or seasonal staff integrated into training/development/promotion system
No long-term commitment to seasonal staff	Long-term commitment to key seasonal staff
Career mobility seen as disloyal/disruptive	Career mobility recognised as beneficial to the individual
Opportunities limited for minorities on basis of gender, ethnicity, disability etc.	Full equal opportunities in promotion and career development
Rewards and benefits	
Company offers minimum rewards and benefits	Company offers competitive rewards and benefits
Employment conditions are designed to suit employer's needs only	Employment conditions are designed to balance employer's and employee's needs
Rewards and benefits reflect centralized company policy and practice	Rewards and benefits are sensitive to local and individual circumstances and needs
Workplace flexibility designed to suit employer's requirements	Workplace flexibility designed as an employer-employee partnership with mutual benefits
Staff attitudes to company a matter of indifference	Staff attitudes closely monitored

Table 10.2	continued

Old human resources practice	Sustainable human resources paradigm
Employees not valued	Employee commitment and feelings of belonging fostered
Initiative and responsibility not encouraged	Organizational citizenship behaviour encouraged and rewarded
Pilfering and theft accepted by 'turning a blind eye'	Rewards and benefits mean pilfering and theft is not a temptation
Education, training and development	
Training focuses on technical skills development	Training recognizes generic skills as complementary to technical skills
Training and development is not planned	Planned training and development policies and strategies
Training seen as the responsibility of training specialists	Training recognized as the responsibility of all supervisors and managers
Lack of senior management commitment to training	Full commitment by senior management to training
Training operates in isolation from other human resources practices	Training and development linked to opportunities for promotion and job enrichment
Dislocation between education system and industry	Partnership between education system and industry
Education programmes have limited industry application	Education programmes based on identified needs
No progression and learning opportunities	Progressive learning opportunities for all employees
Inflexible and location/time constrained learning opportunities	Flexible learning opportunities, using range of learning technologies
Industry-developed skills and competencies not recognized by education system	Full credit given for skills and competencies developed in industry
Management culture	
Employee seen as short-term expedient	Employees seen as a key resource
Employees perceived as a cost	Employees seen as an asset
Authoritarian, remote management culture	Democratic, participative management culture
Authority vested in management alone	Responsibility widely delegated to all levels of staff
Employees remote from decision-making	Employees actively involved in decisions that affect their area of responsibility
No sensitivity to local culture and traditions	Sympathetic adaptation to local culture and traditions
Inflexible imposition of corporate culture	Corporate culture responsive to local culture and needs
Labour-market planning	
No labour-market planning at company or national level	Detailed labour-market planning process in place at company or national level
Human resource issues ignored in strategic planning	Human resource issues central to strategic planning
Fragmentation of labour-market planning	Integrated approach to labour-market planning
Labour-market considerations not considered in planning for tourism, hospitality and leisure	Labour-market considerations to the fore in planning for tourism, hospitality and leisure
Quality in tourism, hospitality and leisure seen in purely product terms	People central to the delivery of quality in tourism, hospitality and leisure
Community detached from/hostile to tourism, hospitality and leisure	Community integral to support of tourism, hospitality and leisure

And yet, as we noted Chapter 3, there is a definite link between how employees at all levels in the tourism and hospitality industry are perceived by their managers, the delivery of quality service to customers and the outcome in terms of profitability. Within the traditional paradigm outlined in the left-hand column of Table 10.2, employees are an afterthought to the main focus of the business. Within the sustainable or integrative organizational model, business functions are designed around people. Schlesinger and Heskett (1991) argue in favour of the approach implicit within the sustainable model which they term the 'cycle of quality service':

> Capable workers, who are well trained and fairly compensated, provide better service, require less supervision and [are] more likely to remain on the job. For individual companies, this means enhanced competitiveness. (Schlesinger and Heskett 1991, p.72)

One good example of how key aspects of the model of sustainable human resource development has been broadly applied comes from Taj Hotels in India (Mahesh 1993). This relates to the preparation for opening of a 34-bedroom Taj Gateway Hotel in Chiplun, a rural community halfway between Bombay and Goa. The location was one with no tradition of employment in the tourism sector and considerable social and cultural antagonism to the idea. The hotel's 11-step human resource development plan is, clearly, very culturally specific, but that is the essence of sustainable human resource development in tourism. The plan is outlined in the case study that follows.

This book addresses the application of the 'right-hand' principles from the model in Table 10.2 in a wide-ranging sense so that the reader will acquire a rather clearer understanding of their implications by the end. The theme of sustainability within the management of human resources is underpinned by assumptions about managerial, corporate and governmental responsibility, depending on which level the sustainable model is applied. Indeed, it draws in essence upon the notion of a social contract between, on the one hand, businesses and an industry sector and, on the other, the community in which they operate and the people that they employ. In this context, this book derives its inspiration from the eighteenth century, from writers like Locke and Rousseau who argued for the notion of responsible coexistence between people, their endeavours and the wider environment.

Case Study *The Taj Gateway Hotel, Chiplun, India: Human Resource Development Plan*

The Gateway concept was introduced by Taj to complement their five-star properties in rural areas and smaller cities. They offer a good quality and simple form of hospitality, designed for leisure and business travellers from both the international and domestic markets. Gateway hotels operate in locations where there is no tradition of hotel work within the local community. As a consequence of their remote locations, Taj's human resources approach to their Gateway properties includes a number of key features:

1. Human resource requirements for the hotel had to be finalized a full year before opening.

2. With the exception of the positions of hotel manager, the heads of food production, service and rooms division and a temporary training manager, all other positions were to be filled through recruitment of local personnel, following appropriate training.

3. All schools within the area were to be visited and graduating students inducted into what a hotel is all about, and what kinds of jobs and careers are available. Given the orthodox and, primarily, rural background of the local community, the very concept of a hotel was so unfamiliar that this first communication was far more complex than would have been the case in an urbanized, more developed region.

4. After considerable persuasion designed to overcome local prejudices against the hotel and catering industry in general, interviews were set up and a tentative shortlist of candidates was prepared. As most of the candidates could speak only their local dialect and had no knowledge or experience of the hotel industry, the criteria for selection were restricted to personality, ability to smile, the ability to contribute to teamwork (demonstrated through games participation), average intelligence and physical fitness.

5. Among those selected were many who had difficulty in communicating to their parents or guardians what they had been selected for; in these cases the hotel manager and the training manager visited the homes in order to help communicate with the parents.

6. Those finally selected were put through a rigorous medical examination to ensure that only those in perfect health were hired. This process also helped to communicate the high priority given to health and hygiene by the hotel company.

7. Commencing with the very simple procedures (in this case, the use of forks and knives as the local population were unfamiliar with these), the very raw and inexperienced recruits were educated and trained in different aspects of hotel work. With the objective of facilitating easy job rotation and mobility, many were trained as multi-skilled employees; for example, a resort attendant could work as a room boy, gardener, waiter or utility assistant.

8. Within six to eight months of joining, most of the employees were adequately trained for the opening of the hotel; for example, those trained in kitchen work could not only prepare a range of basic dishes but could also complete a portion control format and an itemized cost sheet.

9. In anticipation of possible attrition, a number of supernumerary staff were recruited and trained and, in the event, this provision proved vital as a number of staff did leave before the hotel opened.

10. Internal systems for grievance management and counselling were established, wages were formalized and all personnel systems were in place from the outset so that potential causes of labour unrest were anticipated and minimized.

11. The training manager was withdrawn only after all systems had been established and the small management team was in position with a fully trained staff. For the first two years, thereafter, central support was provided in the area of industrial relations and associated personnel concerns but, in all other respects, the hotel was able to function independently in the human resource domain.

Case discussion questions

1. The Taj Gateway case presents an example of human resource planning from India. In what ways and with what modifications might this human resource model be applied to the following new tourism and hospitality developments?

   (a) A beach bar and restaurant in Lindos, Rhodes, Greece.

   (b) A budget hotel and restaurant on the outskirts of Bochum, Germany.

   (c) A five-star resort hotel on the Black Sea in Constantia, Romania, recently renovated and operating under a Western European management contract.

   (d) An international theme park, due to open outside Barcelona, Spain.

   (e) Event caterers contracted to provide for 500 000 visitors to the three public days of the British Grand Prix at Silverstone, England.

   (f) A start-up Malaysian airline formed to compete on major domestic and international business routes within South-East Asia.

   (g) A duty-free shop in Paris, established to cater exclusively for the Japanese visitor market.

   (h) The first overseas representative office located in London to be operated by the National Tourist Board of a small Pacific nation.

2. Identify how and the extent to which the Taj Gateway case illustrates the practice of sustainable human resource management that was proposed in Table 10.2.

Sustainable human resource management in tourism, hospitality and leisure – a broader perspective

Thus far, we have considered sustainability in tourism, hospitality and leisure from a relatively practical level, with a focus on organizations and, to a lesser extent, on sectors at a national level. There is a debate that emanates from the discussion in this book which raises broader themes and, by way of conclusion to this book, we will consider some of these here. At its heart, sustainable human resource management can be viewed from a number of perspectives.

A moral dimension

Sustainability by its nature has an underlying moral dimension in the humanist tradition which, at its simplest, argues that people respond positively to good treatment and negatively to poor management. This is an approach that contrasts markedly with that espoused by the narrow Puritanism which has dominated much industrial development in Western Europe and is at the root of the traditional human resource model. The traditional approach is represented by the attitude that individuals are lazy, self-seeking and basically dishonest with the result that close supervision and punitive behaviour are seen as the only means by which to ensure productive and honest work. The implicit outcome of the implementation of sustainable human resource policies is one in which the employees are seen in positive terms as assets within a company and are treated, managed and rewarded accordingly.

What is argued for here reflects a rejection of the extremes of unsustainable human resource policies, as encapsulated by Orwell in the 1930s but still readily found in some sectors of the tourism, hospitality and leisure industry today. The origins of this argument, thus, have much in common with the objectives of some of the great nineteenth-century industrial reformers, who looked to create alternatives to the existing working conditions in the 'dark satanic mills'. Practical reformers such as Robert Owen with his New Lanark Project and Lord Leverhulme with Port Sunlight, as well as the Cadbury, Rowntree and Wills families, were motivated by religious and moral factors but at the same time did not neglect the business dimension of their projects. Their endeavours were not purely philanthropic but driven by a belief that it was possible and desirable to invest in people in order to increase their contribution to the enterprise and, thus, to enhance profitability. The concern of men such as Leverhulme and Owen was wider than the workplace alone. They saw the responsibilities of employers in paternalistic terms to include the total social and moral well-being of their employees and their families and thus their projects went considerably beyond the immediate workplace to include housing, educational, health, social, welfare and religious dimensions. They were, thus, sustainable in the context of community in that they recognized the links between a stable and contented wider community environment and efficient and profitable production in the workplace.

The moral force of good workplace practices in terms of conditions, remuneration and associated benefits has received the backing of the force of law in many countries and the worst excesses, especially in relation to health and safety considerations, have been ameliorated in developed but not all developing countries. The most extreme practices are, inevitably, those associated with large manufacturing industries. However, as we have seen in Chapter 5, the working environment in some sub-sectors of the international tourism, hospitality and leisure industry is far from exemplary. Exploitative remuneration and conditions, especially in relation to the use of female, youth and minorities labour, is relatively widespread and reflects the application of old human resource practices.

As has already been suggested with respect to the great nineteenth-century reformers, the underlying purpose of sustainability, in moral terms, is not solely altruistic. Provision of good working conditions and competitive remuneration, among other aspects of the total employment environment, are designed to provide long-term benefits to both employers and employees on the basis that a happy working environment is also a productive one. This analysis has additional force in the context of the tourism, hospitality and leisure industry because of the relationship between business profitability, the delivery of quality service and the role of low-skilled, front-line staff. This is the association that we explored in Chapter 4 and provides one of the most compelling arguments in favour of the provision of a workplace environment that is designed to meet employee needs and ensure their contentment and commitment to the company or business. This, in itself, is a major prerequisite before effective internal marketing can be introduced.

Community responsibility

A sense of community responsibility is a second perspective that derives from the sustainable model for human resource management in the tourism, hospitality and leisure industry. Community responsibility emanates from the notion that an employer, large or small, derives profits and a livelihood on the basis of the skills and toil of local labour and that such benefit must be balanced by a sense of responsibility and loyalty to that community. This notion of community responsibility is a commitment that has weakened greatly in manufacturing as the structure and ownership of the great industrial companies has shifted from the individual or family to the faceless conglomerate. In particular, such changes have heralded moves from individual entrepreneurship to corporate ownership, large multinational conglomerates have taken over from individual enterprises, technological substitution has reduced dependency on high levels of unskilled labour, and the perspectives provided by globalization enable companies to base their activity in the most profitable location worldwide, with little regard to local considerations.

The sense of community identity between manufacturing companies and specific locations extends beyond these British examples and includes similar geographical associations throughout Europe, Japan and North America. Ford, traditionally associated with Detroit, now plans its production capacity on a global basis, involving manufacturing plants in the Americas, Europe and Australasia. Volkswagen's investments in Seat of Spain and Skoda in the Czech Republic provide the German company with the potential to move production from its high-cost base in Germany to cheaper locations if necessary and, indeed, this implicit threat has facilitated significant changes to working practices in Volkswagen's German plants.

However, there are fewer such clear links between major service companies and the communities within which they are located. The Littlewoods leisure and retail empire, based in Liverpool, is one exception, with roots deep in that community. However, frequently, where some level of connection and dependency has developed, the links are much more fragile and vulnerable to changes in the business and technological environment. The nature of business in most sub-sectors of the tourism, hospitality and leisure industry is such that little long-term corporate identity with a specific location can be seen. By its nature, the industry is one of dispersal and not concentration, where production and service cannot be centralized. It is, as I have said earlier, an industry of every parish. There are some partial exceptions. Major airlines tend to concentrate their operations in one or, at most, a small number of locations. Thus, a very high proportion of the British Airways workforce is based at or close to Heathrow Airport, London, but increasingly some functions are being sited elsewhere in more cost-effective locations. Likewise, 'honey pot' theme parks such as Disney require a level of investment so that local presence in the business culture is not realistic. Even Disney, however, has dispersed to five major world locations (two in the USA, two in Asia and one in France) and has developed a policy of local retail outlets which both merchandise Disney brands and provide dispersed promotion and access to its products in support of the main locations.

While the scale of many tourism, hospitality and leisure businesses is such that a widely recognized identity between one company and its community is not that common, in another sense the very smallness of most enterprises necessitates a local focus which may be absent in larger firms. A high level of family involvement in the operation and management of many concerns implies a local commitment and such businesses will generally supplement their skills requirements from within the local labour pool – they are unlikely to have the resources to look more widely for expertise. Furthermore, the seasonal nature of many such businesses means that long-term employment commitments to those from outside of the locality are unlikely. In this sense, therefore, the growing strength of multiple unit tourism, hospitality and leisure businesses on a national and transnational level, combined with the market power provided by effective website and reservations management systems, could weaken the local community connection of the industry. At the same time, internet technology allows smaller companies to compete globally for market share to good effect.

In addition, moves towards standardization in the delivery of product and service in larger corporately owned operations has significant implications for the role that a local labour market has to play in meeting the skills demands of such businesses. On the one hand, there is likely to be a reduction in the overall skills levels required in response to automation and standardization, while on the other opportunities for local entrepreneurship will also be reduced and management requirements met from within a central planning process. Such changes will, ultimately, have the potential to undermine the sustainability of the industry in human resource terms especially as demographic pressures increase the competitiveness of the labour market for semi- and unskilled labour, unless the corporate tourism and hospitality sector recognizes the importance of its community links.

There is a sense beyond the individual business in which the tourism, hospitality and leisure industry does have a strong community link and identity and that is as a collective entity. Many locations are identified as tourism destinations, whether we are talking about the great cities of Sydney, Rome or St Petersburg; the Greek islands; the Rocky Mountain ski resorts or touring and sporting terrain such as west Cork in Ireland. In these locations, the tourism, hospitality and leisure industry, if it does exist as a collective body, has strong community associations. In economic terms such destinations to a greater or lesser degree depend upon tourism and hospitality for their livelihood and any significant downturn in business will affect the prosperity of the communities concerned. Tourism, hospitality and leisure also can provide the basis and rationale for investment in infrastructure such as utilities and transportation, which are of direct community benefit and can contribute to the preservation of local historic and cultural resources as well as providing new ones, such as the site of the Tate Modern Gallery in St Ives, Cornwall. In this sense, tourism, as Murphy (1985) rightly argues, is a community resource and also a community responsibility. This responsibility extends to ensuring the sustainability of human resource policies and practices that operate within it. Sustainability, in this context, applies to the manner in which local tourism, hospitality and leisure employers relate to the local labour market, the extent to which they actively encourage local people to work within the industry or, by way of contrast, seek to recruit from possibly cheaper labour pools elsewhere. It also relates to the extent to which the tourism, hospitality and leisure industry and their public representatives ensure that there is educational and training provision locally which is designed to cater for the skills requirements of employers in that resort community, thus enhancing the local skills base and reducing the imperative to attract trained personnel from elsewhere to meet specific needs. The coordinated efforts of the tourism, hospitality and leisure industry and local political interests in Kerry, Ireland, can be given considerable credit in the establishment of specific training courses for the industry at the Tralee Regional Technical College during the late 1980s, thus providing educational and training opportunities within the community as well as meeting skills shortages within the local industry.

The value of intrinsic motivation in the workplace

The sustainable model also has implications for the way in which managers in the tourism, hospitality and leisure industry perceive their employees and understand how they are motivated and what provides satisfaction in the workplace. This perception, in part, derives from the sense of loyalty to a community but also reflects a perspective on the individual that is different from the old model, with its emphasis upon short-term results and externally driven rewards and punishments. Traditional human resource management views people as an immediate and dispensable resource, from which maximum productivity must be extracted with the overall objective of enhancing profitability in the short to medium term. This view can be traced back to Adam Smith and the notion of rational individuality in all things within the economic sphere. Smith's perspective leads to the notion that people will only perform to their optimum through extrinsic motivation, primarily through the allocation or withdrawal of financial rewards or other such benefits. The concept that people may be motivated by other forces than extrinsic rewards, particularly money, is often associated with the United States but is also prevalent in many other countries.

Smith's economic individualism gained support from Darwin's thesis that all species, including humans, adapt to the environment which they face and that those which adapt best survive while those which fail to change become extinct. Applied to the individual and to the economic world, this leads to the notion of the survival of the fittest in a competitive world, where only those companies and those individuals best equipped to succeed will actually do so and those that fail do so as part of the natural order of things. There are also implications of a meritocracy, where all individuals start with an equal chance of success and those that are fittest attract the accolades associated with achievement while those without the necessary attributes will remain stationary or may indeed be cast aside.

The logical outcome of a 'marriage' between Smith and Darwin is a working environment that is designed to maximize profitability while, at the same time, rewarding those individuals who contribute most to the achievement of this objective. At the same time, those unable to make the required level of contribution do not benefit from the company's success or, indeed, may be penalized for their failure to contribute. This approach leads to short-term perspectives on employment, whereby staff are seen as an expendable resource that only have a role to play for as long as their contribution is one towards profitability. The notion of a right to employment on a continued basis which, until recently, formed the backbone of Japanese business practice, cannot reside comfortably alongside Smith's free-market labour environment or the survival of the fittest in business Darwinism.

This combination of Smith and Darwin has a third dimension within the old human resource model and that is the underlying Puritanism to which we have referred earlier. This combines the notion of primarily extrinsic motivating factors in the workplace with competitiveness based on survival, and adds the belief 'that Man was a self-seeking, greedy person whose skills, abilities and miseries at work were to be dealt with as commodities to be supervised, checked, evaluated and traded' (Mahesh 1994, p.27).

The traditional human resource management model can also be linked to the Maslowian model of human motivation. Maslow's model postulates that behaviour is determined in response to a hierarchy of needs. On the basis of this hierarchy, people will only be motivated by a particular level provided that needs with respect to all levels below have been met. As Maslow put it:

> For our chronically and extremely hungry man, Utopia can be defined simply as a place where there is plenty of food. He tends to think that, if only he is guaranteed food for the rest of his life, he will be perfectly happy and will never want anything more. Life tends to be defined in terms of eating. Anything else will be defined as unimportant. Freedom, love, community feeling, respect, philosophy, may all be waved aside as fripperies that are useless, since they fail to fill the stomach. Such a man may fairly be said to live by bread alone. (Maslow 1943, quoted in Mahesh 1994, pp.36–7)

In many respects, the old, non-sustainable model of human resource management is based upon assumptions that an employee's prime motivators at work are those at the base of the Maslow hierarchy, with particular emphasis upon the physiological and safety dimensions. Rewards in this context are primarily extrinsic, tangible and immediate and can readily be equated with an economic return for labour provided. This perspective must be seen in its historical and social context. Mahesh rightly points out that the systemization of work, which is attributed to the thinking of men such as Frederick William Taylor and Henry Ford, occurred at a time when labour in the United States was in considerable surplus and a prime motivator for many immigrant families was the ability to provide food and a home. Rewards beyond these levels on the Maslow hierarchy were, by comparison, relatively unimportant and employees were willing to accept repetitive and demeaning work routines as their only source of income. Such conditions no longer pertain in Western Europe although they have to some extent re-emerged in Eastern Europe.

In an environment where absolute poverty and destitution is not a widespread problem, employees' expectations bypass lower, primarily extrinsically motivated needs in the Maslow hierarchy and look to the satisfaction of personal requirements in terms of the intrinsic, which is belongingness, esteem and self-actualization. Mahesh (1994) reports a number of empirical studies which amply demonstrate that intrinsic motivation has greater force and leads to more permanent modifications in behaviour than is the case with primarily extrinsic motivators located at the base of Maslow's hierarchy. The traditional human resource management model is mainly in its motivation and, therefore, cannot cater fully for more complex human aspirations.

By contrast, the new paradigm seeks to cater for such needs. The sustainable human resource approach requires that both employers and employees take a long-term view of their relationship in the mutual interests of both parties, of their customers and, ultimately, of company profitability. It is a perspective which recognizes that quality service, a key contributor to competitive advantage in the tourism, hospitality and leisure industry, depends for its delivery on committed, well-trained, well-rewarded and, above all, empowered front-line staff. Empowered behaviour, important, in many respects for quality service, cannot be developed on the basis of extrinsic rewards alone. Its achievement depends upon management commitment, from the top, in the form of trust and faith in the capacity of all employees to deliver the desired service and a willingness to invest, through training and development of the individual, in the long-term objective of its attainment. The corollary with respect to employees is a long-term commitment to the company and its objectives and a rejection of mobility for the sake of short-term benefit.

The role in the delivery of service and customer care that is implied by empowerment certainly takes the notion of motivation within the Maslow hierarchy into the realms of belongingness and esteem if not into that of self-actualization. Employees must, within the empowerment model, have a true sense of belonging to the company for whom they work and this sense can be generated both by the faith and trust which employers and management bestow upon their staff and from the implementation of effective internal marketing practices. The reward is esteem in the eyes not only of the employer but also of the customer. The notion of servility and inferiority which dogs so many service encounters in the tourism and hospitality industry is much less likely to occur in an environment of true empowerment, where front-line employees have both pride in what they are doing and the authority to relate to their guests as equals. The Ritz Carlton approach, to which reference has already been made earlier in this book, represents a good example of service on the basis of equal status but different needs and roles in the service encounter.

Belief in the individual

Sustainability goes beyond a perspective on the factors which motivate employees in the workplace and reflects upon the way in which managers and supervisors view the potential for development and the capacity for growth of those with whom they are working. The traditional human resource model sees people in the specific context of the job that needs to be done. Thus recruitment and training strategies are designed to enable a business to meet its immediate skills requirements, to 'plug a gap' in the workforce which results from attrition by a previous post-holder or as a result in growth in demand. This view rarely looks beyond the immediacy of the specific vacancy in question and thus the individual who applies for the job is evaluated in terms of their ability to fill that gap here and now. It is rare to find companies that take this view, giving consideration to their existing human resources for the vacancy in question unless the personnel profile of individuals who are available exactly fit the requirements of the vacancy.

Sustainability in human resource terms, by contrast, means taking a longer-term perspective and considering the potential of the individual to grow within that job towards greater responsibility or skills demands. It also implies recognition that what an individual actually achieves in a job is closely related to the expectations that significant others have of him or her. In the work context, this means managers or supervisors. The consequences of what is known as the 'Pygmalion effect' mean that, in simple terms, low expectations deliver poor performance while high expectations enable individuals to excel. In other words, individual and group performance is significantly affected, in both positive and negative terms, by the expectations that others have for that individual or group. The implications of the Pygmalion effect include a number of elements:

1. What managers expect of their subordinates and the way they treat them largely determine their performance and career progress.
2. A unique characteristic of superior managers is their ability to create high-performance expectations that subordinates can fulfil.
3. Less effective managers fail to develop similar expectations and, as a consequence, the productivity of their subordinates suffers.
4. Subordinates, more often than not, appear to do what they believe is expected of them.
5. The highest output is achieved by jobholders whose supervisors expect high performance.

This argument that people in the workplace perform according to the expectations that are held about them is of considerable importance in the context of the tourism, hospitality and leisure industry. We have seen in earlier chapters that the industry remains one of high labour intensity, with only limited potential for technology substitution and that much of this labour is inputted at a low-skills level. We have also reviewed the role of front-line staff in the delivery of service within most tourism, hospitality and leisure businesses, noting that these staff are frequently the members of the organization with the lowest level of skills and, in terms of remuneration and status, perceived to him the least valued. These staff also deliver the vast majority of an organization's 'moments of truth' to the customer and, in doing so, play a major role in the relationship marketing effort of the company. This delivery of service generally takes place without supervision or direct control.

Yet it is true to say that, within the traditional human resource management model in tourism, hospitality and leisure, companies have relatively limited expectations of their front-line staff. They are readily dispensable at times of reduced demand and are the last to benefit from enhanced rewards and benefits when the company is performing well. It is a widely held expectation that front-line staff will exhibit limited loyalty to the company and will move elsewhere without compunction. Training and development are frequently seen as a wasted investment for this group, as staff will in all probability use their newfound skills as bargaining tools in the search for better employment elsewhere.

Recruitment is based on short-term expectations and in order to meet immediate requirements. All in all, employers have what they would describe as 'realistic' expectations of staff in this category and base their relationship with individuals upon such expectations. The logic of Pygmalion is that front-line staff, faced with such expectations, will deliver precisely what is anticipated, certainly no more and possibly less. As a result, a vicious circle of limited expectations and limited performance is established. The consequences of this scenario, from the employer's perspective, are those which characterize the old human resource model in Table 10.2 and are manifest in terms of:

- limited vision in recruitment;
- a failure to identify the real potential of those who are selected;
- a total lack of, or at best low investment in, training and development;
- a lack of nurturing for future growth and enhancement;
- a disinclination to delegate or give responsibility to front-line staff; and
- expectations of limited capability, low company loyalty and rapid staff turnover.

From the point of view of the front-line employees, this scenario results in attitudes and behaviour such as:

- a low sense of loyalty to a company that appears to place limited value in the individual;
- a frustration at the lack of opportunity for growth or enhancement;
- a reluctance on the part of the highly motivated and ambitious to apply for jobs within the company;
- limited motivation to perform better or to raise productivity or service standards;
- a disinclination to accept delegated responsibility; and
- high levels of staff turnover.

Within the sustainable paradigm, this negative expectation cycle can be broken. Expectations in this context are not driven by the notion that individuals have limitless potential and that all members of staff or new recruits can become a chief executive, an award-winning chef or a top equestrian instructor. Rather it is a perspective which treats each individual on his or her merits, recognizes their individuality and seeks to nurture and develop the potential that exists to its maximum level. It is an approach which does not make generalized assumptions about people based on current employment status/level, gender, race, physical disability, educational background or the level of the post that is currently held. Above all, it is an approach that demands open-mindedness and the ability to recognize the potential for growth in all individuals. From an employer's point of view, recognizing the power of the Pygmalion effect has a number of important consequences which are implicit in the sustainable paradigm. These include:

- recruitment that considers the longer-term needs of the company rather than just filling an immediate gap and thus looks at individuals from the point of view of their potential as well as their existing skills/experience profile;

- recruitment that looks at existing staff and their potential when appointing to positions of responsibility before turning to outside sources of labour;
- management attitudes and style that support individuals in their aspirations for growth and enhancement within the company and, if need be, elsewhere;
- encouragement for staff to participate in training and development in order to meet personal and company needs and objectives;
- management and supervision that seeks to pass responsibility to front-line staff through delegation and empowerment;
- rewards and benefits that encourage performance, loyalty and long service; and
- provision of clear and public criteria for promotion and access to development which do not discriminate on the basis of gender, race, physical disability or any other factor.

By the same token, the Pygmalion effect within the sustainable paradigm has a number of implications from the perspective of the employee. These include:

- viewing employment as a process which provides opportunities for growth, development and enhancement for those that have the skills and aspirations in that direction, but also acknowledging that there may be some delimiters on this process within a specific company;
- recognizing that growth, development and enhancement are earned over a period of time and are not a right bestowed on the basis of specific training or qualifications;
- being realistic in the workplace and recognizing the personal limitations that exist in terms of potential and achievement, or what Mahesh (1994, p.7) calls the concept of 'threshold limitations';
- demonstrating commitment and participating in training and development opportunities in the workplace even though immediate enhancement and rewards may not follow; and
- accepting that managers and supervisors make employment decisions in good faith and without prejudice or discrimination on the basis of gender, race, physical disability or other factors.

Therefore this perspective on sustainability implies a focus on the individual and recognition of the potential for growth and development that exists, to differing levels and in various ways, in each individual. In the absence of this faith, true empowerment is impossible and, as a consequence, genuinely effective service quality cannot be achieved in the tourism, hospitality and leisure industry.

A long-term perspective on the management of people

Sustainability in human resource terms implies a commitment to the individual and his or her potential for growth and development. This, by its very nature, necessitates a long-term perspective with respect to the organization's human resource requirements. The old human resource model in Table 10.2 points to widespread practice in the tourism, hospitality and leisure industry of giving priority to short-term objectives and to viewing people as a readily adjustable resource which can be manipulated in response to market changes, especially on the demand side. This problem is well illustrated by companies in a number of sub-sectors which invest heavily in the development of physical plant and in attendant marketing prior to the opening of a new or expanded tourism, hospitality and leisure facility but only give last-minute attention to meeting the skills requirements of the project. This is true at a regional or national level as well as within individual projects. Schools and colleges are typically built in response to a human resource crisis within a fledgling industry rather than in parallel, or indeed in advance of them. The consequences of a lack of planning in this domain can be considerably in terms of, for example, poor service delivery or the need to draft in expertise from outside of the community, region or even country in order to meet new skills demands. Likewise, traditional deficiencies, especially the lack of human resource planning at times of growth, may necessitate a company to recruit from outside in order to fill positions of responsibility in the organization rather than investing in the planned development of existing staff in anticipation of change.

The human resource development lead time in tourism and hospitality is generally considerably greater than is the case with respect to the product or marketing development of a project or area. The sustainable human resource paradigm within tourism, hospitality and leisure focuses upon the planning needs in this area at all levels, whether relating to a small company expanding or diversifying its markets or to a city or region planning to re-orientate its economic and employment structure in the direction of tourism and hospitality from other, possibly declining, areas of activity. A number of industrial cities in Britain, such as Bradford, Glasgow and Liverpool, are examples of locations where such transition has taken place in recent years. At a national level, the process of transition is something facing many countries in Central and Eastern European as well as in Central Asia. Planning of this nature may be required at the company level or within a wider context and, therefore, frequently will involve a number of agencies and providers, including those within the industry itself, as well as education and training organizations and support funding agencies. The application of integrated planning mechanisms, such as those discussed in Chapter 9, becomes an important contributor to sustainability in this area.

Sustainable human resource planning is also an important factor in ensuring that a community's true potential, in terms of the skills and related attributes that it has to offer, are fully recognized. This has important implications in terms of the discussion in Chapters 6 and 7 about recognizing the potential of all sections of the community and overcoming the limited representation of women and ethnic minorities among senior positions in the industry. We have already discussed the dangers inherent in underestimating the potential of the individual for growth and development. The same principle is true at a community and, indeed, a national level. The long-standing practice of employing expatriate management and technical staff in the major hotels of many developing countries in Asia, Africa and the Caribbean is justified on the grounds that local skills do not exist to take on such responsibilities. Such an assessment may well have been true at the onset when no tourism and hospitality tradition existed in the area and when little or no local training was available. However, such an argument loses its potency in locations such as Hong Kong and Singapore where the skills exist to operate every other kind of complex industrial and service industry, including world-rated airlines, but hotels still preserve their expatriate connection.

Unless the growth and development potential of the local community is fully recognized and acted upon, the original analysis will be come self-fulfilling and, indeed, local expertise will not be recognized. Furthermore, senior positions in hotels will become seen as the preserve of expatriates and ambitious and able young people from the local community will not opt for the industry in their career choices. There is a clear danger that, in the absence of investment in education and training, major tourism, hospitality and leisure companies will continue to fail to recognize and develop local potential to the highest levels.

At a more local level, assumptions are readily made about the ability of a community to respond to changes in the economic structure and provide the required expertise for the tourism, hospitality and leisure industry after the decline of other, traditional industries. On the basis of such assumptions, companies may neglect to test local potential and look elsewhere for the necessary skills. Such assumptions become self-fulfilling as members of the local community see that quality opportunities and those offering scope for development and enhancement are taken by outsiders.

McDonaldization and sustainability

In this book we have encountered a number of conundrums and their satisfactory resolution has only in part been addressed. One of the more important of these is that of how to reconcile two seemingly incompatible trends within the international tourism, hospitality and leisure. On the one hand, the service revolution has established quality in this domain as a prime market demand, and differentiation in terms of service has increasingly been shown to be a major factor in consumer choice. This in turn has led to articulation of the concepts of internal marketing, staff empowerment and organizational citizenship behaviour, essential ingredients in the effective delivery of quality service in the tourism, hospitality and leisure industry. These, in turn, are also concepts that have close associations with the application of sustainable human resource policies and practices.

The counter-balancing weight on the scales of this conundrum is that of McDonaldization or the rational standardization of product and service delivery within the tourism and hospitality industry. McDonaldization, a term which Ritzer (2004) introduces to the vocabulary and so clearly articulates, is a natural development from earlier Taylorism and Fordism in the manufacturing context. However, according to Ritzer's thesis, McDonaldization represents a process which has impacted upon the wider social domain beyond the workplace and created a culture which cherishes speed and convenience of delivery, labour-saving attributes and the certainty and confidence provided to the consumer by the standardization of product and service delivery.

The logical consequences of McDonaldization in human resource terms involve the de-skilling of many jobs in the international tourism, hospitality and leisure industry. The process of standardization in terms of product and service delivery, combined with the implementation of computerization in accounting, control, sales and marketing and a host of related areas, means that the nature of work is changing in most sectors of tourism and hospitality, especially in those operations affiliated to the larger, multinational companies. This impact applies at all operational and management levels and reduces the pre-entry and qualification levels required by the company. It also limits the investment that companies need to make in order to prepare new entrants as well as in anticipation of promotion or change.

As a result of these changes and their impact, McDonaldization contributes towards the perpetuation of a low-wage and low-status environment in the tourism, hospitality and leisure industry and this is a trend that is likely to be maintained despite demographic pressures in the labour markets of developed countries. McDonaldization does not sit comfortably with the concept of sustainable human resource development in the tourism, hospitality and leisure industry. It reduces the skills requirements of work thus contributing to a lessening of the overall skills base within a community and eliminates from the industry local people are able to take on many of the more qualified, professionally focused positions within the workforce which tend to offer higher remuneration and better career prospects. McDonaldization also has an in-built acceptance of some of what have been described as the negative dimensions of the old human resource model, notably high labour turnover and a lack of opportunities for enhancement and development.

McDonaldization views labour as a transitory resource, readily replaced, and because of the low skills and training requirement, such turnover has little impact on the delivery of product or service. Because labour is transitory, there is little need to avoid repetitive and demotivating routines in the workplace because tolerance will not be tested in the relatively short period of time that most individuals will spend in the job. Employees, in turn, accept the parameters of the jobs that they are undertaking and do not look for anything beyond short-term outcomes from their work and the satisfaction of lower-order motivational needs. This short-termism, in turn, contributes to the overall image of the industry as an employer and deters many of the potentially more able among school and college leavers from applying for other than temporary and transitory positions. Little by way of a long-term commitment is made or stake taken within the local labour market by companies which have focused on standardization, and this is the antithesis of the sustainable paradigm. The alternative and undoubtedly much more expensive focus of investing in the individual and in the community is of long-term benefit to both the company and the people it works with, and through this process to the quality of product and service that is delivered to the consumer. It is only with long-term commitment to the individual and, through him or her, to the community, that true empowerment can he achieved which, in turn, allows employees to obtain more than lower levels of motivational benefits from the workplace.

At the end of the day, there is no clear resolution to the McDonaldization–sustainability conundrum. While considering the impact of standardization in the European tourism and hospitality industry and its growing importance at a macro level, it is important not to forget that the majority of small businesses in the industry remain inured from its immediate effects. However, the not inconsiderable effects of budget hotels upon traditional small-town accommodation establishments in France and Britain as well as the consequences of fast-food restaurants on more traditional competition point to some of the areas of potentially significant impact which cannot be ignored. The eventual outcome with respect to this conundrum may be a wide and growing gulf between those operations, on the one hand, which focus upon depersonalized systems and the delivery of low-cost products and services with a minimal skills input, and those, on the other, which focus on high-cost, premium service delivery in a personalized, customized format, with an emphasis on quality and empowered front-line staff and management.

Sustainability and social responsibility

We commenced this chapter with a consideration of sustainability in the context of its moral dimension from a largely humanist perspective. The morality of the argument is also entirely compatible with the teaching of most mainstream religions and, indeed, with common sense. Its only possible source of conflict comes in relation to the short-term cost of sustainable policies and the impact that such approaches have on the somewhat blinkered judgement of financial investors. There is no doubt that the human resource practices which sustainability implies can be costly to implement and maintain in the short term and there remains reluctance on the part of stock market investors to view investment in people as a worthwhile risk. Indeed, pressures have been inexorable in the other direction in recent years with plaudits awarded to those companies which have succeeded in reducing the labour requirement and downsizing their workforce. It is the argument in this book that such strategies cannot work in the long term within those sectors of the tourism, hospitality and leisure industry which seek to maintain a quality product and service, and that investment in human capital is the only viable and profitable strategy that companies in this market can adopt.

This argument draws much of its strength from the wider debate about the social and corporate responsibility of business in general and how industry and late-twentieth-century capitalism in general relate to the wider physical, social, economic, cultural and political environment in which they exist. Much of the discussion in this debate has focused primarily on physical and ecological concerns and the sustainability of industry in the context of finite natural resources and the degradation of the environment. However, similar arguments in terms of social and corporate responsibility go beyond this dimension and impact upon how companies and the corporate sector in general relate to their host communities and the responsibilities and loyalties that they have at that level. The record of many major companies, in this respect, has not been particularly good in recent years. The relationship of the corporate sector to people in the workplace and in the community is a central aspect of the social responsibility of the business sector. This theme emerges as important in the discussions of writers in this area such as Schumacher (1975), Cannon (1992), Sorell and

Hendry (1994) and, indeed, Mahesh (1994), to whom considerable reference has already been made in this chapter.

Ethical human resource policies are sustainable human resource policies. Their implementation requires commitment and, above all, a vision of the future within European tourism and hospitality which recognizes the increasingly competitive global environment with which the industry is faced. The human resource vision that will support the competitive position of tourism, hospitality and leisure is derived from the sustainable paradigm as the main tenets of the traditional model have increasingly been shown to be flawed. Connock (1991) articulates the need for vision in this respect when he argues as follows:

> Developing the HR vision is about articulating the long-term HR goals, core values, key behaviour and underlying philosophy which derive from, support and complement the business mission and strategies. It will be realistic yet visionary; specific enough to be meaningful yet general enough to be applicable in different parts of the business. It will appeal to staff at all levels by demonstrating a clear direction which captures the emotions. From the HR vision will come HR strategies, objectives, milestones, performance measures. All will be integrated and cohesive, deriving from the business mission and ultimately judged on the success of the business in fulfilling that mission. (Connock 1991, p.172)

If we transpose the corporate context which Connock considers to that of the wider tourism, hospitality and leisure industry but apply the same principles, we have the arena for the sustainable human resource vision which this book has sought to address.

Case Study *Scandic Hotels*

Scandic started out with the idea of offering hotels for the general traveller in places where many people wanted to be. At that time, in 1960s Sweden, motels were the latest idea, giving many people access to things that previously had been for the few, such as TV in every room and swimming pools at hotels. The idea of providing easy accommodation along major travel routes still lives on. Today it is complemented by hotels in central city locations. Now the business idea is to offer 'easy and accessible travel for all'.

Ecological and ethical sustainability are two crucial principles in Scandic's operation. We observe and value these principles in everything we do. The decision to award the Swan, the Nordic eco label, for all Scandic hotels in Sweden before the year end of 2004 was made in early 2003. The Swan, one of the world's toughest eco labels, is another token of Scandic's long-term effort towards an ecologically and ethically sustainable society. This effort involves Scandic's guests in taking responsibility for the environment and the wider world.

Scandic was acquired by the London-based Hilton Group plc for £620.2 millions in 2001 and successfully integrated into the Hilton hotels portfolio.

Scandic offers an integrated approach to HRM, with a particular focus on employee development. The company's wider ethical principles (especially environmental) translate into a positive and participative approach to HR and HRD.

Scandic's principles and practices are focused on being an attractive place to work where the leadership, through proper motivation and management by clearly defined objectives, gives the team members opportunities for their own initiatives, involvement and development. It is important to the company that all staff take care in their work to live up to Scandic's team member concept: 'We must offer a secure and meaningful job in a developing environment, where your efforts create value for you, the guests, the brand and Scandic.'

- *Secure and meaningful* – Scandic works to create a good, secure working environment, which encourages open communication and long-term working relationships, and where everyone's efforts are significant for the overall experience of guests and customers.

- *A developing environment* – Scandic endeavours to become even more efficient within its various functions. A successful company depends upon people who learn from their successes and their mistakes by constantly recycling experience.

- *Values* – Everyone's efforts at work must be perceived as stimulating and valuable for the individual, for the guests and for Scandic. Every team member at Scandic must be able to be proud of their work and of being part of Scandic.

- *Training and development.*

Skills and commitment are seen as team members' main contributions to Scandic. The potential for challenging and exciting work is Scandic's contribution back to them. Developing skills, therefore, is an important concern for all staff in Scandic. The company, as an employer, is responsible for ensuring that all the necessary conditions, in terms of time, professional support and financial resources, exist for all of our team members to develop within the company. However,

Scandic team member's, are responsible for their own development.

The Knowledge Portal is a technical platform that provides an overview of an individual's development as a team member within the company. It is their entry point to all learning and development opportunities in Scandic. With individual log-in, it is easy to follow a personal path within the company. All the courses and programmes, with their results and any follow-ups from the annual review reports, competitions entered, or any other competence development initiatives, are fed into the Knowledge Portal system. The Knowledge Portal is therefore an excellent tool for team members, managers and in fact the whole organisation to keep on track of personal and overall targets within Scandic's competence development programme.

Each individual's competence is seen as a very important success factor for Scandic. The company has developed a large number of initiatives and programmes in the competence development area, which are bundled under one name – the Scandic Business School. There are several methods of delivery within the SBS portfolio, ranging from leadership and upselling courses to advanced technical courses, e-learning, meetings, mentorship, literature, seminars, networks.

The Scandic learning culture, within its wider HRM policies and environmental good practice, is a major factor in achieving one of the most productive workforces within the European hospitality sector, offering excellent 3*–4* service to customers at a staff to rooms ratio of about 1:0.25. Scandic is also seen as a desirable place to work, both among younger people within urban locations and by more mature, part-time employees in suburban and rural locations.

The Scandic approach to HR is joined up and integrated. It sits alongside an ethical environmental policy that is second to none in the hospitality sector. The Scandic approach places particular value of learning within the

▶

organisation at all levels and at all stages within careers in the company. This linked approach to learning is what sets Scandic aside as a model worth replication in the Irish context.

Case prepared by the author from personal research and published sources for Fáilte Ireland. Reproduced with permission.

Case discussion questions

1. In what ways do Scandic demonstrate integration in their approach to the key business functions of finance, operations, marketing and human resource management?

2. How do Scandic use ICT to support a learning environment?

3. How relevant is Scandic's approach to environmental management to its application of sustainable HR principles?

Review and discussion questions

1. How are the changes in the working environment, discussed in this chapter, likely to impact on tourism, hospitality and leisure in a location with which you are familiar?

2. Are moral and ethical considerations unrealistic luxuries to employers in the highly competitive tourism, hospitality and leisure industry?

3. In what ways might tourism, hospitality and leisure companies have both a more detached and a closer relationship with the local community than a heavy manufacturing plant?

4. What strategies could a tourism, hospitality and leisure company employ in order to strengthen its community links?

5. Identify situations where the Pygmalion effect may have worked to the advantage or disadvantage of yourself or friends?

6. What steps can managers take to reduce the potentially negative impacts of Pygmalion?

7. How useful is Maslow's motivational model to understanding the needs and aspirations of staff at all levels in the tourism, hospitality and leisure industry?

8. What motivational levels will empowerment in the workplace satisfy?

9. Is sustainable human resource management incompatible with Ritzer's idea of McDonaldization?

10. How important is a sense of social responsibility to a tourism, hospitality and leisure company in formulating its human resource policies and practices?

11. Referring to Table 10.2, how might you edit, revise or expand the sustainable paradigm in the light of reading this book?

References

Ackroyd, S. and Thompson, P. (1999) *Organizational Misbehaviour*, London: Sage.

Adkins, L. (1995) *Gendered Work. Sexuality, Family and the Labour Market*, Buckingham: Open University Press.

Adler, N.J. (1993) 'Women managers in a global economy', *HR Magazine*, 38, pp.52–5.

Adler, P.A. and Adler, P. (2004) *Paradise Laborers. Hotel Work in the Global Economy*, Ithaca, NY: Cornell University Press.

Airey, D. (1994) 'Education for tourism in Poland', Proceedings of the EuroCHRIE Conference Hospitality Schools East–West, Vienna.

AIS (Australian Institute of Sport) (undated) 'Sports nutrition – survival of the fittest' accessed at http://www.ais.org.au/nutrition/ClubSandwich.asp on 5 June 2005.

Aitchison, C., Jordan, F. and Brackenridge, C. (1999) 'Women in leisure management: a survey of gender equity', *Women in Management Review*, 14(4), pp.121–7.

Akyeampong, E. and Ambler, C. (2002) 'Leisure in African History: An Introduction', *The International Journal of African Historical Studies*, 35(1), pp.1–16.

Albrecht, K. and Zemke, R. (1985) *Service America*, Homewood, IL: Dow Jones-Irwin.

Albrecht, K. and Zemke, R. (2001) *Service America in the New Economy*, New York: McGraw Hill Education.

Andrew, R., Baum, T. and Morrison, A. (2001) 'The lifestyle economics of small tourism businesses', *Journal of Travel and Tourism Research*, 1, 16–25.

Apostolopoulos, Y. and Gayle, D. (eds) (2002) *Island Tourism and Sustainable Development: Caribbean, Pacific and Mediterranean Experiences*, Westport, CT, and London: Praeger.

Association of Flight Attendants (undated) '*History of the Association of Flight Attendants*', accessed at http://news.airwise.com/stories/2000/05/958386227.html on 19 May 2005.

Atkinson, J. (1984) 'Manpower strategies for flexible organisations', *Personnel Management*, August, pp.28–31.

Atkinson, J. (1985) *Flexibility, Uncertainty and Manpower Management*, Brighton: Institute of Manpower Studies, IMS Report No. 89.

Azzaro, L. (2005) 'The potential of the human resources in the Malaysian tourism environment: the way ahead in the 21st century', Proceedings of the APacCHRIE, Conference, Kuala Lumpur, pp.777–88.

Baldacchino, G. (ed.) (2006) *Extreme Tourism: Lessons from the World's Cold Water Islands*, London: Elsevier.

Balmer, S. and Baum, T. (1993) 'Applying Herzberg's hygiene factors to the changing accommodation environment: the application of motivational theory to the field of guest satisfaction', *International Journal of Contemporary Hospitality Management*, 5(2), pp.27–31.

Barksdale, K and Werner, J. (2001) 'Managerial ratings of in-role behaviours, organizational citizenship behaviours, and overall performance: testing different models of their relationships', *Journal of Business Research*, 51, pp.145–55.

Bateson, J. and Hoffman, D. (1999) *Managing Services Marketing*, Fort Worth, TX: The Dryden Press.

Baum, T. (1987) 'Introducing educational innovation in hospitality studies', *International Journal of Hospitality Management*, 6(2), pp.97–102.

Baum, T. (1988) 'Towards a new definition of hotel management', *Cornell HRA Quarterly*, 29(2), pp.36–40.

Baum, T. (1989a) 'Managing hotels in Ireland: research and development for change', *International Journal of Hospitality Management*, 8(2), pp.131–44.

Baum, T. (1989b) 'Scope of the tourism industry and its employment impact in Ireland', *The Service Industries Journal*, 9(1), pp.140–51.

Baum, T. (1990) 'Competencies for hotel management: industry expectations of education', *International Journal of Contemporary Hospitality Management*, 2/4, pp.13–16.

Baum, T. (ed.) (1993a) *Human Resource Issues in International Tourism*, Oxford: Butterworth-Heinemann.

Baum, T. (1993b) 'Human resource concerns in European tourism: strategic response and the EC', *International Journal of Hospitality Management*, 12(1), pp.77–88.

Baum, T. (1994) 'The development and implementation of national tourism policies', *Tourism Management*, 15/3, pp.185–92.

Baum, T. (1995) *Human Resource Management in the European Tourism and Hospitality Industry*, London: Chapman and Hall.

Baum, T. (1996a) 'Unskilled work and the hospitality industry: myth or reality?', *International Journal of Hospitality Management*, 15/3, pp. 207–209.

Baum, T. (1996b) 'Tourism in Aland: a case study', *Progress in Tourism and Hospitality Research*, 1/2, pp.111–118.

Baum, T. (1997) 'Tourism education at the crossroads?' *Insights*, 11(12), A34.

Baum, T. (2000) 'Education for tourism in a global economy', in (eds) Wahab, S. and Cooper, C., *Tourism in the Age of Globalisation*, London: Routledge.

Baum, T. (2002a) 'Skills and training for the hospitality sector: a review of issues', *Journal of Vocational Education and Training*, 54(3), pp.343–63.

Baum, T. (2002b) 'Dilemmas facing mature tourism destinations: Cases from the North Atlantic', paper for the International Tourism Congress, University of Girona, Lloret de Mar, April.

Baum, T. (2004) 'Low cost travel: social inclusion or social exclusion?' *Insights*, May, pp.A12–A14.

Baum, T. (2007 forthcoming) 'Low cost air travel: social inclusion or social exclusion?' *Tourism, Culture and Communication*.

Baum, T. and Hallam, G. (1996) 'Contracting out food and beverage operations in hotels: a comparative study of practice in north America and the United Kingdom', *International Journal of Hospitality Management*, 15(1), pp.41–50.

Baum, T. and Lundtorp, S. (eds) (2000) *Seasonality in Tourism*, London: Elsevier.

Baum, T. and Odgers, P. (2001) 'Benchmarking best practice in hotel front office: the western European experience', *Journal of Quality Assurance in Hospitality and Tourism*, 2(3/4), pp.93–109.

BBC (2005) *Destination Scotland*, BBC2 Scotland, 29 May.

Becherel, L. and Cooper, C. (2000) 'Human resources, development, employment and globalization in the hotel, catering and tourism sector', paper commissioned by the ILO, Geneva: ILO.

Bemelmans, L. (1942) *Hotel Splendide*, London: Hamish Hamilton.

Berry, S. (1992) 'The impact of the British on seaside resort development in Europe', Proceedings of the Tourism in Europe conference, Durham.

Bird, B. (1989) *Langkawi – from Mahsuri to Mahathir: tourism for whom?* Kuala Lumpur: INSAN.

Blanning, R., Bui, T.X. and Tan, M. (1997) 'National information infrastructure in Pacific Asia', *Decision Support Systems*, 21(3), pp.215–28.

Blythman, J. (2004) *Shopped. The Shocking Power of British Supermarkets*. London: Harper Perennial.

Borer, M. (1972) *The British Hotel through the Ages*, London: Lutterworth.

Bradley, H., Erickson, M., Stephenson, C. and Williams, S. (2000) *Myths at Work*, Cambridge: Polity Press.

Bramham, J. (1982) *Practical Manpower Planning*, third edition, London: Institute of Personnel Management.

Bramham, J. (1983) 'Manpower planning', in (eds) Guest, D. and Kenny, T., *A Textbook of Techniques and Strategies in Personnel Management*, London: Institute of Personnel Management.

Bramham, J. (1994) *Human Resource Planning*, second edition, London: Institute of Personnel and Development

Bramwell, W. and Lane, B. (1993) 'Sustainable tourism: an evolving global approach?', *Journal of Sustainable Tourism*, 1(1), pp.1–5.

Braverman, H. (1974) *Labor and Monopoly Capital*, New York: Monthly Review Press.

Brotherton, B. and Wood, R. (2000) 'Hospitality and hospitality management', in (eds) Lashley, C. and Morrison, A., *In Search of Hospitality*, Oxford: Butterworth-Heinemann.

Bryman, A. (2004) *The Disneyization of Society*, London: Sage.

Buchanan, J., Watson, I. and Briggs, C. (2004) 'Skill and the renewal of labour: the classical wage-earner model and left productivism in Australia', in (eds) Warhurst, C., Grugulis, I and Keep, E., *The Skills that Matter*, Basingstoke: Palgrave.

Burns, P.M. (1997) 'Hard-skills, soft-skills: undervaluing hospitality's "Service with a Smile"', *Progress in Tourism and Hospitality Research*, 3, 239–48.

Burton, R. (1994) 'Geographical patterns of tourism in Europe', in (eds) Cooper, C. and Lockwood, A.. *Progress in Tourism, Recreation and Hospitality*, Volume 5, Chichester: John Wiley and Sons.

Butler, R. (1980) 'The concept of a tourist are cycle of evolution', *Canadian Geographer*, 24, pp.5–12.

Buzzard, J. (1993) *The Beaten Track: European Tourism, Literature and the Ways to 'Culture', 1800–1918*, Oxford: Clarendon Press.

Byrne, D. (1986) *Waiting for Change? Working in Hotel and Catering*, London: Low Pay Unit.

Calder, S. (2002) *No Frills. The Truth behind the Low-cost Revolution in the Skies*, London: Virgin Books.

Cannon, T. (1992) *Corporate Responsibility*, London: Financial Times/Pitman.

Canny, A. (2002) 'Flexible labour? The growth of student employment in the UK', *Journal of Education and Work*, 15(3), pp.277–301.

Carlzon, J. (1987) *Moments of Truth*, Cambridge, MA: Ballinger.

Cassee, E. (1983) 'Introduction', in (eds) Cassee, E.H. and Reuland, R., *The Management of Hospitality*, Oxford: Pergamon.

Castley, R. (1996) 'Policy-focused approach to manpower planning', *International Journal of Manpower*, 17(3), pp.15–24.

CBS News (2005) 'Pilots' joyride turned to tragedy', accessed at http://www.cbsnews.com/stories/2005/06/13/national/main701381.shtml on 22 June 2005.

CEC (Commission of the European Communities) (1991) *Community Action Plan to Assist Tourism*, Com (91) 97 final, Brussels: CEC.

Chang, Richard (2005) 'An investigation of the Chinese tourists' meal experience in Australia and its contribution to tourist satisfaction', Proceedings of the APacCHRIE Conference, Kuala Lumpur, pp.88–96.

Chant, S. (1997) 'Gender and tourism employment in Mexico and the Philippines', in (ed.) Sinclair, T., *Gender, Work and Tourism*, London: Routledge.

Cheung, C. (2006) 'The impact of employees' behaviour and the implementation of total quality management on service quality: a case study in the hotel industry', unpublished PhD thesis, Glasgow: University of Strathclyde.

Christou, E. (1999) 'Hospitality management education in Greece: an exploratory study', *Tourism Management*, 20, 683–91.

Christou, E. (2001) 'Revisiting competencies for hospitality management (contemporary views of stakeholders)', *Journal of Hospitality & Tourism Educator*, 14(1), 25–32.

Christou, E. and Eaton, J. (2000) 'Management competencies for graduate trainees of hospitality and tourism programs', *Annals of Tourism Research*, 27(4), pp.1058–61.

Churchill, D. (1994) 'Time to upgrade', *Sunday Times*, style and travel section, 22 May, p.38.

Clark, J. and Lai, V. (1998) 'Internet comes to Morocco', *Association for Computing Machinery. Communication of the ACM*, 41(2), pp.21–4.

Conlin, M. and Baum, T. (1994) 'Comprehensive human resource planning: an essential key to sustainable tourism in island settings', in (eds) Cooper, C. and Lockwood, A., *Progress in Tourism, Recreation and Hospitality*, Volume 6, Chichester: John Wiley and Sons.

Conlin, M. and Baum, T. (1995) *Island Tourism. Management Principles and Practices*, Chichester: John Wiley.

Conlin, M., Lynn, M. and O'Donoghue, T. (2004) 'The norm of restaurant tipping', *Journal of Economic Behaviour and Organization*, 52(3), pp.297–312.

Connock, S. (1991) *HR Vision. Managing a Quality Workforce*, London: Institute of Personnel Management.

Cooper, C., Fletcher, J., Fyall, A., Gilbert, D. and Wanhill, S. (2005) *Tourism. Principles and Practice*, third edition, Harlow: Pearson.

Cullen, R. (2001) 'Addressing the digital divide', *Online Information Review*, 25(5), pp.311–21.

Dale, S. (undated) 'Mama-san's babies', accessed at http://akasenkuiki.homestead.com/files/babies.html on 19 May 2005.

D'Annunzio-Green, N. (2002) 'The hotel expatriate in Russia: competencies for cross-cultural adjustment', in (eds) D'Annunzio-Green, N., Maxwell, G. and Watson, S., *Human Resource Management. International Perspectives in Hospitality and Tourism*, London: Continuum.

Deegan, J. (2005) 'Tourism in the Republic of Ireland', Proceedings of 'Tourism and hospitality research in Ireland: exploring the issues', University of Ulster, Portrush.

Deegan, J. and Dineen, D. (1993) 'Irish tourism policy: targets, outcomes and environmental considerations', in (eds) O'Connor, B. and Cronin, M., *Tourism in Ireland: A Critical Analysis*, Cork: Cork University Press.

Deery, M. and Jago, L. (2001) 'Managing human resources in heritage visitor attractions', in (ed.) Yeoman, I., *Quality Issues in Heritage Visitor Attractions*, London: Cassell.

Deissinger, T. (1997) 'The German dual system – a model for Europe?', *Education and Training*, 39(8), pp.297–302.

Devine, F. and Baum, T. (2005) 'Skills and the service sector: the case of hotel front office in Northern Ireland', Proceedings of 'Tourism and hospitality research in Ireland: exploring the issues', University of Ulster, Portrush.

Dewey, J. (1916) *Democracy and Education*, London: Macmillan.

Diaz, P. and Umbreit, W. (1995) 'Women leaders – a new beginning', *Hospitality Research Journal*, 18(3), pp.49–60.

Din, K. (2005) 'The tao of hospitality and tourism management: what, why how', Proceedings of the APacCHRIE conference, Kuala Lumpur.

Dirks, D. and Rice, S. (2004) '"Dining while black": tipping as social artifact', *Cornell Hotel and Restaurant Administration Quarterly*, 45(1), pp.30–48.

Ditton, J. (1977) 'Perks, pilferage and the fiddle: the historical structure of invisible wages', *Theory and Society*, 4(1), pp.39–71.

D'Netto, B. and Sohal, A. (1999) 'Human resource practices and workforce diversity: an empirical assessment', *International Journal of Manpower*, 20(8), pp.530–47.

Donald, B. (1974) 'Manpower and a planned future', in (eds) Margerison, C. and Ashton, D., *Planning for Human Resources*, London: Longman.

Dowling, P. and Welch, D. (2004) *International Human Resource Management. Managing People in a Multinational Context*, fourth edition, London: Thomson Learning.

Dronfield, L. and Soto, P. (1982) *Hardship Hotel*, London: Counter Information Services.

DTI (Department of Trade and Industry) (2001) 'Creating a work-life balance. A good practice guide for the hospitality industry', London: DTI, accessed at http://www.dti.gov.uk/SMD3/pdfs/wlbhospitalityguide.pdf on 5 June 2005.

Du Boulay, C. (1996) 'What does it take to manage volunteers', *Australian Journal on Volunteering*, 4, p.15.

Eaton, J. (2001) *Globalization and Human Resource Management in the Airline Industry*, second edition, Aldershot: Ashgate.

Eaton, J. and Christou, E. (1997) 'Hospitality management competencies for graduate trainees: employers' view', *Journal of European Business Education*, 10:1, 60–8.

Eironline (undated a) 'Female employment and EU employment policy' accessed at http://www.eiro.eurofound.eu.int/2004/06/feature/es0406205f.html on 22 May 2005.

Eironline (undated b) 'Migration and industrial relations', accessed at http://www.eiro.eurofound.eu.int/2003/03/study/tn0303105s.html on 22 May 2005.

Espiritu, A. (2003) 'Digital divide and implications on growth: cross-country analysis', *Journal of American Academy of Business*, 2(2), pp.450–4.

EURHODIP (European Hotel Diploma) (2003) *Euroformation*, White Paper, Brussels: EURHODIP.

Fáilte Ireland (2005a) *Cultural Diversity. Strategy and Implementation Plan*, Dublin: Fáilte Ireland.

Fáilte Ireland (2005b) *A Human Resource Strategy for Irish Tourism. Competing Through People, 2005–2012*, Dublin: Fáilte Ireland.

Fáilte Ireland (2005c) *Report of the Tourism Career Promotions Group Including a National Recruitment Plan for Careers in the Irish Tourism Industry*, Dublin: Fáilte Ireland.

FEFC (Further Education Funding Council) (1998) *Key Skills in Further Education*, Coventry: FEFC.

Feiffer, M. (1985) *Going Places*, London: Macmillan.

Fletcher, J. (1993) 'Input-output analysis and employment multipliers', in (ed.) Baum, T., *Human Resource Issues in International Tourism*, Oxford: Butterworth-Heinemann.

Friedman, A. (2002) 'Tip for U.S. restaurateurs: study European gratuity system', *Nation's Restaurant News*, 36(27), p.60.

Fuller, J. (1971) *Chef's Manual of Kitchen Work*, London: Batsford.

Gabriel, Y. (1988) *Working Lives in Catering*, London: Routledge and Kegan Paul.

George, J. and Jones, G. (1997) 'Organizational spontaneity in context', *Human Performance*, 10, 153–70.

Getz, D., Carlsen, J. and Morrison, A. (2004) *The Family Business in Tourism and Hospitality*, Wallingford: CABI.

Gilg, A. (1991) 'Switzerland: structural change within stability', in (eds) Williams, A. and Shaw, G., *Tourism and Economic Development: Western European Perspectives*, second edition, London: Belhaven Press.

Goodenough, P. (2005) 'Pakistan police arrest runners in mixed-sex road race', CNSNews.com, 16 May, accessed at http://www.cnsnews.com/ViewForeignBureaus.asp?Page=%5CForeignBureaus %5Carchive%5C200505%5CFOR20050516c.html on 2 June 2005.

Gröschl, S. and Doherty, L. (1999) 'Diversity management in practice', *International Journal of Contemporary Hospitality Management*, 11(6), pp. 262–8.

Guerrier, Y. and Adib, A (2001) 'Working in the hospitality industry', in (eds) Lashley, C. and Morrison, A., *In Search of Hospitality*, Oxford: Butterworth-Heinemann.

Guerrier, Y. and Lockwood. A. (1989) 'Core and peripheral employment in hotel operations', *Personnel Review*, 18(1), pp. 9–15.

Guerrier, Y., Baum, T., Jones, P. A. and Roper, A. (1998) *In the World of Hospitality ... 'Anything They can Do, We can Do Better'*, London: Joint Hospitality Industry Congress/Council for Hospitality Management Education.

Hall, D. (1991) *Tourism and Economic Development in Eastern Europe and the Soviet Union*, London: Belhaven Press.

Hall, E. and Hall, M. (1990) *Understanding Cultural Differences*, Yarmouth, MA: Intercultural Press.

Harker, M (1999) 'Relationship marketing defined? An examination of current relationship marketing definitions', *Marketing Intelligence & Planning*, 17(1), pp.13–20.

Harley, B. (1999) 'The myth of empowerment: work organisation, hierarchy and employee autonomy in contemporary Australian workplaces', *Work, Employment and Society*, 13(1), pp.41–66.

Harris, H. (1995) 'Organisational influences on women's career opportunities in international management', *Women in Management Review*, 10(3), pp.26–31.

Harris, R. (2003) *Scottish Jobcentre Survey 2002: Analysis of Vacancies Within the Catering, Leisure and Tourism Sector*, Glasgow: Scottish Low Pay Unit.

Hearns, N. (2004) 'Statutory smoking bans and tourism destinations: opportunity or threat?', *Tourism and Hospitality Planning and Development*, 1(3), pp.195–200.

Hemdi, M.A. and Nasurdin, A.M. (2005) 'Procedural justice, citizenship behaviour and service quality: an agenda for hotels', Proceedings of the APacCHRIE, Conference, Kuala Lumpur, pp.589–98.

Hochschild, A.R. (1983) *The Managed Heart: Commercialisation of Human Feeling*, Berkeley, CA: University of California Press.

Hofman, W. and Steijn, A. (2003) 'Students or lower-skilled workers? "Displacement" at the bottom of the labour market', *Higher Education*, 45, 127–46.

Hofstede, G. (1985) 'The interaction between national organizational systems', *Journal of Management Studies*, 22(4), pp. 347–57.

Hofstede, G. (2001) *Culture's Consequences: Comparing Values, Behaviours, Institutions and Organizations Across Nations*, Newbury Park, CA: Sage.

Holloway, C. (1993) 'Labour, vocational education and training', in (eds) Pompl, W. and Lavery, P., *Tourism in Europe: Structures and Development*, Wallingford: CABI.

Hoque, K. (2000) *Human Resource Management in the Hotel Industry. Strategy, Innovation and Performance*, London: Routledge.

Houellebecq, M. (2003) *Platform* (translated from the French by F. Wynne), London: Vintage.

HtF (Hospitality Training Foundation) (2000a) *Hospitality Sector Workforce Development Plan 2001*, London: HtF.

HtF (Hospitality Training Foundation) (2000b) *Delphi Study of the Hospitality Industry – Final Summary*, London: HtF.

Hutton, W. and The Work Foundation (2005) *Where are the Gaps? An Analysis of UK Skills and Education Strategy in the Light of the Kok Group and European Commission Midterm Review of the Lisbon Goals*, London: The Work Foundation.

ILO (International Labour Office) (1979) *Tasks to Jobs – Developing a Modular System of Training for Hotel Occupations*, Geneva: ILO.

ILO (International Labour Office) (1989) *Conditions of Work in the Hotel, Catering and Tourism Sector, Such as Hours of Work, Methods of Remuneration, Security of Employment*, Geneva: Hotel, Catering and Tourism Committee of the ILO.

ILO (International Labour Office) (2001) 'Human resources development, employment and globalization in the hotel, catering and tourism sector', report for discussion at the Tripartite Meeting on Human Resources Development, Employment and Globalization in the Hotel, Catering and Tourism Sector, Geneva: ILO, accessed at http://www.ilo.org/public/english/dialogue/sector/techmeet/tmhct01/tmhctr2.htm on 24 June 2005.

Isles, N. (2004) *The Joy of Work?* London: The Work Foundation.

ITV (Independent Television) (2005) *Airline*, episode aired 29 April.

Jackson, S., May, K. and Whitney, K. (1995) 'Understanding the dynamics of diversity in decision-making teams', in (eds) Guzzo, R., Salas, E. and Associates, *Team Effectiveness in Decision Making in Organizations*, San Francisco, CA: Jossey-Bass.

Jafari, J. (1990) 'Research and scholarship: the basis of tourism education', *Journal of Tourism Studies*, 1(1), pp.33–41.

Jago, L. and Deery, M. (2002) 'The role of human resource practices in achieving quality enhancement and cost reduction: an investigation of volunteer use in tourism organisations', *International Journal of Contemporary Hospitality Management*, 14(5), pp.229–36.

James, J. (2005) 'The global digital divide in the Internet: developed countries constructs and third world realities', *Journal of Information Science*, 31(2), pp.114–24.

Jameson, S., Walmsley, A. and Ball, S. (2005) *A Review of Hospitality Management Education in the UK*, Leeds: Council for Hospitality Management Education (CHME).

Jithendran, K.J. and Baum, T. (2000) 'Human resource development and sustainability – the case of Indian tourism', *International Journal of Tourism Research*, 2, pp.403–21.

Jordan, F. (1997) 'An occupational hazard? Sex segregation in tourism employment', *Tourism Management*, 18(8), pp.525–34.

Kandola, R. and Fullerton, J. (1994) *Managing the Mosaic*, Trowbridge, Wiltshire: The Cromwell Press.

Keating, M. and Harrington, D. (2005) 'The contribution and experience of hotel middle-managers in quality implementation', proceedings of 'Tourism and hospitality research in Ireland: exploring the issues', University of Ulster, Portrush.

Keep, E. and Mayhew, K. (1999) *Skills Task Force Research Group. Paper 6. The Leisure Sector*. London: DfEE.

Keiser, J. and Swinton, J. (1988) 'Professionalism and ethics in hospitality', *Florida International Hospitality Review*, 6, pp.23–31.

Kemp, S. (2002) 'The hidden workforce: volunteers' learning in the Olympics', *Journal of European Industrial Training*, 26(2/3/4), pp.109–16.

King, R. (1991) 'Italy: multi-faceted tourism', in (eds) Williams, A. and Shaw, G., *Tourism and Economic Development: Western European Perspectives*, second edition, London: Belhaven Press.

Korczynski, M. (2002) *Human Resource Management in Service Work*, Basingstoke: Palgrave.

Kua, J. and Baum, T. (2004) 'Perspectives on the development of low cost airlines in South East Asia: evidence from the regional press', *Current Issues in Tourism*, 7(3), pp.262–76.

Ladkin, A. (2000) 'Vocational education and food and beverage experience: issues for career development', *International Journal of Contemporary Hospitality Management*, 12(4), pp.226–33.

Lai, P.C. (2005) 'Workplace Flexibility and Labour Supply Chains in Hospitality: The Role of Employment Agencies', unpublished PhD thesis, Glasgow: University of Strathclyde.

Lai, P. and Baum, T. (2005) 'Just-in-time labour in the hospitality sector?', *Employee Relations*, 27(1), 86–102.

Lall, S. (2003) *The Employment Impact of Globalization in Developing Countries*, QEH Working Paper Series 93, Oxford: Queen Elizabeth Hall.

Lane, B. (1992) *Sustainable Tourism: a Philosophy*, Bristol: The Rural Tourism Unit, University of Bristol.

Lashley, C. (1997) *Empowering Service Excellence. Beyond the Quick Fix*, London: Cassell.

Lashley, C. and Morrison, A. (eds) (2000) *In Search of Hospitality*, Oxford: Butterworth-Heinemann.

Leeds, C., Kirkbride, P. and Duncan, J. (1994) 'The cultural context of Europe: a tentative mapping', in (ed.) Kirkbride, P., *Human Resource Management in Europe: Perspectives for the 1990s*, London: Routledge.

Leiper, N. (2000) 'Tourist', in (ed.) Jafari, J., *Encyclopaedia of Tourism*, London: Routledge.

Lennon, J. (2002) 'Tourism training in developing countries: a commercial solution to training needs', in (eds) D'Annunzio-Green, N., Maxwell, G. and Watson, S., *Human Resource Management. International Perspectives in Hospitality and Tourism*, London: Continuum.

Lester, R. (1960) *Manpower Planning in a Free Society*, Princeton, NJ: Princeton University Press.

Lewis, R. and Chambers, R. (1989) *Marketing Leadership in Hospitality*, New York: Van Nostrand Reinhold.

Lindsay, C. and McQuaid, R. (2004) 'Avoiding the "McJobs": unemployed job seekers and attitudes to service work', *Work, Employment and Society*, 18(2), pp.297–319.

Lloyd, C. (2003) *Skills and Competitive Strategy in the UK Fitness Industry*. SKOPE Research Paper 43, Oxford/Warwick: ESRC SKOPE.

Lockhart, D. and Drakakis-Smith, D. (eds) (1997) *Island Tourism: Trends and Prospects*, London and New York: Pinter.

London Canals Museum (undated) *Volunteer Work*, accessed at http://www.canalmuseum.org.uk/volunteering.htm on 23 May 2005.

Long, V. and Wall, G. (1996) 'Successful tourism in Nusa, Lombongan, Indonesia', *Tourism Management*, 17(1), pp.43–50.

Longman Dictionary of Contemporary English (2005) Harlow: Longman.

Low Pay Commission (2005) 'National minimum wage', London: Low Pay Commission, accessed at http://www.lowpay.gov.uk/lowpay/lowpay2005/index.shtml on 15 June 2005.

Low Pay Unit (1976) *Low Pay in Hotels and Catering*, London: LPU.

Lynn, M. (1996) 'Seven ways to increase servers' tips', *Cornell Hotel and Restaurant Administration Quarterly*, 37(3), pp.24–30.

Lynn, M. (2004) 'Ethnic differences in tipping: a matter of familiarity with tipping norms', *Cornell Hotel and Restaurant Administration Quarterly*, 45(1), pp.12–23.

Lynn, M., Zinkhan, G. and Harris, J. (1993) 'Consumer tipping: a cross-country study', *Journal of Consumer Research*, 20(3), pp.478–89.

Mahesh, V.S. (1988) 'Effective human resource management: key to excellence in service organizations', *Vikalpa*, 13(4), pp.9–15.

Mahesh, V.S. (1993) 'Human resource planning and development: micro and macro models for effective growth in tourism', in (ed.) Baum, T., *Human Resource Issues in International Tourism*, Oxford: Butterworth-Heinemann.

Mahesh, V.S. (1994) *Thresholds of Motivation*, New York: McGraw-Hill.

Mars, G. (1973) 'Chance, punters and the fiddle: institutionalized pilferage in a hotel dining room', in (ed.) Warner, M., *The Sociology of the Workplace*, London: Allen and Unwin.

Mars, G. and Mitchell, P. (1976) *Room for Reform*, Oxford: Oxford University Press.

Maslow, A. (1943) 'A theory of human motivation', *Psychological Review*, 50, pp.370–96.

Mathieson, A. and Wall, G. (1982) *Tourism: Economic, Physical and Social Impacts*, London: Longman.

McDonald, R. (1994) 'The nature of tourism-related employment in urban areas: the Liverpool experience', paper presented to 'Tourism. State of the art', Glasgow: The University of Strathclyde.

McGrath, G. (2005) 'Consumers know more about destinations than agents', *Travelmole*, accessed at http://www.travelmole.com/stories/103969.php on 20 May 2005.

McIntosh, R. and Goeldner, C. (1996) *Tourism: Principles, Practices and Philosophies*, seventh edition, New York: John Wiley and Sons.

McNabb, J. and Hearns, N. (2005) 'The smoking ban in hospitality: a cross border perspective from Ireland', *International Journal of Contemporary Hospitality Management*, 17(2), pp.181–90.

Mind/Social Firms UK (2004) *Tackling Mental Health Issues through Enterprise*, London: DTI.

Mok, C. (2002) 'Managing diversity in hospitality organizations', in (eds) D'Annunzio-Green, N., Maxwell, G. and Watson, S., *Human Resource Management. International Perspectives in Hospitality and Tourism*, London: Continuum.

Mole, J. (1990) *Mind Your Manners: Managing Culture Clash in the Single European Market*, London: The Industrial Society.

Mulcahy, J. (1999) 'Vocational work experience in the hospitality industry: characteristics and strategies', *Education and Training*, 41(4), pp.164–74.

Münz, R. and Fassmann, H. (2004) *Migrants in Europe and their Economic Position: Evidence from the European Labour Force Survey and from Other Sources*, Hamburg: Hamburg Institute of International Economics (HWWA) for the European Commission, DG Employment and Social Affairs.

Muroi, H. and Sasaki, N. (1997) 'Tourism and prostitution in Japan', in (ed.) Sinclair, T., *Gender, Work and Tourism*, London: Routledge.

Murphy, P. (1985) *Tourism. A Community Approach*, London: Methuen.

Ng, T.S., Boo, H.C. and Ingram, A. (2005) 'Effect of job redesign on employees' job satisfaction and commitment in the Singapore hotel industry', proceedings of the APacCHRIE conference, Kuala Lumpur, pp.295–300.

Nickson, D. and Warhurst, C. (2003) 'The new "Labour Aristocracy"? Aesthetic labour in the service economy', paper delivered to the Third Critical Management Studies Conference, Lancaster.

Nickson, D., Warhurst, C. and Witz, A. (2003) 'The labour of aesthetics and the aesthetics of organization', *Organization*, 10(1), pp.33–54.

Noon, M. and Blyton, P. (1995) *The Realities of Work*, Basingstoke: Macmillan.

Odgers, P. and Baum, T. (2001) *Benchmarking of Best Practice in Hotel Front Office*, Dublin: CERT.

O'Driscoll, F. and O'Connell, K. (2005) 'Hospitality students' attitudes and expectations toward the hotel industry', proceedings of 'Tourism and hospitality research in Ireland: exploring the issues', University of Ulster, Portrush.

Organ, D.W. (1988) *Organizational Citizenship Behavior: The Good Soldier Syndrome*. Lexington, MA: Lexington Books.

Organ, D.W. (1990) 'The motivational basis of organizational citizenship behaviour', in (eds) Staw, B. and Cummings, L., *Research in Organizational Behavior*. Greenwich, CT: JAI Press.

Orwell, G. (1933, reprinted 1986) *Down and Out in Paris and London*, Harmondsworth: Penguin.

Owens, M. (2005) 'Tourism and hospitality education: recent developments', proceedings of 'Tourism and hospitality research in Ireland: exploring the issues', University of Ulster, Portrush.

Oxford Quick Reference Dictionary and Thesaurus (1998) Oxford: Oxford University Press.

Page, E. and Kingsford, P. (1971) *The Master Chefs: A History of Haute Cuisine*, London: Edward Arnold.

Pender, L. and Baum, T. (2000) 'Have the frills really left the airline industry?', *International Journal of Tourism Research*, 2(6), pp.423–36.

Pizam, A. (1982) 'Tourism manpower: the state of the art', *Journal of Travel Research*, 11(2), pp.5–9.

Plüss, C. (1999) *Quick Money – Easy Money? – a Report on Child Labour in Tourism*, SDC Working Paper 1/99, Berne: Swiss Agency for Development and Co-operation (SDC).

Pompl, W. and Lavery, P. (1993) *Tourism in Europe: Structures and Developments*, Wallingford: CABI.

Poon, A. (1993) *Tourism, Technology and Competitive Strategies*, Wallingford, Oxon: CABI.

QCA (Qualifications and Curriculum Authority) (2000) 'Key skills 2000', http://www.qca.org.uk/nq/ks/keyskills

Quay, R. (2001) 'Bridging the digital divide', *Planning*, 67(7), pp.12–17.

Quinn, U., Kinsella, E., McCullough, A., McRory, B. and Quigley, L. (2005) 'The role of foundation degrees in addressing the skills gap in the hospitality and tourism sector – a Northern Ireland perspective', proceedings of 'Tourism and hospitality research in Ireland: exploring the issues', University of Ulster, Portrush.

Rafaeli, A. (1989) 'When cashiers meet customers: an analysis of the role of supermarket cashiers', *Academy of Management Journal*, 32(2), pp.245–73.

Rao, N. (1999) 'Sex tourism in South Asia', *International Journal of Contemporary Hospitality Management*, 11(2/3), pp.96–9.

Richards, G. (1992) 'European social tourism: welfare or investment', proceedings of the Tourism in Europe 1992 conference, Durham.

Riley, M. (1985) 'Some social and historical perspectives on unionization in the UK hotel industry', *International Journal of Hospitality Management*, 4(3), pp.99–104.

Riley, M. (1993) 'Labour markets and vocational education', in (ed.) Baum, T., *Human Resource Issues in International Tourism*, Oxford: Butterworth-Heinemann.

Riley, M. (1996) *Human Resource Management in the Hospitality and Tourism Industry*, Oxford: Butterworth-Heinemann.

Ritzer, G. (2004) *The McDonaldization of Society*, revised new century edition, Thousand Oaks: Pine Forge Press.

Roberts, K. (1978) *Contemporary Society and the Growth of Leisure*, London: Longman.

Ruiz-Mercarder, J., Ruiz-Santos, C. and McDonald, F. (2001) *A Contingency View of Numerical Flexibility: the Case of Spanish SMEs*, Manchester: Manchester Metropolitan University, Business School Working Paper Series, November, 2001.

Russell, B. (1926) *On Education*, London: Unwin.

Ryan, C. and Bates, C. (1995) 'A rose by any other name: the motivations of those opening their gardens for a festival', *Festival Management and Event Tourism*, 3(2), pp.59–71.

Ryan, C. and Hall, C.M. (2001) *Sex Tourism: Marginal People and Liminalities*, London: Routledge.

Saunders, K. (1981) *Social Stigma of Occupations: The Lower Grade Worker in Service Organisations*, London: Gower.

Scanlon, N. (1998) 'The American attitude toward hospitality service employment', in (eds) Cummings, P., Kwansa, F. and Sussman, M., *The Role of the Hospitality Industry in the Lives of Individuals and Families*, New York: The Haworth Press.

Schlesinger, L. and Heskitt, J. (1991) 'The service-driven company', *Harvard Business Review*, September–October, pp.71–81.

Schlosser, E. (2001) *Fast Food Nation: The Dark Side of the All-American Meal*, Boston, MA: Houghton-Mifflin.

Schumacher, E. (1975) *Small is Beautiful*, London: Harper and Row.

Scottish Museums Council (2003) 'Volunteer Development', http://www.scottishmuseums.org.uk/members_services/volunteering_intro.asp accessed 23 May 2005.

Sergeant, G. and Forna, A. (2001) *A Poor Reception. Refugee and Asylum Seekers: Welfare or Work?* London: The Work Foundation.

Seymour, D. (2000) 'Emotional labour: a comparison between fast food and traditional service work', *International Journal of Hospitality Management*, 19(2), pp.159–71.

Shackleton, R. (1998) 'Part-time working in the "super-service" era. Labour force restructuring in the UK food retailing industry during the late 1980s and early 1990s', *Journal of Retailing and Consumer Services*, 5(4), pp.223–34.

Shamir, B. (1980) 'Service and servility: role conflict in subordinate service roles', *Human Relations*, 33(10), pp.741–56.

Shaw, G. and Williams, A. (1994) *Critical Issues in Tourism: A Geographical Perspective*, Oxford: Blackwell.

Shaw, J. and Barrett-Power, E. (1998) 'The effects of diversity on small work group processes and performance', *Human Relations*, 51(10), pp.1307–25.

Sheldon, P. (1989) 'Professionalism in tourism and hospitality', *Annals of Tourism Research*, 16(4), pp.492–503.

Shin, S. and Kleiner, B. ((2003) 'How to manage unpaid volunteers in organizations', *Management Research News*, 26(2/3/4), pp.63–71.

Simmons, D. (2000) 'Recreation', in (ed.) Jaffari, J., *Encyclopaedia of Tourism*, London: Routledge.

Smith, S. and Mannell, R. (2000) 'Leisure', in (ed.) Jafari, J., *Encyclopaedia of Tourism*, London: Routledge.

Sorell, T. and Hendry, J. (1994) *Business Ethics*, Oxford: Butterworth-Heinemann.

Sparrow, P., Brewster, C. and Harris, H. (2004) *Globalizing Human Resource Management*, London: Routledge.

Sparrowe, R. (1994) 'Empowerment in the hospitality industry: an exploration of antecedents and outcomes', *Hospitality Research Journal*, 17(3), pp.51–74.

Stainer, G. (1971) *Manpower Planning: The Management of Human Resources*, London: Heinemann.

Steele, D. (1991) 'From manpower planning to labor market analysis', *International Labor Review*, 130 (4), pp.459–74.

Steinecke, A. (1993) 'The historical development of tourism in Europe', in (eds) Pompl, W. and Lavery, P., *Tourism in Europe: Structures and Developments*, Wallingford, Oxon: CABI.

Stradley, L. (2004) 'History of club sandwich', accessed at http://whatscookingamerica.net/History/Sandwiches/ClubSandwich.htm on 5 June 2005.

Sturman, M. (2001) 'Does the hospitality industry shortchange its employees – and itself?', *Cornell Hotel and Restaurant Administration Quarterly*, 42(3), pp.70–6.

Subramonian, H., Wong, P.W., Kwong, W.C. and Vathsala, N. (2005) 'Disaster detection, prevention and recovery using tourism intelligence (TI)', proceedings of the APacCHRIE conference, Kuala Lumpur, pp.270–80.

Tas, R.E. (1988) 'Teaching future managers', *The Cornell Hotel and Restaurant Administration Quarterly*, 29(2), pp.41–3.

Taylor, R., Airey, D. and Kotas, R. (1983) 'Rates of pay in the British hotel and catering industry', *International Journal of Hospitality Management*, 2(3), pp.157–9.

Tesco (1999) *Critical Success Factors*, London: Tesco plc.

The Work Foundation (2004) *UK Domestic Workers and Their Reluctant Employers*, London: The Work Foundation.

Tideman, M.C. (1983) 'External influences on the hospitality industry', in (eds) Cassee, E.H. and Reuland, R., *The Management of Hospitality*, Oxford: Pergamon.

Tomkins, A. (2004) 'Best of both worlds: An exploration of key skills required for graduate work in the leisure and sport industry and links to Personal Development Planning', LINK 11, accessed at http://www.hlst.heacademy.ac.uk/resources/link11/contents.html on 20 June 2005.

Towner, J. (1985) 'The history of the Grand Tour', *Annals of Tourism Research*, 12(3), pp.310–16.

Turner, L. and Ash, J. (1975) *The Golden Hordes: Tourism and the Pleasure Periphery*, London: Constable.

Turnipseed, D. (2003) 'Organizational citizenship behaviour in the hospitality and tourism industry', in (ed.) Kusluvan, S., *Managing Employee Attitudes and Behaviours in the Tourism and Hospitality Industry*, New York: Nova Science Publishers.

UNEP (undated) 'Negative socio-cultural impacts from tourism', accessed at http://www.uneptie.org/pc/tourism/sust-tourism/soc-drawbacks.htm on 12 June 2005.

Urry, J. (1994) 'Europe, tourism and the nation-state', in (eds) Cooper, C. and Lockwood, A., *Progress in Tourism, Recreation and Hospitality*, Volume 5, Chichester: John Wiley and Sons.

Veal, A.J. (2002) *Leisure and Tourism Policy and Planning*, second edition, Wallingford, Oxon: CABI.

Veal, A.J. and Lynch, R. (2001) *Australian Leisure*, second edition, Frenchs Forest, NSW: Pearson Australia.

Vikhanski, O. and Puffer, S. (1993) 'Management education and employee training at Moscow McDonalds', *European Management Journal*, 11(1), pp.102–107.

Wall, G. (2000) 'Travel', in (ed.) Jafari, J., *Encyclopaedia of Tourism*, London: Routledge.

Walsh, T. (1991) '"Flexible" employment in the retail and hotel trades', in (ed.) Pollert, A., *Farewell to Flexibility?*, Oxford: Basil Blackwell.

Warhurst, C., Nickson, D., Witz, A. and Cullen, A.M. (2000) 'Aesthetic labour in interactive service work: some case study evidence from the "New Glasgow"', *Service Industries Journal*, 20(3), pp.1–18.

Warhurst, C., Grugulis, I. and Keep, E. (2004) *The Skills that Matter*, Basingstoke: Palgrave.

Watson, I., Buchanan, J., Campbell, I. and Briggs, C. (2003) *Fragmented Futures: New Challenges in Working Life*, Sydney: Federation Press.

Weaver, D. and Oppermann, M. (2000) *Tourism Management*, Brisbane: John Wiley and Sons.

Westwood, A. (2002) *Is New Work Good Work?* London: The Work Foundation.

Whitelaw, B. (2005) 'Hospitality management education in Ireland: meeting industry needs? A competency based approach', proceedings of 'Tourism and hospitality research in Ireland: exploring the issues', University of Ulster, Portrush.

Williams, A. and Shaw, G. (1991) 'Western European tourism in perspective', in (eds) Williams, A. and Shaw, G., *Tourism and Economic Development: Western European Perspectives*, second edition, London: Belhaven Press.

Williams, C. (1988) *Blue, White and Pink Collar Workers: Technicians, Bank Employees and Flight Attendants*, London: Allen and Unwin.

Williams, M. (2002) *The Political Economy of Tourism, Liberalization, Gender and the GATS*, Occasional Paper Series on Gender, Trade and Development, Washington DC: International Gender and Trade Network.

Wong, K.Y. (2004) 'Foreign direct involvement: the case of the Malaysian hotel industry', unpublished PhD, University of Strathclyde.

Wood, R. (1993) 'Status and hotel and catering work: theoretical dimensions and practical implications', *Hospitality Research Journal*, 16(3), pp.3–16.

Wood, R. (1997) *Working in Hotels and Catering*, second edition, London: Routledge.

WTO (World Tourism Organization) (1994a) *Aviation and Tourism Policies: Balancing the Benefits*, London: Routledge.

WTO (World Tourism Organization) (1994b) *National and Regional Tourism Planning: Methodologies and Case Studies*, London: Routledge.

WTO (World Tourism Organization) (1995) *Compendium of Tourism Statistics, 1989–1993*, fifteenth edition, Madrid: WTO.

Young, G. (1973) *Tourism: Blessing or Blight*, Harmondsworth: Penguin.

Zhang, H.Q., Pine, R. and Lam, T. (2005) *Tourism and Hotel Development in China. From Political to Economic Success*, New York: The Haworth Press.

Zimmerman, E. (undated) 'On the road in the new republic', accessed at http://xroads.virginia.edu/~HYPER/DETOC/europeans/road.html on 2 May 2005.

Index